PROVERBS AND FOLKLORE OF KUMAUN AND GARHWAL

Introducing the Author

Pandit Ganga Datt Upreti

(Dec.1,1834–Aug.1,1910)

Rai Bahadur Pandit Ganga Datt Upreti was a gifted thinker and keen observer of people's lives and their cultural ethos. He was a profound scholar of Archaeology on the one hand and Folklore on the other. From a modest beginning in 1855 as the 4th Clerk of Senior Assistant, he rose to the position of Deputy Collector 3rd Grade sub-protem in about three decades.

His retirement from service provided the opportunity to read and write extensively. Some of his better known works are :

(1) *A Treatise on the History of People who Originally Settled in Garhwal*
(2) *Precept of this World and the Next*
(3) *A Treatise on the Improvement of Agriculture in the Hills*
(4) *Proverbs and Folklore of Himalayan region* (Kumaun-Garhwal)
(5) *Pharas-Ke-Maharaja-Ki-Rani-Astar-Ko-Itihas* (the History of Rani Astar, Queen of the King of Persia)
(6) *Hill Dialects of the Kumaun Division*
(7) *Parvatiya-Bhasha-Prakashak*
(8) *Dictionary Pahari/English*
(9) *History of Kumaun*
(10) *The Martial Caste of Almora District*

About Panditji's literary contributions, G.A. Grierson comments.
"Of late years several patriotic gentlemen of Almora have endeavoured to give their native language the honour of literature by writing books in Kumauni. Those who have come under my notice are recorded in the following list of them : Pandit Jwala Dutt Joshi's translation of the *Dasa-Kumara-Charitra* and Pandit Ganga Datt Upreti's *Hill Dialects of the Kumaun Division* have been frequently used in my account of the languages, and I am much indebted to them for the permission kindly granted to reprint extracts from their works. I would also call attention to Pandit Ganga Datt Upreti's *Proverbs and Folklore of Kumaun and Garhwal,* which is the most valuable collection affording a Mine of Information regarding the habits and customs of hill people....."

In recognition of his ethnological and linguistic researches, a certificate was awarded to Pt. Ganga Datt Upreti, by command of His Excellency the Viceroy and Governor General in Council in the name of His Most Gracious King Edward VIII, Emperor of India, on 11 Jan. 1903.

On 1st Jan. 1910 Lord Minto, Viceroy and Governor General of India conferred the title of Rai Bahadur to Pt. Ganga Datt Upreti as personal distinction. Needless to mention, Panditji was read by researchers widely.

A.N. Upreti

PROVERBS AND FOLKLORE OF KUMAUN AND GARHWAL

Collected and Edited by
Pandit Ganga Datt Upreti

INDIRA GANDHI NATIONAL CENTRE FOR THE ARTS,
NEW DELHI-110001

Concept

CONCEPT PUBLUBLISHING COMPANY, NEW DELHI-110059

ISBN 81-7022-894-8

First Published 1894

New Edition 2003

Printed in India

Publishers
Indira Gandhi National Centre for the Arts,
Central Vista Mess, Janpath, New Delhi-110001.

and

Ashok Kumar Mittal
Concept Publishing Company
A/15-16, Commercial Block, Mohan Garden
New Delhi-110059 (India)

Phones: 25351460, 25351794
Fax: 091–(11)–25357103
E-mail: publishing@conceptpub.com

Dedicated
to Edmund White ESQ, C.S.,
Late Director of Public Instruction
N.W.P. and Oudh

Pandit Ganga Datt Upreti
(Dec. 1, 1834 - Aug. 1, 1910)

FOREWORD

Proverb is a revelatory reminder. As a universal subject of the human way, it reflects the light of reason, experience, and contemplation. Rich in structure and vocabulary, it reveals the perceivable world in general and the pragmatics of social behaviour in particular. Horizontally, it concerns the phenomenal world; vertically it moves toward the metaphysical order. Hence, on the one hand it is practical; on the other it is essential, absolute. Widely held as voices from afar, it serves as a guiding code that dispels the shadow and fetters of imagination. Grounded in revelational wisdom, it helps cultivate human nobility. Like music, it is transmitted orally to make life better through its own inherent power. Like myths, dispersed throughout the world, it refers to an invisible horizon on which people project their ideology. Like scriptures, it cultivates divine nobility (truth and virtue) in order to obtain human nobility. Like *axioma*, it is a proposition, principle or maxim that has found general acceptance or is thought worthy thereof. Claiming intrinsic merit, it has an appeal to self-evidence. Only in an extraordinary state of cultural consicousness can one read its message for life. Comparable with the *suktas* in Sanskrit and the sayings in Confucian classics, it is the wisdom of the people that can never exhaust.

Proverbs and Folklore of Kumaun and Garhwal by Pandit Ganga Datt Upreti is a remarkable accomplishment, not only for its comprehensive sweep but also for its ability to bring imaginative insights and food for thought. Perhaps first of its king, appearing toward the end of the 19th century, the book is gifted with rich collection of proverbs, axioms, sayings and phrases for particular occasions as well as the customs and manners out of which they arise. Clustering more than 200 themes, arranged in alphabetical order, it is written in the devanagari letters, followed by English translation with due regard to the hill accentuation. Apart from classified themes, an Appendix with 114 new proverbs has been suitably provided at the end. The author of this comprehensive survey was a resident of the sub-Himalayan region serving the British Government as Deputy Collector in Garhwal and Kumaun. His pioneering work was approved by many learned Europeans of that time—both in England and India. Rev. E.S. Oakley's Introduction to the book reads as "...a picture of primitive manners and a native self-revelation which will be delightful to

* With the end of the colonial era, the usage of ' primitive ' as a pejorative term (crude, pre-civilized) has given place to new meaning (ancient, promordial).

the student in human nature, and will be of special value to all who are called on in the course of duty to enter into close relations with the people of India ". What anyone can say about the great work of this self-made folklorist is far too little.

The Indira Gandhi National Centre for the Arts (IGNCA) has been engaged for more than a decade in exploring all dimensions of culture in its widest and deepest conotations. Its objective is to explore all fields of cultural knowledge with a view to understanding various communities in their totality. So far societies have been studied in linear unidimensional form by such disciplines as anthropology, sociology, folklore and others. The Centre is evolving a model for lifestyle studies based on the premise that life is not fragmented into separate dimensions, neither can a model replicate in full a total picture of the cultural lifestyle of the diverse groups and communities. At the heart of the construction of this model is the intention to visualize a multilayered and multidimensional system operating in defined or demarcated social space. The Janapada Sampada Division of the IGNCA undertakes fundamental research in the socio-cultural and metaphysical context of the rich variegated heritage of rural cultures of India. It has endeavoured to explore the many dimensions of the cultural facets of Himalayas.

When Shri A.N. Upreti stuggested that the IGNCA should reprint his grand-father's pioneering work on the proverbs and folklore, we happily responded. Over a century has passed since this book was first published. Our object to bring out the first reprint was to make it readily available and to revive a classic in Indian Folklore. Without the extraordinary generosity of Shri A.N. Upreti and Shri B.M. Pande's gracious help in formidable editing, this book would not have seen light of the day. I would particularly thank my colleague Dr. Nita Mathur for her superhuman patience in seeing the book through the press.

Baidyanath Saraswati

New Delhi

PREFACE

The present collection of proverbs has been made in the remote and secluded districts of Kumaun and Garhwal, which form the integration of the Sub-Himalayan region, formerly considered a portion inaccessible by the people of the rest of India on account of their difficult natural features, and which exhibit both in physical aspect in the manners and customs of the people some remarkable divergences from the rest of India. Its folklore may therefore be considered specially interesting.

I have been induced to collect and translate the proverbs, maxims, sayings and to illustrate folklore of these hills during the course of years in the service of Government as a Deputy Collector in Garhwal and Kumaun, where I sought and obtained information from old men of respectability and knowledge.

A part of this work was submitted to Mr. Edmund White, C.S., Director of Public Instruction, N.W.P. and Oudh, I was encouraged by him to complete it for submission to Government. When the specimen pages were submitted the work was approved by many learned Europeans both in England and in India. It may not be out of place to quote the opinions of a few of these gentlemen :

On submitting the specimen copies to Government N.W.P. and Oudh, the Director of Public Instruction N.W.P. and Oudh said:

"The work of Pandit Ganga Datt is one of much interest and value in connection with the Folklore of the Province and well deserves the encouragement of Government."

Sir W. Muir, Late Lieutenant Governor N.W.P. and Oudh writes:

"Your letter and pamphlet and sheets received. They are very creditable to you."

Sir A.E. Elliott, Lieutenant Governor of Bengal, says:
"I have read your proverbs with much interest. They are well worth publishing."

C.J. Connell, Esquire, C.S., Collector and Magistrate of Bareilly, says:

> "Many thanks for the specimen pages of your collection of proverbs. They should be very useful and interesting when they are published in a complete form."

D.C. Baillie, Esquire, C.S. Superintendent of Census Operation, N.W.P. and Oudh writes:

> "A collection of one thousand five hundred proverbs of Kamaun and Garhwal explained and illustrated on the same lines as the specimen proverbs you have sent would certainly be most interesting."

S. Eardley Wilmot, Esquire, Conservator of Forest, writes:

> "Many thanks for sending me the specimen pages of your proverbs and Folklore of the Provinces of Kamaun and Garhwal. I am sure the subject is one which cannot fail to be of interest not only to those, comparatively few in number, who reside in or visit these districts but also to those who wish to improve their knowledge of the people of India."

W. Young, Esquire, C.S., Judicial Commissioner and High Court Judge Allahabad, says:

> "I think that the collection of proverbs is exceedingly interesting judging from the specimen shown to me by the Author, and he tells me that they are quite original and not to found in Fallon's look."

The specimen pages have also been kindly approved of by the North West Provinces, Madras, Bengal, and Punjab Governments.

My collection (under instructions from the Director of Public Instruction N.W.P. and Oudh) includes all the proverbs which are in vogue amongst the hill people without any reference to the fact that parallel proverbs are also in use in the Plains. At the same time I have not included those Sanskrit verses, generally used by the learned class, nor those verses in the Plains Hindustani dialect which are used by others.

These proverbs give an insight into the character, habits, customs and traditions of the people who inhabit the districts of Kumaun and Garhwal. To enable European gentlemen to understand them better I have briefly explained the appositeness of the proverbs, axioms, sayings and phrases to particular occasions, as well as the customs and manners out of which they arise.

A description of the country where the proverbs are used is briefly given in the Introduction (hereafter printed) kindly contributed by the Rev. E.S. Oakley, Principal of the Ramsay College at Almora, who has also helped me by revising the work and correcting the Proof-sheets. I must also acknowledge my indebtedness to H.O. Budden Esq. the Revs. J. Messmore and G.M. Bulloch, and Mr. M. Harris, Almora, who have at different times assisted me in preparing the volume.

The transliteration of the proverbs is according to Duncan Forbes' Hindustani Grammar (vide pages136 and 137) with due regard to the hill accentuation, so that the pronunciation of the same by any European may be clearly intelligible to hill people.

This is my first attempt to put my collection of proverbs and illustrations of Folklore into type: should this first edition find sale the second one will apppear in an improved and more attractive form.

In conclusion, I must say a word about the difficulty of classifying under appropriate headings such a collection as this. No one unless he had actually attempted such a task, could appreciate the difficulty. I have done what I could in this direction, and must ask indulgence from those readers who may see imperfections in this or in other features of my work.

Perhaps it is hardly necessary to caution my readers against misunderstanding some of these homely sayings, and regarding as indications of the "depravity" of the people, maxims which are obviously framed in an ironical sense and not seriously meant.

Kapina, Almora GANGA DATT UPRETI
9th November, 1892.

CONTENTS

D

E

F

G

H

I

J

K

L

M

N

O

P

Q

R

S

T

U

V

INTRODUCTION

The Oriental must have his epigram. It is one of the chief necessaries of his life, and an untold solace. With a shrewd apophthegm for every occasion he can defy all "the slings and arrows of outrageous fortune;" and a sententious phrase robs even defeat and disappointment of their sting.

The wisdom of the East consists in such sentences and proverbs rather than in any sustained effort of the reason and consequently they assume much greater importance than in Western lands, and furnish better materials for a thorough study of the character and conditions of an Asiastic people than any other source of information can supply. We are indebted to Pandit Ganga Datt Upreti for a complete collection of the proverbs and folk-sayings of Kumaun and Gaṛhwál, which he has diligently gathered together during a life-time of public service. Himself a native of the province, and having spent long periods in different and sometimes remote parts of it, he has enjoyed peculiar advantages for carrying out such a task. These researches have been the favourite relaxation of his leisure hours: and the result which appears in this volume is a valuable addition to our knowledge of the people, and cannot fail to be interesting to many readers not only in India, but also, it is hoped, in Britain and America. They present a picture of primitive manners and a naive self-revelation which will be delightful to the student of human nature, and will be of special value to all who are called on in the course of duty to enter into close relations with the people of India.

The great merit of this collection is that it has been gathered entirely from original sources—taken down, in fact, from the lips of the people and is in no sense a mere literary compilation. Those who have a wide acquaintance with Indian folklore will at once perceive that many of the sayings and proverbs included here are not peculiar to the province of Kumaun and Gaṛhwál, but are common, sometimes in slightly altered form, throughout

Northern India, and not a few of them will be found scattered about in various works of reference. The Pandit is aware of this, but his intention has been to make a complete collection of the proverbs of his own province, omitting nothing that is commonly prevalent; and on the whole this seems the most satisfactory plan. Each proverb and story is a genuine popular saying, derived not from books, but from the living speech of the people, and so possesses an intrinsic value. The stories given are such as are usually related by villagewise acres and rustic philosophers in illustrating or expanding a particular proverb, and many of them, as well as many of the proverbs themselves, are quite peculiar to the province, and are now printed for the first time.

By translation into another language it is inevitable that popular sayings should lose much of their force and pungency. Ingenious plays on words are completely lost, rhythm and rhyme are both sacrificed, and nothing is left but the bare bones of the proverb. The present collection forms no exception to the rule. The brevity, point, and ingenuity of many a saying have vanished in the English translation, nor was there, as a rule, any possible means of retaining them. If poetry cannot be satisfactorily translated into another language, still less can proverbs. Their power often depends on subtle associations of thought and language which no earthly skill can render into another tongue, while cumbrous attempts to throw them into poetical form are only so much time wasted.

The proverbs are translated from the Kumauni and Gaṛhwáli dialects, which are off-shoots or rather sisters of the Hindi, and differ from the high or standard form of that language only in grammatical forms and a few peculiarities of pronunciation. In many cases a saying current in the plains of India seems to have simply been turned into the dialect, though there are many others which are quite local, and from their nature and allusions could only have become current in a mountainous country.

The province of Kumaun and Gaṛhwál extends for about one hundred miles east to west and one hundred and ten miles north to south along the sourthern slopes of the Himalayas, beyond which lies the mysterious land of Tibet, from which the province is separated by the snowy range. In this part of the range there are several peaks exceeding twenty thousand feet in height. These stupendous features in the landscape are visible from most parts of the province and add a striking grandeur to the scenery. The whole country consists of an intricate maze of mountains and glens, through which flow several rivers and innumerable streams, all tributary, either directly or indirectly, to the Ganges. The hilly ranges of this sub-Himalayan region vary in height from eight thousand to five thousand feet, the valleys often descending to a level of only two thousand or three thousand feet above sea level, The hill-sides are usually very steep and frequently quite precipitous, clothed in most part with forests of fir, and above the level of six thousand feet, with giant rhododendron, holm-oak, and beech. Towards the south the higher ranges of hills abruptly descend, being succeeded by a narrow stretch of low broken country called the Bhábar, and then by a gradual slope towards the great plain of Upper India, which is named the Terai. This lower belt is from two to fifteen miles broad, and is part of the province, having always been much used by the hill people, who drive their herds of cattle thither for forage during the dry months. In some parts of the province, especially around the capital town Almora, the hills are very barren. Bishop Heber sang of

"Bleak Almora's barren steep;"

but generally Kumaun may be called a forest land. After and during the rains the grass-covered slopes and verdant valleys are a lovely sight. Himalayan landscapes are distinguished more especially by their vastness: range after range of mountains fade away into the blue distance, crowned towards the north by the towering "snowy summits old in story", with their well-defined peaks of Nanda Devi, Pánch Chule, Trisúl, and Badri Náth. As the traveller advances into the province new vistas are disclosed at every turn of the road, as it winds along the steep mountain sides; and the mingled charms of forest, cliff, glen, and distant snowy peak combine to form landscapes of singular beauty. The only drawback, as a rule, is the absence of water from the scene, though near Naini Tal this defect is abundantly supplied, and the blue waters of two or three lakes glancing in the brilliant sunshine amongst the fir-clad hills make the view from any of the neighbouring heights one of the finest in the world.

The Pindari glacier, at the base of the great snowy ranges is a favourite object for tourists, and a moderately good road with rest-houses placed at suitable intervals, leads to it. The scenery at some points is indescribably grand. The celebrated shrines of Badri Nath and Kedar Nath in Gaṛhwal, also situated among the snows, are yearly visited by many thousands of Hindu pilgrims from all parts of India and even from the extreme south. These temples are specially sacred as being intimately associated with the leading deities of Hindu mythology. Indeed, the Himalayas, as might be expected from their striking physical features, play a large part in Hindu story and legend, and may be called the Olympus of India; every peak, pool, and river has its tradition relating to the gods, and such a degree of sanctity pertains to these mountains that even the sight of them is said, in one of the sacred books, to remove the sins of the beholder, as the dew is dried up by the morning sun.

The population is distributed mostly in small hamlets, perched here and there on the steep sides of the mountains, and often almost inacessible, so that the proverbs in this collection which refer to people who have never been away from their native villages are no exaggeration. When one looks at some of these villages hanging like birdnests on the sides of the precipitous hills, approachable only by the faintest goat-track, one cannot help wondering how human beings can either reach them or get away from them. There are a few larger towns, among which we may mention Almora, the capital, Srinagar and Pauri in Gaṛhwal, and the two European health-resorts, Ranikhet, occupied by British troops, and Naini Tal, the beautiful summer headquarters of the North West Provinces Government.

The agriculture of the province is necessarily of a limited character, owing to the hilly nature of the ground. Yet it is wonderful what human perseverance has done to overcome these difficulties. The hill-sides are scooped into a number of terraces, supported by rough walls. In some places as many as a hundred of these narrow terraces, each of which is a cornfield, may be seen one below another, occupying the whole of the steep side of a hill. The principal grains grown are difficult kinds of millet, wheat, and rice. Tea is succesfully grown in several parts of the province by Europeans. The best kinds of tea are of excellent quality and are preferred by many to any other growth.

The population of the province presents great variety as regards caste and origin. The aborigines exist in the servile race of Doms, who are dark, short and somewhat negro-like in appearance. They have for centuries been in a state of subjection to the Hindu castes, and are still regarded by them as unclean and degraded. In former days a Dom who touched the drinking-vessel or huqqa (tobacco pipe) of a Brahmin was at once put to death. A Dom was not allowed to wear a garment which reached below the knees. One of their customs which especially causes them to be abhorred by the fastidious Hindu is that of eating the carcases of cows or bullocks which have died a natural death. They are chiefly employed as carpenters, masons, black-smiths, and day-labourers of various kinds. It would be interesting to know something of their religious beliefs, but little has yet been determined on this point. They have adopted Hinduism to a large extent, though they generally worship the Deity under the name of Nirákár (for Formless). These Doms have a tradition that they were the original inhabitants of the country, and that they were employed by Mahadev as drummers on the joyful occasion when he adopted the Himalaya mountains as his residence.

According to a tradition of the Doms, as well as from other evidence, it appears certain that the next comers into the country, were the Khasas or Khasiyas, whose descendants form the principal part of the population. They were probably among the first invaders of India—an Aryan race hailing from central Asia and at one time widely spread over Northern India—though distinct from and earlier than the well-known Aryan invasion of the Punjab. They now form a separate race or caste only in Kumaun and Gaṛhwál. They have been influencd greatly in the course of ages by contact with the Brahmins and other Hindus of the plains, and differ little from the orthodox Hindu. They are distinctly Aryan in features, and are the cultivators of the soil and the coolie caste of Kumaun.

The third class of inhabitants may be included under the general designation of immigrants from the Plains of India. It is related that a certain rajah named Kanakpal belonging to the Lunar Race visited Garhwál in the seventh century with his followers on a pilgrimage to the sacred shrines of Kedar Náth and Badri Náth, and afterwards conquered the country. The successors of his dynasty still rule in Tihri or Independent Garhwál. At that time Kumaun was broken up into a number of petty Khasiya kingdoms, until a dynasty was founded in the tenth century A.D. by Som Chand, said to be a scion of a royal family residing at Jhansi. There are very conflicting accounts of the manner in which he established his power in Kumaun. What is certain is that the Chand dynasty reigned in the country (not always over the whole of it, and with interruptions of Khasiya revolts, Rohilla invasions etc.) until the end of the last century, when the Gorkhális of Nepál invaded the country and established their rule in Kumaun. So violent were the methods of the conquerers and so oppressive their government that to this day any act of tyranny is spoken of as "Gorkhiyáni" (rule of the Gurkhas). In 1815 the British took possession of the province, in retaliation for aggressions by the Nepál Kingdom.

As an example of the *legendary* history of Kumaun, (regarding which a large collection of stories and traditions has been gathered by Pandit Ganga Datt Upreti, and will probably be issued by him in a separate volume), the following account of the foundation of Almora, the capital town, may be found interesting:

About six hundred years ago, when the Chand Rajahs held their court at Champawat in eastern Kumaun, the reigning king was one day hunting on the Almorah hill, which was at that time covered with dense forest, a hare suddenly started up before him, and he began to pursue it, whereupon it was transformed into a tiger, and on reaching the top of the hill disappeared. The king consulted his Brahman astrologers concerning this strange event. They all accepted it as a most favourable omen, and counselled the king to found his capital on the spot where the tiger had disappeared. The site was accordingly examined, prior to beginning building operations, and a large crowbar was driven into the ground. It sank so deep that the astrologers declared it has pierced the back of the Seshnág; or great serpent which the Hindus suppose to support the universe, and they accepted the fact as a sign that the king's dynasty should endure for ever. But the king, impelled by curiosity, insisted on the bar being dragged out of the ground, and, sure enough, the point of it was seen to be stained with blood. Thereupon the astrologers in wrath declared that as a punishment for the rajah's presumption and unbelief, his descendants should reign but for a few generations.

Were it not for this valuable information, we should naturally suppose that the real reason of Almora's selection as the capital was the abundant supply of water there, and the excellent quality of the soil on the slope below the ridge, where an immense amount of grain is grown for the food-consumption of the people.

The Chand dynasty attracted many Brahman families from the plains, who settled in Kumaun and have multiplied exceedingly, so that this province contains an unusually large proportion of the Brahman caste. Many of them have entered Government service and prospered. Perhaps nowhere in India is the worldly as well as the spiritual predominance of the Brahman so marked as in Kumaun and its capital Almora.

The Bhoteas are a Mongolian tribe inhabiting the northern parts of the province. They carry on a trade between Tibet and India, conveying borax and other commodities on the backs of their sheep and goats over the high passes of the snow range, from Tibet. They have a distinctly Chinese appearance, and their residence in the cold climate of the snows gives many of them quite a fresh colour. They dress in thick woollen garments and woollen mocassins, and are a cheery good-humoured folk, though unfortunately somewhat given to ardent spirits. They say that if they washed themselves they could never endure the intense cold of those altitudes, consequently they remain unwashed. They own much land (mostly fallow) in the northern part of Kumaun, and some of them are quite wealthy, the Hindus in some places being their labourers and servants. Another industry which they practice is that of weaving carpets and blankets, which they also bring down to the markets of Bageshwar and Almorah. They still acknowledge some kind of fealty to the Tibetan government, though they are really British subjects. Through contact with the Hindus they are rapidly adopting Hindu customs and ceremonies, but are looked down upon by the Hindus and reproached for drinking tea with the Tibetans when visiting Tibet. This custom, though contrary to Hindu caste rules, they cannot avoid, as the merchants of Tibet will conclude no bargain without the friendly preliminary of drinking tea.

In character the (Hindu) people of Kumaun and Gaṛhwal, as becomes a mountain race, are sturdier and more independent than the Hindus of the plains. They have enjoyed great advantages, particularly under the long and benevolent rule of the "King of Kumaun", Sir Henry Ramsay, late Commissioner of the province. In former days the Kumaunis bore an excellent character for honesty, simplicity, and good-nature, and it is to be hoped that they will continue to keep this reputation.

It would be an enjoyable task to give a sketch of the history of the country from early times, abounding as it does in the romantic incidents always to be met with in the history of a mountain people. But such an account would take up too much space, and we can only recommend the reader who desires further information to consult the large and valuable treatise on the subject (*Gazetteer of the North West Provinces*, vol. XI) written by the late Mr. E.T. Atkinson. Kumaun is closely connected through its early history, and by reason of its containing the sacrosanct Himalayas, with the entire legendary system and mythology of India, (the references to it in the ancient Sanskrit scriptures being very numerous) while in many ways the story of the country illustrates and throws light on the most interesting questions of history and archaeology.

Almora, Nov. 7th 1892. E. S. Oakley

PROVERBS AND FOLKLORE OF KUMAUN AND GARHWAL

ABILITY

1. सड़ी शिकार मसुरै कि दाल बराबर के निहो। Sarhî shikára masurai ki dála barábara ke niho.

Is not even rotten meat better than dála of masúra (vetch) ?

E.g. Ability, though of a very inferior kind, is better than incompetence. *Masúra* is a kind of pulse. (*Lentil urvum hirsutum or cicer lens*).

2. चोर जै मोर मारनात भाबर रितो है जानु। Chora jai mora máranáta bhábara rito hai jánu.

If thieves killed peacocks the jungle would have become clear of them.

I.e. If fools are to do the work who will ask for wise men?

3. कवा शिकार मारना त बाज को पाल। Kawá shikára máraná ta bája ko pála.

If a crow could hunt, what need could there be for keeping a falcon?

Used to show that if illiterate and ignorant people could be of use there would be no necessity for getting the services of learned and wise people

ABSENCE OF MASTER

1. जख बिलि नी तख मूसा नाचनी। Jakha bili nî takha músá náchanî.

When there is no cat mice dance.

C. f. "When the cat is away the mice will play." People are liable to go wrong when there is no control whatever over them.

ABSENT MINDEDNESS

1. गोदि में लड़का शहर में ढंड़ोला। Godi me laṛaká shahara me ḍhanḍolá.

The child is in one's arms, but search is made for him throughout the town.

Applied to one's missing a thing which is near at hand all the time—like the old lady looking for her spectacles, which are all the time on her own nose.

2. बान बानैं बलद हराणो। Bána bánai balada haráno.

The bullock disappeared while in the act of ploughing.

One wonders at his own carelessness when he loses sight of the tool with which he is working.

ACCIDENT

1. अनलै कि चोट कनाला। Analai ki choṭa kanálá.

One who aimed at the analá (i.e. the lower edge of a field) hit the kanálá (i.e. the upper edge).

Applied to some attempt which has resulted differently from what was intended or expected.

2. बयाला को लागणो वोट को ढलनु। Bayálá ko lágano boṭa ko ḍhalanu.

The tree fell down as the wind blew.

E.g. An old rotten tree fell before the blast of an ordinary wind. Used by an innocent person saying that he was blamed for nothing, for the ruin or catastrophe was certain to occur. Every effect must have a cause. People must find an explanation (in a wrong sense) for every misfortune.

ADVERSITY

1. नाव नौ इतरो ततरो पाणी पेण को फुटयुं पतरो। Náwa nau itaro tataro páni pena ko phutyun pataro.

Such a great name and such a great fame but a broken vessel (loṭa) to drink water with.

Applied by one who bemoans present adversity following former prosperity.

2. एक रिख की डरले भूड़ पैठो वांतीन रीख निकला। Eka rikha kí ḍarale bhúrha paiṭho wán tína ríkha nikalá.

To save himself from one bear he entered a hedge where he found three.

Out of the frying pan into the fire.

3. थोड़ि उधरियो ज्यादा उधर लो जो सुधारनो लगै सो पुरो होलो। Thorhî udhariyo jyádá udharalo jo sudhárano lagai so puro holo.

The portion of the wall which has given way is sure to fall, and also to fall further; and the portion which is being built or repaired is sure to be finished.

C.f. Adversity and prosperity do not come alone but in train. "It never rains but it pours."

4. घर की जली बण गयुं बण में दूणि आग। Ghara ki jali baṇa gayun̲ baṇa men dúni ága.

Being burnt out of my home I fled to the jungle where I found a fire twice as fierce.

C.f. Out of the frying pan into the fire.

5. थोड़ि जगा गिलो आटो। Thoṛi jagá gilo áṭo.

Narrow quarters and thin gruel.

Used to denote wretched circumstances.

6. फांड फुटली त करदोड़ी क्या थांभली। Phán̲ḍa phuṭali ta karadorhî kyá thámbhalî.

If the stomach is ruptured, the waist chain (worn by men as an ornament) will not be able to support it.

This means that if one's fate is adverse his friends and relatives cannot help him: they are only ornaments in prosperity.

7. कमबखती को आटो गिलो। Kambakhtî ko áṭo gilo.

The dough of an unlucky man is too thin to make bread with.

I.e., Nothing prospers in the hand of an unlucky man. Illustrated by the following story :—

There was a family which consisted of husband, wife, and son. The family being in very poor circumstances began to offer their prayers and penances to *Mahádeva* a god who seeing their sustained piety and devotion was pleased with them. He appeared to them and said he would grant one boon to each. On this they asked permission to be allowed to present their requests the next day, accordingly the wife asked that she might become a queen; instantly she became a most beautiful woman. Just then a king passing by that way became enamoured of her, and carried her off. After this the husband's turn came. He on hearing that his wife had been taken away by the king, was sore distressed and moved the deity to change his wife (who had already become a queen) into a sow and send her to him. This also came to pass. After this the son, who saw what had happened before to his father and mother, went to Mahádeva and said that he wanted nothing but to have his mother become the wife of his father as before. The deity granted this also.

ADVICE (BAD.)

1. तेरो घर हालिद्यूंलो मैके देलै। Tero ghara hálidyun̲lo main̲ ke delai.

What will you give me if I ruin your house ?

Applied to one who gives bad advice.

AGGRAVATION OF EVILS

1. डाडा मा लूण। Ḍáḍá má lún̲a.

Applying salt to a burn.

"To add insult to injury."

Used by one whose feelings are hurt when he is in distress.

2. मरिया स्याप का आंखा खचोरना। Mariyá syápa ká áṅkhá khachoraná.

To pick the eyes of a dead snake.

Applied to one who slanders or insults an enemy who is dead or is in distress or poverty. Hitting a man when he is down.

AGRICULTURE

1. उत्तम खेती मध्यम बणज अखट चाकरी बिकट जोग। Uttama khetí madhyama baṇaja akhaṭa chákarí bikaṭa joga.

Agriculture is best, commerce comes next, service is full of trouble, but the life of an ascetic is the most difficult of all.

Advice to all to follow the professions of agriculture and commerce, and dissuading them from taking service, or becoming hermits.

2. धान पधान मडुवा राजा ग्यूं गुलाम। Dhána padhána maduwá rájá gyún̲ gulám.

Rice the head man, millet the king, and wheat the slave.

Applied by hill people to indicate the varying amounts of their staple crops. Also interpreted thus, that the paddy is sold and the proceeds of it go to the head-man of the village in payment of revenue or rent : the wheat is utilized in satisfying *Chaprásis* (peons) and government messengers &c, whereas the millet is the only support of the family.

3. दूर को सेरो नजीक को केरो। Dúra ko sero najika ko kero.

Irrigated fields at a distance are of no more value than the small plots of ground near the house.

The plots close to one's house are as valuable as irrigated land which is far off, inasmuch as it requires more trouble and expense to cultivate it.

4. मैला की बाल खाया की गाल। Mailá kí bála kháyá kí gála.

Manure produces fine crops and good food fat cheeks.

Spoken in praise of good tillage and generous diet.

5. खेति खसम सेति। Kheti khasama seti.

The tillage (prospers only) when the master is there, or it needs close personal attention.

Applies to other business also.

6. मडुवा राजा जब सेकौ तब ताजा। Maḍuwá rájá jaba sekau taba tájá.

Maḍuwá (millet) is a king, for it becomes fresh when heated.

Poor people make bread of the maduwá flour which they take with them on a journey. They heat the cakes before they eat them. This process makes them as fresh as if they were cooked at the moment.

7. बरखे ह्यूं त को समाल ग्यूं। Barkhe hyún̲ ta ko samála gyún̲.

If snow falls, who will be able to gather in all the wheat! (it will be so plentiful).

This is applicable to high tablelands; for the rain that falls there runs down the slopes, but the snow melts gradually and soaks into the ground, and thus causes better crops.

8. मल खेती बल राज। Mala kheti bala rája.

The tillage depends on manure, and the reign on strength (army).

Used to appreciate the power of manure.

ALTERNATIVES

1. जैले नि देखो स्यू उ देख बिरालु जैले नि देखी वौ उ देख बौको भाई जैले नि देखो ठग उ देख नाइ। Jaile ni dekho syú u dekha biralu jaile ni dekhi bau u dekha bauko bhái, jaile ni dekho ṭhaga u dekha nái.

Whoever is anxious to see a tiger, or a bride or a cheat should gratify his curiosity by looking at their miniatures—viz., a cat, the bride's brother, and a barber.

This is quoted when for some greater thing or business a lesser is made to answer. *E.g.*, if a priest prescribes a buffalo for sacrifice the man offers only a cock.

ANGER

1. गुस्सा बड़ो होस्यार। Gussá barho hosyára.

Anger is very wise.

I.E. Anger breaks out against one's subordinates, not against those who are one's superiors.

2. चबौणा का दांत और देखूणा का और। Chabauṇa ká dáṇta aur dekhúná ká aur.

The molar teeth are different from those that are seen.

To show one's teeth represents anger, but to grind the teeth is a sign of great rage—represents different degrees of anger.

3. गुस्सा खोव अपणी मो बुद्धि खोव बिराणी मो। Gussá khowa apaṉi

mo buddhi khowa biráṉí mo.

Anger ruins one's own family, but wisdom that of one's enemy.

Caution against losing one's temper.

BANIYÁS OR SHOP-KEEPERS

1. गंगोलि को कणकिया भलि कै दण किया। Gangoli ko kaṉa kiyá bhali kai daṇa kiyá.

This man who brings flour (to sell) is of Gangoli (a pargana of the Kamaun district) you should cheat him well.

A resident of Gangoli, though seemingly simple, is very cunning. Once a man of Gangoli brought some flour to Almora for sale. The Baniyá who was to buy it had received a hint from his friend (another Baniyá) in the words of the proverb, "to deceive him well". The man, though he understood the hint, kept silent, keeping his own counsel, but when he sold his flour and received the price, he replied to the baniyás as below, and disappeared.

2. गंगोलि को लाटो पांच बांट खड़ि येक बांट आटो। Gangoli ko láṭo páncha bánṭa khaḍi eka báṉṭa áṭo.

The dumb (simpleton) of Gangoli (who has brought) 5 parts of powdered chalk mixed with one part of real flour for sale.

This mortified the Baniyás and gave them a good lesson.

Illustration. This trait extends even to the bullocks of Gangoli. A story is related that once a Gangoli bullock was pitted against another bullock, the contest consisting in drinking from a pool. The animal which drank the most water was to be declared the victor. The Gangoli bullock kept his mouth in the water feigning to drink without intermission. The other animal thinking his antagonist was continually drinking exerted himself to the utmost, and, being unable to endure the strain, fell down and died.

3. बणिया है सयाणो बौलो। Baṇiya hai sayáṉo baulo.

Any man more acute than a Baniá (merchant) is a madman.

Another name for a Bania is "*Sau*" or "Sáha" which also means *one hundred*, and so villagers say he is called "*Sau*" because he has a hundred cunning ways.

4. सौज्यू गुड़ खावौ लेख, लेख, लेख. Sau jyú gurha kháwau lekha, lekha, lekha.

O Sir, come and eat some treacle ! write it down, write it down, write it down.

(The Baniyá invites a simple fellow to come and eat his wares; but at the same time instructs his servants to make an entry in the account-book against him, for the price of the article eaten). An ironical phrase used against Baniyás, who are outwardly very polite when offering their commodities for sale, but internally wishing to deceive their customers or visitors or guests.

5. सबन है सयाणो बणिया बणिया है सयाणो गवार. Sabana hai sayáṉo Baṇiyá Baṇiyá hai sayáṉo gawára.

The Baniyá who is most sly is exceeded by a villager in craft.

I.e., The Baniyá is the most cunning of all, but he is no match for a villager.

This is used to imply that no one can cheat a Baniyá except a villager, or that no respectable man can cheat a Baniyá (shop-keeper).

6. कुड़ा पैठो सौ गड़ा पैठो झो. Kurhá paiṭho sau garhá paiṭho jhau.

The entry of a Baniyá into one's house and that of jhau (a kind of wild plant which overgròws fields) into a field (is ruinous).

Applied to debt contracted, or credit accounts entered into with a Baniyá, since the transaction will surely ruin the person concerned, just as a single plant of *Jhau* rooting itself in a field will overgrow the whole field.

BETRAYERS

1. भलो होलो कै भागा बुलाइ भागाले भद्रा में ताइ लगाइ. Bhalo holo kai Bhágá bulái Bhágá le bhadrá men tái lagái.

Bhágá was sent for in order to do good, but she on the contrary put the pan on the fire in an inauspicious moment.

The cooking of sweetmeats for festivities such as tonsure marriage &c, &c, must be commenced in an auspicious moment. "Bhadra" is an unlucky portion of a certain day or night which is always avoided by consulting an almanack.

Used of one who, being depended on for help, betrays one.

2. गुड़ दीबेर ईंट मारणो. Gurha ďibera iṇṭa máraṇo.

To allure one with gurha (treacle) and then to smite him with a brick.

Applied to one who betrays another after having taken him into his confidence. Such persons are generally likened to a jar which is full of poison, but a little milk is put on the top of the jar to tempt people with.

3. गुड़ का साथ बिष दिणो. Gurha ká sátha bisha ďino.

With the sweet, poison is given.

A pleasant manner covering an intention to deceive.

BITTER FEELINGS

1. अडिठ भेट दुखन ठेस. Aḍiṭha bheṭa dukhana ṭhesa.

We are sure to meet with a man we dislike and hate, and a sore part of the body is sure to be hit.

2. पैले त उल्लू बासनी बास त गु खौं कर. Paile ta ullú básá ní básá ta gú khauṇ kara.

Owls generally remain silent, but whenever they open their mouths they make a very melancholy and horrid sound.

A gruff and surly person.

3. तेलची को तेल जलौ मशालची की गाण फाटौ. Telchî ko tela jalau mashálachî kî gána phátau.

The master's oil is being used, but the torch-bearer is afraid of wasting it.

Applied to one who is jealous of another's generosity.

4. राजा को भंडार जाव महता को हियो फाटौ. Rájá ko bhaṇḍára jáwa mahatá ko hiyo phátau.

As the treasure of a king is being spent the heart of the treasurer is rent.

This refers to one who prevents another from giving to a third person, or his being benefitted by another.

Story: Once a king gave an order for a large sum of money to be given to a poor man, who taking the order went to the treasurer to ask for the money. The treasurer having refused payment wrote back on the order to the king saying that the sum ordered to be paid was too much, a king ought to store money to be used in time of distress. The man took the paper back to the king, wrote on the same paper that a fortunate man has no distress at all, and sent it again to the treasurer, who returned it to the king, having written on it thus. "If at any time God (fortune) should forsake you?" The king read the remarks of his treasurer, and wrote on the paper again, "If God is against me at any time, the wealth will also vanish." As soon as the treasurer read the final order he was quite convinced of the truth of the king's remark, and paid the money. Hence the proverb.

BRAVERY AND COURAGE

1. बलिया देखि भूत भाजौ. Baliyá dekhi bhúta bhájau.

A ghost even flies before a strong man. No one can oppress the strong.

Once a man having become bankrupt left his village and went away to another country with his family and goods in search of a livelihood. One night he happened to stop at a place where dead bodies were burnt, called *Shamashána* which is supposed to be full of ghosts and evil spirits. As soon as the night came on a murderous ghost appeared before him. The man at once told his daughter-in-law to bind the ghost. She lost no time in running after him with a cord for the purpose. He also told his son and wife to cut off the head of the ghost. As soon as they got this order from the old man they both ran after the ghost with a sword and an axe, and having caught him were about to behead him. The ghost implored them, and said if they spared him he would shew them five jars of gold coin buried in a certain place. On this the old man was shown the place and took possession of the money, and then told the members of his family to let the ghost go uninjured. Thus having possessed himself of the wealth the man returned to his home, where he began to live comfortably. This procedure of his struck his neighbours with amazement and suspicion as to how he had become rich. On close enquiry the story leaked out to some one who had become very envious of the old man. The envious man having come to know how the other man became rich, sold his house and land to others and went away with his family to the spot haunted by the ghost. As the night came on the devil appeared before him; he told his daughter-in-law to have him bound, but she fled away and hid her face; he also at the same time told his wife and son to cut off the ghost's head, but they also ran away for fear of the ghost. The man himself was also frightened at his appearance, and thus the ghost, seeing them all timid and cowardly, killed them one by one. This illustration is also applied to the following proverbs.

1. He who is not afraid of dying will do every thing (vide under the head "Consolation and Encouragement").
2. He who is afraid will die, (vide under the head "Consolation and Encouragement").

2. मारी तलवार नाम गुलदार. Mári talawára náma guladára.

Whoever wields a sword is called Guladára (a chief).

This is applied to a soldier (hero) and also to one who does mischief and is therefore dreaded and called a champion.

3. जुंवां के डर ले घागरि निखोलीनि. Ju̲nwán ki ḍarale ghágari nikholíni

One should not take off her skirt for fear of lice.

Caution against unnecessary alarm.

4. तुमले चुचो पेछ मैले के घुनो पेछै. Tumale chucho pechha maile ke ghuno pechhai.

Did you alone suck the breast of your mother? and did I suck the knee of my mother instead of her breast?

Used to intimidate. Are you a man and am I not?

5. नामरदि परमेश्वर ले देछ मार मार तौभि कौणो. Námardi Parmeshwara le dechha mára mára taubhi kauno.

God has made you a coward, but why do you not threaten to beat?

I.E. Brave words sometimes frighten people. They should be used to effect one's purpose.

Story: Once a he-goat in spite of the remonstrance of his master, an agriculturist, went to a jungle in the evening. While in the jungle he was seen by a leopard, who followed him, and asked him, "Why do you wander in the jungle at night?" To this the goat said, "I have killed many elephants, but I am now in search of a leopard, that I may kill him also." At this the leopard took fright. On hearing the conversation a jackal went after the leopard and said "Shame to you, leopard, that you are frightened by a goat. Let us go and kill the goat." To this the leopard said, "O Jackal, you are a very sly creature, and consequently not worthy of confidence, the goat is such a hero that he has killed many elephants." To this jackal rejoined. "If you do not trust me, let us tie our tails together so that we may help each other in time of need, and kill the goat, which is a tasty morsel for both of us." After this they both set off to kill the goat. As soon as the goat saw these two fierce animals approaching him he said, "Well, my dear friend jackal, you have done well in bringing the leopard to me, for I have just come here in search of him." This speech so frightened the leopard that he fled towards a precipice, while the jackal ran towards the goat. But, owing to the leopard being a stronger animal, he dragged the jackal with him, and falling down the steep precipice both were killed. This story also explains the proverb. "The taste of eating *Auṇla* (a wild fruit used for medicines) and the reason of an old man's warning are experienced afterwards." Vide under head "Old People".

BRIBERY AND GIFTS

1. चांदी को जोतो मारनो. Chánḏi ko joto márano.

To beat a man with a silver shoe.

Applied generally to getting a purpose accomplished through bribery, gifts, or by offering rewards.

2. चांदी को मेख तमाशो देख. Chándi ko mekha tamásho dekha.

Drive in a silver nail and see wonders wrought.

The power of money, which is called the "Assistant God".

3. मृदंग का मुख लेप ले भली आवाज औंछ्य. Mirdanga ká mukha lepa le bhali áwája auṉchhya.

The kettledrum sounds well when its mouth is smeared with flour.

By giving alms or bribes you can get any amount of praise.

4. खालि हाथ मुख में निजानु. Kháli hátha mukha me nijánu.

An empty hand (fingers with no food in them) does not go into the mouth.

Natives of India convey their food to their mouths with their fingers, in other words, they do not enter the mouth without food, *i.e.*, one will not thrust his fingers into his mouth except when taking food.

No one will do any work without remuneration; or used by one who is unwilling to do work without wages as an excuse for his denial.

CALAMITY

1. ऊपर मे चापर, उकल मे ताकुल. Úpara me chápara, ukala me tákula.

Sorrow upon sorrow, perplexity upon perplexity.

E.g., One calamity or perplexity treading upon the heels of another. "Misfortunes never come single."

2. दैब कि मार खबर न सार. Daiba ki mára khabara na sára.

A judgment from God—one cannot provide against or remedy it.

Applied to sudden loss without any opportunity of remedying or preventing it.

3. थाती हरण पिता मरण. Tháti hara̱na pita mara̱na.

Birthright gone and father dead.

An overwhelming calamity. This is also used to represent that the death of one's father is as ruinous as the confiscation of his hereditary home.

4. कख तें बोदूं बिपत कि बात एक एक बिपता नौ नौ हाथ. Kakha te̱n bodú̱n bipata ki báta eka eka bipatá nau nau hátha.

How shall I describe my misfortunes? Each of them is nine cubits long.

Used by one complaining of great misfortunes.

CASTE

1. मागाल सहेव गोच गाल नि सहेव. Má gála sahewa gotra gála ni sahewa.

One can tolerate the slandering of his mother, but not that of his caste.

Showing the high estimate in which caste is held.

CHARACTER

1. बेटा क्या देखणो बेटा का यार देखणा. Betá kyá dekhaṇo betá ká yára dekhaṇá.

A son's character is to be judged by the character of his companions.

2. धानू को गांव़ पराल तें सूज. Dhánú̱n ko gá̱nwa parála te̱n sújha.

A village in which paddy is grown can be recognized by the straw it has produced.

3. नामी सौकार कमाय खाव नामी चोर पकड़ा जाव. Námí saukára kamáya kháwa námí chora pakarhá jáwa.

A noted merchant earns more and more, but a reputed thief will be arrested again and again.

C.f. "Give a dog a bad name and hang him."

4. गौं को लक्षणम्यूं तें. Gaun̲ ko lakshyaṇa gyún̲ḍá ten̲.

The condition of a village is known by the path which leads to it.

A man's character is known by his conduct.

5. हांडी को सीत पछ्याणिद्. Hán̲ḍí ko síta pachhyáṇida.

The potful of rice is judged by one grain taken out of it (as to whether the whole potful is well cooked or not).

A man's character or disposition is known from a single deed.

6. जैकी छ बात तैकि छ साख. Jaiki chha báta taiki chha sákha.

Only a man of good repute is trusted by all.

So one ought to be very careful that his character should remain stainless.

7. सौण सपूत न भादो कपूत. Sauṇa sapúta na bhádo kapúta.

Neither is Sawana (July) a good son, nor Bhado (August) a bad son.

Used in comparing two characters equally noted for wickedness.

8. सौण सूखो न भादो हरो. Sauna súkho na bhádo haro.

Neither Sauna (July) is dry, nor Bhado (August) green.

Used in comparing two characters equally noted for wickedness.

9. ताप्यूं घाम के तापणों देख्यूं मैंस के देखणों. Tápyún̲ gháma ke tápan̲o dekhyún̲ main̲sa ke dekhan̲o.

He who has felt the heat of the sun knows what sunshine is, and he who has once had dealings with a man knows what his character is.

10. गौं का लक्षण गल्याठ बट. Gaun ká lachhyaṇa (lakshyaṇa) galyáṭha baṭi.

One can foretell the condition of a village from the path leading to it.

A man's character is evident from his dealings.

CHARITY AND ALMS

1. रख पत रखाव पत. Rakha pata rakháwa pata.

Be charitable to others, and you will be treated charitably.

This is generally used in exhorting one not to expose the faults of others, so that they should do the same to you.

C.f. "Judge not that ye be not judged."

"Blessed are the merciful, for they shall obtain mercy."

The story related below illustrates the proverb.

Story: One morning in the month of May, the Emperor Akabar the great, his son, and Bírabal his prime minister went out for a walk together. They walked several miles. As soon as the sun had risen the monarch felt his cloak heavy and relieved himself of it by putting it on the shoulder of Bírabal. As soon as he had done this, his son also followed his father's example. On this the Emperor looking at Bírabal said ironically that the load was enough for one ass. To this remark Bírabal said, "No sire, the load I am bearing is properly speaking the load of two asses. "Tit for tat."

2. आदर का चाणा बेआदर का दाख. Ádara ká cháṉá be-ádara ká dákha.

Even gram given with courtesy is better than grapes bestowed with contempt.

I.e. A little given kindly is better than much bestowed with harshness or disdain.

"Every man according as he purposeth in his heart, so let him give: not grudgingly, or of necessity; for God loveth a cheerful giver" (2 Corin. 9.7).

3. भीख में भीख दिणो तीन लोक जीत लिणो. Bhíkha me bhíkha diṉo tína loka jíta liṇo.

He who gives alms out of what he has received as alms (begged) wins three worlds.

This proverb is generally quoted to encourage a poor person to give alms, or support others.

4. भूजि बोणो सताइ दीणो. Bhúji boṉo satái díṉo.

To bestow an alms after many repulses is like sowing parched grain (i.e., bears no good fruit).

This is appiled to one who gives help to another after putting him to great trouble and inconvenience. This kind of giving will meet with no reward (merit), just as parched grain will not grow. *C.f.* "He doubles his gift, who gives in time." "He gives twice, that gives in a trice." "The Lord loveth a cheerful giver."

5. स्वर्ग सों टेक नि धर्म सो छेक नि। Swarga so<u>n</u> ṭeka ni dharma so<u>n</u> chheka ni.

Heaven (the sky) needs no props, and a virtuous act needs no special time, or alms need no future promises, (for its performance).

This is used to encourage one to do good deeds without procrastination.

6. जैकों चुन्न उइ को पुण्य। Jaiko chunna ui ko pu<u>n</u>ya.

The reward is his who gives (the flour) not of the one who receives.

Used to encourage charity.

7. दिन्यूं दान थुक्यूं थूक। Dinyú<u>n</u> dána thukyún thúka.

An alms once given, is as phlegm which has been expectorated, not worth taking back.

8. जसो बोलो तसो लवालो। Jaso bolo taso lawálo.

As much as you sow so much you will reap.

Applied only to giving charities. In a future existence one will be blessed in proportion to one's gifts in this life. "Whatsoever a man soweth that shall he also reap." (Gal. 6, 7.)

Illustration. Once there was a poor, simple, and virtuous beggar living with his wife in a town. He used to earn only three *chhatáks* (six ounces) of flour a day, whether he begged at five houses or fifty, but never more. One day, when they had cooked 1½ cakes with the three *chhatáks* of flour, a saint arrived there who said that he was very hungry. They gave him the 1½ ready-made cakes, which the saint ate and departed. The hermit then went to God and interceded for the poor man, but God shewed him the Account Book and said that, since he had given only 1½ Rupees in his former existence, he was not entitled to more than what he received, and, if he got that 1½ Rupees at one time, after that he would get nothing more. The kind-hearted saint then petitioned God to let him have the 1½ Rupees at once, and God gave it to him. Then the saint came back to earth again and advised the poor man that the 1½ Rupees should be spent on charity, and whatever he got thereafter should also be devoted to the help of poor persons. The beggar did as he was told. The very next day having spent 1½ Rupees on charity he earned Rs.3, and, this sum also having been given to poor people, the next day he got Rs. 6. In this way as his income increased he increased his alms also spending all that he received on charity. After this the same saint went to paradise again and saw God in form of an old man sitting in a bending posture. On his enquiring the cause of this, God said that the man who has received 1½ Rupees, some days ago, had become very charitable and that whatever he got he gave it away to the poor, and that his charity had thus put a heavy burden upon himself. After this the saint came to the man again, and said that he was a very pious man and gave him advice as to his saving something for times of need. The man being puffed up with pride began to withhold his hand from charity, and the consequence was he became poor again very soon. *C.f.* "Much is expected when much is given." "As you sow, so you shall reap."

9. भला काम अैबन कणि ढकनि। Bhalá káma aibana kaṉi ḍhakani.
The good deeds of a man cover his imperfections.
C.f. "Charity covereth a multitude of sins."

10. मुसा घानि लगै दुला पैठ कवा घानि लगै देश फिर। Musá ghńi lagai dula paiṭha kawá ghńi lagai desha phira.

Put a bell on a crow and he flies to distant limits; put a bell on a mouse and he runs to his hole.

Used to induce people to extend their charities to strangers. If you do a kindness to a stranger he will praise you for it far and wide; if you help a fellow countryman he will be ashamed to speak about it and will keep silent.

11. दिनेर है दिवोनेर बड़ो। Dinera haí diwonera barho.

The person who induces another to give is better than the giver (himself).

Used as an inducement to charity.

CHASTITY AND UNCHASTITY

1. रौ तौ अपणा आप नि रौ तौ अपणा बाप। Rautau apaṇá ápa ni rau tau apaṇá bápa.

A woman will remain chaste himself, but not by her father's command.

I.e., only her own sense of honour can be depended on.

2. बुबा घर त चारै खुटा बुबा घर नात चारै खुटा। Búbá ghara tau chárai khuṭa búbá ghara náta chárai khuṭá.

When my father is at home my mother is a quadruped and when he is away still she is the same.

An unchaste woman.

3. रांड सांड की क्या परतीत। Ráṉḍa sáṉḍa kí kyá paratíta.

A woman and a bullock are not to be trusted.

I.e. Neither the chastity of a woman nor the behaviour of a bull can always be depended on.

4. स्यैणि ले खोला दंत बैक ले पै अंत। Syaîṇi le kholá daṉta baika le pai aṉta.

When a woman shows her teeth (speaks) man finds her motive.

Used to show the impropriety of a woman conversing with men, as it is not the custom among native women to converse freely with men other than their own relatives.

CHEATS

1. लालची देश में बगड़ा भूख नि मरना। Lálchí desha me bagarhá bhúkha ni maraná.

Cheats never starve in an avaricious country.

This is applied to one who is tempted to lay out money at interest in an unsafe speculation by offers of high interest. The story noted below illustrates the proverb. In a certain city a cheat once borrowed a small vessel from a rich merchant for cooking his food and after making use of it returned the vessel in the evening with another new vessel smaller than the first one. The merchant took back his own, but refused the other. On this the cheat said that he could not help it, as his (the merchant's) own vessel had given birth to it, and it justly belonged to him. After this argument the merchant was glad to take the other vessel, alleged to be the offspring of his own vessel. Such a bargain was repeated by the cheat several times, entirely to the profit of the merchant, who in the meantime became quite convinced of the man's honesty. Later on the cheat began to borrow from him many things of higher value and return them (with the several offspring of each) in the same way as he used to do with the smaller things. Finally one day the cheat pretended that there was a marriage in his family, for which he wanted to borrow much jewellery and many silver vessels; the merchant without any hesitation lent him all he had; the cheat took them all away as usual, and never appeared again.

2. सबन है ठगनाई। Sabana hai ṭhaga nái.

A barber is the greatest cheat of all.

Used to represent the craft of a barber. The following story illustrates the proverb.

Illustration. Among the 36 arts and crafts a certain king was skilled in 35. He went to an ascetic to learn the 36th or the art of metamorphosing. Contrary to the advice of his ministers he took with him a barber who was a favourite of his. Though the king learnt the art in secret, the barber somehow managed to become acquainted with it, but feigned ignorance. Once at night he entreated the king to shew him the wonders of the 36th art that he had learnt. The king accordingly after instructing the barber to constantly fan his body when he left it, and to prevent its being touched by a single fly, left his own body and entered into that of a parrot, and turned the jungle into a large city full of men, women, elephants, horses, camels &c. In the meantime the barber lost no time (as he had also learnt the art) in entering the king's body and returning to the metropolis. He began to reign over the country, but the Prime Minister of the empire perceived that some other soul had entered into the king's body. As his own body was already taken possession of by the barber, the king remained a parrot. He was caught by a fowler, but entreated the fowler to spare him, promising him nine lacs of rupees as a reward. The fowler did not kill him, but took him to a great city for sale, and, while there, took the parrot to a meeting of literary men. All of them were very much surprised at the parrot, and at the knowledge of science and literature which he displayed. One of the richest of the savants paid nine lacs of Rupees for the parrot and bought him. The parrot's fame for learning soon spread far and wide, and eventually reached the Prime Minister of the said kingdom, who came to the city and saw the parrot and found him no less wonderful than fame had reported. The Vizier then gave many jewels and immense wealth to the rich man, who in return presented him with the parrot. Thereupon the Vizier, returning to his own country, took occasion to say to the false king, "Sire, you were wont formerly to assume the disguise of various animals, but I do not understand why you do not now do so." On this the new king to prevent suspicion ordered a ram-fight, and having caused one animal to be suffocated, entered its body, and began to fight with the real ram, thereupon the real king left the body of the parrot and entered into his former body. Hence the proverb that a barber is an emblem of a cheat.

CLEAR CONSCIENCE

1. मन चंगा त कठौति में गंगा। Mana chan̲gá ta kaṭhauṭi me Gan̲gá.

To a pure mind the water in a shoe-maker's washbowl is as pure as the Ganga's water. (This water is considered so unclean that if a drop of it touches a Brahman he will fast for three days before he is considered a clean person).

This proverb is generally made use of to show strong faith. It has its origin in the story related below.

A shoe-maker named Rai Dás is said to have been a very pious man. Whenever he knew of any one going on a pilgrimage to Hardwár he was in the habit of sending through him two pice as a present to the Ganges, on the condition that she (the Ganges) would put forth her hand to receive it. Once the present was sent through a poor *Brahman*. After having received the shoe-maker's present, the Ganges, pitying the Brahman's poverty, presented him with a single gold bracelet which was richly embroidered and beautifully made. The Bráhman being unable to sell that bracelet was at last obliged to take it to a king for sale. The king bought it at the price demanded by the Bráhman and sent it to his queen consort, who was so highly pleased with it that she insisted on having another one of the same make. The Bráhman was consequently commanded to produce another at the risk of his life. The Bráhman went to the Ganges and prayed to her, but in vain. After that he went to Rái Dás and representing the case to him, begged him to save his life. Rai Dás prayed to the Ganges and plunged his hand in his water pot (in which he used to soak his leather), and brought up another bracelet of the same kind, and gave it to the Bráhman to present to the king.

Kaṭhauṭi means a wooden cup. *C.f.* "To the pure all things are pure."

COMFORTS AND DISCOMFORTS

1. हुना त ग्युं रूना क्यु। Huná ta gyun̲ rúná kyun̲.

If there had been a good crop of wheat, why should I complain?

E.g. No one cries or complains without some cause of suffering.

2. रूंदि रांड चूंदि पांड। Rún̲di rán̲ḍa chún̲di pán̲ḍa.

A weeping woman and a leaking upper story.

Applied to person or things that become very troublesome. *C.f.* "It is better to dwell in the wilderness than with a contentious and an angry women." "Continual dropping in a very rainy day, and a contentious woman are alike."

3. जैकी ज्वे नै तैको क्वे नै। Jaiki jwe nai taiko kwe nai.
He who has no wife has no one.
I.e. A man without a wife has no comfort.

4. चढ़ना हुणि लिगयो बोकणो पड़ो। Chaḍhaná huṇi ligayo bokaṇo parho.
One has to carry the horse, which he had procured for the purpose of riding, on his own shoulders.
Applied to bad trade or business, or to work which instead of being profitable proves to be ruinous.

5. आग तें अंगार मीठो। Aga ten angára míṭho.
Red coals are better than a blazing fire.
This means that moderate and lasting comforts are better than those of a more imposing kind and of a transient nature.

6. खटाइ में पड़नु। Khaṭái me parhanu.
To be immersed into acid.
A hobble. A nasty business. One entangled in an unnecessary trouble, and being unable to rid himself of it ironically uses this phrase. Acid is representative of inconvenience and trouble.

7. खांदी बखत की कल सींदा बखत को धुवां। Khándí bakhata kí kala síndá bakhata ko dhúnwán.
Quarrelling at dinner and smoke at bed-time.
Sources of discomfort.

COMMON PROPERTY

1. गाड़ को छालो धूर को पालो। Gárha ko chhálo dhúra ko pálo.
The banks of a river and the vegetation of a mountain peak.
Applied to denote that these things are nobody's property, every one having a common right to them.

CONSOLATION AND ENCOURAGEMENT

1. हुणा कि रीस जाणा कि खीस। Huṇá ki ŕisa jáṇá ki khísa.
One on the increase in envied, and one on the decline is laughed at.
Used to console people concerned on appropriate occasions.

2. औता धन प्यारो कोढ़ि ज्यू प्यारों। Autá dhana pyáro koḍhi jyú pyáro.
Wealth is dear to a childless man, life is dear to a leper.
This is spoken ironically of the above defects. A person having no descendants consoles himself with his wealth, and in the same way a leper having no enjoyment in life, wishes to live long to see the world. The perversity of human nature.

3. जो डरौ सो मरौ। Jo ḍarau so marau.
He who is afraid will die.
Once in a jungle a man seeing a tiger coming climbed up a large tree to save himself. A monkey followed his example. The tiger came near the shadow of the man, and attempted to grasp it, but as the man knew that his shadow was not himself, he did not fear the tiger's approach. After this the tiger attacked the shadow of the monkey, and as soon as he had stretched forth his claws to catch the shadow of the monkey, the monkey thought that he was being caught, and falling down in terror was eaten up by the tiger.

4. जैले शिर दैछ उइ सेर लग देलो। Jaile shire dechha ui sera laga delo.
He who has given the head, will give also a seer (of grain to support the man)
God supports every creature he has created. Encouragement to the poor and distressed. He who provides the mother's milk for him at his birth will still supply his wants.

5. जै कुं देव जगदीश तैकी क्या रीश। Jai kuṇ dewa jagaďisha taikí kyá ŕisha.

One favoured by God (the ruler of the world) should not be envived.

Good people console themselves by this proverb even in view of the prosperity of their enemies.

6. वो नि रइ त यो लग नि रव। Wo ni rai ta yo laga ni rawa.

As my former condition or circumstances have not lasted up to this time so the present state also will not last.

E.g. A man poor before has become a rich man now, and vice versa, and so speaks as in the proverb. Used to console one in adversity and make him careful and conscientious in prosperity.

7. वखल में शिर देणो मुशल देखि के डरनो। Wokhala me shira deṇa mashala dekhi ke ḍarano.

If you put your head in a mortar, why should you fear the pestle?

Used to encourage one to cope with the difficulties and dangers of a business already started by him.

8. रांड का दिन जावन छोरा का दिन आवन। Ráṉḍa ká dina jáwana chhorá ká dina áwana.

The day of widow has gone, but the day of the orphan boy is to come.

Often used to encourage an orphan son and his mother to try their best to help themselves.

9. श्याल कि बुद्धि शेर को तरण। Shyála ki buddhi shera ko tarṇa.

Slyness of a jackal and courage of a tiger.

Encouragement to try one's best.

10. सुवा मारी कौणि कैले ब्वे। Suwá mári kauṇ kaile bwe.

No one sowed kauṇi (a kind of millet) after killing parrots.

Applied to one who needlessly anticipates the difficulties and obstacles to be met with in a work not already commenced, as *kauṇi* is generally eaten when growing by parrots.

11. सिखीक स्याणा पढ़ीक पंडित। Sikhíka syáṉá paḍhíka Panḍita.

Observation makes one cunning, and study makes one learned.

Used to pursuade children, ignorant and inexperienced people to become clever and learned men.

12. शकरखोर सों शकर पैदा। Shakarakhora so<u>n</u> shakara paidá.

God gives sugar to him who cannot eat without it. "God tempers the wind to the shorn lamb."

Story: A great monarch once obtained God's permission to feed for one day all the animals within his kingdom. Accordingly he collected different kinds of food necessary for each animal on a stupendous scale, so that at last great mountains of food were collected. Just at this time a certain creature came out of the ocean bordering upon the monarch's empire and complained of great hunger. By permission of the monarch the animal was allowed to eat as much as he desired from the provision made ready. The animal within a few hours' time consumed the whole amount. This fact made the Ruler mortified and penitent. He asked God for forgiveness and said "O Lord, thou alone canst supply all thy creatures with food adapted to the nature of each, and secure to each the quantity daily required. No man in the world can support so great a charge even for a second."

13. मन कि हार ले हार मन की जीत ले जीत। Mana ki hára le hára mana kí jíta le jíta.

One has won if in his heart he feels so, and is defeated if he thinks so.

14. सौणि कठिन देखणि हाल हज़ूर। Sauṇi kaṭhina dekhaṇi hála hazura.

It is very difficult for one to endure injustice, but the wrong doer will certainly be requited.

"It is better to suffer wrong than to do it."

15. परमेश्वर कि लंबी बांह। Parmeshwar ki lambí bá<u>n</u>há.

God's arm is long—(to help or to punish).

16. भागी को माल जाव अभागी की ज्यान जाव। Bhági ko mála jáwa abhágí ki jyána jáwa.

One who is fortunate loses his property, but the unfortunate loses life (either his own life, or the lives of other persons in his household).

Consolation derived from Fatalism.

17. दाढ़ बाजे काल भाजे। Ḍáḍha báje, kála bháje.

Death flies away when the jaws work (literally sound).

Sick persons, who have lost their appetite, are thus induced to eat as much as they can so that they may get well soon.

18. काम कणि काम सिखौ। Káma kaṇi káma sikhau.

Work teaches work.

I.E. One who is initiated in or is made to do work will naturally find out how to do it.

Used to encourage one to undertake work and not to be afraid of it on account of ignorance or inexperience.

"Experientia docet".

19. लागि गयो भूतिया नि लागो चूतिया। Lágo gayo bhútiyá ni lágo chútiyá.

If I hit the mark it is like a lance; if I miss I will only be laughed at.

Encouragement to venture boldly.

20. जो मरना है निडरौ सो सब कुछ करौ। Jo maraná hai ni ḍarau so saba kuchha karau.

He who is not afraid of dying will do every thing.

Used to encourage people to chivalry.

21. डर का पास जैबेर डर जांछि। Ḍara ká pása jaibera ḍara jánchhi.

Fear or danger vanishes only when it is faced or coped with.

Used to encourage people not to fear or flee dangers.

C.f. "Better face a danger once than be always in fear."

CONTENTMENT

1. औतो चाइ सौतो प्यारो। Auto chái sauto pyáro.

Better to have a stepson than to be childless.

This is used by a woman who has no son of her own but finds comfort in the fact that her rival wife has one, so that her husband will not be childless.

2. थोड़ि खाणो बनारस में रौणो। Thorhi kháṇo Benares men̲ rauṇo.

It is better to live in Benares with a little food than with much food elsewhere.

E.g. Benares being a sacred city, living there is considered a meritorious act.

3. कभैं घ्यु घणा कभैं मुठि भरि चणा। Kabhain̲ ghyu ghaṇá kabhain̲ muṭhi bhari chaṇá.

Plenty of ghi at one time and a handful of gram at another.

Denotes that no one, in any circumstances, can expect to have all days alike with regard to food, comfort, &c.

4. थोड़ि खाणो सुखि रौणो। Thori kháṇo sukhi rauṇo.

To eat a little and be contented and happy.

C.f. "A little with quiet is the best of all diet." This is used in deterring one from aspiring after a higher thing which will entail hardship and trouble, or in advising one to remain contented with his own circumstances, and not to envy others in better condition.

5. घर कि आधि भलि। Ghara ki ádhi bhali.

Half a loaf at home is better than a whole one abroad.

Used to make one contented with his own lot at home in comparison with that of others abroad, though they may be in better circumstances.

6. रोटि का सांटा रोटि के माड़ि के मोटि। Roṭi ká sánṭá roṭi ke márhi ke moṭi.

Bread is bread, who cares whether it is thick or thin?

E.g. If one has to eat bread what does it matter whether it be made thick or thin.

Used of one who is contented with his circumstances whether good or adverse.

7. नीति जाइक थींति। Níti jáika thíti.

One wishes to stop after getting to Niti (a village in Bhoṭ in the snows in Garhwal on the borders of Thibet).

Applied to one who has accomplished his purpose and is satisfied.

8. आदर का चाणा बे आदर का दाख। Ādara ka cháṇá beádara ká dákha.

Even gram given with courtesy is better than grapes bestowed with contempt.

I.e. A little given kindly is better than much bestowed with harshness or disdain.

COURAGE UNDER DESPAIR

1. मरता क्या न करता। Marata kyá na karatá.

Once about to be killed, what will he not do?

Applied to one who is in a desperate plight. *C.f.* "The drowning man catches at a straw."

COWARD

1. हाणदार का पाइथर भागदार का आइथर। Háṇadára ká páiṭ-hara bhágadára ká áiṭhara.

Behind one who is attacking, and in front of one who is running away.

Applied to a coward

2. स्यैणि का लेखन मैस का लेख। Syaiṇi ká lekha na maiśa ká lekha.

Neither like a man nor woman.

An effeminate, home-staying person.

CRITICAL PERIODS

1. घड़ि बचि त घड़ो बचो। Ghari bachi ta gharho bacho.

If a small pot escapes, the large jar may escape.

I.e. If the critical or dangerous moment is passed then there is no danger thereafter for years.

2. ये जतकाल बचुं तौ खसम थैंब्बा कूं। Ye jatakála bachun̲ tau khasama ṭhaiṇ babá kún.

If I survive this confinement I will treat my husband as I do my father.

The anguish of child-birth:

Applied to any trouble which a man has brought on himself and of which he repents.

DEBTS, LOANS AND SURETY

1. ओछी पूंजी खसम खाणी। Ochhí púnji khasama kháṇi.

Small capital is (a fruitful source of) swearing.

I.e. To borrow money from a man of small capital is dangerous, because he will give much trouble in connection with the debt.

C.f. "A poor man's debt makes a great noise."

2. लेणो एक न दोणो दुइ। Leṇo eka na deṇo dui.

Neither take one, nor pay back two.

One who borrows has to pay back with interest. There was once a washer-man in the service of a king. He was well off before he borrowed. As the king used to give money on interest to his other servants the washer-man was pursuaded by his wife (though not in need) to ask for a loan. He did, and received one gold *Mohara* which he brought to his wife. Though he did this, he was always fretting himself to make up the second *Mohara* required for interest. He spent only half his pay, refused delicacies, and overworked himself until he had earned the second *Mohara*. When the day for payment came the king noticed how thin he had grown, and asked the reason, to which he replied that, *"To borrow one and to pay back two,"* made him lean. A caution against incurring debt: also used by one who repudiates a loan or denies having borrowed.

3. हाथ को दीन्यू पाथा को भरियूं। Hátha ko dínyú páthá ko bhary'n̲.

Given by one's hand, and measured in a measure.

Bona fide loans which cannot be absolved either in this or the next world.

4. रिण मुच्यते न काशी। Riṇa muchyate na Káshí.

Debt is not absolved even at Kashi (by visiting and bathing at Benares).

The story given below is used to illustrate the proverb:

Once a man in very poor circumstances brought home Rs. 2,000 which he had borrowed from a man who did not know how poor he was. At night while he slept among the cattle, as is usual among the poor, he overheard one of the bullocks saying to the others that as the man was quite unable in his life time to discharge the debt he had incurred, he would have to come and serve as a bullock to the lender of the money for years in his next existence. At this the man got frightened, and asked advice from the bullock about the matter, who told him to return the money and advised him to go to the king and wager Rs. 2,000 with him on a fight between his bullock and the elephant of the king. The king thinking his elephant far superior in strength to the lean bullock accepted the wager of Rs. 2,000. Both the animals were brought before the king to fight, but no sooner did the elephant see the bullock than he turned tail and ran away from him. Attempt to get up a fight was repeated thrice, but the elephant could not stand the snorting and pawing of the bullock. The king at last, finding his elephant thus vanquished by the bullock, paid the sum of Rs. 2,000 according to agreement; on inquiring the cause of the elephant's fright both of the animals admitted that the elephant haḍ owed and had not repaid Rs. 300 to the bullock in his former life and so he could not face the bullock.

C.f. "Out of debt out of danger." "Better go to bed supperless, than rise in debt."

5. मोल लेणी सुख सेणी। Mola leṇí sukha seṇí.

Buy for cash and sleep well.

Never borrow.

6. जो पड़ भर सो देव घर। Jo parha bhara so dewa ghara.

He who stands surety will have to give up his own house.

7. एक गुलि का दुइ गुलि टयूं अलाइ बलाइ शिर पर ल्यूं। Eka guli kấ dui guli dyúṇ alái balái shira para lyún̲.

Why should one pay two bullets (two Rupees) for one borrowed, and take the extra dangers and trouble on his head.

E.g. Generally in former times, and even now to a certain extent, one who borrows money another becomes in from a manner his vassal.

C.f. "The borrower is a servant of the lender." The usage is still prevailing in the country for borrowers to work in the fields of their creditors for a certain number of days without wages in each season. This is over and above the high interest stipulated for the loans.

8. खाणि बखत खाब लाल दिणि बखत आंख लाल। Kháṇi bhakata khába lála diṇi bakhata áṇkha lála.

The mouth gets red when the betel nut is eaten, but the eye becomes red when it has to be paid for.

E.g. The people of India are very fond of chewing betel nuts; these they geneally get from the dealers on credit, so that when betel nuts are eaten (chewed) the chewers' mouths get red, but when a bill for the price of the same is received by them their eyes get red (they become angry). Hence the proverb is used to condemn the practice of contracting debts. The borrower is glad when he gets the money but is angry when he is requested to repay it.

9. बैरी को एक ऋण को शेष। Bairi ko eka riṇa ko shesha.

Of enemies not one, of debt not even a little (or enemies and debts should be totally destroyed).

E.g. A single enemy not destroyed, and a little debt left unpaid will increase in time and prove troublesome.

10. मरूं भूक रूं सुख। Marún̲ bhúka rún sukha.

May I starve but remain comfortable (without anxieties).

Used as a caution against incurring debts or against extravagance.

11. ब्याज रात लग चलदौ। Byája ráta laga chaladau.
Interest runs even at night, i.e., some animals move about in the day and others at night, but interest never ceases to accumulate.
Used as a caution against getting into debt.

12. कुकुर ले दौड़नु छ मरनो कांकड़ ले छ। Kukura le daurhanu chha marano káṇkarha le chha.
The dog has only to hunt, it is the wild sheep that is killed.
"Used by one to induce another to stand security for him as the former (the principal) is incurring the primary liability but the latter (the security) has only the secondary responsibility.

13. पाथो फुटद उधारो नि बगदो। Pátho phuṭada udháro ni bagado.
The measure breaks, but the loan remains.
Means that a debt must be repaid even if the men dealt with or the witnesses to the transactions are dead.

14. टका दियो गजि फाड़ि। Ṭaká diyo gaji phárhi.
Pay cash and tear the cloth (so much as you want) from the piece (belonging to merchant), i.e. pay and purchase.
Caution against getting anything on credit.

DECEIT

1. मारद बाखरो पंकाद कुकुड़ो खांदी दांव लिगुड़ा को थुपुड़ो। Márada bákharo pakáṇda kukurho kháṉdi dáṇwa lingurhá ko thupurho.
One kills a goat, cooks a cock, but for dinner gives only a heap of Lingurhá (a wild vegetable).
Applied to deceitful persons who make great profession but do little or nothing.

2. आपुं खाणु औरन चुठोणु। Āpuṉ kháṇu aurana chuṭhoṇu.
He himself eats, but makes another wash out his mouth, as if the latter had eaten.
Clearing himself from his own guilt by implicating another. (Chuṭhana=to wash one's hands and mouth after a meal eaten with the fingers.)

3. आग लगै बेर पाणि सों दौड़नु। Ága lagai bera pári son̲ daurhanu.
One sets fire, and then runs for water to quench it.
Applied to deceitful persons and mischief-makers.

4. मुंड काटिक रेंड की बड़ाई। Mun̲ḍa kátika renḍa kí barhái.
After having cut off the head, to praise the corpse.
To eulogise a man after ruining him.

5. चोर थें चोरि करौ सौकार थें जाग दिलौ। Chora then̲ chori karau Saukára then̲ jága dilau.
Telling the thief to steal, and the rich man to guard his house.
Applied to tricky and deceiptful people who collude with both parties.

6. धान का दाणा भीतर चावल को गूदो। Dhána ká dáṇa bhitara cháwala ko gudo.
There is a grain of rice inside the husk (of paddy).
It is said, that once the son of a king had conceived a strong friendship for the son of a minister. The king, for some reason of his own, wished that his son should give up this friendship, but failed to make him do so. At last he offered a great reward to any one who would accomplish this object for him. Many wise and clever people accordingly tried various devices to effect this, but in vain. Whatever either of the friends was told by any one he informed the other of it, and thus strengthened the friendship day by day. After this a cunning woman contracted close intimacy with both of them, and one day while the two were sitting together, she went in and said she wished to tell a secret to the son of the minister, and then took him away for a minute to a private place when she whispered in his ear. "There is a grain of rice inside the husk of the paddy." As soon as this was done she left the kingdom for good. The minister's son immediately repaired to his friend, and as usual, informed him of what the woman had really said to him. But the king's son did not believe it, and suspected his friend of having concealed the real matter told to him

by the woman; and from that time the king's son became alienated from his friend. Hence the proverb.

Used to warn against deception, and applied to one who makes too much of a very little thing.

7. चड़ा का मड़ा मड़ा का चड़ा। Charhá ká marhá marhá ká charhá.

Representing living birds as dead bodies, and dead bodies as living birds.

Calling black, white; and white, black.

8. नौ तेरो गौं मेरो। Nau tero gaun mero.

In your name, but my village.

The village is in your name but is really mine. Giving one nominal authority in order to impose upon him.

9. घर बार तेरो कोठड़ि में हाथनि लगा। Ghara bára tero koṭharhi men hátha ni lagá.

The house is yours but do not use the room.

Applied to nominal trusts.

10. मुख में राम पेट में और काम। Mukha men ráma peṭa men aura káma.

God's name in the mouth, but another motive in the heart.

"A wolf in sheep's clothing."

E.g. A magnanimous man has the same thing in his heart, mouth, and actions, but a wicked man has one thing in his heart, another in his words, and a quite different one in his deeds.

DEFERRED HOPES

1. हइया मरिगया हुणा कि आस। Haiyá marigayá huṇá ki ása.

My sons already born are dead: I can therefore hope to have more born to me.

One bases his hopes on past experience. Also used ironically to denote the precarious state of a thing which has already failed.

2. पैणा को पैणो चुकायो सारो भीतर बथाउं न फुकायो। Paṇá ko paiṇo chukáyo sáro bhítara baṭháuṇ na phúkáyo.

I was repaid for my present, but the wind blow through my house all night.

Paiṇá = any thing good that is distributed among the neighbours and kinsmen.

I.E. One in hope of such a return from his neighbour kept his doors open at night, so that the wind blew through the house to the inconvenience of the occupants.

This is applied to one who instead of being benefitted by any transaction is put to extra troubles or loss; also spoken of hopes which are deferred.

3. दाता है सूम भलो जो पैली दीदे जबाब। Dáta hai súma bhalo jo paili díde jabába,

A miser who rejects one at once is a better man than a liberal man who keeps one long in suspense.

This is used in regard to inconveniences that trouble one whose hopes are not realised for a considerable time

C.f. "Hope deferred maketh the heart sick."

4. कब थोरि ब्याली कब खोरि खाली। Kaba thori byáli kaba khori kháli.

When will the yearling buffalo calve and when will my skull eat?

An expression of impatience used when some desired good seems to be long deferred. For instance, a widow anxiously and impatiently waits for her infant sons to grow up when they will contribute to her support.

DEPENDENCE

1. दादा ले बहू बहू ले सगली मउ। Dádá le bahú bahú le sagali mau.

The Bahú (elder brother's wife) depends on my elder brother, and the whole family depends on her.

The chief person or moving spirit in a concern.

2. ठुलो गोरू लूण बुकाब नानो थोबड़ो चाट। Ṭhudo gorú lúṇa bukáwa náno thobarho chaṭa.

Full grown cows eat salt, but the calves lick their (mother's) lips.

Applicable to one who maintains an establishment.

3. पाणी का सास घुतड़ो बास। Páṇi ká sása ghutarho bása.
The frog croaks by the aid of the water.
A poor and weak person can only achieve anything by the patronage of a greater man, or a poor man lives his life by support or in hope of support from some great man.
C.f. "Quench not hope, for when hope dies, all dies."

4. स्याप को जियो मुंडला में। Suápa ko jiyo muṇḍalá meṉ.
The soul or life of a snake is in its head.
This is applied to the head of a family on whom all the members of the family are dependent.

5. अपणो खोरो अपणा हाथ ले नी मुडीनो। Apaṉo khoro apaṇá háṭha le ní muḍíno.
No one can shave his head with his own hand.
Applied to mutual need of help.

6. स्यूड़ा दगड़ि को धागो। Syúrhá dagarhi ko dhágo.
The thread follows the needle.
Used by a member of one's family or by a dependent, or to one who is the head of a family or to a patron on whose movements all depend. Usually spoken by women in regard to their respective husbands.

DILATORY HABITS

1. तोपाल की तोप ताप चौंडाल को राज। Topála kí topa tápa chauṇḍála ko rája.
While the Topál was getting ready his cannons, the Chauṇḍála came and seized his kingdom.
These two petty kings reigned over Pargannah Chandpur (Garhwal) in the seventh century A.D. Used in advising one to be always ready for any thing that may happen, and not to let matters slide. (A pure Garhwali proverb).

2. जांतक भाटले पाग बांधि तांतक पेठै उठि। Jáṉtaka Bháṭa le pága báṉdhi táṉ taka peṭhai uṭhi.
While the bard was dressing his turban the market broke up.
E.g. Bards or buffoons dress themselves up before they go to

a public place, and if they are delayed in dressing they lose the opportunity of displaying their arts and making money.

Applied to failure in any business due to dilatoriness.

DILEMMA

1. आटा को दियो भीतर रंदत मूसा खांदान भैर कवा लीजांदान। Áṭá ko diyo bhítara randata músá khándána bhaira kawá lijáṇdana.

A lamp made of flour (paste) if placed inside the house is eaten by mice, and if kept outside is taken away by the crows.

(A dilemma).

2. ये तरफ रौ रभाड़ वी तरफ भेल कफाड़। Ye tarapha rau rabhárha wí tarapha bhela kaphārha.

On one side a deep stream and a raging torrent, on the other a sheer precipice.

C.f. "The sea in front of them, and the Egyptians behind them." or "between Seylla and Charybdis."

3. तातो दूध थुकेव न घुटेव। Táto dūdha thukewa na ghuṭewa.

Hot milk one cannot either spit out or drink.

I.e. If you spit it out it is wasted, if you swallow it, it burns you.

4. रोवेन हंसै गिज ताणै। Rowai na ha̲nsai gijá táṇai.

Could neither weep nor laugh.

This is applied to one who is astounded at some sudden unexpected incident.

5. ये तरफ कुवा वी तरफ खाइ। Ye tarapha kuwá wí tarapha khái.

Hither a well, and thither a ditch.

A dilemma.

6. तातो दूध हाथ में राखेव न भीं छाड़ेव। Táto duḍha hátha me̲n rákhewa na bhí̲n chhárhewa.

Hot milk neither worth retaining in one's hand, nor worth dropping on the ground.

E.g. Signifies a dilemma which in either way suggests loss.

7. कौंछू त मै मारिजांछ्य नि कौन्यु त बाप कुत्ता खांछ। Kauṉchhú ta mai mári jáṇchhya ni kaunyu ta bápa kuttá khháṇchha.

If I speak out my mother will be beaten, if I keep silence my father will feed on dog's flesh.

"On the horns of a dilemma."

Story : A certain man had a son (a boy of 12 years of age) by a former wife, and a young wife whom he had married after the death of the lad's mother. This woman had a paramour who instigated her to feed her husband with the flesh of a dog so that he might become mad. (For they suppose that when a man eats the flesh either of a dog or of an owl he becomes insane). So, following his advice, she one day killed a dog and prepared the food and placed it before her husband. The boy, who had observed all this, was in great doubt whether he should tell his father or not. He said, "If I tell my father he will surely kill my mother; but if I remain silent he will eat dog's flesh."

8. मैं और बापू एक चोर और लाठी दो। Maiṉ aura bápú eka chora aura láṭhí do.

I and my father are one, but the thief and his stick are two.

E.g. In a certain house at night there were only father and son; a thief came there with a stick in hand; the son says to himself. "If my faher is killed it is a loss, and if I am killed it is also a loss." The stick is quite a separate thing from the thief, and so they are two. For if the stick is broken it is no loss to the thief, and if the thief be beaten it is also no real loss to the stick.

9. कुजगा को दुख जेठाणो वैद। Kujagá ko dukha jaṭháṇo baida.

Abcess in the private part to be treated by her husband's elder brother, who is the doctor or physician.

A younger brother's wife is looked upon as a daugher, and she in turn looks upon her husband's elder brother as a father, *i.e.* one is not allowed even to touch the other. So she feels ashamed or finds it difficult to expose herself to her husband's elder brother.

Used to represent a difficult position, a dilemma.

10. भुरा का लाडू खाला त पछताला निखाला त पछताला। Bhurá ká ládhú khálá ta pachhatálá ne khálá ta pachhatálá.

The sweet balls of sawdust you will repent of whether you eat them or not.

I.e. If you taste them you will regret your buying and tasting them, on the other hand you will also repent for not purchasing and tasting them, because they are elegantly made and tempting in appearance. Such balls used to be made to deceive the hill people who went to Hardawár in former times.

A dilemma.

DISAPPOINTMENT

1. हारो मियां दाढ़ी हाथ। Háro miyán dadhí hátha.

One who is vanquished seizes his beard.

I.e. In disappointment or chagrin.

2. जोगी कु छारो कुम्हार कु माटी कख नी। Jogí ku chháro kumahára ku máṭi kakha ní.

Is there any place where a Jogi (ascetic) cannot get ashes? and a potter earth?

It is a very easy matter to become a *Jogi*, if a man fails in all other efforts to get a living.

3. तुमड़ि फुटि लस्कर कि बिदा। Tumarhi phuṭi laskara ki bidā.

As the gourd is broken the people depart.

I.e. The people who were in hopes of getting some of the seeds of the gourd went away on its being broken, either with their hopes realized or disappointed, for it was in existence no longer. When the matter is decided all the candidates go away.

4. जैकि करि बड़ि आस वीले दियो झुगरा को गास। Jaiki kari barhi ása wíle diyo jhungará ko gása.

He in whom I had a great hope gave me only a morsel of millet (inferior grain).

Applied to disappointment from a person in whom trust was placed.

5. ममा आलो तौलि छुटालो निजाणि नौ टका और डंडयालो। Mamá álo tauli chhuṭálo nijáṇi nau ṭaku aura ḍaṉḍyálo.

I thought that when my maternal uncle came, he would redeem my (pledged) vessel, but did not think that he would cause me to be robbed of nine Ṭakás (four and half annas) more.

Used of bad treatment when help was expected.

6. आकाश चाणो। Ákásha chaṇo.

Looking to heaven (the sky); i.e., one having na hopes looks to the sky.

Used of utter disappointment.

7. खायो न पायो मरण सो आयो। Kháyo na páyo maraṇa so áyo.

Neither ate nor received any thing but come to die.

Used by one mourning over great disappointment.

DISHONESTY

1. दै का पहरा बिरालु। Dai ká pahará birálu.

A cat set to watch the curds.

Applied to dishonest persons who are entrusted with property.

2. दमड़ि कि हांडि कुत्ता को इमान। Damarhi ki hánḍi kuttá ko imána,

The trustworthiness of a dog is tried even by a small pot (of food) worth 1/8 of pice.

Used in reference to petty dishonesty.

3. डूम ग्वेर बाग बखरवालो। Ḍúma gwera bága bakharwálo.

To make a Dúm cowherd, and a leopard a shepherd.

Dums will eat beef, and so cannot be trusted with the care of cows.

Applied to dishonest persons in charge of property.

4. सुंगणसों दियो निगलि गयो। Suṇgaṇa soṇ diyo nigali gayo.

The thing given to one for smelling has been devoured by him.

Applied to one who misappropriates a thing lent to him for temporary use, or in his capacity of an agent or guardian &c.

5. सोठों का बीज कुजांद फोलि खांदइ ओंद। Sonthon ká bíja kujáṇḍa pholi kháṇḍai auṇda.

One who goes to collect pulses comes home eating the beans.

Applied to dishonest persons or servants.

DISINTERESTEDNESS

1. डूम को ब्या आंखन डा। Ḍúma ko byá áṉkhana ḍá.

The marriage of a Dúm (simply) pains the eyes.

The Hindu *Biṭha* (patrician) castes do not participate in any ceremony or feasts held by a *Dúm*.

Applied to things in which one has no concern at all and which instead of being beneficial turn out to be troublesome to him.

2. मेरा घर है नहैगेछी मेरा लेखा तेरा चेलै है जान। Merá ghara hai nahaigechhí merá lekhá terá chelai chelá hai jána.

If you leave my house you may be blessed with so many sons (I do not care).

The thing left or got rid of should be forgotten. Loss of interest in any thing with which we are no longer connected.

3. सौ को साई वौ को भाई। Sau ko sái bau ko bhái.

Neither related to my father-in-law nor to my mother.

Applied to one who is no relation at all, or with whom one has no concern whatever.

4. तु कोली मै लोहार तेरो के ब्योहार। Tú koli mai lohára tero mero ke byohára.

You are a weaver, I am a blacksmith, what dealings are there between us?

This is said by one who thinks himself quite separate from the person addressed.

5. तेरो पैलागो मेरा कथप। Tero pailágo merá kathapa.

Your salutation is nothing to me.

Expresses extreme hatred, contempt, or indifference. Ironically applied to one by whom the speaker is not properly treated.

6. तीन लोक है मथुरा न्यारि। Tína loka hai Mathurá nyári.
Mathurá is quite separate from the three worlds.
Mathurá is considered highly blessed because Krishna was born there.

7. आपुं मरि गयोत कवा राज बैठि जाव। Ápuṇ marigayo to kawá rája baiṭhi jáwa.
One who is about to die does not mind if a crow becomes king.
Spoken in reference to any thing in which one is no longer concerned.

8. भौत बिरालुनले मूसा नि मरना। Bhauta birálunale Músá ni maraná.
Too many cats do not kill rats.
C.f. "Too many cooks spoil the broth."

9. छोड़ियो गौं को नातो के। Chhorhiyo gauṉ ko náto ke.
What relation with a village one has deserted?
Used to indicate one's disinterestedness in a matter with which he has no concern.

DISTRESS

1. डुबनेर कणि तिणका को सहारो। Dubanera kaṉi tiṇká ko saháro.
A drowning man clings to a straw. (Also an English proverb. Which was the borrower?)
I.e. One in distress is neglected and forsaken by all, and so if one gives him any small help in that state it is greatly appreciated.

2. निरपाणि को माछो। Nirapáṇi ko máchho.
A fish out of water.
Out of one's element.

3. निखाणा घर चौमासि जर। Nikháṇá ghara chaumási jara.

No food in my house, and besides I am down with fever (of the rainy season).

Accumulated woes. *C.f.* "Misfortunes never come singly."

4. गांठ न दाम मुख न चाम। Gáṉṯha na dáma mukha na cháma.

No money in hand, and no skin on the face.

An old and poor man's plea.

5. रात नींद नै दिन भूख नै। Ráta nínda nai dina bhúkha nai.

No sleep at night, and no hunger in the day.

A distressful state.

6. सौ घड़ी को सुख एक घड़ी को दुख। Sau gharhí ko sukha eka gharhí ko dukha.

An hour of misery is equal to a hundred hours of pleasure.

7. जगन में बिघन। Jagana meṉ bighana.

A calamity during a sacrifice (merry festival).

E.g. During the marriage, tonsure, and other like ceremonies, when all the kinsmen and guests are being feasted, if any one falls sick or dies, or some other adverse circumstance occurs, the people concerned are much troubled and use this phrase expressive of great sorrow and regret.

8. अलूणि मर्च को बर बराट। Alúṇi marcha ko barabaráṭa.

Red pepper taken without salt causes greater irritation.

I.e. Any inconvenience or distress shared with others is less painful (or more endurable) than when suffered alone.

Used by one thus affected, and also by one imposed on or tasked for nothing (without any compensation for his work) or by one who receives punishment or reproof without any fault or offence committed by him.

DISUNION

1. आठ पटियाल नौचुला। Áṭha paṭyála nau chúlá.

Eight Brahmins of the village of Paṭiyá, but nine ovens.

I.e. Eight Brahmin kinsmen of the village of Páṭiyá, Kumaun, and one man, their coolie (a *shudra* or *khassiá* by caste) went on a journey. At the first stopping place, each of the Brahmins began to build a separate cooking place for himself, no one being willing to eat the food cooked by another. The *khassiá* coolie, who could not possibly object to eat the food cooked by a Brahmin, became suspicious and disgusted at their unexpected disunion, thinking they must all be of a low caste. So he determined to cook his own food separately by having a separate, or ninth, *chúlá* for himself. Hence this proverb. Whenever, there is want of unity among one set of people others suspect them. This proverb is also often quoted by the people of Garhwal against the Kumaunis, who are much more fastidious in such matters than the Garhwalis.

2. झगुला दुई मुख दुई। Jhagulá duí mukha duí.

Where there are two Jhagulás (long robes) there are two mouth-openings, (i.e. the part round the neck through which the head goes).

I.e. Each person, in a family, or community, has his own bent or motive.

3. आधा गौं चैतवाल आधा गौं बगबाल। Ádhá gaun̠ chaitwála ádhá gaun̠ bagwála.

One half the village keeps the festival in one month, the other half eight months after.

Illustrates the evil of disunion.

DOG IN THE MANGER

1. बूढ़ो बैल आप लग न औरन कणि लगणदे। Búḍho baila ápa laga na aurana kaṇi lagaṇade.

An old bullock will not himself woo, nor will he allow any other bullock to do so; i.e. putting hindrance in the way of others without gaining any benefit yourself.

C.f. "Dog in the manger."

DUPLICITY

1. झुठा ब्या सांचा न्या। Jhuṭa byá sánchá nyá.

Marriages will be effected by false representations, but justice will be obtained by speaking the truth.

It is difficult to get a poor man married unless he is falsely represented to be of a high caste and a man of property and wealth.

ECONOMY OR FRUGALITY

1. भीत ढोली भितनाइ। Bhíta ḍholí bhitanái.

The wall was thrown down, but it fell inwards (and so all the stones were available for use again).

If it had fallen outwards into the neighbour's field he might have taken away the stones for his own use.

E.g. One who is bound to give alms bestows them on his own relatives.

2. जां चालीस तां घवतालीस। Ján̲ chálísa tán̲ ghabatálisa.

If there are 40, one or more can be included without making any material difference; (so small a difference is of no importance.)

"Six of one and half a dozen of the other."

3. पात मुगतो भात जुगतो। Páta mugato bháta jugato.

A broad leaf, but the rice in moderate quantity.

This suggests that full provision should be made for any thing before-hand, but the expenditure should be carefully limited, and also that if one brings a broad leaf (for begging rice) we should give him rice or any food in limited quantity or according to our circumstances.

4. जतुक लंबो सौड़ ततुकै पैर पसारना। Jatuka lambo saurha tatukai paira pasarná.

One should stretch out his feet only so far as his quilt may cover them.

C.f. "Cut your coat according to your cloth."

5. तेल तुरक्योणा लूण बुरक्योणा। Tela turkyoṇá lúṇa burkyoṇá.

Oil to be used in drops, and salt to be used in pinches.

The smallest items of expenditure in a family amount to a great deal in the end, and so one should be cautioned against extravagance.

6. पगड़ी रखि क घ्यू खाणो। Pagarhî rakhi ka ghyú kháṇo.

One should eat ghi without dishonouring his turban. An economical maxim.

One should not indulge in pleasure to the injury of his wealth or reputation. *C.f.* "Hast thou found honey? eat so much as is sufficient for thee, lest thou be filled therewith and vomit it." The turban or *Pagarhi* is an indispensable article of a respectable man's dress and honour, and is often the most costly part of it.

7. तोपो तोपो कै छांस बियों बियों कै रास। Topo topo kai chháṇsa biyon̲ biyon̲ kai rása.

Drop by drop the vessel (of curds) fills, and grain by grain the corn-heap grows.

C.f. "Many a mickle makes a muckle." (Scotch proverb).

8. धणियां का दाणा में राइ को दाणो। Dhaṇiyon̲ ká dáṇá me rái ko dáṇo.

Adding a grain of mustard to that of coriander.

This is applied either to one who is thrifty and thus adds to his possessions or to one who earns much with a small capital prudently invested in wise speculations.

9. और दिन चंगा त्योहार नंगा। Aura dina chan̲gá tyohára nan̲gá.

Well fed and clothed on ordinary days, naked and hungry on festival days.

Bad economy, not saving for needy days. (On festive occasions the best of clothes and food obtainable should be used).

10. जख इतगा तख ततगा। Jakha itagá takha tatagá.

When so much, then that much will do.

E.g. The difference of one or two in a large quantity is no difference *i.e.* is of no moment.

This is used to induce a man to spend a little more than what has already been estimated or spent with a view to have an auspicious completion of the business.

11. तेल देख तेल कि धार देख। Tela dekha tela ke dhára dekha.
Look at the oil (i.e. see how much there is) and then regulate the flow (i.e. how much you will pour out).
I.e. Restrict your expenses within your income, *C.f.* "Cut your coat according to your cloth."

ENVY

1. अपणा जायां कि नी कका की रयां की छौ। Apaṇá jáyán̲ ki ní kaká kí rayán̲ kí chhau.
I do not complain of my own ruin, but why in the world has my uncle escaped?
The regret of one fallen into misfortune that others do not share with him.

2. हो पड़ोसिण मैं जसि। Ho parhosiṇa mai jasi.
O, neighbour be like me.
Story : Once a man who had his nose cut off for some offence happened to come to a certain city, where he was teased by being given the nickname *"Nakatá"* (noseless). For some time he patiently endured the disgrace, but at last invented a plan for revenging himself upon the residents of the town. So he sat down like a saint in a conspicuous place in the city, and acted as if he was absorbed in the contemplation of God. Now and then he would address the Gods thus. "O Vishnu you are welcome," "O Mahádeo you are welcome," "O Brahma you are welcome," "O Lachhmi, O Parbati," O Brahmáni, you are welcome." "Come and sit down here (pointing out in a respectful manner with his two hands a place for each), and thanking them for their trouble and condescension in manifesting themselves to him. He did this everyday for some time attracting the attention of the passers-by, and gradually the news spread throughout the city and the country. At first the people did not believe him, but seeing him so firm in

his faith, piety, and adoration, some began to pay more attention and feel curious about the matter, and so they enquired from the feigned saint what it meant, as they could not see the deities with whom he had converse. To this he replied that no one could see the gods (with the bodily eye) until he got heavenly eyes by becoming a devotee. This naturally induced some to become devotees in order to have a constant vision of God like the saint, and consequently many of them wished and asked him to have mercy on them. The man said that they must become his disciples by learning the religious enchantments (power to fascinate the deities) from him. Whereupon many of them volunteered to be his disciples, but the noseless man said to them, "O, my dear brothers, it is very difficult for one to become truly religious amidst the luxuries and endearments of worldly things. No one can ever see the deities until he divests himself of all worldly honours and subdues his senses for the sake of his God. The chief sense or pride of these worldly honours is the nose (the root of haughtiness and vanities) which ought to be got rid of first of all in order to render man a humble and worthy being in the sight of the deities. This is the first and most important ordeal one has to go through in order to merit personal conversation with the deities. For as soon as one's nose is cut off he becomes absolved of all sins and sinful sensations. One man at first fell a victim to this plot, and submitted to the loss of his nose, and to his utter grief found his hopes of seeing the deities to be utterly false. On enquiry from his *Guru* (spiritual guide) the new disciple was told, "My dear son, do you not know that a leper wishes to have the whole world become like himself, and so also a sinner; since you have been unfortunately imposed upon now you must also make the same professions, so that more may become like ourselves, and then no one will be able to cast a slur on any of us." After this both the *Nakatás* united in persuading others to follow their example, and succeeding in tricking many of their neighbours, until the news reached the king and his wise statesmen, who at once put a stop to this scandal of the noseless sect by driving them out of their city and country.

EVIL PROPENSITIES AND HABITS

1. छाती में सांप चल्यो बाटा कुबाटा लग्यो। Chháti me sánpá chalyo báṭá kubátá lagyo.

If a snake has crept into one's bosom it has taken a wrong road.

Applied to one who attempts improper acts which ought to be stopped at once before any injury is done. *C.f.* "Ill examples are like contagious diseases." Evil habits should be nipped in the bud.

2. बाग गोठ है बाकरो लिगयो फिकर नै पर बाग गोठ पलको यो फिकर छ। Bága goṭha hai bákaro ligayo phikara nai para bága goṭha palako yo phikara chha.

The leopard has carried away a goat out of a cowshed; I do not care for that, but I do care that the leopard has found a relish in (or way to) the cowshed.

Applied to future apprehensions or dangers from the lure or clue someone has found to injure us.

EXTRAVAGANCE

1. घर फूकि तमाशो देख। Ghara phúki tamásho dekha.

For the sake of a show he burns his own house.

Applied to extravagant persons.

2. पांच अंगुल घ्यू मा छटो शिर कढ़ाइमा। Páncha angula ghyú má chhaṭo shira kaḍhái má.

Five fingers in Ghi but the sixth head on the pan.

This is an ironical phrase applied to imprudent, extravagant and voluptuous people. *C.f.* "Short pleasure long lament". "He burns the candle at both ends."

A pan is a kind of oven in which cakes are cooked and grain parched. Food is eaten with five fingers and it is also taken with *Ghi* mixed with it by rich and well-to-do persons, and so the fingers are besmeared with *Ghi* at dinner time, but the head of the eater of the *Ghi* is responsible for its price, for which (if not paid) the head will be troubled (arrested).

3. चख डालौ माल और धन कणि कौड़ी निराखौ कफन सुणि जो देलो तन सुणि सो देलो कफन सुणि। Chakha ḍalau mála aurá dhana kaṇi kaurhî nirakhau kafana suṇi, jo delo taṇa suṇi so delo kafana suṇi.

Enjoy all your property and wealth, leaving nothing for your coffin, for God who gives for the nourishment of the body is sure to provide for the coffin also.

Carpe diem.

4. काज कौणि अकाज भात। Kája kauṇi akája bháta.

Kauni (an inferior millet) on a festival day (for meal) and rice on ordinary days.

Used of extravagant or improper conduct in regard to expenses.

Poor people eat *kauni* as a general rule, but keep a small quantity of rice for festive occasions. An extravagant person will use up his stock of rice for ordinary consumption, and thus when the feast comes round he will have to eat the meagre *kauni*.

5. भैंसो मारी तोड़ो कूडो ढाली वोड़ो। Bhainso mârî torho kúrho ḍháli worho.

He kills his buffalo for the sake of "Torhás," and pulls down his house for the sake of stones for a boundary mark.

"Torho" is a musical horn made of the horns of a buffalo and used as a trumpet. "Worho" is a boundary mark made of a stone or stones which separate one's field from that of another.

Applied to one foolishly extravagant.

6. नौपल बाछरू दशपल घांट। Nau pala báchharu dasa pala ghánṭa.

A calf weighing nine chhatākas wears a bell of ten chatáks' weight.

Applies to one who wears sumptuous clothes and valuable jewelry beyond his position or means.

7. रांड का छोरा लग्यो लोई होई मौ ढुंगा में धोई। Ráṉḍa ká chhorá lagyo loí hoí mau ḍhuṉgá me dhoí.

The pampered son of a widow in his arrogance and excess brought the wealthy family to ruin.

This is applicable to one who has no one to look after him or control his bad conduct.

8. मादिरो कौंछ यो धमा धम कैका उपरछ। Mádiro kauṇchha yo dhamá dhama kaiká upara chha.

The millet (while being threshed or husked out) says where does the sound come from, or on whom is the threshing being done (i.e. on me).

Used by the head of a family when he finds the members of his family extravagant.

FALSEHOOD

1. काना खुरी। Kánákhurí.

One hits the ear and foot at one shot.

E.g. A sportsman said that he hit a deer on its ear and foot with one bullet while the animal was scratching its ear with its foot.

Applied to liars who try to make their stories as plausible as they can. The story below will illustrate the proverb.

Story : A man addicted to telling lies once went to Hardwára to bathe in the Ganges, with an express vow that after the bathing he would no longer tell lies. When he came back from the shrine his friends and kinsmen came round him, and asked him how he performed his pilgrimage. The man said he had no trouble at all on his journey to and from that place except once when in the jungle he saw seven tigers, who, on seeing him, came towards him. But being frightened at the sight of the tigers, he climbed up a tall tree by the side of the road. All the tigers came up to the trunk of the tree and seeing him seated at a safe distance beyond their reach became very furious, and began to roar and jump upwards, but in vain. After this, with a view to catch him, one tiger in an erect posture stood on the head of the other, in this way the seventh animal attained a certain height, but still could not reach the bough on which he was. This frightful scene terrified him so much that the perspiration ran from his face in a stream. On this the tigers began to climb up the stream he was making, whereupon with great presence of mind, he whipped out a *khukari* (a kind of short sword) from his belt, and cut off the stream. This caused them all to fall on the ground and die. After that he descended the tree and calmly resumed his journey homewards.

2. सौ रूपयां राजा का भंडार कि खंकल का गिचा। Sau rupayán rájá ká bhanḏára ki khaṇkala ká gichá.

One hundred Rupees is either in the treasury of the king, or in the mouth of a liar.

This is an old saying belonging to the time when money was very scarce. That so much could only be found in the treasury of king or in the mouth of a liar refers to the way in which liars exaggerate. *C.f.* "Liars begin by imposing upon others, but they end in deceiving themselves."

3. झूट कि जड़ ने। Jhúṭa ki jarha nai.

A falsehood has no roots.

C.f. "Falsehood has no legs."

4. जो झूटो सो टूटो। Jo jhúṭo so ṭúṭo.

One who resorts to lies is sure to be in poverty.

I.e. Evil deeds must result in evil consequences.

FALSE ALARM

1. जूंआ की भैंस। Juṇwáṇ kí bhainsa.

A louse exaggerated into a buffalo.

In a certain village lived a man and his wife. The man was simple, cowardly, and lazy person, while his wife was a wise and energetic woman. Whenever the husband was told to work he used to become angry with his wife and frighten her by saying that he would leave his house for good and go to some foreign country. For some years the woman lived in great terror of being deserted, at length becoming callous of his threats she allowed him to go. On the day he was to set out to the Plains she equipped herself like a policeman with a sword and gun and waylaid her husband, whom she threatened with instant death if he did not return home and pledge his word never to come again that way. (It being the only pathway from the village to the Plains). The poor coward returned home at once. She managed to reach home unobserved before the arrival of her husband. When the man returned she enquired of him the cause of his return. "O dear wife," said he, "how could I go to the Plains, for a hundred policemen came to kill me?" To this she said, "Alas! a hundred is too great a number, perhaps you mean fifth." "Yes you are right, fifty." On this the wife said again, "I think twenty-five even would have been more than sufficient to deter you," to which he said that there were indeed twenty-five. Thus the wife mentioned ten, then five, then two, and finally one, the husband admitting each number, and finally confessing that it was only one constable who had prevented his going away the story is also applicable to other Proverbs viz.,

1. A falsehood has no roots (under heading Falsehood).
2. The remedy of poison is poison (Do. Remedy).
3. Worms cannot be extracted without charming (under heading Remedy).

2. बाग डूठ। Bága duṭha.

Leopards and ghosts.

This phrase is used to frighten children from going out in the evening when leopards and ghosts are said to be moving about.

3. कमल को भालु। Kamala ko bhálu.

A bear made of blanket.

Monkeys and deer are kept from the fields by a scare-crow in the shape of a bear made with a black blanket.

Applied to any false alarm; a canard.

4. कांडे क्लेश बामसु उल्केश। Kánde klesha Bamsu uklesha.
Sickness in Kande but anxieties and fears in Bámsu.
Used in teaching that no one unnecessarily entertain fears for a danger which is not at hand.

FALSE MODESTY

1. छांसकु जाणो टिटरो लुकोणो। Chháṇsa ku jáṇo ṭiṭaro lukoṇo.
Why should one, who goes to ask for butter-milk, conceal the pot in which he had to bring it?
Applies to one who goes to another to ask for a thing, but is ashamed to make his request.

FALSE PROMISES

1. सुवा सिमल धरी गयो बड़े फलन की आश, फल पाको रुवा भयो सुवा भयो निराश। Suwá Simala dhaŕigayo barhe phalana ḱi ása, phala páko ruwá bhayo suwá bhayo nirása.
A parrot (which is very fond of eating fruit) seeing the big buds and flowers of a Simala tree in the month of February, left the place (where the Simala tree grew) hoping to come back when the fruit was ripe. But when the parrot returned in April to eat the fruit he found to his utter despair that there was nothing but cotton in the pods.
Used of false promises.

2. बांज ब्यायो गो बिड़ो भयो। Báṉja byáyo gobirho bhayo.
An oak tree gave birth to Gobirha (a worm often found in the cracks of an oak tree).
Applied to one whose many promises end in nothing, or in something which is of very little use.
"Parturiunt montes, nascetur ridiculus mus."

3. बिना दूदि छ मैना पालदौ। Biná dúdi chha mainá páladau.
Fostering a child for six months, without milk.
Applied to one who puts off another with promises and never fulfils them.

4. तेरो ब्या करूंलो सौ बरस में। Tero byá karuṇlo sau barasa meṉ.
I will get you married a hundred years hence.

Applied to promises to do a thing after an unnecessary delay or at a time when it will not be needed.

FALSE HOPES

1. मन का लाड़ू खाणा। Mana ká lárhú kháṇá.

Eating the sweetmeats of fancy. Equivalent to "Building castles in the air."

The story below illustrates the proverb.

Story : Once a poor man had a jar of oil to convey from one place to another at a wage of four annas. The man as usual took the jar on his head, and began to walk with it, amusing himself with his imaginings, as follows : "For the conveyance of this load I will get four *annas,* with which I will buy a hen, which will in due time produce eggs and chickens. The sale of these will procure me a few rupees, which will enable me to purchase a herd of goats. After this the sale of the goats and their kids will supply me with money sufficient to purchase and keep cows, the sale of which, with their offspring, will make me possessed of money to buy buffaloes and herd them. The last occupation will give me money enough to marry. When I get married I will have children who will call me, "Father dear, come and take your meal;" then I shall reply. "No, no." Suiting his action to his words he shook his head, (by this time he had arrived at the shop where he had to deliver the load) and threw the jar on the ground and spilt the oil. The owner of the oil began to blame the coolie for the loss of his oil. But the coolie said to the man to whom the oil belonged. "O my dear friends, alas! you should not mourn over the oil, which is of very little value; for I have lost my family through the destruction of your oil." On being asked what he meant, the coolie narrated the imaginary prospects which he had based on the four *annas* that he had to receive for carriage of the oil jar. *C.f.* "He that lives upon hopes will die fasting," and the story of Alnaschar in the "Arabian Nights."

2. उइणा धुबीणा झूटा मूत ढांढ सची। Uiṇá dhubíṇa jhútá múta ḍhánḍha sachí.

The dream was false, but the pool of urine is a reality.

Said by one who has had a terrifying dream, on awaking.

This proverb is made use of to distinguish between the realities of life and the false fears and anticipations which are like dreams.

3. राजा भोज भरम का भुला, घर घर मट्टिका चूला। Rájá Bhoja bharama ká bhulá ghara ghara maṭṭi ká chúlá.

Rájá Bhoja is under an illusion. Every house has earthen hearths.

I.e. all human beings doomed to death, pleasure, pains, prosperity and adversity.

Rajah Bhoj was a famous King of Malwá, supposed to have flourished about the end of the tenth and beginning of the eleventh century. He is said to have been a great patron of learning, and is the hero of many stories and anecdotes, the best known of which is the beautiful story called "Rájá Bhoj ká Swapná" or "King Bhoj's dream."

4. भरम कि टट्टि। Bharama ki ṭaṭṭi.

Illusion's veil.

Applied to worldly honour and wealth which intrinsically are fallacious. *E.g.*, it is used of a seemingly wealthy or great man who on examination turns out to be a man of straw. A man who possesses one lakh of rupees is often reckoned to have ten lakhs.

5. माया का तीन नाम, फरसि फरसा फरसराम। Máyá ká tína náma Pharasi, Pharasá, Pharasaráma.

Wealth has three names, (Maya=illusion, that which tempts all men), viz Pharsu, Pharsá, Pharasrám.

One who has a competence is called Pharsu, a wealthier man is called Pharsa (a better name), if he is very rich people will call him Pharasrám (a very respectable name).

Degrees of wealth and corresponding honour.

FAMILY OR HOUSEHOLD

1. घर करौ घर करौ सौ बलाय खोरा में धरौ। Ghara karau ghara karau sau baláya khorá me dharau.

Set up house, get married, and bring one hundred troubles on your head.

Used to dissuade one from marrying, or used by one who becomes disgusted with the troubles and discomforts he is having on account of his family.

FATE OR DESTINY

1. आपणो वोइयो लओणो। Ápaṇo boiyo lawoṇo.

One is sure to get the fruit of what he has sown.

"Whatsoever a man soweth that shall he also reap."

A reference to the doctrine of transmigration. A man will receive the fruit of the deeds done by him in former existences. This is so certain that a man should be prefectly patient under all circumstances.

2. पढ़ि फारसि बेच तेल यो देखौ किसमत को खेल। Paḍhi phárasi becha tela yo dekhau kismata ko khela.

A Persian scholar, yet obliged to sell oil; such is the tyranny of fate.

The story below is used to illustrate the proverb.

Once when India was under the sceptre of the Mohamedan Rulers every one who knew Persian could get a post of some importance in the administration. But an unlucky man thoroughly educated in that language not having been able to get such a post was obliged to take up service with a *Baniyá* (merchant) who assigned to him the work of selling oil.

An accomplished but unlucky man.

3. हुनी छत एकै सपक नि हुनी त सारि रात घेपलो। Huni chhaṭa ekai sapaka ni huní ta sári ráta ghepalo.

The khíra (rice pudding) is prepared by stirring it with one stick; and an event which is fated not to occur cannot be brought round even if a whole crowd of men work all night to accomplish it.

Fate will accomplish itself in its own way.

4. नाज खाणों साग राज खाणो भाग। Nája kháṇo sága rája kháṇo bhága.

One eats his meal (grain) with vegetables and enjoys his kingdom by his luck.

Fortune decides all.

Used as a caution against envying others who are in better positions.

5. कु नलि के देखणि मुनलि देखणि। Kunali ke dekhaṇi munali dekhaṇi.

Why should one consult one's horoscope rather than (be contented with) his skull or fate.

At the time of birth an astrologer is employed to draw out a chart or horoscope predicting the course of the child's life. The sutures of the skull are also supposed to indicate a man's lot. This proverb is a warning against constant and useless reference to one's horoscope (which is always carefully preserved, but which often turn out false) instead of being content with the course of one's life.

The predictions of horoscopes are so unquestionably believed by illiterate people of these hills that they regard the things therein predicted to take place as already in their possession.

The under-noted fact is used to illustrate the matter. Once a man enquired of a youth (bachelor) of his acquaintance whether he was married. The latter replied to the query in the affirmative. But the other persons of his household present then and there contradicted his statement, saying that he was yet a bachelor. On this the youth said "Friends how do you say this? you know that our Pandit (astrologer) has put down 2 wives for me in my horoscope."

6. खसम सोहाग लेलो भाग निले। Khasama sohága lelo bhága nile.

My husband, if angry, can deprive me of sohága (of his society) but not of my luck.

Applied to one who cares nothing for his superior's wrath, since every thing depends on one's fate.

The extreme of fatalism.

7. जाणो नैपाल खाणु कपाल। Jáṇo Nepál kháṇu kapála.

Though one may go to Nepal yet he cannot escape the decrees of fate.

8. बाकरि आपणा बच्चा की खैर कब तक मना। Bákari apaṇa bachchá kí khaira kaba taka maná.

How long shall a she-goat pray for the life of her kid? (i.e. no one can escape his fate).

A bad man will certainly at last meet with punishment. There is a strange story current about kids which illustrates the proverb.

Story : There are nine festival days called *Nabratrí* or *Durga Pujá* generally occurring either in September or October every year. During these festivities he-goats or kids are killed or sacrificed by almost every family. Twenty-two days after this there is another festival called "Go Púјá" or "Gobardhan" on which day all the cows, bullocks, and calves are fed with human food (viz., rice, dal, cakes &c). One day some kids saw calves playing and jumping merrily on account of the feast they were looking forward to on the day of the ensuing "Go púјá." The calves informed the kids of the approaching feast and the latter also began to dance for joy, in expectation of that day. On seeing them so ignorant of their impending fate, the old goats said to them. "O kids, you are very foolish, you are unaware of the fact that the Go púјá festival will come a long time after you will have been killed during the Durgá pujá, which is drawing near now. On hearing this all the kids playing so joyfully became very sad.

Also used in the sense that the things of this world are uncertain and fleeting.

9. ढाक का तीन पात। Dháka ká tiná pátá.

The Ḍhaka tree has three leaves only.

The *Dháka* is considered a very sacred tree. It has only three leaves. These are supposed to represent the three universal stages of birth, life, and death. The proverb applies to any or every thing which is written in one's fate as inevitable. It is also used to represent insufficient or fallacious arrangement. It is also used to represent that no king howsoever pleased with one can give him more than what is destined in his fate, as any amount of rain will not produce more than 3 leaves in the *Dháka* tree.

10. जंगल में मंगल बस्ति में कड़ाका। Jangala me mangala basti me karháká.

Feasting in the jungle and starving in a town.

Good fortune spreads a table before us even in the wilderness, while evil fortune reduces us to misery even in the most favourable circumstances.

11. पूरब जाव पछम करम का उई लक्षण। Puraba jáwa pachhama karama ká ui lakshyaṇa.

Whether I go east or west the same fate follows me.

Change of place will not change one's fate. *C.f.* Horace's "Patriae quis exsul se quoque fugit."

12. चल भाग आग। Chala bhága ága.

"O fate, move on."

E.g. One wishes to try his fortune elsewhere by leaving the place where his fate has failed to do anything for him. "Better luck another time."

13. अग्रे किं किं भविष्यति। Agre kiṇ kiṇ bhabishyati.

What becomes hereafter.

Once the skull of a man was found by a *Pandit* on which the under-noted inscriptions (sutures) were written. "This man will remain in poverty during the whole of his life, and undergo 10 years imprisonment; after this he will die on the banks of the ocean; what will become of him hereafter no one knows." The Pandit, who understood the divine writing, felt curious about the fate of the skull, since all other things which were written thereon had passed away, and he was quite unable to test its accuracy by comparing it with the real events of the man's life. So the *Pandit* wrapped the skull in a clean cloth and locked it in his box. After travelling for some time in foreign countries he at last returned home. There also he took proper care of the skull and kept it locked in his own safe. Some time afterwards being laid up with illness, his wife got possession of the key of her husband's safe. Intending to take out some money or valuables she opened it and found the skull. Suspecting it was the skull of her rival wife who had died many years before, and becoming jealous on account of her husband's attachment to the dead woman as evinced by the fact of his keeping her skull so safely, secretly she threw it into a latrine. She did this because it is supposed that when the bones of a deceased person are thus defiled that person's spirit will remain for ever in hell. The outcome of the skull's fate, when made known to the *Pandit,* convinced him that the writing on the skull was correct.

14. धूणि पाणि। Dhúṇi páṇi.

Fire and water, i.e. ministering to a Fakír.

E.g. The fire used by a Fakír (ascetic) for warming himself is known as a *Dhúṇi*. A Fakír needs only a fire to warm him, and water kept in a gourd, for he gets cooked food from other people by begging. Those who help him by supplying fuel and water are considered to have earned his favour. Ascetics who perform penances, and abstain from worldly affairs in this life are supposed to become kings, ministers, and wealthy people in the next life, and so in that existence they will repay the service rendered them in this world by giving good posts &c in their Government to those who gave them food, water and fuel. In the same way the people who now find favour with great men are believed to have served them in the former life when the great officers and kins were ascetics.

15. उफलि उफलि द्यूं फाले करम कि दुइ नाले। Uphali uphali dyún phále karama ki dui nále.

No matter how hard I dig I can only get two nalis (four seers).

Used to dissuade people from excessive toil, and also used by one who is discouraged by the failure of his own efforts.

16. नानि खोरी ठुलि निहुनी। Náni khorí ṭhuli ni huni.

Whose fate (Qismat) is small can never become great.

Applied to a poor man who after once having become prosperous relapses into his former wretched condition.

Illustration 1. Once there lived a sage hermit in a certain forest far away from human habitations, where he had no other creature but a small mouse now and then playing around him. One day the mouse having been pursued by a cat entered the blanket worn by the hermit for covering. The hermit having pity on the helpless little creature wished him to be a cat. The mouse instantly became a cat. After a little time the transformed animal was pursued by a dog, when the sage was kind enough to turn him into a dog. On the dog being hunted by a leopard the sage made him also a leopard. The leopard used to move about fearlessly during the day-time and returned to the jungle in the evening. In course of time the leopard came to be known by the people of the neighbourhood as "the hermit's leopard." This epithet the leopard considered as a disgrace to himself, and thought that it would be uttered no more if he killed the hermit. So he went to kill the sage, who, knowing his evil intention, turned him again into a mouse.

Illustration 2. Once a king while journeying in a foreign country saw a most beautiful girl whom he took to his harem though ignorant of her parentage. Soon after this it was observed that the girl was waning and losing her beauty day by day. On enquiry it was found that she did not take her food properly. Many learned and experienced physicians were employed to benefit her, but in vain. She could not give any clue to her disorder. At last a wise man, having somehow found out the parentage of the damsel, volunteered to bring her food if he were allowed to feed her. The offer was accepted. After this the man having put a little food on a leaf began to feed her at short intervals, and she began to eat, as she was accustomed so. (For she was the daughter of a sweeper, a class who do not cook their own food, but live on what they get from the people they serve. Thus they take a little food as they receive it many times a day. (The girl also was accustomed to the habit). Under the regimen the girl began to grow fat and plump. But when the facts were made known to the king he was obliged to drive her out of his seraglio.

17. अपणो दिनेर अन्यारा क्वाड़ा। Apaṇo dinera anyárá kwarhá.

One who wishes to bestow a gift will give it even if the recipient is shut up (hidden) in a dark corner.

Fate must fulfil itself whatever the outward circumstances may be. In other words, any one who wishes to give help to another will do so without regard to the other's position.

18. कै सों सिपि कै सुं घोगा। Kai so̱n sipi kai so̱n ghogá.

One gets shells, another pearls. (In diving for pearls).

One man is fortunate, another unfortunate.

19. आपणा भाग को खाणो। Ápaṇá bhága ko kháṇo.

One will eat (suffer) what there is in store in his destiny, or what fate has decreed.

This means that no relatives are of any help to one in either prosperity or adversity.

The story narrated below is quoted to explain the proverb. It is said that there was once a king who had seven daughters, all of whom were very dear to him. One day while sitting among them he enquired of each of them through whose luck she got her maintenance. All of them except the youngest said "O Father, we as well as the world under your sceptre depend on your good luck for maintenance and protection." The seventh and youngest differed from the others and said, "O Sire, though you have given me birth, still I shall have to undergo whatever there may be in my luck. I do not at all depend on your luck." This statement made the king indignant against this daughter, and he ordered her to be expelled from his palace and placed where four roads meet, to be taken away by any body who might wish to have her. But he gave the other daughters to powerful and wealthy princes in marriage with an excessive amount of dowry, so that it might last for generations. The banished girl, as soon as she was thrown on the road far off the town of her father made a vow in her mind to make the first man she met her husband. The man who first came turned out to be a woodman, who used to earn his bread by selling firewood daily. According to her vow the girl took him for her husband and went to his home, where she began to live as his wife, doing the necessary domestic work for him. One day while he was about to take his load of firewood to the town she saw that the load consisted of sandal wood. On enquiry she found that her husband had supplied that kind of wood to the king of the city (her own father) for many years past on credit, and received only two annas (about 1-1/2 pence) a day. She prepared a bill for him, which, after deduction of what he had already received, amounted to a lac of rupees as the price of the sandal, and instructed her husband to demand this the sum from the king. The wood-man did as he was told, and received a lac of rupees, with which he came home. With such a large sum in her possession she did not like to remain in the wretched hovel she and her husband were living in. So she selected a nice site for her palace and ordered it to be dug out, squared and levelled. While this was being done she found in the place four invaluable large rubies, besides immense wealth in gold, buried under-ground. The rubies on sale fatched her four lacs of rupees. This wealth she invested in prudent speculation as well as in buying innumerable villages in the neighbourhood and in various kinds of trade. All these transactions in time greatly added to their wealth, and her husband began to be called a king. Once after this, the hereditary king was assailed and would have been defeated and driven out of his kindom had it not been for the help the new king gave in defeating the assailants. This event put the original king under obligation to and made him acquainted with the new king. He was yet ignorant of the fact that his own daughter was the wife of the new king, and that the latter was his old woodman. After this one day the king with his royal family and train was invited by the woodman to a feast. The wife having put a drop of curd on her right foot (among the Hindus food is distributed with naked foot) served each course herself, disguising herself each time by putting on a different costume. The guests were astonished that instead of one the host had so many waiters. As soon as the feast was over the king and the royal family were seated in another apartment. The king was astonished to find here a woman saluting and addressing him as her father. He recognized his daughter and acknowledged that every one ought to depend on his or her own *kismat* (fate) and shewed her other sisters, who, having lost all they had, had become dependant on him, and was convinced that no relation howsoever wealthy and powerful or poor he may be can make a man either prosperous or otherwise.

20. गैणो बापु देलो लेणो को देलो। Gaiṇo bápu delo laiṇo ko delo.

My father will give me jewelry (gold and silver ornaments) but who will give me the luck in store for me?

Used to teach people that they should depend on their lot, and not on getting from others.

21. करतुत का नल कर्म का फल। Karatúta ká nala karma ká phala.

The stalks (of crops) come by industry, but the yield depends on luck.

E.g. A cultivator can only make the crops grow, but if he has ill luck the crops will be damaged or destroyed in some way or other.

22. खा कपाली सह शरीर। Khá kapálí saha sharíra.

Eat O skull, and endure O body.

Used by one who is angry with his ill luck. By skull he means his evil destiny. The sutures of the skull are supposed to be written words in which a man's destiny is recorded.

FAULT-FINDING

1. अपणा गांडको लेखो न जोखो पराया गांड को जांठी को टेको। Ápaṉá gáṉḍa ko lekho na jokho paráyá gáṉḍa ko jáṇṭhí ko ṭeko.

Unmindful of his own large goitre he tells another to support his on a stick.

We see the faults of others, but not our own. *C.f.* "The faults of our neighbours with freedom we blame, but tax not ourselves though we pactise the same."

Illustrated by the following story:

While sitting in Court before the Emperor Akabar the Great, his chief minister Birbal was guilty of an act of indecency. At which the other ministers present being envious of his position cried out that Bírbal had committed a very disrespectful act in the august presence of the Emperor, and that he deserved capital punishment. The king agreeing with them ordered Birbal to be impaled. Birbal being thus convicted of his unavoidable fault did not refute the charge at that time. But a few days before the date fixed for the execution of the sentence he presented himself to the king and said to him that he had already instructed him in all the arts and sciences of which he was possessed, but the art of sowing pearls he had no opportunity of imparting to him, and that after his death there was no one who would be able to instruct him in this mystery. The emperor being interested in this speech ordered that he should be executed after he had shown him this art. So Birbal was allowed to sow the pearls. In order to revenge himself upon his enemies (the other ministers) he selected the sites on which their houses were built for the sowing of the pearls. The houses were ordered to be razed to the ground and made into fields. He then asked for lacs of rupees in order to provide the seed pearls. Having so far accomplished his purpose, he sowed barley on the fields prepared for the purpose. After some time the barley sprung up and grew, when Birbal himself went to the Emperor and told him that the pearls were now ready for reaping early in the morning. (For in the early morning each dew-drop on the barley appeared like a beautiful pearl). He also recommended that the Emperor should reap them with his own hands, as the pearls would turn into water if touched by any one who was not in the habit of committing the act of indecency of which he had been guilty. Whereupon the king was sorely troubled and confessed that he was unable to reap them, and the ministers and the other servants of the *Darbára* all confessed their inability to undertake the delicate work of reaping the pearls, not being free from the fault of which Birbal had been found guilty. Birbal then said, "O Lord of my soul and property, if no one is free from the fault of which I have been guilty, why should I lose my life for a habit common to all?" The king was then obliged to grant him pardon. Compare the

Sanskrit proverb. "The wicked blame others for small faults, though they be small as mustard seeds, but will not see their own faults, though they be large as the bel fruit."

Also the mote in another's eye and beam in one's own eye of the Gospel story.

2. आपुं कोड़ी गन गन पाकौ औरन नौ धरौ। Apuṇ korhi̇́ gana gana pákau aurana nau dharau.

A leper rotting and full of sores blames another on the same score.

I.e. Exposing the faults of others with a view to conceal one's own.

FEAR OR SERVILITY

1. डर कि स्वस्ति। Ḍara ki swasti.

Giving salutation of "Swasti" through fear.

E.g. The salutation *"Swasti"* is only uttered by a Brahmana to a king, or to those who are of royal family after they have bowed down before or saluted him. But generally through fear the same word is used by a Brahmana before a king salutes him (in order to please him) or to any one in power though not entitled to it.

Hence the proverb is applied to one who from fear acts contrary to his conscience and custom.

2. बस पड़ो कलाल का बिन मद रई निजानु। Basa parho kalála ká bina mada raî nijánu.

One in the power of a distiller cannot abstain from wine (through fear or in order to please him).

FOLLY AND IMPRUDENCE

1. उन पना का चुला पन चुला पना का उन पन। Un paná ká chulá pana chulá paná ká un pana.

To bring in outsiders and place them near the hearth, and to drive away those of the household.

The custom among Hindus prohibits persons, other than kinsmen and relations, to approach their kitchen, otherwise their food is rendered unholy and useless; and thus by "hearth-people" is meant the members of the same house and near relations. So foreigner if taken into one's house, are sure to ruin the house, having no sympathy with the family. For instance when a concubine is taken into the house and the married wife expelled from it.

2. अपणि माणी बिराणा डेरा जाईक खाणी। Apa̠ni máṇi birá̠na ḍerá jáika kháṇí.

To eat one's own grain in another's house.

Refers to one who is independent and not under obligation to others. In another sense this is also quoted of one who foolishly maintains independence, *E.g.* a man who is visiting another, is expected to live at the expense of his host.

3. अकल को टप्पू पिछाड़ि ढाल अघाड़ि अप्पू। Akala ko ṭappú pichhárhi ḍhhála aghárhi appú.

One who loses his presence of mind holds his shield behind him and puts himself in front.

4. बाबाज्यु कि जै आशीरबाद मे गै। Bábájyu ki jai áshirbada me̠n gai.

The "Jai" (blessing) of a Jogi (ascetic) goes in blessings.

This is applicable to one who neglects his own affairs for the sake of others.

This proverb is a slur on an ascetic, who instead of devoting his time and attention to the contemplation of the Almighty with the object of attaining the chief end of man, wastes his life in profusely throwing away his blessings saying *"Jai"* (victory) to every one he comes across. An ascetic when saluted is bound to express his good wish (*Jai*) to the person making an obeisance to him. He wishes triumph to others but does not triumph over his own desires (lower nature).

5. भेकुवा कुल्याड़ौं Bhekuwá kulyárho.

A dull head is a blunted axe.

Applied to a very stupid person.

6. जात्री हरद्वार गया हुमणा दगड़ा लागा। Játri Haridwára gayá Humaṇá dagarhá lágá.

The pilgrims go to Haridwára, but the ghosts also go with them.

"Humaṇas" are spirits that take human forms, but cannot perform human acts, and so cannot perform any religious rites at Haridwara (a famous place of pilgrimage). Applied to one who tries to do what is beyond his power; imitating greater persons. Superstitious people suppose that evil spirits accompany human beings invisibly in order to take possession of them and also to imitate them, merely because they were human beings themselves before they died.

7. गोबर ल्या कयो गू लीबेर ठाड़ो। Gobara lyá kayo gú líbera ṭhárho.

One deputed to bring cow dung has brought human excreta.

Applied to a very stupid man.

8. गांडू हाथी घर कि फौज मारौ। Gáṇḍú hathí ghara ki phauja marau.

A wicked elephant destroys its own army.

Fouling one's own nest.

9. गुड़ दीक गुडलो चूक दीक रुठलो। Gurha dika guḍalo chúka díka ruṭhalo.

One gets angry with a man who gives him treacle, and pleased with him who gives a sour liquid.

Applied to a foolish man who is annoyed with another's good advice, but pleased with him who gives him bad advice. This corresponds with what it elsewhere said, that good advice to a foolish man makes him angry rather than wise, just as milk given to a snake will only increase the quantity of its poison.

10. हगणि बखत म्वाल ढुनुणौ। Hagaṇi bakhata mwálá ḍhunuṇu.

One begins to look for the door when he is under the necessity of easing himself.

Applied to imprudent persons who do not provide for future necessities.

11. जोर थोड़ी गुस्सा भौत मारखाणा का लक्षण। Jora thorí gussá bhauta márakháṇá ká lakshyaṇa.

One who has little strength but much anger carries the marks of one who will be beaten (i.e. will surely get a licking).

Used as a caution to poor persons against shewing anger. *C.f.* "if you cannot bite, never shew your teeth."

12. बणिया बोल कि मेरि हाटि ना बैठ पहाड़ि बोल पूरो तोल। Baṇiyá bola ki merí háṭi na baiṭha pahárhi bola púro tola.

The Baniyá (shop-keeper) says "Do not sit in my shop." The Pahárhi (hill man) answers, "please weigh me the full weight." (for the grain he has brought to sell)."

This is applied to one who in spite of his being very much disliked by another asks him to do some thing for him which the other will not do.

13. भात खाइक जात पूछद। Bhaṭa kháika játá púchhadá.

After having eaten rice from a man's hand to enquire about his caste.

A man generally enquires about another's caste before he intermarries in his family or eats rice from his hand. If he has already entered into such an alliance without previous enquiry he should make no enquiries afterwards. If he does so, he exposes himself to ignominy and disgrace; for after eating *rice* (not other kinds of food) from a man's hand you can refuse him nothing.

14. सिखाईं अकल चढ़ायुं पाणि। Sikháin̲ akala chaḍháyuṇ páṇi.

Borrowed wisdom and water thrown upward (cannot be depended on).

Applied to one who being devoid of wits is instructed for a certain occasion, but fails to use properly the words taught him. Illustrated by this story.

A villager had a younger brother who was a simpleton. One day, wishing to hear news of his father-in-law's family he sent him thither, instructing him to talk cheerfully and politely, and not sit like an owl, as was his usual custom. On arriving at the house, the members of the family gathered round him and began relating several misfortunes which had happened to them lately, such as the death of their father, the loss of their irrigated land by a flood etc. The simpleton, remembering his brother's instructions, replied to each recital, "Really now, that's very nice. I am glad to hear this," whereupon the family were enraged, thinking he was making fun of them. Returning home, he told his brother what he had done. His brother called him all the fools and idiots under the sun, and told him that he ought to have expressed his sorrow and sympathy for their misfortunes. After some months the simpleton was again sent to the same house. This time they began telling him good news, about four sons born in the family, large profit made by dealing in bullocks etc, to which the fellow kept replying, "Good God! I'm very sorry to hear this;" whereat the people of the house were so angry that they kicked him out, and ordered him never to show his face there again.

15. शिकारि शिकार खेलनि चूतिया गैल फिरनि। Shikári shikára khelani chútiyá gaila phirani.

Sportsmen hunt for game, but the foolish aimlessly follow them.

Applied to people who idle away their time in the hope of profiting by the labours of others.

16. कनाली खाइक कनाली की जड़ निपहच्याणदो। Kanáli kháika kanáli ki jarha ni pahachyaṇado.

One who eats the nettle but does not know its roots.

Applied to one who is utterly ignorant and never asks the reason or origin of the most ordinary things.

17. लेखि बेर दिणु हाथ काटि बेर दिणु। Lekhi bera diṇu hátha káṭi bera diṇu.

Giving writings is the same as cutting off the hand.

I.e. He who gives written obligations is in the power of another.

Compare Proverbs, 22,26. Be not one of them that are sureties for debts.

"If thou art surety for thy neighbour, thou art snared." Pro. 6.1.

18. सीख पाइ बेचि खाई। Síkha pái bechi khâî.

He happened to learn something but sold his wisdom.

Applied to one who makes poor or improper use of his resources. *C.f.* "Buy the truth, and sell it not; also wisdom, and instruction and understanding."

19. लछुवा कोठारि का चेला। Lachhuwá koṭhári ká chelá.

Lachhuwá koṭhari's sons.

Lacchuwá was, many years ago, living in a village known as "Koṭhyárá (Patti Bherang, Pargana Gangoli, District Kumaun). He had nine strong, stout, and good looking sons, but all dull-headed, foolish and stupid. They have become proverbial, and their names are used by people to bring home to their own young sons and relations their follies and imprudences, when they have not the common sense to do a thing properly, to encourage them to sharpen their wits.

A recital of a few of their acts will illustrate the proverb.

Once their father proposed to build a house, and desired them to cut beams, sleepers and planks in the jungle for the purpose, and convey them home by a hand or a span, (as the phrase goes in the hills when a thing is to be done at one's convenience) to the spot where the house was being built. Accordingly they went to the jungle, and cut trees, but instead of bringing them home they cut them into pieces of a cubit or span in length. The father (who was expecting the timber daily) on enquiry after many days found to his regret and astonishment that the timber had been completely spoiled.

Again one day while cutting trees in the jungle they were panic-struck by seeing a tiger at a distance. Unnecessarily apprehending that perhaps one of them had been taken away by the tiger, one of them began to count their number to ascertain whether they were nine or not. He counted and found eight only, because he did not count himself. The others tried and found the same result. They then began to lament and cry out that one of them had been taken away by the tiger. As soon as their father heard their cries and lamentations he was paralysed, and became as one thunder-struck. But on coming out and seeing all the nine present he began to mourn over the stupidity of his sons.

A third time their father gave them cloth and desired them to make skirts for the women of his household. Instead of measuring the cloth on the person of each of the women before the skirts were sewn, they measured cloth round the trunks of *Chir* trees, and sewed the skirts around them, and reported to their father that the skirts were ready, but could not be taken off. The father went to see what was really the matter, and was disgusted to find how stupid his sons were.

Again, on another occasion, their father, in order to make them of some use, gave them a large sum of money to deal in cloth. They brought cloth from Kashipur (a market in the Tarai district adjoining Kumaun) and began to sell it. After some months the father asked them whether they were getting any profit by the traffic. They replied "O father, we are getting immense profit from the sale of the cloth; what we purchased at only eight yards for the rupee at Kashipur, we are selling here at the enhanced rate of twelve yards for the rupee."

On the fifth occasion the father requested them to dig some wells for the sake of merit as he himself had become very old and was about to die. The sons went out and had a talk among themselves. The arrived at the sage conclusion that there was scarcely any need of digging wells in the village, where there were already many water springs, so they had better furnish water on the tops of high mountains where it was most needed. Therefore, they dug many ditches on the peaks of mountains to get water, but to no purpose. These ditches or dry holes or wells are still in existence in Pargannah Gangoli and are called after them, "Lachhuwa Kothari's sons' wells."

Lastly, when their father died, all of them proposed to amuse themselves by flying about as birds. Knowing that they could not fly without wings, they tied large *"Súps"* with which corn is sifted, to their bodies and arms, and leaping down a high precipice perished like Icarus of old.

20. वखल को भाई मुशल हुमा को भाई थुमा। Wokhala ko bhâî Mushala Humá ko bhâî Thumá.

The brother of a mortar is a pestle and Humá's brother is Thumá.

Two persons who are alike foolish and illiterate.

21. सकणि न पकणि बंदूक तकणी। Sakan̲î na pakan̲i bandúka takan̲i.

One unable to shoot straight aims at another with a gun.

Applied to one who vainly attempts any thing beyond his capacity or power. *C.f.* "If you cannot bite, never shew your teeth."

22. काला सीख दीनि सिलकदोरयो। Kálá shikha d́ini silaka-do rayo.

A foolish man broods over all he hears.

Illustration. A foolish man once heard some one say that people about to die become cold in the hands and feet. This saying took hold of him so that he never forgot it. One day he went out to dig *Tairhu,* an edible root highly prized by the villagers, and which is often dug from a depth of 3 or 4 feet in the ground. When the fool had finished digging and collecting the roots, his hands and feet became very cold, as it was the winter season. Remembering the saying that cold hands and feet are signs of approaching death, he left the basket of roots in the jungle and went home, telling his friends that he was about to die. He then laid himself down and soon assumed all the appearance of a dead man. His friends thinking he was really dead carried him to the junction of two streams, where they slightly scorched the body and left it. That evening two travellers passing that way, and not knowing the road, began to speak about the way they should take to reach a certain village. The fool hearing them said, "When I was alive I used to go by such a path, but I am dead now." The travellers were frightened, and supposing that the man was a ghost, stoned him to death.

23. बौली मा का बौला पूत औंदि गंगा पराल का सूत। Bauli má ká baulá púta áuṉdi gangá parála ká súta.

The foolish son of a foolish mother wishes to cross the swollen torrent on a bridge of straw.

Foolish people do or attempt foolish things.

Illustration. Once the Emperor Akbar the Great desired his vizier B́irbal to produce three fools before him within a week. B́irbal accordingly went about in search of them. While thus engaged he saw a man riding a pregnant mare with a heavy load of fuel on his head, and enquired of him why he was doing so. The man replied that he did so only to spare the mare as it was pregnant. Amused at his reasoning, Birbal noted him down as one of the three fools he was in search of. So he took him to the Emperor, who, after hearing from the man the reason he had to give for his conduct, declared that the man was right. After this he asked B́irbal why he had brought only one fool instead of three. B́irbal said "O Sire, this is the first (natural) fool; your majesty is the second, who has declared his conduct to be right; and I am the third, who have brought him before your majesty to be judged."

24. चोर भलो बेकूफ बुरो। Chora bhalo bekúpha buro.

A thief is better than a stupid man.

I.e. A stupid man is worse than a thief to deal with.

25. जबान तरास खांदो नजदीक। Jabána tarásha khándo najadika.

A cutting tongue and the term (within which a debt is to be repaid) will be short.

No one can get his work done or purpose accomplished by using harsh words, or taking severe and improper measures. For instance, if one were to accost a woman as "mother" she would feel highly pleased, but would be greatly incensed if one in saluting or addressing her were to say to her "O my father's wife" though both terms have the same signification.

26. आपणा खुटा मैं कुल्याड़ि मारनि। Ápana̲ khuṭá me kulárhi márani.

One strikes an axe against his own foot.

To do a thing which ruins one's own interest.

27. चुतिया मरिगया औलाद छोड़िगया। Chutiyá marigayá auláda chhorhigayá.

The foolish man is dead, but has left offspring.

By this proverb the father is still accused of foolishness through his foolish son. His follies live after him.

28. गांठ को पूरो, अकल को हीनो। Gánṭha ko púro akala ko híno̲.

Full of knots but witless.

The villagers keep their money tied up in knots in their clothes; so full of knots means very rich.

Applied to one who is rich, but destitute of wit, and so deceived and cheated by every one. One who has more money than wit to use it properly.

29. शुक्र औरन सौं साणौं आपुसौं कांणो। Shukra aurana so̲n sáṇo ápu̲n káṇo.

The planet Venus (in Hindu̧ astronomy, of the male sex) is two-eyed to other people, but blind (one-eyed) to himself.

E.g. This planet is said to have only one eye, the other has been put out. In spite of this defect, according to astrologers he bestows good furtune while in the ascendant, but is unable to repair his own loss. This proverb is thus quoted in reference to a man who is engaged in doing good to others but neglects his own affairs. The lesson usually drawn from this is that a man ought first to look to his own welfare and then try to do good to other people. *C.f.* "Physician, heal thyself."

30. जाण न पहचाण भकअंग्बाल। Jáṇa na pahachyáṇa bhaka aṇgwála.

To embrace at once one who is a perfect stranger.

Applies to one's revealing his secrets or making requests to another with whose conduct and character he is unacquainted.

31. पौणा पूछि पकोड़ा। Pauṇá púchhi pakorhá.

He asks the guest what food he prefers.

E.g. To enquire from the guest as to the kind of food he likes to eat. It is improper and against etiquette for the guest to say what he will eat. He who is to receive a gift should not be asked what is his choice.

32. तू क्यान गये हाय का को कमाये अपणो खाये। Tú kyána gaye háiká ko kamaye apaṇo kháye.

Why have you been ruined? because you earned for others, but fed yourself at your won expense (you did the work of others without food and wages).

E.g. The custom is for the employer to feed the labourer and also pay his wages.

Applied to foolish squanderers who do not care for wages.

33. देख हाले सहुर बुवारी को मुतणै बटी। Dekha hále sahúra búwári ko mutaṇai baṭi.

I have seen the conduct of my daughter-in-law from the manner she performed the offices of nature.

An unchaste woman reveals her character by trifling actions; or, more generally, we can judge a person's nature by small indications, *e.g.* untidiness or carelessness.

34. अघिन दौड़ पछिन चौड़। Aghina daurha pachhina chaurha.

He runs forward but neglects behind.

Applies to one who makes advancement or progress in his lesson or work, but neglects what he has already attained.

35. लाटो आपणि जसि धोति लगा। Láṭo ápaṇi jasi dhoti lagá.

The dumb (in spite of other's admonitions) will cover his loins (or dress himself) in his own (clumsy) way.

That is an idiot will not follow or act upon the good advice given to him by others superior to him in every respect. *C.f.* "Fools despise wisdom."

36. गै कसाइ कणि पत्यांछ्य। Gai kasái kaṇi patyáṇchhya.

A cow trusts in a butcher.

Used of persons void of intellect who trust in cheats and thus suffer in consequence.

37. बोलीक कुमहार घोड़ा मा लगनी चड़दो। Bolika kumahára ghorá má ní charhado.

A potter will not ride a horse even if told to do so.

A potter always rides an ass, hence the proverb.

I.e. Foolish people do not listen to any advice, even if for their own comfort or benefit.

FOOLISH AMBITION

1. गाणसौं लंगोटि नै तंबू सों मन। Gáṇa so͟n la͟ngoṭi nai tambú so͟n mana.

One who has no cloth for his loins (to hide his nakedness) longs for a tent.

Preposterous desires.

2. बदन पर लंगोट नी मोत्यु की खरीद। Badana para laṇgota ní motyú͟n kí kharída.

One who has no cloth to cover his loins wishes to purchase pearls.

Preposterous desires.

3. मन बोद मरगलखौं स्यूंदी माकु डडेलनिपौं। Mana boda margala khau͟n syúṇḍí má ku ḍaḍela ni pau͟n.

I have not even the ḍaḍela (oil) for my head but I have a longing for sweetments (cooked in oil).

(Ḍaḍel=the oil left after cooking púris (cakes) in the cooking vessel *i.e.* burnt oil).

Applied to one who longs for things beyond his means. Women apply oil to their head in order to decorate and tie their hair.

4. तनको नो धोती मन बोद लावो मोती। Tana ko ni dhotí mana boda láo motí.

Nothing to wear, yet wishes for pearls.

5. तन को नी लंगोटी तंबु की फरमायश। Tana ko ní laṇgoṭi tambu ki farmáyasha.

Nothing to wear, yet asks for a tent.

6. तन को नी लत्ता पान चबोंछ अलपत्ता। Tana ko ni lattá pána chabaun̲chha alapattá.

No cloth to cover his person, yet he wants to chew betel nut.

7. मन हौसिया करम गंडिया। Mana hausiyá karama gan̲ḍiyá.

Heart ambitious, but fate unlucky.

Used when poor people indulge in impossible wishes.

8. सभी श्यालों सींग निहोंदा। Sabhí shyálon̲ síṇga ni hon̲dá.

All jackals have not horns.

Applied ironically to those who aspire to some dignity and pretend to importance. *C.f.* "All that glitters is not gold."

The jackal who is supposed to possess a horn in his head is made king of the jackals. The horn comes out and becomes visible only at the time when it cries, at other times it shrinks and is therefore not seen. Whenever the king of the jackals cries, all the jackals are obliged to acknowledge him as their lord by their howling response. If any one does not do this his head breaks and he dies. The king of jackals is said to yell out to the other jackals. "Main̲ Dilli ká Bádsháh hún̲, Main̲ Dilli ká Bádsháh hún, Main̲ Dilli ká Bádsháh hún̲." (I am emperor of Delhi.) To this all the jackals say Ho, ho, ho. (Yes you are, yes you are, yes you are). People attribute many strange properties to the horn of the jackal (Shyála siṇgí). Whoever is in possession of the horn will get the king in his own power, will defeat his enemy, will draw men to his side, make women love him, will be prosperous; will not die even if struck with a deadly weapon &c. &c.

The Shyála Siṇgi (horn of the king of jackals) is reckoned as one of the *Nidhis* (talismans or charms) by virtue of which one can get everything he desires.

9. गेड़ी न पल्ला दुइ ब्याव करूला। Geḍi na pallá dui byáwa karulá.

Nothing in his pocket and purse, yet wishes to marry two brides.

In Garhwal no one can get a bride unless he pays smartly for her. Applied to one ambitious beyond his position and power.

10. रसि गला लाग हाड़सों हाथ पसारनु। Rasi galá lága hárha soṉ hátha pasáranu.

Soup sticks in the throat, but he stretches forth his hand for a bone.

Applied to one who cannot do what work is already in his hands yet asks for more, or being unable even to do an ordinary thing attempts matters beyond his power.

11. राजा का जसा ग्रह मेरा लगकर। Rájá ká jasá graha merá laga kara.

Make my stars the same as those of a king.

By stars literally is meant circumstances or luck. This is applicable to a very insignificant person who aspires after high things totally beyond his reach, or competes with his superiors.

Stars = fortune. High ambition.

FOPS, BOASTERS AND FASTIDIOUS PEOPLE

1. गुड़ खाणो गुलगुलान को परहेज। Gurha kháṇo gulgulána ko paraheja.

One who eats gurha (treacle) but abstains from sweet loaves (made with gurha).

Foolish scruples.

2. हाथि निगलि जाणो मच्छर गला लागणो। Háthi nigali jáṇo machhara galá lágaṇo.

To strain at a gnat and swallow an elephant or camal.

E.g. to make much ado about the performance of unimportant duties, but to make no difficulties about neglecting much more important affairs.

3. डेड़ टटु बाग में डेरो। Derha ṭaṭu bága me ḍero.

Encamped in the garden, but having only a pony and a half.

Pride and poverty.

4. मारनि दिल्लि हगनि चुलि। Márnai Dilli hagani chuli.

Professes to conquer Dehli but never stirs out of his own house.

A great boaster.

5. मारनै मारनै दिल्लि जांछ जोखड़ो हाथ क्वे निकर। Márnai márani Dilli janchha jo kharho hátha kwe nikara.

He would fight his way to Dehil, but does not wish to strike a blow.

A great boaster.

6. बूढ़ि घोड़ि बनाति जीन। Búrhi ghorhi banáti jína.

An old mare with a saddle of broad cloth.

A beggarly fellow in fine clothes.

7. दिल्ली को दिलवाली मुख चुपड़ो पेट खालि। Dilli ko dilwálî mukha chuparho peṭa kháli.

Like the inhabitants of Delhi, who, though hungry (try to) look well fed.

Applies to fops.

8. बदन को नि लत्ता मिस्सी लगाव अलपत्ता। Badana ko ni lattá missî lagáwa alapattá.

Has no cloth for his person, but, needs Missi (a powder) used for coloring the teeth by fashionable native women).

9. गांड गरीबिणि रेशम को तणियां। Gáṉḍa garibiṇi reshama ko taṉiyán.

A poor man, but uses a silk thread to tie his trousers with.

10. सौकीन बुढ़िया चटाइ को लहंगा। Saukína buḍhiyá chaṭái ko lahaṇgá.

A foppish old lady has a skrit made of a mat, (when she cannot get anything else).

I.e. One accustomed to luxuries or comforts cannot give them up.

11. डेढ़ पौ चन तेबारि में रसोइ। Deḍha pau chún tebári meṉ rasoi.

One six chhatáks of flour (the smallest quantity necessary for one person) but cooked in the Tebári.

The *Tebári* is that portion of a house which is visible to all who pass by.

This is used of one who being very poor has haughty airs and makes vain show.

12. ऊंचि दुकान फीका पकवान। Úṉchi dukána phíká pakawána.

A lofty shop, but tasteless or worthless sweets.

A man of note whose dealings are not good, or one who is great in name, but has no wealth or property to maintain it.

13. मन मन भौ शिर हिलौ। Mana mana bhau shira hilau.

The heart desires, but the head is shaken in denial.

14. नाम को बड़ो दर्शन को छोटो। Náma ko barho darshana ko chhoṭo.

Well reputed, but bad to deal with (literally, great in name, but little to look at).

Descriptive of a man who has managed to get a good reputation, but in private dealings is found to be roguish, selfish etc.

FORBEARANCE

1. एक चूल बिषकी वी कि पिणि जैकि एक सौ चूल अमृत कि पीराखीछ। Eka chúla bisha ki wíki piṇi jaiki eka sau chúla amrita ki pí rákhí chha.

One cup of poison should be accepted at the hands of the man who has already given one a hundred of nectar.

We should be willing to bear somewhat with the abuse or ill-treatment bestowed on us by a benefactor.

2. पांच लाइ निखोणी डूमन दसलाइ निखोणी बीठन। Páncha lái ni khoṇí ḍúmana dasa lái ni khoṇí biṭhana.

A Dum (a low caste man) ought not to quarrel for the sake of five rupees, and a Biṭha (patrician) for ten rupees.

This is used to show that one ought to forbear quarrelling with others for small amounts. *C.f.* Go not forth hastily to strife, lest thou know not what to do in the end thereof, when thy neighbour hath put thee to shame.

3. हिसालु की बाण बड़ी रिसालू नजीक जैबेर उधीणि दिंछ। ये बात को कैले गटो नि मानणो दूधाल की लात सौणी पड़यंछ्य। Hisálu ki báṇa barí risálú najíka jaibera udhíṇi diṇccha. Ye báta ko kaile gaṭo ni manano dúdyala ki láta sauṇi. parhyaṇhhya.

The temper of Hisálu, a thorny wild berry (wild raspberry), is very bad; for it pierces one who touches the plant; no one ought to mind this, for the kicking of a milch cow must be endured by every one.

All the field-terraces are full of this wild plant, the branches and leaves of which are full of sharp and crooked thorns. It is loaded with ripe berries in the months of May and June. The berries are soft, pulpy, and sweet, and afford a nice treat to the poor people, but every time a berry is plucked the fingers are in danger of being pierced with thorns.

One ought not to mind the ill temper of those we are benefitted by.

4. खाणिगम पैरणि शरम। Khani gama pairani sharama.

One ought to forbear and be modest.

Used to admonish children or others not to be fastidious or quarrelsome, but to lead a respectable life.

FORCE OR COMPULSION

1. भूतन लखा देवतन धक्का। Bhútana lakhá dewatana dhakká.

Ghosts have large goats sacrificed to them, but the deities are pushed aside.

Ghosts are supposed to frighten and take possession of people by making them sick and die, so people thus attacked worship ghosts, and sacrifice big goats to them, whereas deities, who, though they have far greater power to bless their devotees, and who do not thus trouble and attack people, are forgotten or neglected on the score of their being harmless.

2. निमडियो गौं को घिनौडो पधान। Nimarhiyo gauṇ ko ghinaurho padhána.

The headman of a deserted village is the sparrow.

E.g. In an inhabited village sparrows find a few nooks or holes to live in, but in the village abandoned by human beings they can occupy any place without fear.

Applied to a small man who exercises great authority, or oppresses others with inpunity, there being no great men or authorities in the locality.

3. दूण निसकदो बीस पाथा। Dúṇa ni sakado bísa páthá.

Cannot lift up 32 seers, but can lift 40 seers.

Applied to one who is not willing to do a little work, but will do much more by being goaded to it.

4. हो मेरी स्वेण नतर कादूं तेरो नाख। Ho merí swe_na natara káṭ ú_n tero nákha.

Be my wife, or I will cut your nose off.

Obtaining one's object by threats and violence.

5. रांड की मुडली ढोल की कुंडली कसीक भलो बुलांद। Ráṇḍa kí muṇḍalí ḍhola kí kuṇḍalí kasíka bhalo buláṇda.

The head of a woman and that of a drum give good sound when well tied and beaten.

Material authority commended.

6. मारि मारि बेर मुसलमान। Mári mári bera musalamána.

Made a Musalman by force.

Applied to any one who is compelled to do anything contrary to his wishes. Adverting to the manner in which Hindus were forced to become Mahomedans by the Mahomedan rulers.

7. मुलैजै मुलैजा जेठाणा की स्वेण। Mulaijai mulaijá jeṭháṇá kî sweṇa.

To become by pressure the unwilling wife of her husband's elder brother.

E.g. According to custom a younger brother's wife is not allowed even to touch her husband's elder brother, and vice versa. So to become his wife is a most atrocious incest.

Used of one who commits sin under compulsion.

8. मेरी अंगुली तेरी आंख में तेरी मेरे मुख में। Meri aṇguli terî án̲kha me teri merá mukha me.

My finger is in your eye, and your finger is in my mouth.

I.e. you are in my power every way; you are in a periloús state.

9. लातौं को यार बातौं ते नि बुझदौं Láton̲ ko yára báton̲ ten̲ ni bujhado.

A man who needs blows to move him, will pay no attention to mere words.

Applied to foolish and illiterate people who will not be anything without coercion or force.

FRIENDSHIP AND ESTRANGEMENT

1. वालाणी मिताईं जोरव निताईं। Wáláṇî mitâîn jo rawa nitáin̲.

Make that kind of friendship which will last forever.

Caution against temporary friendship which are generally not sincere, but entered into from some selfish motive.

"Those friends thou hast, and their adoption tried".

"Buckle them to thy soul with hoops of steel." *Shakspeare.*,

2. कैको आप होइ रहणो कोई अपणो बणाइ राखणो। Kaiko ápa hoi rahan̲o koî apaṇo baṇái rákhaṇo.

Act as a friend to another and have another as your friend.
"Do unto others as you would have them do unto you."

3. रुपया कि दोस्ति दवाइ को शरीर। Rupayá ki dosti dawái ko sharíra.
Friendship for money's sake and the body fed on medicine will not last.

4. तेरी मेरि प्रीत कोलाई काटुकू। Teri meri príta kolaín̠ ká ṭukú.
Your love and mine is on the top of a pine tree.
This is used when friends are completely estranged from each other.

5. बबा को मित्र गुड़ को काठ। Babá ko mitra gurha ko káṭha.
The friend of one's father and the treacle-wood (dry sugarcane).
E.g. One's father's friend will do him good, *i.e.* not injure him, as the sugarcane though dried up will prove to be sweet.
Used to encourage one's father's friend to do some favour.

FUTURE APPREHENSIONS OR CONTINGENCIES

1. पेट मैं लड़का करदोड़ बट। Peṭa men̠ larhaká karadorha baṭa.
Twist a chain for the boy who is yet in the womb.
As soon as a boy is born, a chain either of silver or of thread is put round his waist. An imprudent or impatient person wishes to make unnecessary provision for him while it is yet uncertain whether the unborn child will be a boy or a girl. (In the case of a girl, the waist chain is not required).
Used of needless apprehensions.
This is illustrated by an incident which took place during the time of one of the Native Princes at Almora.
Once a contingent force composed of the *Banias* of Almora was ordered to go and fight with the army of an enemy, who had arrived at Haldwani (at the foot of the hills) to invade the hill-country. The raw recruits, in a great fright, drew out their swords from the sheaths and started on the expedition. The Rájá asked the reason of their so doing,

when they replied "Sire, we shall have hardly any time to draw our swords when we come in face of the enemy, and so we must keep them ready for the emergency." From this the Raja saw that they were a set of cowards, and so packed them off home again.

2. जै बखत को द्यो तै बखत कौ पाणि। Jai bakhata ko dyo tai bakhata ko páṇi.

When it rains, there will be water.

One should not be anxious about the future.

"Sufficient unto the day is the evil thereof."

3. बाप मरलो बैल बटला। Bápa maralo baila baṭalá.

The bullocks (property) will be divided (among the brothers) on the death of the father.

The son imagines he will do many wonderful things with the property that comes to him, builds castles in the air. But all is contingent on his getting the property.

GAMBLING

1. जुवा मीठी हार। Júwá míṭhí hára.

Gambling losses are like sweets.

I.e. One wants more, or the loser wants to try again.

GIFTS FROM RELATIVES

1. पौणा कि पकौड़ी स्वाद। Pauṇá ki pakorhí swáda.

Dainties brought by a guest who is a relative are delicious.

Other peoples' food, possessions, &c seem to us better than our own. Or, the gift of a beloved one is sweet.

Also that any dainty which one may have in plenty is not so delicious nor so highly appreciated as that which he has not himself, but receives a little of from another person.

GIFT OF THE GAB

1. जैको गीचो तै को सब कुछ। Jaiko gícho taiko saba kuchha.

Whoever has a tongue has everything.

The power of eloquence.

Once an illiterate but crafty and talkative man, professing himself to be one of the greatest of Pandits, took his abode in a certain city where he was much respected, and regarded as a saint by the people. When his fame spread far and wide, another *Pandit* who was a real scholar came to see him with a view to test his learning, and sent him a letter in *Sanscrit* through his servant. As soon as the letter was handed to the illiterate man he opened it and then threw it towards the servant saying that his master had no ability to address him in *Sanscrit*. After this the real *Pandit* sent him word that he would meet him in a literary contest. To this the pretended *Pandit* said "Alas! how can a mouse stand before a cat, but let the mouse come to the cat at any time he likes." A day was fixed for their contest. In the meantime the pretender was asked by the people whether he would require any books for reference, and how they would be able to know which of the two was victorious. The false *Pandit* said that all books they had in their houses should at once be sent to him, and that they should consider him defeated who was first silenced. After this the crafty *Pandit* separated all the leaves of the books the people had sent him, and on the appointed day sat almost buried under the heap of papers. The other *Pandit*, as soon as he saw the talkative man, gave his salutation (Namaskára) to which the latter replied by saying "Namaskára, Chamatkára, Dhamatkára," (mere meaningless words uttered in mimicry). The true *Pandit* was rather astonished at such behaviour on the part of the false *Pandit*. However, he asked him again "Kiṇchit Shástra Charchá," "Will you have some discussion of learning?" The false *Pandit* answered him by howling "Charchá, marchá, kharchá," (absurd mimicry). At this the true *Pandit* was astounded and could not say a word more, but silently withdrew from the place. By this the people, who were interested in the false *Pandit*, were fully convinced that he had won the victory, and began to beat drums, ring bells, and blow conch shells and trumpets.

Illustration No. 2. A she-fox being pregnant desired her husband to build her a house for her young ones. The fox agreed to do so, but as soon as he got his food he went out to another jungle, and there basked in the sun the whole day, and returned to his wife in the evening in time to eat the evening meal provided by her for him. In this way he loitered for days and months, always telling his wife that he was engaged in building a shed for her offspring. At last his wife gave birth to the young ones, and asked him to shew her the house. He took her and the young ones into the jungle to a den occupied by the cubs of a tigress, and placed them there, instructing his wife what to do and say on the approach of the tigress, *viz.*, to squeeze the young ones so that they might scream out, and to tell him (the husband), on his enquiring the cause of their crying, that the young ones were crying for the fresh flesh of a tiger which they could not get, and that they would not eat the stale flesh of a tiger killed the day before. He then went and sat down on a ridge above the cavern. Just as the tigress came the she-fox caused her young ones to cry out, which enraged the tigress, who saw that her den was taken possession of by some other animals. The fox (as arranged) enquired why her young ones were crying, to which his wife replied as she was told to do. On hearing this the tigress, thinking that her young ones had been killed and that now she herself would be killed, took fright and ran away. While thus running through the forest the tigress met with a monkey, who, having heard why she was running, told her that her panic was groundless, since she was queen of all the animals of the forest, and offered to accompany her to her den. So the tigress appeared again before her den accompanied by the monkey. The she-fox repeated the process of squeezing and pinching her young ones, and her husband made the same enquiry and the she-fox the same reply as before. This time the fox said to his wife. "Tell the young ones to have a little more patience: they will soon get the flesh of a live tiger, which his friend the monkey is kindly bringing for them." This last speech of the fox put the tigress into such terror that she left the place never to return.

GOD'S JUDGEMENTS

1. दैबी बिचित्रा गति। Daívî bichitrá gati.
The ways of Providence are wonderful.
C.f. "Man proposes, God disposes."
Once a pair of doves, seated on a tree, were aimed at with an arrow by a fowler on the one hand, and on the other a falcon darted on them from the sky. At this crisis, while the she-dove was lamenting to her husband and telling him that they would surely be killed either by the one or the other, the shaft discharged by the hunter killed the falcon, and the sportsman himself was bitten by a venomous snake. So the pair, thus providentially preserved, narrowly escaped with their lives.

2. राई को पर्बत, पर्बत कि राई। Rái ko parbata parbata ki rái.
A grain of mustard into a mountain, and a mountain into a grain of mustard again.
Used to represent God's power, or providence, or the transient nature of things in this world.

3. परमेश्वर कि माया कैं धूप कैं छाया। Parmeshwara ki máyá kai̲n dhúpa kai̲n chháyá.
Illusion of God, sun-shine at one place, and shadows at another.
The transient nature of wordly things, and the unequal distribution of human happiness and misery, regarded as "Maya" or Illusion. Used to teach patience.

4. एक दिन हुणा को एक दिन जाणा को। Eka dina huṇá ko eka dina jáṇá ko.

A certain day is ordained for one to rise, and another day to sink.

Used to warn in prosperity and console in adversity with the thought that Fate rules all.

5. परमेश्वर का घर मु देरछ अंधेरनी। Parmeshwara ká ghara mu dera chha aṇdhera ní.

There is delay in God's judgment, but there is no injustice in him.

6. नर समजे और नारायण करे और। Nara samaje aura náráyaṇa kare aura.

Man proposes one thing, but God does another thing.

C.f. "Man proposes but God disposes."

GOOD LUCK

1. अंधा का हाथ बटेर लागौं Anḍhá ká hátha baṭera lágo.

A blind man happened to catch a quail.

It is almost impossible to catch a quail, and for a blind man to catch one must be a great chance. Some events are entirely the result of the favour of Providence or fortune. Used to one who is puffed up, through having gained any thing by chance.

2. बिरालू का भागले सीको या छिंको टूटो। Birálú ká bhága le síko yá chhiṉko ṭúṭo.

It was the cat's good luck when the net broke.

Milk and curds are generally kept in a vessel which is hung up in a net to one of the beams of the roof, to be out of the way of children and cats, but when the string breaks, the cat has a feast. Description of a stroke of unexpected good luck. *C.f.* "It is an ill wind that blows nobody good."

3. एक बाट दुइ काज। Eka báṭa dui kája.

One road, two jobs.

This is used when one sets out for one business, but fortunately accomplishes another object on his way. *C.f.* "To kill two birds with one stone."

4. परमेश्वर छप्पर फाड़ि बेर दिंछ । Parmeshwara chhapara phárhibera dinchha.

God gives even through the roof of one's house.

This means that if one's fate is good he will get every thing he needs without care and trouble.

5. लाटा का पौ बाटा। Láṭá ká pau báṭá.

The feet of a simple man (lit. dumb) man are in the path (of profit).

A simple man often prospers by good luck.

Story: In a certain village there lived a very simple man who had a hut and some cattle. His neighbours being envious of him, and taking advantage of his simplicity, tried to drive him out of the village. So one day, while his cattle were grazing in a jungle, they drove them down a precipice, and thus killed them. The poor simple man skinned the dead cattle and conveyed the skins for sale to a certain town. While on his way he was overtaken by the darkness, and stopped in a cave in a jungle; after midnight some thieves with stolen property arrived and took shelter at the mouth of the same cave. Hearing their tread in the cave, the man become much alarmed, and tried to conceal himself under the hides he had brought. The rattling of the hides inside the cave startled the thieves, who, panic struck, ran away leaving all the money they had brought with them. The simple man took possession of the money and went home. In order to measure the amount of money he had received he asked for the loan of a wooden measure from one of his neighbours. The neighbour, being curious to know what he had brought, placed some tar at the bottom of the measure. As soon as the simple man had measured his money he returned the measure, but a few rupees had stuck to the tar at the bottom. This aroused the avarice of his neighbour, who asked the simple man how and whence he had obtained so much money; he said that it was from the sale of the skins of his cattle. The envy he bore to the simple man, and greediness for money, caused his neighbour to kill his own cattle and take their skins for sale, but to no purpose, for he received only a few rupees by the bargain. Being enraged he set fire to the hut of the simple man, and reduced it to ashes. The simple man collected the ashes and put them in a bag, and set off to sell them. While on his way, he left his load by the road side and went to drink water at a spring which was at a little distance. In the mean time another man who had also left a load of flour there, went to drink water too. On returning he took up the load of ashes leaving his own by mistake and went his way. The simple man also returned and took the load left by the other man. Seeing some strange marks on the load he opened it and found that it contained flour. Then he took the load to his home where he again asked his neighbour's measure to ascertain the quantity of the flour. His neighbour, having found that the simple man received flour in lieu of the ashes of his shed, set fire to his own shed, but could not sell the ashes.

This story is also applicable to the proverb. "Whoever digs a pit for another will himself fall into it."

6. हेलु का भागले मेलु पाका। Helu ká bhága le melu páká.

(Wild) pears have ripened to the good luck of a jackal.

The jackals, when other food is scarce, in the cold season, have wild pears to eat.

Applied to one who, when on the brink of ruin, is saved by a lucky accident.

7. किसमत का अगाड़ि इलम पाणि भरद। Kisamata ká agarhi ilama páṇi bharada.

Knowledge will bring water (is a servant) before a lucky person.

Story : A very learned and a very lucky man by chance met each other in a foreign country, and being strangers there they agreed to divide equally whatever they might be able to earn. For some months they subsisted entirely upon the earnings of the learned man. But at last his income failed, and both were in danger of starvation. Whereupon the learned man said to the other, "Now it is your turn to do some thing for our support."

The lucky man then went to the court of a king, and with his club knocked the crown off the king's head. When the courtires went to pick up the crown they saw a venomous snake entwined about it. Thinking the man had saved him from the snake, the king was very grateful, and asked what reward he should give him. The man replied. "I want nothing." The next day the man again went to the king's court, and taking the king by the hand, dragged him out of the building, the roof of which fell in as soon as the king had got out. The king now more than ever thinking himself under obligation asked the man to name his reward, and when half of his kingdom was asked, he freely gave it to him.

8. काला गोरू का सपना बाछरू। Kálá goru ká sapaná báchharu.

Perfect calves of a dumb cow.

Applied to a clever man whose father is an idiot or a simple man. Used ironically.

GOOD OR BAD SIGNS OR OMENS

1. हुन्यारि डाली का चला चला पात। Hunyári ḍálī ká chala-chalá páta.

A promising tree bears shining leaves.

Applied to promising boys or girls.

2. जैका मुख सुबाक तैको करम भाग। Jaiká mukha subáka taiká karama bhága.

One who has good words in his mouth has good luck in store.

I.e. Whoever is affable will be fortunate.

3. अणहोति कला बेतैण कि माला। Aṇahoti kalá betaiṇa ki málá.

To attempt impossibilities is like wearing a garland of the Betaiṇa fruit or flowers. (Melia sempervirens).

The *Betaina* tree is supposed to be haunted by an evil spirit.

A garland of the fruits or flowers of the tree is suggestive of an evil spirit, and so they are never used for this purpose. In the same way to attempt a work which is beyond one's power is suggestive of ruin.

4. बांजागौं की घिनौड़ो पधान। Báṇjagau̱n ko ghinaurho padhána.
Sparrows are the headmen of deserted villages.
C.f. "Among the blind the one-eyed is king."

5. जामना बटि कामना। Jámaná baṭi ˙kámaná.
No sooner up than it quivers.
If a plant, as soon as it has sprouted up from the ground, quivers, it is sure to wither; the proverb is applied to boys and girls who learn bad habits from their childhood, and so are sure to be ruined.

6. जेठो चेलो बोदलो गांति। Jeṭho chelo bodalo gáṇti.
The eldest son is clothed in sackcloth.
This is spoken by parents grieving for their eldest son who is in adverse circumstances; or in regard to the first crop or the first attempt at anything which has proved a failure.

7. त्याड़ि देखा जोशि देखा मरनि बखत करड़िया देखा। Tyárhi dekhá joshi dekhá marani bakhata kararhiyá dekhá.
While well all castes of Brahmans (Tyarhi, Joshi &c) came to me, but when at the point of death the Kararhiyá Brahman only comes.
In the first instance this was used by the *Banias* of Almorah who employ Kararhiyá Brahmans as their priests. While well they have dealings with all sorts of people, but when they are at the point of death, no one, except the Kararhiyá Brahmans, who have to perform the last religious ceremony for the dying man, will come near them. Hence the proverb.
This is applied to adverse circumstances or evil omens which fill one with apprehensions of ruin or downfall.

8. एक घर का नौमता कुशल कां बटहो। Eka ghara ká naumatá kushala ká̱n bata ho.

If there are nine opinions in a household what peace can there be?

"A house divided against itself cannot stand."

9. ब्याह को सगुन रंगवालिबट। Byáha ko saguna rangwáli baṭa.

The prospects of a marriage are known from the time of the Raṇgwali (beginning).

E.g. When a marriage day is fixed the women of the households of both parties as a preliminary rite prepare a purple dye made of the infusion of *Kusumbha* flowers (safflower, carthamus tinctorius) in which first of all they tinge the sheet of the would-be bride and after that their own sheets. If the color on the sheets turns out brilliant they take it as a good omen, and if otherwise they interpret it accordingly.

One applies this proverb to himself when he is disappointed by the failure of his first efforts in an undertaking

10. नमडुवा गौं को चमडुवा पधान। Namarhuwá gaun ko chamarhuwá padhána.

The head man of a decaying village is chamarhuwá (pinched and destitute).

The village is as its headman, i.e., suffers from his incompetency etc.

11. निहुणियां पूत घुंडौं गांड़। Nehuṇiyán púta gnunḍon gánḍá.

Boys doomed to be ruined get goitres on their knees.

Applies to one who is attacked early with diseases, or is addicted to bad habits from his boyhood.

12. गौं को सयाणो चोरी। Gaun ko sayáno chorí.

If the headman of a village is a thief than all will steal.

Evil example.

13. जानी डालि का खसखसा पात। Jání ḍáli ká khasakhasá páta.

A tree decaying has stiff leaves.

Early signs of evil.

14. जब शाल कि कमबखति औंछ्य तब बस्ति का तरफ औंछ। Jaba shyála ki kambakhti au͟nchhya taba basti ká tarafa au͟nchha.

By ill luck a jackal has to run towards a populous place, (where it is hunted by dogs or men).

One struggling with a stronger antagonist or superior numbers.

15. उगटदी गोठ को काटै काटा। Ugataḍí goṭha ká kaṭai kaṭa.

He-buffaloes are only born in the cattle shed that is about to be ruined.

Used of one who is baffled in all his purposes.

16. पुनरपि शत्रु शंकर जागे उगटदिकिरमोली पंखरलागे। Punarapi shatru shankara jáge ugaṭadi kirmoli paṇkhara láge.

The ant gets wings just before its death. When Kámdeo awoke Mahádeo, he himself was killed.

When men begin to act in a strange manner their ruin is near. Judicial blindness.

Note : Kámdeo, the Indian Cupid, a child of Brahmá, or as some represent, of Vishnu and Lakshmi, was promised by Brahmá dominion over the hearts of the inhabitants of the three worlds. On one occasion he ventured to discharge a shaft at Shiva or Mahadeo when he was engaged in ascetic meditation in the forest. Mahadeo was so incensed that with a glance from the eye in the centre of his forehead he consumed the god of love to ashes, though he afterwards took birth again.

17. नौड़ी का नौ बाटा। Naudi ká nau báṭá.

Nine paths to Naudi (a village in Garhwal having a separate path from each of the neighbouring villages by which it is surrounded).

Applied to members of a family each having his own different opinion.

18. चाल सुकाल ग्रहण अकाल। Chála súkála grahaṇa akála.

An earthquake (foretells) abundance of crops, but an eclipse (foretells) scarcity and famine.

19. बूढ़ा बमत्याला तनसुत्याल्या। Búḍhá bamatyálá tana sutyálá.

If the old men of a household become mad (by marrying young wives, or doing something else totally unbecoming their age) the younger men of that house are ashamed and mortified.

(For they are not in position to reprimand their elders).

20. पैलो गास मक्खी पात। Pailo gása makhî pátá.

A fly fell on the first morsel.

I.e. Misfortune overtook his first venture, an ill omen of future success.

21. के जौ बेटिवालि कुड़ि केजौ रोटिवालि कुड़ि। Ke jau beṭi wáli kurhi ke jau roṭi wáli kurhi.

The house where there are many girls (daughters) and the house which has to supply relatives with bread are sure to be ruined.

Respectable people have to give a large dowry on the marriage of their daughters, and so whoever has many daughters has heavy expenses on their account. A rich or well-to-do man who is obliged to feed all his relatives at his own expense is also liable to be ruined.

22. गौं कि सिरि गल्याठबटि। Gain̲ ki siri galyáṭha baṭi.

The condition of a village can be judged or guessed from the path which leads to it.

A man's character can be judged from one of his actions.

23. बाग को गोठबटि बाकरो ली जाणा कि नै बाग पलकि याकि। Bága ko goṭha baṭi bákaro líjáṇa ki nai bága palakiyá ki.

The leopard has carried away a goat but of the cow house : I do not care for that, but I care that the leopard has found a relish in (or way to) the cowshed.

Apprehension of injury from an enemy who has hit on a means of doing one an ill-turn.

GOOD WORDS

1. भलि बात सुना कि रात। Bhali báta suná ki ráta.

A pleasant talk is like a golden night.

A golden night, that is, a night during which one sleeps soundly. "Ointment and perfume rejoice the heart: so doth the sweetness of a man's friend by hearty counsel." Proverbs 27, 9.

GRATITUDE

1. पाणी पीणो मगरो नी पटियूंणो। Pá<u>n</u>i pí<u>n</u>o magaro ní paṭyú<u>n</u>o.

Drink all you want, but do not spoil the springs.

This means that the things from which benefit is derived should not be injured. Censure of ingratitude.

C.f. "Let every man praise the bridge he goes over."

2. जैको भात खाणो तैको गीत गाणो। Jaiko bháta khá<u>n</u>o taíko gíta gá<u>n</u>o.

Sing the praises of the man who feeds you.

Story : Once a man with his servant arrived in a foreign city. Soon after their arrival the servant bought along with the other necessaries for food some egg plants. He kept an egg plant with him to shew to his master, and made of the others a dish of vegetable curry. On taking his meal, the master having exceedingly relished the vegetable praised it to his servant, and directed him to have the same every day for him. To this the servant said, "Very good Sir, I shall do so, you are quite right in admiring the vegetable. Let me shew you the raw plant. It is the best of all vegetables in the world, consequently God has made it after his own color and form (referring to the black stones, *Saligráma* which are worshipped and which the egg-plant resembles), and with a view to save it from sun and water. He has attached an umbrella to it, (referring to the *Bhinda* or small twig to which the vegetable is fastened)." In consequence of eating the vegetable for many days in succession the man was attacked severely with a complaint which made him disgusted with the vegetable, and so he told his servant not to buy the vegetable any more, as it was a nasty thing. To this the servant rejoined. "Very good Sir, I shall not get it again. It is the most obnoxious in the world, as is evinced by the verdict of God, inasmuch as its face is blackened; and in addition to this a stick is thrust into it (as a sign of its being cursed)." On this the man said to him again, "Well servant, you are an odd fellow, you were praising the vegetable the other day so highly, but now you speak ill of it." To this the servant replied. "Sir, I certainly did as you say, but judge for yourself; am I your servant or the vegetable's?"

GREAT MEN

1. पूरो तारौ अदमीरो मारो। Púro tárau adamíro márau.

An efficient man saves, but the ineffecient one kills.

2. ठुला थुपड़ा को ठुलोसेत नाना थुपड़ा को नानो सेत। Ṭhulá thuparhá ko ṭhulo seta náná thuparho ko náno seta.

The greater the dunghill the greater the heat, the smaller it is, the less heat.

Great and rich men have more anxieties than other people.

3. जो बिधिगया सो मोति। Jo bidhigayá so moti.

All that are pierced are pearls.

E.g. The pearls which have been pierced and are ready to be worn are considered real pearls, and more valuable than those not pierced.

Applied to men who having received some high position are afterwards always regarded as great men.

4. बड़ा लाठ कि बड़ि खाट। Barhá laṭha ki barhi kháṭa.

Big timber makes a big bed.

I.e. Great people should do noble deeds.

This is often applied to great people either to encourage them to noble deeds or to dissuade them from doing a mean thing.

5. बड़ा को गुस्सा चूतड़ तली। Barhá ko gussá chútarha talí.

The anger of the great is under their haunches.

I.e. They hide it by sitting upon it. A great man suppresses his anger, and does not give vent to it.

Illustration : Once a scoundrel threw a stone at a nobleman who was taking a drive on his own estate. The nobleman's attendants and companions were so angry with the man that they began to abuse him and threatened to beat him, but the nobleman checked them, and threw a gold *Mohara* towards the man, saying "A fruitful tree, is generally pelted at by poor people for the sake of the fruit on it, and so the poor man, considering me to be a fruitful tree threw the stone at me in the hope of getting something from me; and so he should have it." This noble conduct of the gentleman filled all with admiration for his gracious and forgiving disposition.

6. छोटो खोटो बड़ा समाइ। Chhoṭo khoṭo barhá samái.

छोटा बिगाड़नि बड़ा माफ करनी। Chhoṭá bigárhani barhá máfa karaní.

Small men (i.e. subordinates) err, and great men (i.e. superiors) have to forgive.

C.f. "To err is human, to forgive divine."

7. हाथि का पैणा हाथी। Háthi ká pauṉá háthi.

An elephant must be the host of another elephant.

E.g. The great can be entertained only by the great.

8. टोटा खै बुड़ा हुनी। Ṭoṭá khai barhá huni.

A barhá is made by being pierced in the centre.

E.g. A man becomes great by willingly sustaining loss for the good of others. *Barhá* is a cake of flour of *Urda* (a kind of pulse), with a hole in its centre, cooked either in *ghi* or oil. It is called *"Barhá"* only when it is pierced. This is cooked only on festival days.

9. हाथि ज्यूनो खाक को मरियो लाख को। Háthi jyúno khaka ko mariyo lákha ko.

An elephant either alive or dead is worth a lac of Rupees (equally valuable in either state).

A dead elephant is very valuable on account of its bones which are so much in demand that they are worth nearly as much as the living animal.

Used of great men, who, whether in power or out of power are equally weighty and useful.

10. स्यू कि खाल। Syu ki khála.

The skin of a tiger.

Applied to exalt the value of a man formerly great, though now reduced to an ordinary level, comparing him with the skin of a tiger which though an inanimate thing (powerless or harmless) is still made use of for frightening animals.

GREED

1. भिंडे खाण कु जोगी होयो पैला बास भूखो रयो। Bhiṇḍe kháṉa ku jogí hoyo pailá bása bhukho rayo.

One became an ascetic (a wandering beggar) in order to get much food given him, but starved on the first stage of his journey.

Beware of covetousness.

2. लालचि बेचैन। Lálachi bechaina.

A covetous man is always restless.

C.f. "Covetous men are bad sleepers."

3. अपणा घर को बुरा निभौ चोरि को गुड़ मिठो। Apṇá ghara ko burá nibhau chori ko gurha miṭho.

The sugar of one's own house is not liked, but the treacle obtained by theft is found sweeter.

"Stolen waters are sweet."

4. औरै खौं गाबै खौं। Au̱nrai khau̱n gábai khau̱n.
Should I eat the covering of an embryo or the embryo?
E.g. It is prohibited for any one to eat an embryo of an (edible) animal but if one eats it he does so for greediness.
C.f. "Is thy servant a dog that he should do this thing?" The reply of one charged with an act of great impropriety.

5. लालच बुरि बलै। Lálacha buri balai.
Covetousness is a great curse.
That is, it brings one into trouble; as when a fly in its greed for honey loses its life in the honey-pot.

GUILTY CONSCIENCE

1. चोर का दाढ़ि मैं तिणको। Chora ká dáḍhi me̱n tiṇako.
A straw on the beard of a thief.
A thief is suspicious of the slightest movement made by others, fearing he may be detected. It is said that once when many people suspected of theft were brought together, to find out the culprit a wise man cried out, "There is a bit of straw on the beard of the thief." No sooner was this said than the real thief put his hand on his beard with a view to remove it, and in this way was detected.

2. मृग आपी हगौ आपी चौंकौ। Mríga ápí hagau ápí chauṇkau.
The deer is frightened by the noise of his own droppings, (on dry leaves).
A guilty conscience.

HABITS AND NATURE

1. मासु खाणू पर हडको गला निबांधणु। Másu kháṇú para harhako galá ni bá̱ndhaṇu.
Eat animal food if you will, but do not tie the bones round your neck.
I.e. No one should be a slave to his passions or make a show of his evil habits.

Note : The eating of animals, especially the cow, is regarded by all Hindu castes as extremely wicked.

2. मौ गइ पर लौ निगई। Mau gai para lau nigai.

Even when one's family is ruined the evil passion does not cease.

3. चोर चोरि है गयोत के हेरिफेरि है लग गयो। Chora chori hai gayata ke heripheri hai laga gayo.

If a thief gives up stealing, will he also give up looking about him? (as a thief looks about stealthily for articles to pick up).

Applied to one who claims something on the merit of his having given up evil deeds, but who cannot be entirely trusted.

4. चाई का बेड़ा चाई बांस का बेड़ा बांस। Chái ká berá châi bán̠sa ká berhá bán̠sa.

Cháі will spring from the roots of Cháі, and bamboo from the roots of bamboo.

The son will be as his father. *"Cháі"* is an inferior kind of bamboo.

5. बिराणा घर ताता कि बाण। Biŕn̠á ghara tátá ki bán̠a.

One expecting to have fresh and warm food even at the house of another, or one accustomed only to warm food, suffers in a strange house.

Used of one who becomes a slave to some habit, or who cannot change his habits easily; want of adaptability.

6. चूतिया मन बतासान बिननि रौनु। Chútiyá mana batásána bina ni raunu.

A self-indulgent and foolish fellow cannot live without batáshan (a sweet made of sugar).

Applied to one who is addicted to self-indulgent habits.

7. दींदो गुड़िया गुड़ निखाव पाछ उठीक लड़ो चाट। Dín̠do gurhiyá gurha ni kháwa páchha uṭhika larho chátau.

One fond of gurh (treacle) will not eat it if it is given, but afterwards (secretly) he will lick even the stone or the wood with which the sugarcanes are pressed.

People addicted to certain (even harmless) habits are often ashamed of them in public.

8. मोर सिंगाड़ बदला जावन स्वभाव निबदलेव । Mora singárha badalá jáwana swabhába ni badalewa.

Door posts and arches can be changed, but not one's habits.

I.e. when a man's character is formed, it is hopeless to expect any radical change or improvement in him.

9. कुत्ता को पूछ थोला घाल्यो परबांगोहि बांगो । Kuttá ko púchha tholá ghályo para báṉgo hi báṉgo.

In order to make the tail of a dog straight it was put in a hollow bamboo and kept there for 12 years, but when it was taken out of the bamboo it again became crooked.

Applied to natural defects or the stupidity of a man which is not changed by training or education.

C.f. Proverbs 27, 22: "Though thou shouldst bray a fool in a mortar among wheat with a pestle, yet will not his foolishness depart from him."

C.f. "What God has made crooked cannot be made straight."

Illustration : A Brahman finding his boy stupid and thick-headed sent him to Káshi (Benaras) where he put him under the tuition of a *Pandit* so that he might turn out a learned man. After studying for 12 years at Benares he at last came home professing to be a learned *Sanscrit* scholar. As the people of his family and neighbourhood were very anxious to hear some good doctrines expounded by him, they brought a book and placed it before him for the purpose. He took up the book and began to turn over the leaves, and at last fixing his eyes on a certain page tears began to flow from his eyes. The audience seeing him in this condition thought that he had met with a pathetic passage which had made him feel so deeply. They waited for some time that he might explain it to them, but when they found him still absorbed they asked him. "O honourable *Pandit*, purify our ears by explaning what has affected you so keenly." On this the *Pandit* cried out. "I am very sorry to see that all the letters (of the alphabet) which were so big and large at Káshi have become so thin and small here. This has made me sorrowful and anxious."

On further examination it was found that during the 12 years the man resided at Káshi he was learning the alphabet alone, in which, for beginners, the letters are written very large either on a table or slate. When he saw the same letters written so small in the book he could not make out what made them so, and so he began to cry.

This is something like a story told by Montaigne in his Essays, of a youth who was sent by his parents to Paris to be educated, and on his returning to his home in the provinces, his father gave a great feast and invited all his friends and neighbours to meet his son and observe his wonderful accomplishments. The young man, however, never opened his mouth, until, as the guests were departing, he caught sight of the moon rising, and exclaimed "Bless my soul! I do believe you have got the same moon here that we have at Paris."

10. होड़ बुद्धि न कोड़ औषध। Horha buḍḍhi na korha aushadha.

There is no wisdom or wit for an idiot, and no medicine for leprosy.

Illustration : Once an idiot with a basket of cakes was sent by the head of the family to one of his relatives living at some distance in another village. When he had travelled a mile or two he happened to look back and saw his own shadow. Thinking the shadow to be another man following him in hope of getting something he threw a cake behind him and continued his way. After going on a few steps he again looked round and seeing the shadow he again threw a cake. In this way he went on throwing out cakes till, a little before sunset, he had emptied the whole basket. Looking back at his shadow again, he asked "What would you have now?" He then threw away the clothes he had on. Just at this time the sun went down. Then the idiot referring to his shadow (of course supposing him to be another person following him) said. "Now he has gone, when he saw that I had nothing more to give him."

11. हीरा को कीरा बिगाड़ता। Hirá ko kirá bigárhatá.

A diamond is spoiled by a streak (flaw) in it.

C.f. Ecclesiastes x.i "A dead fly causes the ointment of the apothecary to stink: so doth a little folly him that is in reputation for wisdom and honour." "A little leak will sink a great ship."

And Tennyson. "It is the little rift within the lute."
"Which, slowly widening, makes the music mute."

12. जो डाढो सो डाढ़ो जो रयो पुन गाडो। Jo ḍaḍho so ḍáḍho jo rayo puṇa gáḍo.

Whatever has been burnt is burnt, but the rest should be saved.

Used to pursuade one to abstain from evil habits which have already caused him much damage or loss, in order to save himself from further ruin. "Never too late to mend."

13. मैकम्मल कणि छाडुं कम्मल मै कणि निछोड़नु। Mai kammala kaṇi chhoruṉ kammala mai kaṇi ni chhorhanu.

I wish to leave the blanket, but the blanket does not leave me.

E.g. Once a black bear was seen floating down a river on the bank of which some people were washing and bathing. Thinking that it was a black blanket, one of them swam to it, but no sooner did he come near it than the drowning bear tightly embraced the unfortunate man, who also began to sink with it. Seeing matters in that way the people on the shore called out to the man to leave the blanket and save himself. But the man being unable to rid himself of the supposed blanket replied as in the proverb.

This phrase is generally used in reference to old habits which cannot easily be given up.

14. मरि रे रांड खटाइ बिना। Mari re rá<u>n</u>ḍa khaṭáî biná.

A widow dying for want of acid.

Used in condemning bad habits. Acid is the most insignificant part of one's food, and can easily be dispensed with. To die for want of acid is to die for want of some thing that is not necessary, but one addicted to it cannot remain happy or contented without it.

15. इल्लत धोई जाव पर आदत कख जाव। Illáta dhoî jáwa para ádata kakha jáwa.

One can clear himself of his guilt, but how can he get rid of his habits?

Habit is second nature.

"A wicked man is his own hell."

The mind is its own place and in itself.

"Can make a hell of heaven, a heaven of hell." —*Milton*

16. जो तृण हर सो कंचन हर जो कंचन हर सो प्राणहर। Jo tri<u>n</u>a hara so ka<u>n</u>chana hara jo ka<u>n</u>chana hara so prá<u>n</u>a hara.

One who steals grass will steal gold, and one who steals gold will commit murder.

The habit of stealing should at once be checked in a man, to prevent his going on to commit graver offences.

17. ज्योडो जलिगयो पैन निजलि। Jyorho jaligayo paina ni jali.

The cord is burnt up, but the twist is not burnt (i.e. remains visible).

Applied to a man's retaining his proud and grave habits even after his prosperity has gone, or to one who, being naturally proud or conceited, will be so even when he becomes poor.

18. पूड़ि पाल है गयुंत नमो नरायण है लग गयु। Púrhipála hai gayu<u>n</u> to namo náráyana hai laga gayu<u>n</u>.

Though I am excluded from food, yet how can I be precluded from uttering a salutation (namo nárayaṇa)

Literally this is a saying of an ascetic who is entitled to food from other people. The *Jogi* says although he is not allowed the food, yet he will still have the right of uttering his blessings (namo narayana). A *Jogi's* duty is to utter "namo narayana" to the people he goes to, who in their turn have to feed him or give him alms, and so if the *Jogi* does not get anything from any one he will not abstain from his bahit of saluting God, ("namo náráyaṉa" means God be saluted).

This is used regarding one's own relations and acquaintances who are not only unwilling to help, but even to see one.

19. नजर है बचो माल यारनको। Najara hai bacho mála yárana ko.

As soon as a thing is out of sight it becomes the property of my friends (ironically) the thieves.

A caution against habits of carelessness.

20. आज गिजो काकड़ि भोल गिजो बाकरी। Ája gijo kákarhi bhola gijo bákarí.

One who is tempted today by a cucumber, will be tempted tomorrow by a goat.

The beginnings of bad habits should be punished. Nip the sin in the bud.

21. काणो कचबाइ डुंडो अन्याइ। Káṉo kachabái ḍuṉḍo anyái.

A one-eyed person is a slanderer, and a lame man is unjust.

I.e. Such persons are to be feared, since they usually make up for their defects by dishonesty.

22. मा जाड़ो कि मे जाड़ो। Má járho ki me járho.

Whether cold in the month of Má (Mágha, January) or when it is raining.

I.e. Cold is due to rain, but not to the month of January.

Used when some effect is attributed to a wrong cause.

23. कालो बामण गोरो शुद्र इनन देखि कांप महारूद्र। Kálo Bámaṇa goro shúdra inana dekhi ká̲npa mahá Rudra.

A dark-hued Brahman and a fair-skinned Shudra frighten even god (Rudra).

Generally a Brahman's complexion is fair and a Sudra's dark. The contrary is much dreaded as a freak of nature ominous of disaster.

24. मोछी स्वर्ण गयो फिर मोछी को मोछी। Mochhí swarga gayo phira mocchí ko mochhí.

A shoe-maker went to heaven, but he became a shoe-maker again.

Once in very old times a shoe-maker was taken to the kingdom of heaven by a virtuous king along with his other subjects, but on his arrival there, the shoe-maker, not finding his ordinary food, which consisted of filthy things, asked permission to return to earth, where he became a shoe-maker again. The dog returning to his vomit.

25. ठेट मोछी को मोछी। Ṭheṭa mochhí ko michhí.

The shoe-maker again became a shoe-maker.

The same meaning.

26. माल कि चड़ि येतणि भइ उतणि भइ उताणि भइ। Mála ki charhi yetaṇi bhai utaṇi bhai utáṇi bhai.

The bird of the Plains grew to such and such a size and then fell down.

This is generally applied to wicked habits and conduct which, when contracted, gradually gain ground and eventually end in ruin.

27. ह्यून हिमाल माल बसकाल। Hyúna Himála mála basakála.

Rain comes from the clouds which accumulate in the snowy range during the cold season, and from the plains during the rainy season.

A proverb describing the Kumaun weather.

28. आपणा घर कि चीनि निभौ चोरि को गुड़ मिठो। Apaṇá ghara ki chîni nibhau chori ko gurha miṭho.

The sugar of one's own house is not liked, but the treacle obtained by theft is found sweeter.

"Stolen waters are sweet."

29. बाला की हाती खजांद दाना को गीचो। Bálá kî hátî khajánda dáná ko gîcho.

The hands of a child and the tongue of an old man transgress.

Children seize forbidden things and garrulous old people say many things they ought not to.

30. चौमास को जर राजा को कर। Chaumása ko jara rájá ko kara.

Fever during the chaumása (June to September) is like a tax levied by a king.

Every one has to suffer more or less from such fever, it is common to all. *C.f.* "Necessity has no laws."

31. बिष को कीड़ो बिष मेरौ। Bisha ko kîrho bisha me rau.

An insect which grow out of poison lives on poison.

I.e. One brought up in bad society or in an unhealthy country lives on without any inconvenience or regret.

HEALTH

1. आरोग्य लाभो लाभानां। Árogya lábho labhánán.

Health is the best gain of all.

C.f. "Eka tandurastî hazár nyamata" or "Health is more valuable than a thousand luxuries or dainties." "Health is above wealth."

2. मन बसंत कि खलक बसंत। Mana basanta ki khalaka basanta.

When it is spring time in the heart the whole world is green.

3. मेरि चेलि कुशल मुशलै मुशल। Meri cheli kushala mushalai mushala.

When my daughter is well, there are pestles without number (to husk out paddy and millet).

I.e. A man in health has no want of employment or tools to work with and if he is sick his tools are useless to him.

Used to encourage one not to despair of finding work.

HELP

1. मरनि बखत बाकरो गुसैं का मुख चांछ। Marani bakhata bákaro gusain̲ ká mukha chán̲chha.

A goat when being sacrificed looks round at its master.

I.e. When a man is in straitened circumstances he resorts to his master or friend for help.

HELPFULNESS (TRUE)

1. सौ साग लूणमिठो सौ छुईं देण मिठि। Sau sága lúṇa miṭho sau chhuin̲ deṇa miṭhi.

Salt alone is better than a hundred vegetable dishes, and one gift is better than a hundred words.

Deeds are better than words.

HOME

1. अपणो घर दिल्ली तें भी सूझ। Apaṇo ghara Dilli ten̲ bhí sújha.

Even at Delhi one remembers or thinks of his home (native land).

C.f. "There is no place like Home."

2. घोरड़ कन चांत प्यारो। Ghorarha kana chán̲ta pyáro.

To the wild goat the precipice (where it is born and where it lives) is dear.

A man is fond of his native land however bad it may be.

3. घर कि आधि भलि। Ghara ki ádhi bhali.

Half a loaf at home is better than a whole one abroad.

Applied to dissuade one from leaving his home for a foreign country.

4. बनजारा कणि टांडै सुजंछ। Ban̲jára kaṇi Ṭán̲ḍai sujan̲chha.

A Banjára looks always towards Ṭánḍá.

I.e. The place from which he set out. Banjárás are Plains grain dealers who take grain to sell in the hills. The Banjárás of Tánḍá, a village on the road to Moradabad, are indefatigable grain dealers, but they love their home. Every one always looks forward to the accomplishment of his undertaking.

HOPE

1. पाणि का सास घुतुड़ो बास। Páṇi ká sása ghuturho bása.

The frog croaks by the aid (in hope) of the water.

A poor and weak person can only achieve anything by the patronage of a greater man, or a poor man lives his life by support or in hope of support from some great man.

C.f. "Quench not hope, for when hope dies, all dies."

HYPOCRITES

1. बृद्धा बेश्या पतिब्रता। Briddhá beshyá patibratá.

An old harlot becomes chaste (literally, faithful to her husband).

C.f. One who loses the power (of doing evil) becomes discreet and pious.

2. खांद खेरी कंदमूल हगद खेरी मूसा गला तेरा कठुल मठुल क्वीड़ा तेरा ऊसा। Khán̲da kherí kan̲da múla hagada kherí músá, galá terá kaṭhula maṭhula kwírhá terá úsá.

To all appearance the cat is living on mere roots and vegetables, but hairs of mice and feathers of birds are found in her dung. There is a necklace on her neck but her speech is pious.

Applied to hypocrites and deceivers.

Story : Once a cat thrust her head into a pot of *ghi*, but could not extricate it again. In the attempt to free himself the pot was broken, but its neck remained round her neck as a necklace. Being in this plight she was unable to catch her prey. She however contrived a plan to obtain food, and went boldly to the birds and mice, and said, "O friends, I have sinned much, but now repent for what I have done, and have therefore, in order to get forgiveness and mercy, put on this necklace and vowed never to eat animal food, or kill any animals whatever in future. We animals are all sinners, let us now go to Hardwára (a famous place of pilgrimage) and get our sins washed away in the Ganges. When the birds and mice protested against this statement of their adversary, she swore to her abstinence from flesh, and began apparently to live on roots and vegetables. She thus overcame the suspicions of the birds and mice and started with them for the shrine. On the evening of the first day they encamped in a cave; the cat occupied the innermost part of it, telling her companions, with a view to frighten them, that the jungle was full of lions and tigers, and that they might escape if they liked, but that she herself being fatigued would remain in some safe corner of the cave (wishing all the time that the animals might ask to be allowed to occupy the inner part themselves). To this the animals objected and said, "Friend, our safety depends on you, you are the most powerful among us. We are powerless to defend ourselves; do you sit at the entrance to defend us, and let us occupy the safer part of the cave." The cat feigned to dislike this proposal, but eventually consented, and all went to sleep in their respective places. At night the cat quietly ate up some of the birds and mice. In the morning she said to the animals, "O mice and birds, some of you are surely not true to your word, for I saw some of you run away last night, but I dare not arrest them for fear of blame." The animals being quite deceived by his stratagem thought that what the cat said was true. In this way their number began to decrease day by day, but no one disbelieved the cat's story, as in the daytime she apparently lived on leaves and roots. One day, somehow or other, the fact reached the ears of a fox, who advised the mice and the birds to examine the cat's dung. They did so and found it mixed with hairs and feathers. Then they got frightened and blamed themselves much for putting confidence in their natural enemy, and expressed their amazement in the proverb: ("The cat eats only vegetables &c").

Hypocrisy. Wolves in sheep's clothing.

3. बगुला भगत। Bagulá bhagata.

4. बिड़ाल बैष्णव। Bidál vaishnava.

5. गो रूप ब्याघ्र कर्म। Go rúpa byághra karma.

The heron looks like a saint.

E.g. The heron, in order to catch fish, stands on one leg in the water, and looks as if it was praying to God, but as soon as it sees its prey it plunges in after it.

So the cat becomes a vaishnav (i.e. a worshipper of Vishnu, one who abstains from all animal food) and assumes this form the more easily to catch birds etcetera.

So also.

A cow in form, a tiger in deeds.

6. हाथ में माला मन में कैंचि। Hátha meṉ málá mana meṉ kaiṉchi.

In his hands a rosary, but scissors in his heart.

7. नौ सौ मूसा खैबेर बिरालु हजसौं पहुंचौं Nau sau músá khaibera birálu haja soṉ pahuṉcho.

After eating 900 rats the cat has gone on a pilgrimage.

This represents one who, after leading a loose life, falsely professes to be a most pious or religious man.

8. मुखड़ि हसदि पुछड़ि डसदि। Mukhari hasadi puchharhi ḍasadi.

Smiling face and stinging tail.

Applicable to one who is very polite to others in their presence, but in their absence injures them.

"Fair to one's face."

9. मुख मिष्टा पेट दुष्टा। Mukha mishṭá peṭa dushtá.
Sweet mouth, wicked heart.

10. रात को रत बाग दिन को पद बाग। Ráta ko rata bága dina ko pada bága.
Red leopard at night, and a Pada-bága (small leopard) during the day.
I.e. Very humble in appearance but dangerous. "Uriah Heep." "Wolves in sheep's clothing."

HUNGER THE BEST SAUCE

1. भूख मिठि कि भोजन मिठो। Bhúkha miṭhi ki bhojana miṭho.
Is hunger delicious, or the food?
C.f. Hunger is the best sauce.

IGNORANCE

1. अंधा को मुख भीति। An̲dhá ko mukha bhîti.
A blind man turns his face towards wall.
I.e. One ignorant of a matter is always liable to take a wrong direction; a blind man, not knowing whither he goes, is apt to run against a wall, or is often seen turning his face to the wall, perhaps to aviod the glare of the light.
Applied to one who is labouring under wrong views through ignornace.

ILL RECOMPENSE

1. बुति करा का छै माणा गल मारा का नो माणा। Buti kará ká chhai máṇá gala márá ká nau mán̲á.
The labourer gets six mánás (three seers) and he who blows his cheeks (one who talks· but does not work) receives nine mánás (four and a half seers). A máná equals half a seer of capacity.
Used by one who is ill-paid for his work in comparison with another who gets well paid for very little or no work. This is also used ironically of educated men who are highly paid for their work.

2. नाजर बाबा पटवारि है जाव। Názara bábá paṭwári hai jáwa.

O Názir may you become a Paṭwári.

One very much pleased with a man who holds the post of a *Názir* wishes him to become a *Paṭwári* (an inferior post).

Applied by one who is ill-rewarded for his good services by an officer or master.

3. धुपाणा कद अंगोरे डाडन। Ḍhupáṇá kada aṉgore ḍáḍana.

In offering incense he gets his fingers burnt.

Same as above.

4. होम करनामे हाथ जलो। Homa karaná me hátha jalo.

In offering the sacrifice he burnt his hand.

Same meaning as above.

Homa karanu=pouring ablutions of *ghi* etcetera into the sacred fire.

5. जैन गायो विशनु पद उई कुछ नकथ। जैन गायो भगनौलो उइ को रुपयों को थैलो। Jaina gáyo vishnu pada ui ko kuccha na katha, jaina gáyo bhaganaulo uiko rupayoṉ ko thailo.

One who sings the praises of Vishnu (God) gets nothing, but one who sings love ditties (obscene songs) gets bags of money.

Used by one who is ill-rewarded for his good services. Evil is rewarded, but virtue is without recompense.

6. जैन करो पार वीकु पाथा चार। जैन करो नीकाचार वीकु धिकाचार। Jaina karo wára pára wîku páthá chára. Jaina karo níká chára wîku dhiká chára.

One who makes a show of work done is rewarded with eight seers, (2 quarts = 1 seer) but he who has done honest work is driven out.

Applied to one whose good services are not appreciated or ill rewarded.

7. मियांज्यू खुशि भया ईंट खेंचि मारो। Miyáṉ jyú khushi bhayá inṭa khaiṉchi máro.

When my husband is pleased with me he flings a brick at me.

It is generally a custom among the villagers for the husband to throw lightly a small bit of earth, stone &c towards his wife as a token of his being pleased with her. But the person alluded to in the proverb hit his wife with a brick with such force that he hurt her.

Applied to one who having been relied on or entreated for help by another foolishly does something which injures the other. *C.f.* "More zeal than knowledge."

ILL LUCK

1. बागले मारो तौ दौणो रितो भेल पड़ो तौ दौणो रितो। Bágale máro tau dauno rito bhela parho tu dauno rito.

The peg remains empty whether the animal has been killed by a leopard or has fallen down a precipice.

Whatever the cause may be the loss is evident. There are particular pegs called "dauṇá" in a cowshed for each cow and calf, to which they are tied at night. If any animal has been killed or has died, the peg remains empty, hence the proverb.

2. रीतो भरींछ टोटो नि भरीनू। Ríto bharinchha ṭoṭo ni bharínú.

An empty vessel can be filled up, but the vessel with a hole in the bottom cannot be filled up.

Description of a very unlucky or discontented man.

3. नित्या नामको चूतिया नाम पायो ढीस मु छयो बेड़ मु आयो। Nityá náma ko chútiyá náma páyo ḍhhis mu chhayo beḍa mu áyo.

My name is Nityá. I am called Chútiyá (foolish). I was on a height, but have fallen low.

Applied by one who is mourning over his misfortune which has caused him to be nicknamed a fool and brought about his degradation.

4. कला करूं विद्या करूं दाता नि देत मैं क्या करूं। Kalá karun Vidyá karún dátá ni deta mai kyá karun.

I use my skill and learning, but if God does not help me, what shall I do?

Applied by one who finding all his attempts to better his circumstances frustrated, bemoans his bad fortune.

5. मैं जौं वां कर्म लीजौं कां। Mai jaun wán karma lijaun káṇ.
I shall go there, but where shall I leave my ill luck?
I.e. Change of place cannot change a man's ill luck.

6. मन कौंछ दूद भात खौंला कर्म कौंछ दगड़ै रौंला। Mana kaunchha dúda bháta khaunlá karma kaunchha dagarhai raunla.
The heart desires to eat milk and rice, but ill luck says she will not leave me.

7. अकरमि को कपाल बुरूंस को फूल जैकि बासना नै। Akarami ko kapála burunsa ko phúla jaiki básaná nai.
The forehead of an unfortunate man is like the flower of Buruṇsa (rhododendron), being without any scent.

IMMODESTY

1. एक दांत को मोल करो बत्तीस खोल दिया। Eka dánta ko mola karo battisa kholadiyá.
Being asked the price of one tooth he showed thirty-two teeth.
Want of due reserve.
Also applied to shameless women.

2. स्यैणि ले खोला दंत मरद ले पै अंत। Saiṇi le kholá danta marada le pai anta.
When a woman shows her teeth (speaks) man finds her motive.
Used to show the impropriety of a woman conversing with men. It is not the custom among Hindu women to converse freely with men other than their own relatives.

IMPOSSIBILITIES

1. मड़ो मरयो भूखन छुरक्यों कु लावा धान। Marho maryo bhúkhana chhurkyon ku láwá dhána.
One who has died of starvation needs rice for his funeral ceremony.
If he had had the rice before, he would not have starved.

2. वीका ल्याव फौल जैका नी नौल। Wiká lyáwa phaula jaiká ni naula.
Demanding fruit when we have not the fruit tree.

Asking for a thing which is not to be had. *Phaul* also means a copper or brass jar, and *naul* also means a well. So the proverb may be rendered: Demanding a jar of that water of which there is no well—asking an impossibility.

3. न नौमण तेल जल न राधा नाच। Na nau maṇa tela jala na rádhá nácha.

Neither will nine maunds of oil be burned, nor will Rádhá dance.

Used regarding something which seems to be impossible for a man to accomplish by any amount of effort.

4. ह्यूं पड़ो डांडा बुढ़ि मरि पांडा। Hyún̲ parho ḍán̲ḍá buḍhi mari pán̲ḍá.

The snow fell on the ridge, but the old lady died in the upper storey.

Used as an expression of wonder referring to things unintelligible or improbable.

5. जख स्यूड़ो नि अकड़ौ तब साबलौं Jakha syúrho ni akarhau takha sábalo.

To thrust a thick iron bar in a place where a needle cannot go.

Used to denote a small space or accommodation which too many persons wish to occupy; or when a large number has to be supported on a small quantity. "The camel going through the needle's eye."

6. राजा का घर मोत्यूं को अकाल। Rájá ká ghara motyún̲ ko akála.

Dearth of pearls in the house of a king.

This is used to express wonder and impossibility, and is used when a great person claims to be destitute of what every one supposes him to have.

7. तितरो बाणी भाणजो धाणि कख छया। Titaro baṇi bháṇajo dháṇi kakha chhayá.

A partridge never learns to speak, and a maternal nephew never does any work.

Applied to maternal nephews who belong to another caste and therefore do not like to work in their uncles' houses.

8. भौं तेरा भट बुकाणन भौं तेरो हलबाणो। Bhaun terá bhaṭa bukáṇana bhaun tero halabáṇo.

I will either chew your parched grain or plough your field (I cannot do both at the same time).

E.g. A woman employed a ploughman to plough up her fields. According to the custom the ploughman was to get a meal at noon. While eating his food he of course stops the ploughing and unties the bullocks. In order to make up or prevent this interruption she devised a scheme to feed him with parched *Bhaṭa* (pulses) instead of rice or *Chapátis*, thinking that the ploughman while chewing the grain would continue ploughing. But the ploughman, on the *Bhaṭa* being placed before him, said as in the Proverb. This means that no one can do two things at the same time.

Applied by one who is pressed to do many things at the same time.

9. डूम छोरा ब्याखन भूख मरन प्रबाथ कलेउ सुत्यालन। Ḍúma chhorá byákhana bhúkha marana prabátha kaleu sutyálana.

The children of a Dúma (a low caste man) go supperless to bed, and in the morning they ask for what was left from the evenings' meal.

(Breakfast usually consists of what was left from the evening meal). Looking for impossibilities.

10. जो मेरा मुख नि बुलानि सो मेरा घर के आलि। Jo merá mukha ni buláni so merá ghara ke áli.

Will she, who does not talk with me, come to my house?

He who takes no interest in me will not do me any favour.

11. स्यै बिनसर घट। Syai Binasara ghaṭa.

Water-mill on the mountains of Syai and Binasara. (These have no or very little water in them).

An impossibility.

IMPROPER FRIENDSHIP

1. नादान कि दोस्ती फूस कि आग। Nádána ki dosti phúsa ki ága.

Friendship with a fool is like a fire of grass.

I.e. Rises high at first but dies out quickly.

2. मुख लगै डुमणि ल्या गुस्याणि लूण। Mukha lagai ḍumani lyạ gusyaṇi lúna.

If you are kind to a Ḍumani (low caste woman) she will take the opportunity to ask for salt.

A caution against being very intimate with the poor, as they will surely ask for help of some sort.

3. लड्यायूं कूकर जीभ चाटौ। Larhyáyan kúkara jîbha chaṭau.

A dog petted or caressed will lick one's mouth.

Intimacy with poor and mean people should be avoided.

4. रांडकि यारी सदा ख्वारी। Ránḍa ki yárí sadá khwárí.

Association with a (vicious) woman is always ruinous.

5. ओछा कि प्रीत बालु कि भीत। Ochhá ki príta bálu ki bhíta.

The friendship of mean-minded man is like a wall of sand (will not last).

Parallel to what is elsewhere said:that the friendship of a mean man is like the shadow of the first half of the day *i.e.* great at first but declining every moment, while that of a noble-minded person is like the shadow of the second half of the day, *i.e.* very small at first but increasing every moment until sunset.

IMPROPER UNION

1. छरपट की स्यैणी बरपट को खसम। Chharapaṭa ki syaiṇi barapaṭa ko khasama.

A wife picked up by chance (out of the ashes or leavings) and a husband taken out of a number.

Such a wife wishes to ruin her husband, to whom she is not properly married, and the latter in his turn wishes to cheat his wife.

Caution against such unions.

INADEQUATE OR INSUFFICIENT HELP

1. हाथी कि खाब प्यूरहि को फूल। Háthi ki khába pyúrarhi ko phúla.

A flower of the Pyúrarhi of pyúli in the mounth of (i.e. to feed) an elephant.

Applied to inadequate or insufficient help given to another.

INATTENTION

1. बार बरस रामायण सुणिबेर पूछण लागो कि राम राक्ष्यस छ कि रावण राक्ष्यस छ। Bára barasa Rámáyaṇa suṇi bera búchhaṇa lágo ki Ráma rákshyasa chha ki Ráwaṇa rákshyasa chha.

One who has heard the Rámáyana recited for twelve years, at the end enquires whether Ráma or Ráwana was the devil.

Used of one who pays no attention to what he reads or hears. A dullard.

INCOMPETENCY

2. आप कर्म छोड़ि पर कर्म करौ तैकि अकल बिधिना हरौ। Ápa karma chhorhi para karma karau taiki akala bidhina harau.

One who leaving his own profession or work follows that of another is deprived by God of his wit or wisdom.

Story : Once a fox having found an elephant drowned in a marsh mounted upon the corpse in order to eat its flesh. Seeing one of their brethren in that position and allured by the corpse, other foxes approached him. Seeing them come there he began to act boastfully over the dead body of the elephant, and forbade them to touch it, saying "How can you be allowed to eat the elephant killed by me alone?" This speech struck them with awe and astonishment. But hunger and natural rapacity for animal food compelled them to implore the fox again for permission to share the treat with him. He granted their petition on the condition that they acknowledged their allegiance to him as their future king. All agreed to do so. As soon as they all had devoured the flesh of the elephant the crafty fox ordered them to convey him on a throne (otherwise there was no distinction between him and the others) and address him as their king, "Hathamalla" or destroyer of an elephant. So he was seated on a big throne made of grass and rags firmly tied to his tail, and was thus borne by the other foxes wherever he went. One day they all entered a sheep-fold, when no sooner was the alarm given than the watch-dogs were set on them. This caused a panic, the foxes dropped the throne and ran away. But the so-called king being unable to run on account of the heavy throne fastened to his tail, was torn to pieces by the dogs.

2. नौला कवा ले गू खायो ठूनै बटि लटपटायो। Naulá kawá le gú kháyo ṭhúnai baṭti laṭa paṭáyo.

A young crow in attempting to eat filth smears its beak with it.

Used to denote one who is caught in doing a sinful or unlawful act, and punished for it.

3. अणजाणले खै भांग नीचे मुंड ऊपर टांग। Anjáṇale khai bhánga níche munḍa úpara ṭánga.

One not accustomed to hemp throws his legs upwards and bends his head downwards (becomes senseless or mad) when he eats it.

Used of one who suffers in consequence of his undertaking business beyond his control.

4. आंडु घोड़ो गांडु सवार। Ándu ghorho gánḍu sawára.

A vicious (uncastrated) horse, and a bad rider.

Applied to one who fails in any new business through ignorance of the matter.

5. काचो बैद ज्यान को खतरा। Kácho baida jyána ko khatará.

A raw (half trained) quack is dangerous to life.

Inefficiency in work.

6. अद खड़ो भानो बाजनै रून्छ। Ada kharho bháno bájanai rúnchha.
An empty vessel continues to make a noise.
C.f. "Empty barrels make most noise."
Shallow-minded and incompetent people.

7. अदपुरि विद्या जिया कि काल। Adapuri vidyá jiyá ki kála.
A little learning is a calamity to the soul.
C.f. Pope's lines "A little learning is a dangerous thing:
Drink deep, or taste not Pierian spring."

8. नाख जोक पोका असेडू। Nákha joka poká aserhú.
Leeches in the noise, aserhu applied to the rectum. (Aserhu is an irritating grass the smell of which causes sneezing).
When leeches enter the nose of any animal this grass is put inside its nostrils so that the leeches may come away with the sneezing which the grass produces. If the grass be applied to the rectum it will of course have no effect on one's nose.
Applied to persons who are inefficient in their professions.

9. हाणि नि जाणि खुटा आइ लागि। Haṇi nijáṇi khuṭá ái lági.
One not knowing how to use an axe cuts his own foot.

10. पेट कि पीड़ा आंखनकि औषध। Peṭa ki pírhá ankhanaki aushadha.
Pain in the stomach and medicine to the eyes.
Inefficiency in any business or profession.

11. सर्प को खायो बिछी को मंत्र। Sarpa ko kháyo bichhî ko mantra.
Bitten by a snake, but treated as if stung by a scorpion.
Incapacity.

12. मार निजाणि कांधा आइ लागी। Mára nijáṇi kándhá ái lágî.
The unskilful woodman strikes his own shoulder.

13. जैको काम उइ कणि छाज दुसरो करत ठींगा बाज। Jaiko káma ui kaṇi chhája dusaro karata ṭhingá bája.
The work is profitable to one who is trained to the profession, but it proves ruinous if undertaken by any other person.

INCONGRUITY

1. छींट कि घागरी गजी को टला। Chhíta ki ghágarí gají ko talá.
A skirt of chintz, patched with a piece of Gaji (coarse cloth).
Applied to inappropriate or incongruous things.

INDEPENDENCE

1. गुड़ खाणो न कान छेड़ोणो। Gurha kháṇo na kána chherhoṉo.
One who does not eat Gurha (treacle) will not have his ears pierced.
E.g. About the age of eight years boys have their ears pierced, and girls their noses and ears at the age of five years, and sweetmeats are given to them at the time to take their thoughts off the pain. But if the sweets are refused, the ears will not be pierced. So if one avoids putting himself under obligations to others he will be saved much trouble.

2. तेरि दाथी तरा जौं जख बटि सकदि तख बटि लौ। Teri dáthí terá jauṉ jakha baṭi sakadi takha baṭi sakadi takha baṭi lau.
The sikcle is yours, and the whole barley field is yours; you can reap wherever you please.
One is master of his own property in regard to its disposal.

3. पैहालो तौ अमीरी नतर फकीरी। Paihalo tau amírí natara phakíri.
Enjoy what is within reach, forget what is unattainable.

4. साटि होला तौ नौला में कुटि खौंला। Sáti holá tau naulá meṉ kuṭi khauṉlá.
If we have paddy we can husk it in our own navels.
Used to denote that if one has enough food he is not dependent on any one. Paddy is husked in a mortar with a pestle but if one has paddy but no mortar he can husk it in his navel.
I.e. He can contrive some way of cleaning the grain.

5. अपणि गाजी बालि तापणि। Apaṇi gájí báli tapaṇi.
One can burn his clothes (or cloth) to warm himself.
(The man would have died in the cold night if he had not burned it).
The good thing of others are of no use to a starving man. A man must use what he has got.

Applied to one's own possession which he can dispose of in any way he likes.

6. बाछि भई न लूति लागी। Báchhi bhaî na lúti lágî.

No calf was born, and hence no skin disease (very common among the calves) attacked it.

E.g. If one has no wealth or property he is not troubled with it. Little goods little care.

7. जां देखि तवा परात तां गबांण रात। Ján dekhi tawá paráta tan gawáni ráta.

Wherever I shall find Tawá Paráta (vessels used for kneading and baking their cakes) there I will stop the night.

These vessels are absolutely necessary to a traveller, who has no vessels of his own, but has to borrow them.

This is applied to one's settling in a place where he finds a means of livelihood.

8. आंखो फुटो पीड़गे। Ánkho phuṭo pîrha ge.

As soon as sore eye is plucked out the pain goes.

One finds relief as soon as he gets rid of troublesome things.

9. आपणो रंग रंग परै रंग धतुरो। Ápaṇo ranga ranga parai ranga dhaturo.

The colour which I chose is the best colour, but the colour which others choose is like that of the poisonous plant called "Dhatúrá." (The thorn apple, Datura).

We think our own advice and opinion the best, those of others worthless.

10. नि मिलिया का त्यागि मिलिया का अनुरागी। Ni miliyá ká tyági miliyá ká anurágî.

He despises a thing which it is impossible to get, but of which he would be fond if it were attainable.

"The grapes are sour."

11. आपणा घर का सब राजा। Ápaṇá ghara ká saba rájá.

Every one is a king in his own household.

This is used when one's actions in his own private affairs are called in question. *C.f.* "Every man's house is his castle."

12. अपणा घर में कुकुर शेर। Ápaṇa ghara men̲ kukara shera.

A dog is a lion in its own house.

Applicable to one who treats others with disrespect while in his own house. *C.f.* "Every cock fights best on his own dunghill."

13. आपणि बारि सबन प्यारी। Ápaṇi bárí sabana pyári.

Every one has to take his own turn, or is willing to undertake his own turn and not the work of another.

14. अपण तान में चिड़िया लग मशतान। Apaṇá tána men̲ chirhiyá laga mashtána.

A bird is regaled by its own song.

I.e. Every man does what pleases him. Every one follows his own bent.

15. अपणी माणि जख मुग जाणी तख मुग खाणी। Apaṇí máṇi jakha mugáján̲í takha muga khán̲í.

If one has his own grain it is available for food wherever he goes.

Said by one who has no friends to feed him while away from home or on a pilgrimage. Expressing his independence.

17. बोझ छोड़ि जगात के। Bojha chhori jagáta ke.

If I give up the load, why should I be taxed for it?

(In reference to the tolls that people have to pay on all sorts of loads &c.)

This is applied to one who gives up any duty or service, and thereby thinks himself freed from all further responsibility.

18. बासि भात में परमेश्वर को के लागंछ। Básì bháta men̲ Parmeshwara ko ke lágan̲chha.

Why should God be thanked for stale rice? (that is, rice left over from a previous meal).

This is made use of in speaking of a thing already got or gained.

19. चल थौला जख जौंला तख खौंला। Chala thaulá jakha jaunlá takha khaunlá.

Come along, wallet, wherever we go we will have food.

E.g. On a journey people take their own grain with them in a bag, and so are certain of food wherever they may go.

Applied to independent people, also used in reference to one's stomach (wallet) saying that he can fill it (with food) wherever he goes.

INDIFFERENCE

1. हाथि का कान का माखा। Háthi ká kána ká mákhá.

As flies to the ears of an elephant.

Applied to one who disregards all advice, orders, or suggestions regarding a matter in which he is concerned. (The elephant is quite indifferent to flies on his ears.)

2. घुना घुना जलिगे कुतराण कखि अै। Ghuná ghuná jalige kutaráṇa kakhî ai.

Where does the smell of burning come from? (Kutarāṇa means the smell of burning cloth).

Applied to one who though already on the point of being ruined is still indifferent to his own interests, or though his character has been stained still he is indifferent.

INDULGENCE

1. बड़ि लाड़ का बड़ि खाड़। Barhi laṛha ká barhi khárha.

The one greatly loved goes to a deeper ditch.

Generally used with reference to children and young people whose ruin is due to the indulgence of their parents and guardians.

2. धी लड़ाइ क दारी पूत लड़ाइ क भिखारी। Dhi larhái ka dári púta larhái ka bhikhári.

A daughter spoilt becomes a prostitute, and a spoilt son a beggar.

Caution against indulging children.

INDUSTRY

1. बेटि न खाणो कुटाई भौं बुवारि न खाणो कुटाई। Beṭi na kháno kuṭáî bhaun buwári na kháṇo kuṭáî.

Both one's daughter and one's daughter-in-law must thresh corn to live.

This is only applicable to agriculturists who make use of this phrase in the sense that every member of their family must work for his living. It is also used to imply that one's daughter must be treated as somebody's wife, as one's daughter-in-law is the wife of one's son.

2. बड़ी फजर चूला मु नजर। Barhî phajara, chúlá mu najara.

The kitchen has to be looked to early in the morning.

One must earn one's food first of all.

Applied also ironically to one who is more eager to eat than work in the early morning.

3. भीखों भारा ओसी घड़ा निहोंदा। Bhîkhon bhárá osí ghará ní hondá.

No one can expect to get much (lit. loads) by begging, or to fill jars with dew.

Necessity of toil.

4. घसकै ल्यालै फसकै पालै। Ghaskai lyálai phasakai pátai.

If you bring much you will get much.

Applied to one who is rewarded according to his labor, or the service rendered by him.

5. जतुकै गुड़ उतुकै मीठो। Jatukai gurha, utukai mîṭho.

The more treacle you put in, the sweeter will be the food.

I.e. The more labor one bestows on his work or business the better result will he have. Equivalent to, the more a field is manured the better will be the crop.

6. खाणो ढिलै बांटी जौ काम ढिलै निबांटीनू। Kháṇo ḍhalai bánṭí jau káma ḍhilai ni bánṭínu.

A meal postponed is shared by others, but the work delayed will devolve on one's self.

Prepared food, if not taken at the moment, is liable to be eaten by other people or thrown to the dogs and cats, but work, if delayed, will fall on himself alone.

7. उंदो को साबण उभोको लूण। Uṇdo ko sábana ubho ko lúna.
Salt comes from the high lands, and soap from the Plains.
E.g. In former times, when the country salt did not find its way to the hills, the people used to be supplied with the salt of the upper country (Tibet), and with soap from the Plains. The head of a family in his old age exhorts his family to be as industrious as he was.

8. रीतो बाटै भरियुं बाटै। Ríto báṭai bhariyuṇ báṭai.
Whether unburdened or with a load one has to travel the length of the road.
This is used to induce one to take a load with him i.e. to lead a busy life. Since life is to be lived whether with work or without it.

9. सांजि धरणो पांजी राखणो। Sáṇjí ḍharaṇo, Pánji rákháṇo.
First earn and then take care of your earnings.
C.f. "Much food is in the tillage of the poor: but there is that is destroyed for want of judgment."

10. सातू खायो सात बगत धौ नि भई एक बगत। Sátú kháyo sáta bagata ḍhau ni bhaí eka bagata.
One ate Sátú (meal of parched grain) seven times, but was not even once satisfied.
Satu represents what is gained from begging; better work and get sufficient to satisfy all needs.

11. तू राणी मै राणी को कूट चीणा दाणी। Tú ráṇo mai ráṇí ko kúṭa chíṇá dání.
You are a queen, I am a queen, but who will husk the millet?
This is applied ironically to members of one's family to induce them to work, for if each thinks himself a lord or master no one will work, and in that case family will be ruined.

12. नाना कि बाण ठुलाकि धाण। Náná ki bána ṭhulá ki ḍhána.

The young ought to accustom themselves to habits of industry, so that when they grow up they may know how to work.

Custom in infancy becomes nature in old age.

13. बिना अपणा मरिया स्वर्ग नि देखीनो। Biná apṇá mariyá warga ni dekhíno.

No one can see heaven without dying.

I.e. If a man wishes to accomplish some good work, or gain some great end, he must do it himself.

14. बेकार है बेगार भलो। Bekára hai begára bhalo.

To work for nothing is better than to remain idle.

E.g. In native states every one is bound to do the work of the state without wages, which is called "Begára". This kind of work is taken by the ruling Prince in lieu of dues, and thereby absolves the subjects for some time from further calls. These services devolve on every one by turn in the native states. The phrase is also made use of and acted upon by one who keeps himself employed in some way or other instead of being idle.

15. मांगणो आपणा बाप थैं लगबुरो। Máṉgaṇo ápṇá bápa thaiṉ laga buro.

To beg even of one's own father is bad.

A censure on begging and laziness.

16. माथा भरी लाणो पेट भरी खाणो। Máthá bharî láṉo peṭa bharî kháṇo.

Bring a full load, and then eat your stomach-full.

This is used to encourage labour or diligence.

17. पूसकि रस्यारि सौण कि घस्यारि। Púsa ki rasyári sauṇa ki ghasyári.

A cook for the month of Púsa (January) and a grass-cutter for the month of Sauṇa (July).

Used to induce one to do the work, saying that it is very easy, and that no one but a fool can refuse to do it.

In January the weather is cold and so a cook is well off near the fire. In July (rainy season) grass grows everywhere in plenty.

18. शिर को जामन पैर। Shira ko jámana paira.

The feet are the surety of the head.

This means to say that as long as one's feet move (are alive to walk) the head is safe.

Used in regard to a business or household which will go on only so long as it is properly managed.

19. नकल में के अकल। Nakala me ke akala.

What genius or intellectual power is required for copying a paper?

Used to pursuade one to do the work he is entrusted with by saying that it is easy to be done.

20. जोड़ि झगुलि न कि फारिकरि झगुलि। Jorhi jhaguli na ki phári kari jhaguli.

One ought to earn money for his clothes, but not to take too much care of it.

21. घर जानी छूं बण जानी छूं तेरि खेति निहुनि त मैं के करूं। Ghara jáńi chhún̲ baṇa jáńi chhúṇ teri kheti nihuni ta main̲ ke karúṇ.

I work at my house and go to the jungle for the purpose; if your husbandry fails what can I do?

I.e. I do my best, if the tillage fails it is not my fault.

22. मरनु को लग सोबतो नहाति। Maranu ko laga sobato naháti.

No leisure even to die.

Used to signify refusal to undertake another business when one is already fully engaged.

23. जो बातो सरालो वीका हाथ चुपड़ा होला। Jo báto sarálo wíká hátha chuparhá holá.

Whosoever will mend a wick will get his hands greased.

An encouragement to industry, for any one who will work will get something from the work.

24. काम प्यारो कि चाम प्यारो। Káma pyáro ki cháma pyáro.
Is one to be valued for his work or for his skin?
Industry is worth more than beauty.

25. कुमहार की सती धोबी को मुर्दा। Kumhára kí satí ḍhobí ko murdá.
The potter's wheel and the washerman's club.
As these two tools are constantly in use they have become proverbial.
Used of one who never has any spare time, being always engaged in work.

26. आधि खेति पाति आधि जत पाति। Ádhi kheti páti ádhi jata páti.
Cultivation of the field is only half the farmer's work, for he must also watch his crops.
Industry must be accompanied by care and thoughtfulness.

27. नाना तिना को जाड़ो ढुंगा में। Náná tiná ko járho ḍhuṇgá men̲.
The cold of children is on a stone.
This means that a stone suffers or bears the cold on behalf of a child who moves about and works.
Used to stir and pursuade children to work even during intense cold.

INFLUENCE

1. हाथ पुजौ एक हाथ हातो पुजौ हजार हाथ। Hátha pujau eka hátha háto pujau hazára hátha.
A hand (hátha) reaches a distance of one cubit, but the Hátá, the influence of relationship reaches thousands of cubits.
The far-reaching power of family influence.

INHERITANCE

1. बबा कि कमाई सपूत खाव न कपूत खाव। Babá ki kamáín̲ sapúta kháwa na kapúta kháwa.
Neither a good son nor a bad one enjoys the property left by his father.

E.g. A good son will earn for himself and thus will not care for his father's property: and a bad son, who does not earn anything will have to sell the property bequeathed to him by his father. Hence the proverb is used to induce fathers not to leave anything for their sons.

2. भायों का बांटा हथगुली का रेखा। Bháyoṇ ká baṉṭá hathagulī ká rekhá.

The shares of one's brothers and the marks on the palms of the hands cannot be obliterated.

INJUSTICE AND OPPRESSION

1. बण सुंगर ले उज्याड़ खै घर सुंगर का थोल थेचा। Baṇa suṉgarale ujyáraha khai ghara suṉgara ká thola thechá.

The trespass was committed by wild pigs, but the snout of the domestic pig was crushed (for it was easier to punish a domestic pig than the wild one).

This proverb denotes injustice in which a real culprit, owing to his being wealthy and crafty escapes the punishment, and an innocent poor person is punished.

2. कैका घलाघला गास कैसों पट उपास। Kaiká ghalághalá gása kaisoṉ, paṭa upása.

One gets pulpy or dainty morsels, and the other has to starve.

Used of mismanagement or injustice, under which one member of a certain community or sect is very much favoured, and others totally neglected.

3. ठग ठठेरो चोर सुनार खौ कोलि डाड ल्वार। Ṭhaga ṭhaṭhero chora sunára khau koli ḍáḍa lwára.

Cheats, vessel-makers, thieves, goldsmiths, and weavers steal, but the blacksmith is scorched.

E.g. The former five steal the precious metal they work in, but the blacksmith is scorched by the heat of his fire.

Miscarriage of justice.

4. कनालि लगै दान मारि बांधि सौदा। Kanáli lagai dána mári báṉdhi saudá.

Causing one to give alms by beating him with nettles, and forcing one into a bargain by beating and binding him.

Applied to oppression.

5. जैले से तैले पै। Jaile sai taile pai.

6. जैले सहारो सो कभैं नि हारो। Jaile saháro so kabhain̲ ni háro.

Whoever endures patiently attains his motive eventually.

Used to console aggrieved people.

7. गरीब कि आह बुरी। Garíba ki áha burí.

The sighs of a poor man are very bad (dangerous).

Used to dissuade people from oppressing poor people.

8. कुमुं सों डीठ गढ़ सों पीठ। Kumuṇ son̲ diṭha Garha son̲ pīṭha.

One looks towards Kumaun and turns his back towards Garhwal.

Said regarding the partiality of one in power who, while in Garhwal, favours those who are in Kumaun.

Used only in Garhwal regarding injustice.

9. बिदा द्यो को बज्र। Bidá dyo ko bajra.

A thunderbolt out of a clear sky.

Applied to one who suffers innocently, or to a sudden unexpected misfortune.

10. बिरालु मारियो सबन ले देखो दूध खत्यों कैले नि देखो। Birálu máriyo sabana le dekho dúdha khatyoṇ kail ni dekho.

The cat killed is seen by all, but the spilt milk is seen by none.

This is used when one's own faults are exposed and those of another are hid.

I.e. The woman is blamed for killing the cat whose dead body is seen, but the milk taken by the cat is not seen by any one.

11. छोठा हुणि बड़ो बड़ा सों करतार। Chhoṭa hun̲i barho barhá son̲ Kartára.

As a great man is to a poor one, so God is to the great man.

I.e. Oppressors of the poor will be punished by God.

Illustration : Once a small cow was pursued by a bigger cow to a jungle where a leopard having caught sight of the big cow began to go after it with a view to kill it, but before he killed it he was pursued by a fire which had caught the forest, and barely escaped with his life.

12. जैको मर तैकु पच्चीस पड़। Jaiko mara taiku pachisa parha.

One in whose family a death occurs, will have to pay Rs. 25/-.

E.g. In old times the kings used to levy a tax on deaths called "*Harha kara*"=tax on bones. Hence the proverb applied to one who in addition to injury inflicted upon him is also punished by the Court.

13. कख उरो कख पड़्यो। Kakha uro kakha parhyo.

What threatens and what happens.

E.g. This refers to clouds which, while hanging over in one place, thunder and lighten in another place.

Used of injustice by which an innocent person is punished.

14. जैका आंखा सौण में गाड़ा वीकन हरियो सुझ। Jaiká aṇkhá sauṇa meṉ gárhá wî kana hariyo sujha.

One whose eyes are taken out in the month of July believes the earth to be green always.

Applied to one who does not try to see the present aspect or state of things but delivers his judgment on his past experience alone.

Once during the prevalence of a certain famine a king, while engaged in hunting deer, happened to stop at night at a peasant's shed, where he was fed by him with *Ghi* and *Khicharhi*, saying that no other edibles were to be had on account of the dearth. After a great many years there was another famine in his kingdom; reports were made to him with prayers that some steps should be taken to prevent the people from starving; but the king took no notice of their entreaty, and said that they could live on *Ghi* and *Khicharhi*. (Two parts of rice and one part of dála (pulse) cooked together).

C.f. The story of the French Queen who wondered how the people could possibly be starving when there were such beautiful tarts to be had for six pence each.

15. जैको जांठो वी को बांटो। Jaikojáṉṭho wî ko báṉṭo.

His is the share who has a club (in his hand).

Used to denote misgovernment and injustice, where might is right.

16. खै गया तितिरा चाखुड़ा जिबाला पड़ा मुसभ्याकुड़ा। Khai gayá titirá chákhurhá jibálá parhá musabhyákurhá.

The grain was eaten by partridges, but the Musabhyákurhás (a kind of small bird) were entrapped.

E.g. Villagers have *"jibálás"* (stone traps for birds) fixed in places frequented by birds, with grain spread underneath them. Partridges being of a very shy nature pick up the grain from a safe distance, and fly away, but the other birds (musabhyákurhás) being of more unwary nature enter the *jibálás* of stones in order to eat the grain, and are crushed by the fall of the stone. A large stone or slate is set up on a stick at the bottom of which grain is placed. The slightest touch of the stick by the beak of the bird displaces it, and the stone falls on the birds feeding below.

Applied to cunning and crafty men who put their evil designs into execution entirely for their own benefit through some simple man, who often suffers for them, but the real culprits escape with impunity.

17. ऊंट कि बलै भेकाना का खोरा। Úṉṭa ki balai bhekáná ka khorá.

The punishment of a camel on the head of a frog.

This is used when in order to save a great man a smaller person is punished or censured, as a scape-goat.

Applied to injustice and partiality.

18. अलसि काचो नाज खा राजा लबार पत्या। Alasi kácho nája khá rájá labára patyá.

A sluggard eats raw rice and a liar finds favour with a king.

I.e. A lazy man will not cook his food, but chews it raw, and a king listens to others who backbite and thus poison his mind against people.

19. उलटो चोर कोतवाल डांड़। Ulṭo chora kotwála ḍán̲ḍa.

The arrest of a person other than the thief causes the police officer to be punished, or, in case the thief escapes, the chaukidar (watchman) being there is caught and punished.

This is used in speaking of a gross injustice done by any one.

20. रांड देखी मपका छोरों देखी दणखा। Rán̲ḍa dekhí mapaká chhoron̲ dekhí daṇakhá.

Opressing the widow and frightening orphan children.

This is used when poor people are oppressed by stronger ones. *C.f.* "He that oppresseth the poor to increase his riches, and he that giveth to the rich, shall surely come to want." "Rob not the poor, because he is poor: neither oppress the afflicted in the gate."

21. सुधा को मुख कुकर चाट। Sudhá ko mukha kukara cháṭa.

The mouth of a simple man is licked even by a dog.

E.g. A simple man is not dreaded even by a dog, and so why should men fear him?

22. पुजा देखिक बाकरो हंस। Pújá dekhika bákaro han̲sa.

The he-goat laughs at the slight worship any one is going to perform, in which its own life is to be taken or sacrificed.

Applied to or by one who is punished more severely for a comparatively trifling offence, or without any formal investigation or trial.

23. कख ओड़ो कख तोड़ो। Kakha orho kakha torho.

Where is the boundary of the field? and where has the crop been reaped?

Applied to gross injustice, as illustrated by the story narrated below:

Illustration: A newly married prince was sleeping with his bride while, according to custom, the officiating priest slept in the next room. At night while the prince was asleep his bride saw a dagger (*Kaṭára*) in his belt, as is the custom among the Rajputs. She being curious about the weapon took it out of its sheath and then after having examined it tried to replace it in its sheath, but missed the sheath, and thrust it into the body of the Prince, who died instantly. The Princess was in great grief. Next morning the king, who was the father of this unfortunate Princess, together with his people, was much distressed on account of what had happened, and without any investigation regarded the priest as the guilty one and ordered his hands and feet to be cut off in punishment for the crime, the Princess meanwhile through fear and shame keeping silent.

24. मैं गिरनेर छ्युं तेरो ढेसो लागो। Mai giranera chhyuṉ tero ḍheso lágo.

I was about to fall myself, but now you have pushed me down.

This means to say that one about to be ruined was finally ruined by the action of another who now gets the blame for what has happened.

Illustration : Once a large palm-tree having all its roots rotten and turned up was about to fall, but it fell down just as a crow sat on one of its branches. Hence the proverb is used by one when he is injured by another.

24. मारो घुंडो फुटो आंखो। Máro ghuṉḍo phuṭo áṉkho.

The knee was struck but the eye was put out.

Indicating injustice, or infliction of penalty upon the wrong person or thing.

25. माघ खाया आम फागुण लागा घाम। Mágha kháyá áma pháguṇa lágá ghāma.

Mangoes eaten in Magha (January) fever caught in Pháguṇa (February).

Applied to unjust or illogical actions.

27. तैडू कंडो पार फुसरो पोको वार। Tairhú kaṉḍo pára phusaro poko wára.

The basketful of "Tairhu" (a kind of sweet wild root which people eat as vegetable food) has gone over the other side, but one his thighs made white (muddy) this side.

E.g. This root is obtained by digging the earth to the depth of the loin, and so the person gets his thighs muddy in the attempt to get the root out of the ground. A man can get a basketful if he works a whole day. If the fruit of his toil is taken away by another he has nothing but the muddy thighs left to show, hence he says as in the proverb. Applied to one who is deprived of his earnings. *C.f.* "One beats the bush, while another catches the bird."

28. एक हाट दुइ भाव। Eka háṭa dui bháwa.

One market but rates two.

Applied to injustice, or favour or disfavour shown by an officer of a court of justice, or by an administrative officer who is considered as the common master of all.

29. नानी खसम कर दोहता डांड भर। Nánî khasama kara dohatá ḍáṉḍa bhara.

The grandmother commits adultery, her granddaughter suffers punishment.

30. दिन कि रात रात को दिन। Dina ki ráta, ráta ko diná.

Day is changed to night and night into day.

Spoken of flagrant injustice.

31. एकारि गाली बज्र कि ताली। Ekári gálí bajra ki tálí.

He who curses another without cause, upon his own head the curse shall come like a thunderbolt.

C.f. "Curses like chickens come home to roost."

32. गरीब का काल बलिया का श्याल। Garíba ká kála baliyá ká shyála.

Like death to oppress a poor person, but like a jackal to fly before a strong and influential one.

E.g. People in the world generally do not hesitate to oppress and rob a poor person, taking advantage of his distressed circumstances, but they would shun a strong man for fear of his avenging himself.

33. घिनौड़ान में सिटौलो पधान। Ghinorhána me Siṭaulo padhána.

Among sparrows the Siṭaulá is head man.

Amongst small men the mediocrity is a king. Generally used of oppression or cumpulsion.

34. औरन सुं और मैं सुं गुजिया शौर। Auran su̲n aura mai su̲n gujiyá shaura.

Others may be under others (their superiors), but a Gujiyá has become my father-in-law (i.e. rules over me).

Gajádhara or Gajey Singh=a man of high position.

Gujá=Do. of middle do.

Gujiyá=Do. of lowest position.

Used by one mourning over his circumstances when he is unexpectedly oppressed even by poor men.

35. अंधेर गरदि पूपा बाइ चारों जुग बटि हुनि आई। A̲ndhera garadi púpábái cháro̲n juga baṭi huni áí.

Injustice, disorder, and oppression have existed from time immemorial; lit. during all the four ages.

One oppressed by others generally consoles himself by quoting this proverb.

36. अंधा चूनि तोतरा धान मारो घुंडा फूटि आंख। Andhá chúni totará dhána máro ghuṉḍá phúṭi áṉkhá.

A blind man gleans (blasted paddy) empty ears of corn, and when he would strike the leg, knocks out the eye.

I.e. One not qualified to do a particular work should not be employed on it, or else he will spoil it. It also illustrates the miscarriage of justice when the wrong man is punished by a biased or inconsiderate judge.

37. अंधानले सिरनी बाटि घरै घर। Aṉdhánale siraní báṭi gharai ghara.

The blind distribute sweetmeats, but among themselves only.

This phrase is used by people regarding a neighbour who feasts his own particular cronies and excludes others, or also of one who pretending to be a gentleman and impartial officer is interested in the good of his own people only, and does not look to the good of others.

38. बड़ो मारौ रुण निदे। Barho márau rúṉa ni de.

The strong man not only beats one but does not allow one to cry in consequence.

This proverb is generally made use of when an officer gets angry at an appeal against his decision, and wrongly takes further steps to prevent the appellant being successful in his appeal.

39. बिर सिंग ले खायो शिव सिंग वसायो। Bira Siṉg le kháyo Shiba Siṉg wasáyo.

Bira Singh ate gluttonously, but Shib Sing's stomach has swelled (with indigestion).

This proverb is made use of when an innocent person suffers because of the bad deeds of another, for want of proper investigation.

C.f. "The fathers have eaten sour grapes, and the children's teeth are set on edge" (Ezek. 18.2)

40. बड़ा को लठ शिर मे। Barhá ko laṭha shira me.

The club of the stronger must be borne on one's head.

There is no remedy for what a stronger person does to the weaker—he must bear it patiently. "Might is right."

41. मारौ वैसणि जैको नी रोदारो। Márau waisani jaiko ní rodáro.

Beat one who has no one to grieve for him (no one to help him).

This is considered safe, whereas to beat a stronger party would bring revenge on oneself. Also beat one who has no one to ask after him.

42. माछो देखी भीतर हाथ सांप देखी भैर हाथ। Máchho dekhi bhitara hátha sánpa dekhí bhaira háthá.

Seeing a fish in the water he puts in his hand, but seeing a snake he pulls it out.

This applies to one who is simple and poor and is therefore oppressed or injured by others; but one who is strong and dangerous is not touched by any one.

43. भूतन लखा देवतन धक्का। Bhútana lakhá dewatana dhakká.

Devils get he-goats offered to them, but deities are pushed aside.

This is applied when an honest and submissive man is driven out, and a dishonest and tricky one is respected.

44. वैकि लीणी स्वेण वे को खायो खाड़ू। Waiki líní sweṇa we ko kháyo khárhú.

His wife was taken and his ram eaten.

Denoting great injustice done to one.

45. दिया का तली अन्यारो। Diyá ká talí anyáro.

Darkness under the lamp.

This metaphor is used of a man who does good to others but does not remember those who are immediately serving under him.

46. नाना गोरू में ठुलो गोरू ठुला गोरू में बाग। Náná goru meṇ ṭhulo goru ṭhulá goru meṇ bága.

A bigger cow assaults a smaller one, and a leopard the bigger cow.

Used to threaten with divine vengeance those who oppress their inferiors.

Illustration : It is related that Brahmá, a god having four faces, became proud on this account, and thought himself superior to other gods who had only one face. With the object of showing off his wonderful figure-head he began to move about in the aerial regions, but to his great chagrin one day met another Brahmá who possessed eight faces, and in the utmost disappointment he retired to his own place. The eight faced Brahmá seeing him thus retreat in despair became very proud in his turn, until he encountered another Brahmá who had sixteen faces, and the last named again become too conscious of his superiority was sent by the Lord of the Universe to a region ruled over by a Brahmá who rejoiced in thirty-two faces. The moral, of course, is that people should be humble.

47. चौरासु गोरु फरासु उज्याड़। Chaurásu goru pharásu ujyárha.

The cattle in the village of Chaurásu are accused of trespassing in the village of Pharásu (two villages in Garhwal 9 miles apart from each other).

Applied to false accusation.

48. चोर कुतिया मिलीगया त पहरो कैको। Chora kutiyá miligayá ta paharo kaiko.

If a thief and the watch dog unite, who will guard the house?

This is generally used in regard to corrupt police officers who are in concert with thieves.

49. दूध खाव बिरालि पकड़ि जाव घर वालि। Dúdha kháwa biráli pakarhi jáwa gharawáli.

The milk is drunk by the cat, but the wife is held responsible.

Applied to one who is responsible for the trust consigned to her.

50. तुस्यारा कि कड़ कड़ धाम औण तक। Tusyárá ki karha karha ghāma auṇa taka.

The frost is hard until the sun rises.

This is applied by one has who has been oppressed at home, but as soon as he resorts to a Court of justice the oppressors tremble.

51. एक गुणो एकै शूल सौ गुणो एकै शूल। Eka guṇo ekai shúla sau guṇo ekai shúla.

The same punishment for one crime or for one hundred crimes.

May as well be hanged for a sheep as a lamb.

"Shúla" is a sharp and long iron bar used by Native Princes to impale with as a capital punishment (as hanging is used by the British Government).

52. शूल मोटि शुल्या पतलो। Shúla moṭi shulyá patalo.

The iron bar (shula) is very thick, but the man ordered to be impaled with it is very thin.

Once a native prince sentenced a convict to death. On the offender being sent to be excuted his person was found unsuitable for the thick iron bar fixed for the purpose. This fact was accordingly reported to the king by the executioners (as said in the proverb). The king ordered that a stout man adapted to the thickness of the bar be secured and executed. The messengers selected a fat ascetic for the purpose, and on his being taken to the scaffold his spiritual guide (another fat ascetic) voluntarily came there and insisted on being put to death in the room of his beloved disciple, and on the other hand his disciple also persisted in being put to death, and so they both quarrelled about the matter to the utter embarrasment of the executioners. On this fact being also reported, the King sent for both the ascetics and enquired the reason why each of them offered himself for death, to which the elder dervish replied thus:

"While absorbed in devotion today, I heard an oracle from heaven saying that any man who should be sacrificed (put to death) on the iron bar would go to heaven, where he would be made a king of deiṭies. Under such circumstances I would eagerly pray that in consideration of my most rigid penances and devotions I may be allowed to be executed, as I alone deserve such a happy and blissful death." This speech of the hermit moved the whole *Darbára*. Every one of the ministers, nay each member of the Royal family came forward and asked to be kindly allowed to suffer this death, but the king said if this was the case he would willingly die himself, and accordingly executed.

Applied to gross injustice and anarchy, and also used by rich people who are unjustly and unnecessarily troubled or oppressed on no other grounds than their being rich, and also by one who innocently suffers only on account of his name.

53. ग्यूं का साथ घूण पिसीनी। Gyún ká sáṇtha ghúna pisíní.

The ghána (weevils) are ground with the wheat.

Wheat is often infested with weevils, which are ground with the wheat. Applied to innocent persons when they are punished along with the culprits, only on the ground of their having been found with them. This is also used as a caution against remaining in bad society.

54. ग्यूं सोल भठ सोल। Gyúṇ sola bhaṭa sola.

Wheat at the rate of 16 seers and Bhaṭa at the same rate (16 seers a Rupee).

(Although wheat is of much more value than Bhaṭa).

Applied to want of discretion or to injustice. *Bhaṭa* is a kind of inferior pulse eaten by poor people alone.

55. गोरख्याणी। Gorkhyáṇi.

Gorkhyáṇi or the rule of the Gurkhas.

Exemplification of oppression and injustice. People use this phrase whenever they complain of oppression or injustice. The province of Kumaun was ruled for a time by the Gurkhas, a courageous though wild Nepalese tribe, before the English occupation in 1815.

56. हमन करीती काल की मेश ये छन चलयूं का देश। Humana karíti kála kí mesha ye chhana chalyún ká desha.

I acted in accordance with the customs of the times, but this is a country of wicked men.

Applied to one who is censured or punished though he has done nothing wrong.

57. जैको लठ तैको भैंस। Jaiko laṭha taiko bhainsa.

The buffalo is that man's who has a club in his hand, i.e. He who has the stick has the buffalo.

Representing oppression of want of proper government or justice. The man who can beat another of his buffalo.

C.f. "Might is right".

58. अंधेर नगरी बेबूझ राजा टका सेर भाजी टका सेर खाजा। Aṇdhera nagarí bebújha Rájá ṭaká sera bháji ṭaka sera khája.

A town full of darkness (or injustice) ruled over by a careless ruler, where vegetables and sweetmeats sell at one and the same rate. (Description of an unjust ruler).

Once a saint and his disciple while sojourning in various countries and cities happened to arrive in the aforesaid town. The saint, who knew the ins and outs of it, did not wish to stay there, but his disciple being tempted and allured by the sweetmeats which were sold very cheap there said to the saint "O *Guru* (spiritual guide) permit me to stay here for some time." The saint did not comply with his request, but said that it would not be safe for him to protract his residence in such a place as that, and the sooner they got out of it the better. But the imprudent disciple again eagerly asked permission from his Guru to allow him to live there for a short time. Thus the saint was at last obliged to leave his disciple there, with great reluctance, and said to him, "Whenever you happen to get into any trouble remember me; I shall help you." After some time a goat was killed there by the fall of a wall. The owner of the goat sent a complaint against the owner of the wall to the King, who ordered the latter to be hanged for having built such *katcha* (imperfect) walls, but the accused man pleaded his innocence, and said that the fault lay in the mason who had built it. The ruler on this representation changed his mind and ordered the mason to be executed in his stead. The mason also in his turn denied his guilt, and reproached the labourer who supplied him with mortar. On this the man who had supplied mortar for the wall was doomed to death, but the labourer set forth his innocence and blamed the *Bhisti* (water-bearer) for pouring too much water into the mortar and making it too soft for use. On this the sentence of death devolved on the *Bhisti* who so cleared himself of the guilt and implicated the *Kotawál* (Police Officer) who had driven his pony rapidly by him, and so frightened him that he happened to throw more water in the mortar than was required. At this the *Kotawál* was sentenced to be executed, and as he had nothing to say in his defence he was brought to the scaffold to receive his doom. The noose of the cord was found too big for the head of the *Kotawál*. The matter was reported to the king, who ordered that a fat man (whose head and neck were adapted to the noose) should be selected and executed instead. The servants of the king after great search found out the kind of man they wanted in the disciple of the saint, who had become fat by eating cheap sweetmeats, and he was arrested and brought to the scaffold, where he remembered his *Guru* the saint, who made his appearance instantly and volunteered to be hanged in lieu of his disciple, but the latter (wishing to save his *Guru* from death) insisted on undergoing the sentence himself. Each persisted in dying for the other and there was a quarrel between them as to who should be hanged. This matter was also reported to the King who sent for both the *Fakirs* (the saint and his disciple) and enquired why one wished to die for the other. The saint said to the king. "O, just king a heavenly vehicle was at hand to take to Paradise the soul of the man who should die this blissful death. Since I have performed various religious acts and have led a long life of penance I alone merit it and no other." On this the King, who coveted the heavenly vehicle for himself, volunteered to die, and was accordingly hanged.

59. कैले खायो खासु मासु कैका आया पाथणा आंसु। Kaile kháyo khásu másu kaiká áyá pathaṉá áṉsu.

Who ate the fat meat and who shed a flood of tears.

Used in regard to an injustice by which a culprit escapes punishment and an innocent person is punished instead.

60. खा कोली डाडौ ल्वार। Khá kolȋ ḍáḍau lwára.

The weaver gains by stealing some of the yarn entrusted to him and makes up the weight with sizing. But all the iron the blacksmith can steal is the sparks that fly off and burn him.

61. खै गया दाड़ि वाला पकड़ी गया जूंगा वाला। Khai gayá dárhiwálá pakarhȋ gayá júṉgá wálá.

Those with beards ate the spoil but those with moustaches were punished.

(Mahommedans wear beards, and Hindus moustaches).

E.g. During the reign of some of the Mahommedan rulers Mahommedans used to commit crimes and charge them upon the Hindus. Hence the proverb applied to gross injustice through which the real offenders were let off and innocent persons arrested and punished.

62. औरन सों नि सकुलो त घर कि ज्वे सों लेक नि सकूं। Aurana son̲ nisakulo ta ghara ki jew son̲ leka ni sakún̲.

If I cannot beat others, shall I not be able to lord it over my wife?

Used to imply that poor people can be oppressed by every one.

INNOCENCE

1. जै आंगुला बिष लागो वी झड़ंछ। Jai án̲gulá bikha lágo jharhaṇchha.

That finger which has been affected with poison shall fall or drop off.

An assertion of innocence by people who have been mixed up with offenders.

2. गालि बाटा हिटली। Gáli báṭá hiṭalī.

The curse (abusive language) will go its way.

I.e. It will fall on the unjust party and not injure the person used if he is innocent.

Used by one who is unjustly cursed.

3. नि खोऊं हाथ नि खोऊं गात पड़ि रौं चौबाटा बाट। Ni khoúṇ hátha ni khoúṇ gáta parhi raun̲ chaubáṭá báṭa.

If my hands and my person do not offend I can lie down without fear on the highway.

I.e. If I do not do anything wrong why should I fear to rest in a public place?

Applied by one who considers himself innocent, and hence secure from all danger.

INOPPORTUNE ACTS

1. मा बाछी बाग लीगयो फागुण दरोजा बंद करो। Má báchhi bága līgayo pháguṇa darojá baṇda karo.

The leopard carried off the calf in the month of Mágha

(January), and in Pháguṇa (February) they put the doors on the cowshed.

C.f. "Locking the stable after the house has been stolen".

2. यार कुं ज्यूं त्यूं जाणो द्वीचेला पछा। Yára kun̲ jyún̲ tyún jáṇo dwí chelá pachhá.

If a woman is determined to go to a paramour, why should she go after she gives birth to two sons in her husband's house?

I.e. She should go while young, not after she has begotten children.

Used to condemn inopportune actions.

3. त्यार खै बैसी का दिन। Tyára khi baisí ká dina.

The day after the festival (i.e. not in time).

The day of the festival is spent in feasting and merriment. Any good thing received on that day is greatly appreciated, and any guest who comes on that day is well received, but not so after the close of the festival.

Used of inopportune occasions.

4. काटो नफांटो ल्यौ मेरो बांठो। Káṭo na phán̲ṭo lyau mero banṭo.

Neither cut nor divided, but one wishes to have his share.

Applied to improper, impossible or inopportune requests made at a time when the other is not in a position to comply with them.

5. झुकि लिणि ठौर बाल जामिगइ। Bhuki liṇ ṭhaura bála jami gaiṇ.

The place to be kissed is overgrown with hair.

Infant children are generally kissed by their relatives. But the latter are prevented from doing so by living at some distance, the former grow up and the time for kissing is passed. Hence the proverb is applied to lost opportunities, and also to one who used to listen to prayers and requests but now turns a deaf ear.

6. बाटा में ल्वार मिलो आफर लगौ। Báṭá meṇ lwára milo áphara lagau.

A blacksmith met on the road is asked to set his bellows to work.

Applied to one who troubles another, to do some work away from home. Inopportune requests.

7. सौण मरि सासु भादो आया आंसु। Sauna mari sásu bhádo áyá aṇsu.

His mother-in-law died in Sáwana (July) but his tears did not flow until Bhádo (August).

Applied to one who wreaks his vengeance for any grievance after a long time, or to one who does a thing inopportunely.

8. नांग जाइक वस्त्र भूख जाइक भोजन। Nánga jáika bastra bhuk jáika bhojana.

One gets clothes after his nakedness has been covered; and then his hunger is satisfied.

Applicable to inopportune aid which is not appreciated. To give in time of need is considered an act of lasting merit, but to give otherwise is in no way a virtue.

9. कपाल पिठाई नी पोका पिठाइ। Kapála paṭhái ní poká piṭhái.

Red colour applied not to the forehead but to the back.

Red colour (called "Piṭhyá" made of turmeric soaked in lemon juice for days to turn it red).

When marriage or tonsure or a son's birth-cermony takes place in a man's house he invites his relatives and gives them a feast. Soon after the ceremony is over, the *Piṭhyá* mixed with water is applied to their foreheads in one oblong streak (upwards) with a pinch of soaked rice put over it, and then money or other gifts are presented to them, and they take their departure. This is considered necessary etiquette. But if the relatives are allowed to go to their house empty-handed, and without receiving the mark on their foreheads, and if presents are sent to them after the ceremony instead of during the feast, this is called applying the *Piṭhyá* to their backs instead of their foreheads. The saying is generally applied to inopportune actions.

10. बूंद गे बिलायत सों। Bún̲da ge biláyata son̲.

The drop has gone to a foreign country.

This proverb arose from the story noted below.

Once some perfumers brought perfumes for sale to a king who bought some, but out of what he had purchased one drop fell on the ground, and the king at once tried to take it up with his own finger from the floor. This act on the part of the king was considered very mean by his ministers and all others, including the perfume sellers. In order to remove the impression, the ministers afterwards purchased many thousand rupees' worth of perfumes from the same strangers and got it sprinkled all over the royal stables, in order to augment their master's fame for munificence and liberality. Nevertheless the news of the drop had already gone to foreign countries through those strangers. Hence this proverb suggests a careful, reserved, and wise dealing with a stranger, and shows that an opportunity once lost cannot be regained. Also, "Ill news travels fast."

11. तेरो ब्या करूलो सौ बरस में। Tero byá karulo sau barasa me.

I will get you married a hundred years hence.

Applied to promises to do a thing when it will not be needed.

12. खांद आव भागी हाथ धोंदा अभागी। Khán̲da áwa bhágí hátha dhon̲dá abhágí.

A fortunate man comes at the time when dinner is ready, but an unlucky one arrives just after it is over, (lit : at the time when people wash their hands after dinner).

Applied to one who asks for anything when it is too late.

INSIGNIFICANT OR UNPROFITABLE BUSINESS

1. कवा मारि हाड़न मास। Kawá mári hárha na mása.

By killing a crow one gets neither flesh nor bones.

It is no use attempting to "squeeze" a *poor* man, by opression &c.

2. डांग में बुत्यो बैठिक लवायो। Dáṇga me butyo baiṭhîka lawáyo.

One who sows seed in stony land has to reap the crop sitting. (Because the stalks of the grain grown on such land are very short).

Applied to a small business which yields very little profit, or to business started unwisely.

3. टोटलिया को हल पिलंगट को बैल। Ṭoṭaliyá ko hala pilaṇgaṭa ko baila.

A plough of grass, and grass-hoppers for oxen.

Applied in derision to one who has made inadequate provision for any enterprise.

INTERFERENCE

1. आम खाणा कि पेड़ गणना। Áma kháṉá ki perha gaṇaná.

Eat the mangoes, do not count the mango trees.

I.e. One ought to restrict himself to the work in hand; meddle not with that which concerns you not.

2. द्वी राजि तिसरो को पाजि। Dwî ráji tisaro ko páji.

When two men have consented, a third who interferes is a fool.

Applied to one who unnecessarily interferes in the affairs of others.

3. गौ में न गधा में। Gau meṉ na gadhá meṉ.

One counted neither among the kine nor among asses.

Applied to one who has no concern whatever in a matter, but

who unnecessarily interferes in it; or to one who is nobody.

4. हिरा को हिरा लाल को लाल। Hirá ko hirá lála ko lálá.
Diamond to diamond, and ruby to ruby.
Used when one is injured by interference in a quarrel in which the principals make friends. Caution against interference with quarrels in which one is not concerned.

5. मैं ल्युं तल्युं नतर भौ खवे द्युं। Mai lyun̲ ta lyun̲ natara bhau khwe dyun̲.
I may or may not buy a thing but I must spoil the rate (increase it).
Applies to one who wishes to injure others in a business in which he himself has no concern whatever.

6. वार गाड़ भट भुटा पार गाड़ चिड़ चिड़ै उठा। Wára gárha bhaṭa bhuṭá gárha chirha chirhai uṭhá.
Bhaṭa (a kind of inferior pulse) being parched on this side of the river, but the crackling is heard on the other side.
Used of one who interferes in a quarrel or business with which he has no concern.

7. बैल नि भर भरानु गूण जै भरभराणि। Baila ni bhara bharánu gúṇa jai bhara bharáṇí.
The bullock does not stir or jump, but the pannier.
(Bullock an animal, but the pannier an inanimate thing).
I.e. Another person is interfering on behalf of the interested party (who is inactive) in a certain matter.

8. काजि ज्यू दुबला केलै शहर का अंदेसा ले। Káji jyú dubalá kelai sahara ká aṇdesá le.
O, Cadi why have you become so thin? Through anxiety for the city. (The Cadi has nothing to do with public affairs).
Applied to one who unnecessarily interferes with matters in which he is not at all concerned.

INTOXICATING DRUGS

1. जो चरस की करौ बदबोइ बी का बंश में निरो कोई। Jo charasa kî karau badaboi wî ká ba<u>n</u>sha me nirau koi.

Any one who speaks against charasa (a narcotic drug), may no one be left to him in his family.

2. जै लड़काले नि पी गांजा कि कलि वी लड़का है लड़कि भली। Jai larhakále ni pî gá<u>n</u>já ki kili wî larhaká hai larhaki bhalî.

The boy who does not smoke charasa, a girl is better than he.

Both the above are used by those in the habit of smoking these drugs.

IRONY

1. अणकाटियो तुमड़ो को मुख। Aṇakáṭiyo tumarho ko mukha.

The mouth of a gourd uncut.

E.g. As long as a gourd is not cut open it cannot be certainly ascertained what is inside it, though every one is practically aware of its contents.

Applied to unnecessary reserve and precaution.

2. सगलो भनार नौ रति सुनो। Sagalo bhanára nau rati suno.

What is nine ratis (18 grains) of gold compared with the whole treasure?

Used to induce another to give large sums by representing that nine *ratis* is a ridiculously trifling sum for a wealthy man. Also as an expresion of wonder that a man reputed to be rich or great should be unable to comply with a small request.

3. श्यालों का टोलका शेर को एक। Shyálo<u>n</u> ká ṭolaká shera ko eka.

A number of jackals but no tiger.

E.g. A she-jackal gives birth to two or three cubs and a tigress to only one. In other words a number of the former are not competent to face one of the latter.

Applied when a number of small men set themselves in opposition to a man of great influence and power.

4. सलाऊं सरदेशि पिलंगट परदेशि। Saláún saradeshi pilangaṭa paradeshi.

He regards locusts as belonging to his own country and grasshoppers as strangers.

I.e. He cannot distinguish between those who are his true friends and those who are not.

5. चार आदिमि मेरी पीठ मलासौ तब मंगल गौलो। Chára ádimi meri píṭha malásau taba manala gaunlo.

Four persons should rub my back, then I will sing the songs of peace.

E.g. According to custom it is the duty of every person to sing auspicious songs, or to join a party of such singers of his own accord on a festive occasion, but if he refuses to do so shows that he wishes to be bribed or earnestly entreated.

Used ironically to induce one to do his own duty.

6. बूढ़ी माथी माथी मेरो हाथ। Búḍhí máthí máthi mero hátha.

Old lady, my hand is uppermost.

Ironically used of a person who either unnecessarily insists on having a thing done by his own will and choice, or pretends to put an obligation on others without any reason. For instance, if his friend is benefitted somehow, without his interference or help, he attributes the incident to his own instrumentality; if his enemy meets with misfortune he wishes people to believe that his adversary was injured through his influence, and so he was revenged.

7. घौत देखा यो रेलो नि देखो। Ghauta dekhá yo relo ni dekho.

I saw Gahata (a kind of inferior pulse) but not in such a heap.

Ironically used to express astonishment at some one's extraordinary conduct which is either against some established custom or contrary to the course of nature.

8. मियां ज्यू केलै रूंछा शिकलै एसी छ। शबब के छ मुहर्रम कि पैदास। Miyán jyú kelai rúnchhá shikalai yesi chha. shababa ke chhao moharrama ki paidása.

Why do you seem to cry? my features were made so. What is the cause of this? I was born during the Moharrama (when all Mahomedans are engaged in fasting and weeping).

Ironically used to condemn people who show their folly by spoiled work.

9. पहाड़ि कवा देशि भाखा। Pahárhi kawá deshi bhákhá.

Hill crow and Plains language.

Ironically applied to one who makes a vain display of his learning in a foreign tongue.

10. ससुरास को जवांइ बुसराड़ को बलद। Sasurása ko jawáni busararha ko balada.

A son-in-law in his father-in-laws's house, and a bullock in the chaff of the threshing floor, are so well fed that they become notorious.

Used of men who stay very long in their father-in-law's houses.

11. समजनेर सो मौत। Samajnera so mauta.

This is death to one who knows what it is.

Said to or of one who is involved in dangerous and disgraceful affair of any kind.

12. बाबा ज्यू कि जटा आशिखा में गे। Bábá jyú ki jaṭá áshikhá meṇ ge.

The hairs on an ascetic's head (an ascetic's hairs are uncombed locks called "Jaṭás") are takeṇ away or distributed as blessings.

The hairs of a *Jogi* are considered sacred and are supposed to act like talismans.

Ironically used of a man who devotes all his earnings to helping other people.

13. कब को जोगि कब कि जटा। Kaba ko jogi kaba ki jaṭá.

Whenever did he become a Jogi, and how old are his Jaṭás (clusters of hair on his head)?

Used to deride a man's newly acquired possessions when he gets proud of them and thinks himself superior to those who have been long in the enjoyment of such possessions.

14. बाग कि मौसि बिरालि। Bága ki mausi birâli.

A cat is a miniature of a leopard or bears the same likeness, (a cat is said to be a step-mother of a leopard).

Used of one who does little with much show or much less than was expected by other people.

15. मैकणि पसक मेरा मधन कणि पसक। Maikáṇí pasaka merá madhana kaṇi pasaka.

Give food to me as well as to my friend Madhan.

This is applicable to one who besides himself brings other people with him to be fed for helped. *C.f.* "Love me love my dog."

16. सैब सच्चा नफर झूटो। Saiba sachchá naphara jhúṭo.

The master is truthful, but the servant (slave) is a liar.

This is an ironical phrase used by servants to their masters. As masters are always in the habit of censuring their servants whether rightly or wrongly, and also of finding faults and flaws in them. Also applied as in the fable of the wolf and the lamb.

17. अंत में सूम और दाता बराबर हुनि। Aṇta me súma aur dátá barábara huni.

The miser's money goes as rapidly as the benevolent man's does.

Ironically used to induce a miser to use his money properly. Money should be used for one's self or for others; otherwise it will fly away.

18. पुतलि का खेल। Putali ká khela.

A puppet show.

E.g. Girls while unmarried play with dolls, have dolls' marriage, and in sport perform all the ceremonies that are enjoined for boys and girls. Used to deride one who spends very little on the tonsure and marriage ceremonies of his children.

19. हाड़ न मास घला घला गास। Hárha na mása galá galá gása.

Having neither bone nor flesh one wishes to have dainty morsels.

Ironically used of those who wish to have comfort and pleasure without taking any trouble to secure them.

20. घर बार तुमरो कोठड़ि में हाथ जन लगाया। Ghara bára tumaro koṭhari men̲ hátha jana lagáyá.

The house is yours but do not use the room.

Applied ironically to nominal trust.

21. आपणि द्यूं त आपणा बाब की ज्वे अरका कि ल्यूं घागरि ख्वे। Apáṇi dyúṇ ta ápaṇá bába kí jwe araká ki lyún̲ ghágari khwe.

I swear by my father that I shall not give anything of my own, but take that of others by stripping them of their skirts (clothes). Extreme selfishness, giving nothing and taking every thing.

A sarcasm against misers and selfish people.

22. कालो अक्षर भैंस बराबर। Kálo akshyara bhain̲sa barábara.

A black character (letter) looks like a buffalo (to an illiterate person).

23. नगर का असवाल बैखइ बैख । Nagara ká Aswála baikhai baikha.

The Aswals (first class Rajputs) of Nagara, a village in Garhwal, consider themselves as masters, and so do not work themselves.

Applied to members of a family who all think themselves lords (above work). An ironical expression used to induce such people to work.

24. झख मारि खिचड़ि खै साजि नि खै बासि खै। Jakha mári khicharhi khai sáji ni khai bási khai.

One kills a fish and then eats the roe not fresh but stale.

(The roe of a fish is called "khicharí" from its appearance).

Applied to one who at first refuses to do what he is asked, but afterwards asks to be allowed to do it.

Story : Once a man travelling to a certain place having missed his way found himself in a desert, where he became very hungry. As he was wandering here and there in search of some village, he found a hut occupied by a man, with a tank before the hut full of fishes. The stranger asked for some food, but the owner said, "My rule is that whoever wants a fish must catch it himself; give me the meat and keep the intestines for yourself." In spite of this, the traveller took a fish out of the pond, but insisted on having the whole fish himself. The owner refused his request. The stranger at this became sulky and lay down to sleep. In the mean time the proprietor cut the fish and set aside the inner part of its body for the other man, and ate up the rest. Next morning the stranger being further compelled by hunger was obliged to take the intestines, which he had refused to eat on the former evening. Hence the proverb.

25. मर रे चोर बिराणा धन पर। Mara re chora biráṇá dhana para.

O thief, why kill yourself for the wealth of others.

An ironical lesson to a thief, telling him to forsake his evil conduct.

26. माघ मास पाका आम। Mágha mása páká áma.

Do mangoes ripen in the month of Magha (January)?

Applies to one who speaks impossible or absured things.

27. डूम त्वे मै राखुलो चोरी जारी नाकरी। Ḍuma twe mai rákhulo chorí járí nákarí.

O, Ḍúma (a low caste man) I shall keep you if you do not commit theft and adultery.

Ḍúmas are very useful to agriculturists inasmuch as they plough, do other works of tillage, make and sharpen agricultural implements, carry loads, build houses &c. But otherwise they are great scoundrels. As long as a Ḍúma is innocent or harmless, everyone will like to have him for his work. Hence the proverb applies to a very shrewd person.

28. बिगडि गे नाथ कि सुधरिगे सिद्ध कि। Bigarhi ge nátha ki sudharige siddha ki.

Failure is ascribed to a Nátha, but success to a Siddha.

Náthas are a sect of ascetics who take an active part in all wordly affairs, but one who makes himself noted by stringent penances by separating himself from the world, and by abstinence is called a *"Siddha"* or "Santa". A *"Siddha"* is believed to be able one to get impossible things accomplished by means of his penance. He is revered and honoured for the sake of his penances and saintliness. Hence the people attribute any thing spoiled or gone wrong to a *Natha,* and blessings to a *Siddha*. Hence the proverb applies ironically either to one who is unfortunate, or to one who is very lucky.

29. बोलणु चेलि सों सुणाणो बुवारिसों। Bola̲nu cheli soṇ suṇáṇo buwari so̲n.

Lecturing one's daughter in order that the daughter-in-law may hear (and get a lesson).

Parents often, even when there is no fault in their daughter-in-law, reproach or lecture her by addressing their own daughter in the presence of the former, for they do not wish to quarrel with the new bride. Hence when a man wishes convey a hint to another he does so by addressing a third person on the subject.

30. नाख न मुख बांज को रुख। Nákha na mukha bánja ko rukha.

Has no nose and no mouth, is an oak tree. (The tree quercus incana or dilatata. A Himalayan oak).

This is used of one who is ugly. The oak tree which is very common, is considered an ugly tree. A proverb ironically used by village women.

31. बाप बिनोलो पूत चौतार। Bápa binolo púta chautára.

The father was a Binolá seed, but the son Chautara, i.e., a beautiful lace made out of cotton.

Binolá is the small seed of the cotton plant. Chautára is a cotton lace.

This is applied as a slur on a great man who is the son of a poor man, and also to denote that great and noble men can come from a poor family.

32. भासरो भासरो क्या बोलन गांडोइ जी बोल्यो। Bhásaro bhásaro kyá bolana gándoi jî bolyo.

Why do you say I am husky? say at once that I have a goitre.

(A man with a goitre talks huskily).

I.e. Do not talk ironically, pretending to think me only husky, when you really mean to say that I have a goitre. Insinuating evil of a person.

33. दमड़ि को साहू टिपडी को राऊ। Damarhi ko sáhu ṭiparhî ko ráú.

The man who has a Damarhi (i.e. 1/8 of a pice) is called a "Sahu" and the man who possesses the top of a hill is called "Rau".

I.e. In former times, in these hills, when money was very scarce a man who had a *Damarhi* (a copper coin = 1/8) of a piece) in cash was considered a rich man, and a man who tyrranized over a few villages by taking possession of the top of a mountain (called a *garhi* or fortress) was called a "Ráú" or Rájá. This was the case in Garhwal (the whole of the district having been portioned out by petty Rajas called Ṭhakuri Rájás) before the conquest of the country by Raja Kanaka Pála in the seventh century. Used to describe the anarchy and poverty of ancient Garhwal. It is also quoted in derision of one who claims to be descended from a Raja.

34. मुफत का चंदन घिस बे ललू। Mufata ká chan̲dana ghisa be Lallú.

O, Lallu rub the sandalwood which costs nothing.

Applied to one who is very fond of things which belong to other people and which cost him nothing.

Sandalwood is rubbed on a stone into a paste, and then applied to the forehead.

35. क्या मैं गोरू का पेटको छूं। Kyá mai goru ka peṭa ko chhúṇ.

Am I born of a cow?

Do you take me for a fool?

36. जां कुकुड़ो निबासनु वां रात नि ब्यानी। Jáṇ kukurho ní básanu wán̲ ráta ni byání.

Will the morn not dawn should the cock not crow?

I.e. If you will not do the work, we can do without you.

37. जात न थात खलो खलो नाथ। Játa na tháta khalo khalo náthá.

No caste and no land, lord of nothing.

Used ironically of poor people who have nothing to care about.

38. तेरि तौली तेरा मुख में रौलि। Teri taulí terá mukha men̲ rauli.

Your tauli (vessel in which rice is cooked) will remain in your mouth.

I.e. I shall not spend anything for you but your own property. When a Hindu dies the Brahmanas get many gifts, but if the man has only a *Tauli*, this only will be given to the

Brahmanas, and only the merit of so small a gift will go with the spirit of the deceased. A term of abuse.

39. त्वे मेरा सौं जो तू मैकन भलो निमानै । Twe merá saun̲ jo tú maikana bhalo ni manai.

You are sworn on my name to love me.

Used as an ironical phrase against another who does not love the speaker. This means to say that one loves another naturally, but not by force.

40. तू मै कनू मानदी जनू तू मै मानदी । Tú mai kanú mánadí janú tú maí manadí.

How do you regard me? I regard you just as you regard me.

Used generally ironically between persons who are not very friendly.

41. कुमया आपुं कमइया औरन सो चुमइया । Kumaiyá ápun̲ kamaiyá aurana so chumaiyá.

Natives of Kumaun earn for themselves, but are miserly to others.

This is a Garhwali proverb showing how the Garhwalis look upon the people of Kumaun, who are very keen in business but also very clannish.

42. परमेश्वर आपणा गधा कणि हलुवा खओंछ । Parmeshwara ápaṇá gadhá kaṇi haluwá khaoṇchha.

God allows his asses to eat sweets.

Applies to ignorant (incompetent) people who are promoted to high posts.

Generally used by those who think that incompetent people have secured the places they themselves ought to have had.

43. एसो त गोबर में लग लागंछ । Eso ta gobara me laga lágan̲chha.

Such use of the world "bara" (best) is also found in "Gobara" (cow dung).

Once the Emperor Akbar the great asked his chief Minister Birabal where the suffix "bara" should be used. The minister replied that it was used in qualifying such names Sítábara, Rádhábara, Bírábara. The Emperor again asked him why not in Akabara? To this Birábara replied as in the proverb. Hence the origin of the proverb. Applied ironically to one to show that his position or power is too low in comparison with another of similar rank or name to cope with him.

IRRETRIEVABLE LOSSES

1. छोड़ दियो त धोखो के लूट पडी त लेखो के। Chhorha diyo ta dhokho ke luṭa parhi ta lekho ke.

Any thing given up should not be thought of, and of that which has been stolen why keep an account ?

Used by one who has lost anything irretrievably.

JEALOUSY

1. बिराणि देखी लाइ पैराइ अपणी देखी नांगी। बाप की अकल गइ वहि न मांगी। Biráṇi dekhi lái pairái apaṇí dekhí náṉgí, bápa kí akala gai wahi na máṇgí.

Seeing his wife naked, and that of another well clothed and adorned, the man says that his father was a fool inasmuch as he did not espouse the other woman to him.

Blaming others for one's own mismanagement or ill luck.

2. हूंदा की रीस जांदा की खीस। Húṇdá ki rísa jáṉdá kí khísa.

A well-to-do person is envied and a ruined man is laughed at.

Used as consolation on appropriate occasions. No one should wonder at such treatment by the world.

JOINT PROPERTY

1. साझी बाकरो बाग नी खाव। Sajhí bákaro bága ní kháwa.

The goat that is the joint property of several persons is not killed even by a leopard.

I.e. Such property is never taken care of by any individual, each leaves it to the care of others than himself and so it is not noticed by the leopard.

C.f. "Everybody's business is nobody's business."

2. सेरो बगो सेरो बगो माणेके मेरो लग बगो। Sero bago sero bago ma̱neka mero laga bago.

The irrigated land was washed away, and a little of mine was also washed away along with it.

Applied to those who do not care for the loss of their own shares in the joint property thus damaged. The application of this proverb is to any joint property which when damaged is not likely to be repaired as no one is much interested in it.

This corresponds to what is elsewhere said that the loss or pain shared along with five or more persons is not painful at all.

KINDNESS

1. बालो बिरालु। Bálo birálu.

Children and cats should be treated with equal kindness.

Used against treating children and cats cruelly.

KINGS AND HIS SUBJECTS

1. जसो राजा तसि परजा। Jaso rájá tasi parjá.

As the king is so are his subjects.

(1) The greatness of the King's station causes him to be imitated by all his subjects, and

(2) The laws which he ordains influence powerfully the character of the people.

2. राजा मारौ जगतर जाणौ। Rájá márau jagatara jaṇau.

When a king punishes, the world knows the fact.

This is used to lessen the mortification of receiving punishment from a ruling authority.

3. राजा को तेल पला में मेल। Rájá ko tela palá me mela.

The oil given by a Rája should be taken in one's skirt.

I.e. Never refuse the gift of a king no matter how much it may inconvenience you. It is also considered as good luck whatever be the value of the gift when it is given by a king.

4. सेला राजा कि घणि परजा। Selá rájá ki ghaṇi parjá.

A kind-hearted king has numerous subjects.

A cruel master and a tyrannical king are very often deserted by people on account of oppression and want of regard, and those of opposite nature are resorted to for the sake of justice and mercy.

C.f. "In the multitude of people is the king's honour but in the want of people is the destruction of the prince."

5. राजा चलद मेघ बरसद कुइ नि देखदो। Rájá chalada megha barasada kui ni dekhado.

No one knows when the king will move, and the cloud rain.

(Alluding to the secret and sudden movements of the old Indian Kings).

C.f. "The heaven for height, and the earth for depth, and the heart of kings is unsearchable."

LAME EXCUSES

1. असकू भारी का काखा कटगड़ा। Asakú dharí ká kákhá kaṭagarhá.

One unable to carry his load complains of the strings, (by which the load is tied on to the back) being tight.

This applies to one who being unable to do a thing, finds faults with or blames others.

C.f. "A bad workman complains of his tools."

2. स्याल को गू चैनु पड़ो सात समुद्र पार। Shyála ko gú chainu parho sáta samudra pára.

Jackals' dung, when asked for, is said to be seven oceans away.

This is applied to a useless person who when told to do any work refuses to do so, or promises to do it afterwards.

Applied both to the lazy man, who is likened to jackal's dung which is very plentiful, and to his excuses.

3. नाकर भाट खणदी खाड़ चौंल बुकाइक भात नि बाढ़। Nákara bháṭ á khaṇaḋi khárha chaunla bukáika bháta ni báḍha.

O, baggar, do not dig a pit for yourself, if you have already devoured the raw rice, how can the rice you are cooking increase?

A small quantity of raw rice when cooked occupies a much larger space. The beggar having eaten some of the raw rice obtained in begging, in excuse for the small quantity he cooks for his companions says the rice was bad, and is rebuked by the above saying.

4. नाच निजाणो आंगण बांगो। Nácha nijáṇo aṇgan bángo.

Not knowing how to dance she complains of the floor being uneven.

C.f. "Bad workmen quarrel with their tools".

5. हल सों मरिगयो रेभड़ को काल। Hala son marigayo rebharha ko kála.

A bullock becomes as dead for the plough, but is death on his food.

I.e. Devours his evening meal.

Applied to one who makes lame excuses about doing any work, but is very fond of food.

6. पोथि का बैंगण। Pothi ká baiṅgaṇa.

The Baiṇgaṇa (egg plants) of the books are quite different from that which is eaten.

This is used as an ironical excuse for doing what is prohibited by the scriptures. A story is connected with this which gave rise to the proverb.

Story : Once a *Pandita* expounded from his book some doctrines to his wife. Among others this, that "one was not to eat *Baingana*" in other words that "any one who eats *Baingana* will go to hell." After hearing the precept the woman became disgusted with the *Baingana,* the only vegetable she had in her field. Next day she cooked bread for her husband, the Pandita, and placed it before him without any vegetable food. At this the Pandita became very angry, and reprimanded her for not having prepared the *Baingana* vegetable. Whereupon she reminded her husband of the doctrine which he had explained to her regarding the vegetable; the Pandita being thus silenced by his own doctrine cleverly explained that the real *Bainganas* are quite different from those spoken of in the book, and are therefore to be eaten.

7. साधु संतन कन कुछ रोक ठोक नहाति जो अपणा आप गिरनि गिरण दियौ। Sádhu saṇtana kana kuchha roka ṭhoka nahâti jo apṉá ápa girani giraṉa diyau.

Nothing is forbidden the Faquire; why do you stop the pieces of meat? Let them come on.

Ironically applied to those who never mind doing an improper or wrongful thing because they are great and rich men or like saints.

A man of business one day invited an asectic (Vaishnaba or devotee of Vishnu, of the sect who rigidly abstain from animal food living in the neighbourhood), to a grand feast. The hermit said he would never come to the dinner, because mutton was being cooked there. The man admitted the fact but assured him that the meat would be cooked quite separate from the other kinds of food. On this condition the ascetic agreed to accept the invitation. The man went to his home and had the animal food cooked in a separate kitchen. When the dinner was ready all the people invited to the feast sat down in rows. The hermit also took his seat among them. All the various kinds of food were put in dishes and placed before them all. The ascetic insisted on each kind of food in sufficient quantity being put in his dishes, so that he might not have occasion to ask for any thing more after the meat had come to the table. (For they think that any food touched by the vessel in which meat is cooked becomes polluted). And so, after getting enough for himself, he permitted the other people to do what they pleased. After this the cooked meat came for distribution. While it was being given to all, the ascetic being tempted by the savoury smell of the meat and soup said "I think the soup consists of nothing but Ganges water" to this all who were present said "Certainly." Then he said "I must have some of it, there is nothing wrong in taking it, for it is made of Ganges water, but the cook should take the greatest care that no pieces of the mutton come to my dish, otherwise I will leave the food and go away." They gave him the soup, which further tempted him, for he had not tasted it before. He again asked for it, by that time very little or no soup had remained in the vessel, and so the cook was obliged to empty the vessel into the Hermit's dish, putting a spoon to the mouth of the vessel so that all the remaining soup in the vessel should flow out, but none of the bits of the meat, as desired by the *Faquira*. Seeing this, the ascetic, wishing to have the taste of mutton also, used the expression which has become proverbial.

8. निमखणा भैंस कि भैंसेनि खीर। Namakhaṇá bhainsá ki bhaiseni khîra.

The Khîra (rice milk) prepared with the milk of a buffalo which one dislikes smells of the buffalo, or the milk of the buffalo which costs him nothing, or the buffalo which has no master or owner (astray) smells of the buffalo.

This applies to the conduct and services of one who is disliked, or to the thing disliked. The following story explains the lame excuses referred to in the proverb.

Story : The temple of Vishnu, where the idol or image is worshipped, is called "Ṭhákurdorá," In the ceremony of worship the idol or image is first of all bathed with water, milk, *ghi,* curds, and sugar mixed together. The water that drops from the image as it is bathed is caught in a vessel, and is called "Charanámrita" nectar of Vishnu's feet). After this the image is adorned with powdered sandalwood, garlands of flowers &c. Subsequently it is illuminated with lights made of cloth soaked in *ghi*, and then sweetmeats and cleansed raw gram soaked in water are placed before it, which are thus called *"Bhoga"* or *Parsháda i.e.* an offering. This last ceremony concludes the worship. When the worship is finished, the water and the *Parsháda* are distributed to the spectators of the worship. Among the spectators once there stood an old woman. As usual, she was also asked to drink *Charanámrita.* To this offer she said she had no teeth to drink it. After this came the distribution of the *Parsháda.* She was asked again whether she would take it, to which enquiry she said "Why not? I am nourished only by this." The proverb implies that anything disliked is avoided with the aid of strange excuses.

9. निदिणो भानो अखाणो नाम। Nidin̠o bháno akháṇo náma.

The vessel which one does not wish to give to another is said to be in use (not spare or empty).

Applied to refusal of another's request for feigned reasons.

10. लोटनेर मैं छ्यूं तेरो ढेसो लागो। Loṭanera mai chhyun̠ tero ḍheso lágo.

I was about to fall down when I came in contact with you (then I fell down at once).

C.f. "Last straw that breaks the camels' back."

A worthless man laying the blame of his misfortunes on other people.

LAZINESS, SLOTH, OR SLUGGISHNESS

1. अलसि कि बाण येकै घाण। Alasi ki bán̠a ekai gháṇa.

A sluggard wishes to have all his work done in a single attempt.

For instance, lazy man will attempt to carry two loads at one time to save himself the trouble of two journeys.

2. अलसि का वांगा जूंगा। Alasi ká báṉgá juṉgá.

A lazy man's moustaches are untidy.

I.e. In all the actions of an idle man his carelessness is apparent. A common rebuke of sloth and negligence.

3. वोटदा कातदा त भेल क्या लोटदा। Woṭadá kátadá ta bhela kyá loṭadá.

Had he worked a spindle, would he have fallen down a precipice?

I.e. If he had worked for his living, he would not have been ruined.

4. बातन बातन घर खोयो चुला पन भांग बोयो। Bátana bátana ghara khoyo chulá pana bháṉga boyo.

One wasting his time in gossipping ruins his house. His hearth becomes overgrown with weeds.

5. छै मैना रयो हड़ी पाछलि दांव लीग्यो खुटो टोड़ी। Chhai mainá rayo harhi páchhali dáṉwa l͂igyo khuṭo ṭorh͂i.

One lay idle for six months, and at the end went away with a broken leg.

Caution against laziness, which often results in a man being compelled to sell his property.

6. छुयाल रांड छुयों भूलि डोखरि पुंगड़ि मलसा फूलि। Chhuyála ráṉḍa chhuyoṉ bhúli ḍokhári puṉgarhi malasá phúli.

A talkative woman, by indulging in conversation, had her fields overgrown with weeds.

Applied to one who lazily leaves his work undone, or indulges in useless amusements.

7. निगलगंड मोटा न नाफा न टोटा। Nigalagaṉda moṭá na náphá na ṭoṭá.

A fat sluggard causes neigher gain nor loss.

8. मेरा खसमे कणि रोजि नि मिलौ मै कणि पकूंणो पंड़लो। Merá khasama kaṇi roji ni milau mai káni pakúṇo parhalo.

My husband must not earn his livelihood, otherwise I shall have the trouble of cooking food for him (starving preferred to the trouble of cooking).

Used to convince persons (of one's own family or household) of the folly of being lazy in helping others.

9. डूम हल न मल खांदि दांव जल। Ḍúma hala na mala khándi dánwa jala.

The Dúma will neither plough nor mansure the fields but at dinner time is envious.

Said of lazy people, who are unwilling to work, but ready enough to eat.

10. अलसि स्यैणि को दूध साग निरबुधो हाकम को कसम भाख। Alasi syaini ko dúdha sága nirabudho hákama ko kasama bhákha.

A lazy woman eats her rice with milk alone, and a dull-headed officer disposes of his cases by making the parties resort to an oath.

E.g. A lazy woman will not take pains to cook curry or vegetables to eat with her rice, and so an incompetent officer will not take the trouble to find out the truth of a case by an exhaustive enquiry and investigation, but will save trouble by making the parties swear, and so deciding the case.

11. टुकुड़ा खाया दिन बिलाया कपड़ा फाटा घर सों भाजा। Ṭukurhá kháyá dina biláyá kaparhá pháṭá ghara son bhájá.

Lives on bits of broken meal, and when his clothes turn into rags runs back to his home.

This is used of vagrants, especially young village boys who out of curiosity or from disinclination to work at home, run away to a town, but eventually come back to their relations, who are obliged to feed them for some time without any return, but they have to go to their own parents for renewal of their clothes. Also used of one who wastes his time unprofitably.

12. मेरि जै सैल करण कि दशा हुनि त मेरा बापु का भैस नि हुना। Meri jai saila karaṇa ki dashá huni ta merá bápu ká bhaisa ni huná.

Were I so lucky as to rove about my father would not have buffaloes.

The speaker complains of his father having buffaloes (property) in grazing which he is employed.

Applied to sluggards who wish to waste their time at any risk whatever.

13. खेति पाति के नै लासण मे जोर। Kheti páto ke nai lásaṉa me jora.

No husbandary, but relies on garlic.

I.e. One who does not do work but talks of costly food.

Applied to sluggards to stir them to be industrious.

14. गाइ न बाछि नींद आई आछि। Gái na báchhí nĩnda ấi áchhi.

One who has no cows or calves sleeps soundly.

Ironically used of one who is idle and will not take on him the responsibilities of life.

15. गमू का कूड़ा कि बिसौण गमू काई कूड़ा मा। Gamú ká kúrhá ki bisauṉa gamú kấi kúrhá má.

Gammu rests, with his load on, in his own house.

A stay-at-home who does no work.

The reference is to coolies carrying load on their backs.

16. जो नि धोव अपणु मुख सो क्या करौ हाइका को सुख। Jo ni dhowa apaṇu mukha so kyá karau háiká ko sukha.

He who cannot wash his own face, how can he be of any use to another.

An idle man is of service to nobody.

17. रांड को सांड सौदागर को घोड़ा खालो भौत कमालो थोड़ा। Ráṉḍa ko sáṇḍa saudágara ko ghorhá khálo bhauta kamálo thorhá.

The son of a widow and the pony of a merchant eat much but earn little.

A widow's son is petted and lives in idleness, and a merchant's (riding) horse has but little work to do. Also used of an indolent fellow who boasts much but does little work.

18. मुशलचंद फिरौ। Mushala chand phirau.

Moving like a pestle;

Applied to a vagrant person. "A rolling stone."

19. कुवा का मेंडक कुवा में रया। Kuwá ká meṉḍaka kuwá me rayá.

The frogs who live in a well remain in the well for ever.

Applied to people who never leave their homes but remain in one place during their whole life.

The following story is told to illustrate the effects of such life.

Story : Some men, who had never moved out of their village before, once went to another village in order to get one of their sons married to a maiden of that place. They arrived there in the evening. The marriage had to be performed in the latter part of the night. But soon after their arrival they saw the moon in the sky, and supposing that the moon belonged to their village only, and no other village had a similar moon over it, and that their own moon had been carried away by the people of this other village on the previous day, all of them became angry and began to return home without performing the marriage ceremony, charging the people of the village with the theft of the moon, which they considered exclusively their own. Seeing this ignorance the magnates of the neighbourhood became surety for returning their moon to the village the next day under penalty of Rs. 10,000. Having been thus assured that their moon would be returned they had the girl of their village married that night. On the next day they returned to their village with the sureties, who showed them the moon over their own village, and were then released.

LITIGATION AND JUSTICE

1. अदालत में चढ़नु गधा में चढ़नु । Adálatá men̲ chaḍhanu gadhá men̲ chaḍhanu.

To have a case in court is like mounting a donkey. (To be made to ride on an ass is the greatest mark of disgrace).

This punishment was awarded by Hindu or Mahomedan rulers for the most atrocious crimes. In like manner a litigant, however respectable, while in court, is liable to be put to great inconvenience and dishonour. He is reprimanded by peons for approaching the officials etc, he has to humble himself before each petty official down to a *Chapŕási,* besides having to attend the precincts of the court like a vagrant. This kind of trouble follows him from the first to the last stage of the case.

2. बाप देव या छाप देव । Bápa dewa yá chhápa dewa.

Either father must give or the Court.

This means that one's own father is to give a man his right, if not, he will obtain it by a decision of a court of justice bearing its seal (chhápa).

3. बाप देव गौं राजा देव न्यौं । Bápa dewa gaun̲ rajá dewa nyau.

A father gives a village and a king does justice.

I.e. A father is expected to give his property to his son, and the king to do justice to his subjects.

4. बाग बाकरो येक घाट पाणि पीव । Bága bákaro eka gháṭa páṉí píwa,

The leopard and the goat drink water at the same pool.

This proverb is cited to represent good government by which the strong are kept from oppressing the weak.

5. कणोदि बिलि चुहों मु कान कतराव । Kaṇodi billi chúhon̲ mu kána kataráwa.

The ears of an entrapped cat are gnawed by rats.

Used to denote one who becomes partial in his judgments, or connives at the wrong actions of one to whom he may be some way or other under obligation.

6. दूध को दूध पाणि को पाणि। Dúdha ko dúdha páṇi ko páni.

Milk by itself, and water by itself.

Applied to impartial justice. In legal cases truth and falsehood are mixed up as milk mixed with water looks like milk, but the judge separates the truth from falsehood and thus gives real justice.

Story : A man owed Rs. 5,000 to another as a simple debt. The money when demanded having been refused by the debtor was sued for by the creditor in a court of justice. There the debtor denied having owed anything at all to the plaintiff. The plaintiff's statement was that there was no other person present when the money was lent. After considering the case the judge asked the plaintiff whether there was any animal there at the time, to which query the plantiff replied that there was a cat. The cat was ordered to be brought before the court. When the cat was placed he took it into his bosom and began to caress it. Just at this moment the defendant exclaimed that that cat was not present at the time (meaning that the one present at the time was some other cat). From this the judge at once concluded that the plaintiff was in the right, and after further inquiry, which still further convinced him, he gave judgment accordingly.

Compare the story of Solomon's judgment. I Kings iii.

Note : The expression Dúdha ká dúdha, pánî ká pánî. "Milk of milk, water of water," is also used to denote the best part or essence of anything. "Crēme de la crēme."

7. पांसो पड़ सो दाव राजा कर सो न्याव। Pa̲nso parha so dáwa rájá kara so nyáwa.

Dice win the bet, and whatever the king does is justice.

This is used in representing the decision of a king as inevitable and final.

8. पूत आपणो न्याव परायो। Pútá ápano nyáwa paráyo.

The judge must not favour the offender even if he is his own son.

9. श्याल कसि बुद्धि स्यू कसो तराण दूब कसि जड़ धरति को जसो छाड आकाश जसो उचो। Shyála kasi buddhi syú kaso tarána, dúba kasi jarha, dharati ko jaso chhárha, ákásha jaso ucho.

The cleverness of a fox, the courage of a lion, the root of Dúba grass, (Bent grass, parricum dactylon or cynodon dactylon) for its evergreen and spreading nature, the length and breadth of the earth, and the height of the heavens are proverbial, and all these wished for by mothers for their sons as blessings.

The cunning of the fox is often illustrated by the following two stories.

Story No. 1 : Once a leopard was caught in a trap set in a jungle. A Pandita passing near was asked by the animal to extricate him. But the man said, "If I release you, you will kill and eat me." The leopard swore on his honor not to injure his benefactor. So the animal was set free. But no sooner was he (the leopard) at liberty than he leapt upon the man who entreated the animal not to kill him after he had so generously liberated him. The contest continuing for some time, at last both parties submitted their case to the arbitration of a cow, the Ganges, a snake, and a fox. The cow condemned the man, saying that he received immense benefit from her, yet beat and starved her. The Ganges also concurred with the cow, saying that men were purified by her water, which they drink and make use of in various ways, yet do not forbear from throwing filth into her. The snake also delivered the same judgment, declaring that men first of all provoke him, and then kill him unjustly. Then came the fox's turn to pronounce judgment, who, after patiently hearing the findings of the other arbitrators, expressed a wish to see the position from which the leopard had been extricated. All therefore went to the place, and desired the leopard to lie within the trap once more, so that the arbitrators might have an idea of the facts of the case. As soon as he did so, the fox, to the great admiration of the other arbitrators, said justice demanded that each party should remain where he was, and told the man to go way, leaving the leopard in the trap.

Story No. 2 : Once a traveller met a fox, who asked the traveller where he was going to. The reply was "Be off, you jackal; don't meddle with me." The fox went away saying that though he treated him with contempt then, he would afterwards feel the need of his help. At night the traveller reached a certain village and there he stopped, tying his pony to the *Kolu* (the oil-press). The villagers wishing to rob him of his horse gave out that their oil-press had given birth to a pony, and in order to make the story public they distributed sweetmeats and congratulated each other on the event. Next morning when the stranger was about to unloose his pony, he was stopped and told that the pony was the offspring of their oil-press. The stranger was obliged to have recourse to the king for justice, who, during the investigation of the case, ordered the stranger to produce his witness the fox. When the stranger went to call the fox the fox said he would go to the king and give evidence, but he wanted the man to carry him on his shoulders (as a revenge for the contemptuous treatment he had received from the man) for fear of the city dogs which would kill him. As soon as the fox arrived in the court of the king he feigned to dose. The king asked him why he was so sleepy. The fox said "Sire, I could not sleep last night, as the sea had caught fire, and I was engaged all night in quenching the fire." The king laughed at the fox, and said "How could the sea catch fire, it is impossible." To this the fox replied "Sire, how can lifeless wood give birth to a pony?" This stopped further proceedings, and the king ordered the pony to be made over to the traveller.

10. जैको बिंद तैको पिंड । Jaiko binda taiko pin̲ḍa.

The body is his of whose seed it is created.

The son belongs to father and the girl to the mother, for it is said that a son is born out of the father's element and a girl out of the mother's.

11. बांटा तें खाणो बोड़ा तें लावणो । Bán̲ṭá ten̲ khán̲o borhá ten̲ lawán̲o.

One must eat one's own allotted portion only, and reap crops up to the boundary mark (i.e. in one's own field only).

This is made use of when one trespasses on another's right. Food is divided out carefully among the different members of a poor family.

12. माणा माथ गौं नी अठार माथ दौंनी । Máná mátha gaun̲ ní aṭhára mátha daun̲ní.

No village beyond Máná (a village in the snowy range in Garhwál) and no number (of dice) above eighteen.

E.g. There are only eighteen spots in dice, and Máná is the last village on the Máná Pass route to Tibet. This proverb is also found in another form, viz. that "no flesh can be found beyond one's nails."

This is used to denote the highest court one can appeal to, or the last remedy one has tried with a view to obtain justice. "Ne plus ultra."

13. जसै मुख उसै थपड़ । Jasai mukha usai thaparha.

As the face so the blow.

E.g. Strike a little child a little blow, a big man a big blow; or, people of the same station should act according to that station, or as the crime so is the punishment. As the man so is the work.

14. आपणु सुनो खोटो परखनेर के दोष। Āpanu suno khoṭo parakhanera ke dokha.

It is no fault of the assayer when one's own gold is counterfeit.

This proverb is generally used of one who rightly loses his case or gets himself punished for his real guilt by a court of justice. (A guilty conscience needs no accuser).

15. काकड़ी को चोर मुठगि घौ। Kákarhî ko chora muṭhagi ghau.

Theft of a cucumber should be punished with one stroke or blow.

This means to say that light offences should meet with light punishment but should not be allowed to go unpunished.

The cucumber is the cheapest of all vegetables and is freely given away.

MANAGEMENT (BAD)

1. उन्ने नून उन्ने नान। उन्ने वखलि उन्ने धान। Unne núna unne nána unne wakhali unne dhána.

As the Núna so is Nána, as the mortar so the dhána (paddy).

The members of a cartain household and the arrangement of their work or business are equally bad. Núna and Nána are proper names, "Tweedledum and tweedledee."

2. रौ खेती सालम पहरो। Rau kheti sálama paharo.

His village is in Rau, and he keeps guard in Sálama.

E.g. "Rau" is ten miles distant from the place known as "Sálama."

This is used of one who lives away from the place where his business is, which in consequence suffers loss.

C.f. "The master's eye makes the horse fat." Rau, a patti (tract or Putwari circle) of Parganná Kali (eastern) Kumaun, and Sálama that of Chaugarkhá Zillah, Kumaun.

3. सातु रैग्यो सासु मु सपड़ाक रैगे बुवारि मु। Sátu raigyo sásu mu saparháka raige buwári mu.

Sátu (flour of parched grain) is with the mother-in-law but the dexterity (skill in management) is in the daughter-in-law.

E.g. The person in charge of property is not competent to manage it, but the one who has the wit to manage it is not in charge of the property.

4. सासु ले बुवारि थैं बवारिले कुकुर थैं कयो कुकुर ले पुछड हिलै दियो। Sásu le buwári thai̱n kayo buwári le kukura thai̱n kayo kukura le puchharha hilai diyo.

The mother-in-law told her daughter-in-law to do something, the latter, instead of doing it, told the dog, and the dog in turn refused to do it by moving its tail.

Want of control in a household.

5. अशरफिन कि लूट क्वेलान में मोहर। Asharfina ki lúṭa kweláná me mohara.

Gold mohars are allowed to be stolen, but charcoal is kept carefully sealed up.

"Penny-wise and pound-foolish."

6. ब्या मे खल खाणु त और दिन के खाणु। Byá me khala kháṇú ta aura dina ke kháṇú.

When chaff is given to be eaten on a marriage day what will be given on other days?

Either great poverty or great stinginess.

7. बिगर रौ कि मौनि। Bigara rau ka mauni.

A swarm of bess without a Rao (queen or leader).

Bees that have no queen to lead them are scattered here and there, but those that have a queen keep together.

Applied to subjects without a ruler, or children without parents, &c.

8. नाई कि बरात ठाकुरै ठाकुर। Nái ki baráta ṭhákurai ṭhákura.

In the marriage procession of a barber every one invited

thinks himself a lord (as the barber is everybody's servants).

Applied to a household or company which fails because none of the members work or help, all considering themselves to be masters.

9. हाथी की लड़ैं इंडि कि बाड़। Háti kî larhain̠ inḍa ki bárha.

An elephant fight within a railing made of the castor-oil tree.

Applied to small or ridiculous preparations for a great business or undertaking.

10. जैकी छ डर सो नी छ घर। Jaikî chha ḍara so nî chha ghara.

The one I am afraid of is not at home.

Applied to mismanagement in a house owing to the absence of the head of the family. "When the cat is away the mice will play."

11. तीन बुलाया तेर आया देखौ यांकि रीत। भैरवाला खै गया घर का गानी गीत। Tina buláyá tera áyá dekhau yán̠ki rîta. Bhaira wálá khaigayá ghara ká gáni gîta.

Three were invited but thirteen came. See the custom of this place. The strangers ate up the food, but those of the house had to sing for it.

Used with regard to unwelcome guests who come in unexpectedly just for the sake of a meal, and to want of proper management in one's household or business.

C.f. "Charity begins at home."

12. सौ कि सौ बियां कि नाट। Sau ki sau biyán̠ ki náṭa.

One hundred from one hundred, no seed left.

I.e. If the whole is taken or spent nothing remains for futher use (or for seed).

Applied to bad management.

13. एक घर का नौ मता कुशल कां बटि होलि। Eka ghara ká nau matá kushala kán̠ baṭi boli.

A household which is governed by nine (different) opinions will not thrive.

C.f. "A house divided against itself cannot stand."

MEANNESS

1. दमड़ि को सौदा बाजार में खलहल। Damarhi ko saudá bázára men̲ khalahala.

One in purchasing only 1/8 of a pice worth makes a great noise throughout the bazaar.

Applies to dealings with a mean man. Very small dealings in business.

2. जतुकै छोटो उतुकै खोटो। Jatukai chhoṭo utukai khoṭo.

The meaner the man the more wicked he is.

3. पौणा पूछी पकोड़ा। Pauṉa púchhî pakorhá.

He asks a guest who is a relative whether he should cook cakes for him.

The guest, though naturally willing to be feasted splendidly, cannot without impoliteness express his wish. If the host puts such a question to him he does it with some mean or impudent motive. Hence the proverb is applied to one who does a foolish and unnecessary thing or acts with the intention of putting another to shame.

4. पाणि सि पतलो धुंआं सि बकलो। Páni si patalo dhun̲wán̲ si bakalo.

Thin like water but thick like smoke.

Used of a mean-minded and selfish set of people who to obtain their own ends become very humble, but when others look to them for favours, turn haughty and offensive.

5. गुलाम हाथि में चढ़ फिर लग माधर चोद। Gulâma háthi me chaḍha phira lega mádhara choda.

A slave though mounted on an elephant is nevertheless a mean man.

Man of low descent or family however great they may become, are to be suspected and dreaded.

6. अफुला को धन डफुआ ले बाज। Aphulá ko dhana ḍaphauá le bája.

The little wealth of a mean person is made public by the beat of a drum.

Used as a caution against borrowing from or dealing with one who is mean-hearted and has very little wealth.

7. कच्यार में ढुंगो हालो मुख अै लागो। Kachyára me ḍhungo hálo mukha ai lágo.

Throw a stone into the mud and you splash your own face.

I.e. Direct communication or conversation or dealing with vile persons should be carefully avoided.

C.f. "You cannot touch pitch and not be defiled."

MERITORIOUS ACTS, GOODNESS OR VIRTUE

1. आंखर भलो को भलो। Áṉkhara bhalo ko bhalo.

A good man's end is good.

2. भीख में भीख दिणो तीन लोक जीत लिणो। Bhîkha me bhîkha diṇo tina loka jîta liṇo.

He who gives alms out of what he has received as alms (begged) wins three worlds.

This proverb is generally quoted to encourage a poor person to give alms or support others.

3. भूजी बोणो सताई दीणो। Bhújî bono satâi dîṇo.

To bestow an alms after many repulses is like sowing parched grain. i.e. bears no fruit.

C.f. "He doubles his gift, who gives in time". "He gives twice, that gives in a trice." "The Lord loveth a cheerful giver."

4. स्वर्ग सों टेक नि धर्म सों छेकनि। Swarga son ṭeka ni dharma son chheka ni.

Heaven (the sky) needs no props, and a virtuous act needs no special time, or an alms needs no future promises (for its performance).

This is used to encourage one to do good deeds without procrastination.

5. नित्य निमाणा धर्म ठिकाणा। Nitya nimáṇá dharma ṭhikáṉá.
Only one who is free from pride always can be (truly) religious.

6. टूटी लागौ पर झूटी नि लागौ। Túṭí lágau para jhúṭí ni lágau.
Let poverty come, but do not be dishonest.
"Tell the truth and shame the devil."

7. धर्म करनै करनै है जौ हाणि तब लग नि छोड़नि धर्म कि बाणि। Dharma karnai karnai hai jau háṉi taba laga ni chhorhani dharma ki báṇi.
Follow righteousness stedfastly though you may be injured by it.

Story : There was a very poor Brahmin beggar in the kingdom of a certain king who was noted far and wide for his munificence and virtue. The Brahmin and his wife being entirely destitute used to live on wild roots and vegetables. Hearing that the king gave money to every beggar who went to him, the Brahmin was constantly urged by his wife to go to the king and ask for alms. But he always refused. At last having been prevailed upon and compelled by his wife, he went to the king one day and stood before him, but did not ask for any thing. On the King's offering to give him a quantity of Rupees the poor man refused to accept them, saying that it would injure him in his next stage of existence. Seeing him so firm and determined in his refusal the king was very grieved and asked him to accept something again and again. At length the Brahmin said that he would not take the money for nothing, but if it would please the king to buy a certain thing from him he would then accept the money as payment. The king agreed to this proposal. Then the Brahmin said that he had nothing else but his poverty, which he would sell for three lacs of rupees. On this the king ordered three lacs of rupees to be paid to the poor man and bought his poverty from him. The Brahmin departed. Immediately after the bargain was completed the king's wealth disappeared from his treasury, his kingdom was encroached upon by neighbouring kings, who left him nothing but his own house. There was constant quarrelling and estrangement among the members of his family. One night, while he was sitting in front of his house and brooding over his misfortunes, a beautiful woman clothed in red came out of his palace and asked leave of him to go elsewhere, saying that she was *Wealth* and could not remain in his house on account of the poverty he had bought. The king gave her permission to go, and she went away. After half an hour another woman in a black robe came out of his house and craved his permission to go, saying that she was his Empire and she could not stay with the poverty he had purchased. The king told her to go and she also went away. After a similar interval a third woman in white clothes came out of his door, who also went away with the permission of the king, saying that she was his Wisdom, that she departed because he had embraced poverty. After this an old man came out of the king's house and asked permission to go saying that he was Righteousness or Virtue, and he wished to depart from his house on account of the poverty he had bought. The king however, refused his permission, for, he said, how could righteousness forsake him when the poverty was purchased only for his sake? Righteousness could give no reply to this reasoning of the king, but having been convinced of its force re-entered his house and stopped there. Later on the three women alluded to also returned to his palace, but the king forbade them to enter. On this they all entreated him to let them into his house where their husband Righteousness was living. They said they left his house as their husband (Righteousness) was also to leave it, but since he did not leave it they must return to remain with him for ever. Then they were also allowed to enter the house and remain with their husband. After this he became an emperor instead of a king, and possessed incalculable wealth.

8. जां धर्म तां जय। Ján dharma tán jaya.

Where virtue, there victory.

I.e. Where there is honesty, truthfulness, and godliness there victory is sure and certain.

9. सौ घड़ि घर की एक घड़ि हरकि। Sau ghari ghara ki eka gharhi haraki.

One hundred gharhis (2-1/2 gharhis make an hour) to the house and one to God.

This means that out of the abundance of time spent on one's own business a few minutes should be devoted to the worship of God.

10. पुण्य रेख में मेख मारंछ। Punya rekha men mekha maranchha.

Meritorious acts drive a nail into the line of evil destiny.

I.e. Into the sutures of the skull which are supposed to record one's fate. The nail obliterates the writing.

Story : There was a pious man who had no son; he longed for one very much, but in vain. Once a saint came to his house, to whom also he prayed that he might have a son. The saint, in order to find out whether or not the man would have children, went first to Brahma, and on Brahma's replying to his query in the negative, went to Mahadeva, who also told him that there were no children decreed in the pious man's fate. After this the saint repaired to Vishnu for the same purpose and received a similar reply. Then the saint came back to the devout man and informed him of his fate, and then went away. A few years after this event another saint came to the house of the religious man, and complaining of hunger told the man he would have as many sons born to him as he would give loaves of bread. The pious man gave him five loaves for his meal which he ate up and then went away. In due time five sons were born to the good man. The first saint after some time came back to the pious man and was amazed to find him possessed of five sons, contrary to the prediction. And consequently he became very angry, and regarded the aforesaid three deities as liars. Being indignant he went straight to the highest God Vishnu. As soon as he approached the God he found him very ill (a form assumed by illusion in order to pacify the saint). Finding Vishnu in such a state the saint's anger subsided, and he asked Vishnu "O God, thou hast never before became sick; now what medicine will cure thee?", To this Vishnu said, "I can be cured only by the blood of saints." So the saint went to other saints with a cup to bring their blood in, and asked them for their blood. Each of the saints after hearing the sad news gave each a drop of blood from his own body, and on the first saint's demanding more, all of them said that he could get more from his own body since he also was a saint. The saint then came back to Vishnu with a little dried blood which Vishnu rejected because there was so little, and it was dry. Then the saint said that he could not get more. On this Vishnu pointed out another saint in the neighbourhood, and told the saint to go to that one and bring to a cupful of fresh blood. The saint went to the hermit, and after representing the whole matter to him asked for his blood. No sooner had he heard this than the hermit, to the utter astonishment of the saint, gladly cut his own body in several places, and filled up the cup. Immediately the saint saw Vishnu standing before him, and heard these words. "O saint, behold the hermit who spared nothing for me, shall I not cause his words to turn out true in that he promised five sons to the pious man. You have been to so many saints and you yourself are a saint, yet none has furnished me with his blood except this hermit."

11. धर्म की जड़ हरी। Dharma ki jarha harī.

The root of virtue is perennial.

Story : There was a pious man in a certain town. He devoted 36 years of his life to the service of God and led a life of piety and righteousness. After this a son was born to him, concerning whom God informed the man that he would live only 12 years. This made the parents sad and anxious. When the boy became 8 years old he one day asked his parents why they were always so dejected and sad. The parents at first wisely and prudently refused to acquaint him with the real state of affairs, apprehending that their doing so would dispirit him, but on his persisting to know the matter they disclosed the secret to him. On this, the son, seeing that he had shortly to die, left his home and went on pilgrimage, resigning himself to the will of Providence. While thus journeying he was seen by a king who was about to marry an ugly faced son to a fair damsel of another king. As this boy was very beautiful the king requested him to do him the service of taking the place of his own son in the marriage ceremony. The custom is that the son goes with a procession of men to the house of the father of the girl who is to be married. After visiting the girl in her house he returns to his own house with the bride. If the son is found to be defective in his person at the time of the ceremony the proposed marriage is rejected by the father of the girl. In that case the bridegroom has to return home without completing the marriage, which is considered a great disgrace. So the short lived boy was taken along with the marriage procession to the house of the other king, to whose daughter the king's ugly son had been espoused. Then the marriage of the girl was celebrated with the beautiful boy, and the procession returned homeward. During the first stage the short-lived boy was dismissed by the king, but, on seeing this, the bride also deserted the camp and followed her bridegroom. By this time the appointed twelve years of the boy's life were nearly ended, and so he went towards the Himalayan snows to die there. (The belief is that one who dies in the snows will go to paradise). But while there he was seen by the deities, who having pity on the very young pair were anxious to avert the boy's death. The age of the girl was found to be fixed at 120 years, and, so they found a way to increase the boy's age to 72 years by taking 60 years from the age of his wife, to whom only 50 years more were then left, during which period they lived happily together and were also blessed with offspring.

12. धन सांजिक रज्जा कु ज्यू सांजिक ज्यूरा कु। Dhan sáṉjika rajjá ku jyú sáṉjika jyúrá ku.

Money gathered or saved is sure to be confiscated by a king, (as was the custom in the time of native rulers), and the body carefully nourished is certain to be seized by death.

13. खांड कि रोटी जख बठि तोड़ि तखं बटि मीठी। Kháṇḍa ki roṭi jakha baṭi torhi takan baṭi míṭhí.

A sugar loaf sweet on all sides.

Applied to good and meritorious works which one ought to do at all times and under all circumstances.

14. गुड़ अन्यारा में लग मिठो। Gurha anyárá me laga míṭho.

Treacle is sweet even in the dark.

E.g. Good deeds though done in secret have the same effect and are appreciated as much as if they had been done publicly.

Used to encourage people to perform good deeds even in private.

15. राजा को दान प्रजा को स्नान। Rájá ko dána prajá ko snána.

Raja's alms, and bathing of a poor person, are equal.

E.g. To give alms is the duty of the rich, but the poor can get merit by bathing.

16. भलि करी खेड़ा निजानी। Bhali karí kherhá nijání.

Goodness (a good deed) is never wasted (or fruitless).

17. कलि पापि लाइ फलि, धर्मात्मा का छोरा छोरी पापी काहली, पर अन्त में धर्मात्मा बली। Kali pápí lái phali, dharmátmá ká chhorá chhorí pápí ká halí, para aṇta me dharmátmá balí.

The Kali yuga or iron age is prosperous to a sinner whom the son of a virtuous man serves as a ploughman, but eventually the latter will be victorious.

Used of strange and adverse results and incidents.

MIDDLE OR MODERATE COURSE

1. आपुं राखि तप घर राखि दान। Apuṇ rákhi tapa ghara rákhi dána.

Perform penance, but without ruining your health—Bestow alms but without wasting your wealth.

Be not "righteous overmuch."

2. दौड़ दौड़ जांदु त धुरिया बतांदन माठु माठु जांदु त सहेल ब्रदांतन। Daurha daurha jáṇdu ta dhuriyá batáṉdana máṭhu máṭhu jaṇdu ta sahela batáṉdana.

If I go quickly, i.e., running, people think me a bad character, and if I go slowly they call me an ass or lazy.

A medium course is best.

3. सिरू सिरधार बिरू बिरधार टुकन्या बिचे धार। Siru siradhára biru biradhára ṭukanyá biche dhára.

Siru to Siradhára (a mountain of that name), Biru to Biradhár, and Tukanyá in the middle of the two mountains.

There were three brothers in a certain village named Siru, Biru, and Tukanyá. When they were full-grown Siru, in pursuit of objects of his ambition, took an extreme course and was ruined, and in the same way Biru, who took the other extreme, was also ruined. But the third brother Tukanyá always chose the middle course and prospered.

4. कानो लग गाड़ी जौ पीड़ लगै नी हो। Káno laga garhî jau pîrha lagi ní ho.

The thorn (which has pricked the foot) should be taken out without pain.

Used to encourage one to go easily in all affairs or to pursue a moderate course.

MISCELLANEOUS

1. आडू बेडू घिंगारू। Árhú berhú ghiṉgárú.

Árhú (apricot), Berhú (wild figs), and Ghingarú.

Wild fruits representing ignorant and mean people who are hardly to be trusted with any responsible work.

2. अंधो अलुणो पहच्याणो। An̲dho aluṇo pahachyáṇau.

A blind man can discern food which has no salt in it.

A man devoid of one sense can be made use of in other ways.

3. अधान में काणो मीर। Aṇdhána men̲ kán̲o míra.

A one-eyed man is a lord among the blind.

A figure among ciphers. A triton among minnows. A castor oil plant is reckoned a *tree* in a country where there are no other trees.

4. अैब करण सों लग गुण चैंछ। Aiba karṇa son̲ laga guṇa chain̲chha.

To commit a crime even requires skill.

This proverb is often cited when an offender evades detection and punishment.

5. बिन गुरू बाटनी बिन कौड़ि हाटनी। Bina guru báṭa ní bina kourhi háṭa ní.

No way (to heaven) without a spiritual guide, and no market (purchaser) without cowries (i.e., money).

This is often made use of by one coming to market without any money with him. Villagers when urged by their wives to go to town and purchase necessaries strengthen their refusal by this phrase. This proverb also reminds them of their need of a spiritual guide.

6. भूल चूक को भारद्वाज गोत्र। Bhúla chúka ko bháradwája gotra.

One who does not know his own descent (gotra) belongs to the Bháradwája gotra.

This is applied to one who is of low birth but becomes a great or notable man, or to one who justifies his actions and mistakes by quoting or inventing traditions which cannot be gainsaid.

7. भूल बिसर जाणो ईश्वर। Bhúla bisara jáṇau Ishwara.

Unconscious errors and mistakes are known to God.

This is a phrase used by pious persons as a prayer for forgiveness. Also by those who have done their best in any undertaking, as an excuse for any mistakes or imperfections.

8. वह न्यापफा की नी जाण क्यात परवाण बींगी नीजाण। Waha nyáfá kí ní jáṇa kyáta parawáṇa bíṇgí níjáṇa.

He who does not know how to tie up his own pantaloons, what kind of a chief will he make? He will not understand his people.

This is applied to the head of a community who does not know even how to look after his own private affairs, and is an incompetent ruler.

9. बैक को देखियूं साग सैणि को देखियूं बाग। Baiká ko dekhyún ságá syaiṇi ko dekhyún bága.

A vegetable seen by a man and a tiger seen by a woman are not to be trusted i.e., should be considered as false reports.

In villages the women cultivate the small fields of vegetables near their houses, and the men know nothing about them. So a man who professes to know where a certain vegetable is to be found is not to be believed any more than a woman who says she has seen a tiger.

10. हाथ काटियो को भाड़ो। Hátha káṭiyo ko bhárho.

One has to pay for having his own hands cut off.

E.g. If hands which are necessary members, are cut off, one has to pay for the operation.

This is used regarding the loss of a thing in constant use expressing a double loss.

11. तीन में न तेर में। Tina men na tera men.

Neither among the "three" nor among the "thirteen": i.e. worth nothing.

E.g. A prostitute was reputed to have thirteen lovers in one direction, and three in another. Over and above the sixteen, she had also contracted friendship with another one secretly, to whom now and then she used to say that he was the dearest of all her friends, and she would leave him a greater share of her property, after her death. In hope of this promise this man rendered her good and constant services. After she was dead all these seventeen appeared to claim her property, but as she had already bequeathed her property, some of it to the thirteen and some to the three, the name of seventeenth man was not found either among the thirteen or among the three, so the man exclaimed that he was neither among the noted thirteen nor the three. This became a proverb for people who think themselves unentitled to a thing, not being included amongst those eligible.

12. घर कि मुरगि दाल बराबर। Ghjara kî muragi dála barábara.

A hen in one's house is like Dála (pulse grain).

Dála is an article commonly kept in the house, and so can be cooked at any time. In the same way one can cook the hen in his own possession at any time he likes.

Applied to things which are easily accessible or procurable and are consequently not much valued.

13. हलका आदमि का नाख में टोसा। Halká ádami ká nákha men̲ ṭosá.

A small-minded man shows anger in his nose.

C.f. "A little pot is soon hot."

14. जुन्यालि रात कुल्यालि थात। Junyáli ráta kulyáli tháta.

A moonlight night and irrigated land.

E.g. A night with the moon shining is equal to irrigated land. Watered land is much valued, as crops on it never fail, and so a man walking in the moonlight will not stumble.

15. सब नर एक सर नै। Saba nara eka sara nai.

All men are not alike.

16. साबास भुलि कंगला पैले पांडा बटि मांगला। Sábása bhuli kaṇgalá paile pán̲ḍá baṭi máṇgalá.

Well done, sister Kan̲galá, we should begin begging from the upper story.

Beg from the rich, the poor have nothing to give.

17. सरप का खुटा हथगुलि का बाल नि देखींदा। Sarapa ká khuṭá hathaguli ká bála ni dekhîṇdá.

No one sees the legs of a snake or the hairs of one's palm.

This means that no one can tell at first glance what genius or skill a man may possess.

18. अपणा हाथ ले अपणो शिर नि मुंडीनो। Apaṇá hátha le apaṇo shira ni munḍîno.

No one can shave his own head himself.

I.e. No one can properly speak his own praise; or in reference to certain actions which cannot be accomplished without the intervention of others (friends or relations).

19. जैकु नि सूझ अपणो घर सो के अकलबर। Jaiku ni sújha apaṇo ghara so ke akalabara.

One who does not take care of his own house, how can he be considered a wise man?

20. पूरब रोग पछम सोग उत्तर जोग दखिन भोग। Púraba roga, pachhama soga uttara joga dakhina bhoga.

The east for disease, the west for sorrow, the north for penance, and the south for pleasure.

This phrase is generally used by the hill people regarding the hills being not a place for enjoyment but a painful place of residence or of penance.

21. सौ सुनार कि एक ल्वार कि। Sau sunára ki eka lwára ki.

One hundred strokes of goldsmith are equal to one of blacksmith.

This is used of one who after much forbearance amply repays another either for good deeds or for bad ones.

22. सबन का गुरु गोबर्धन दास। Sabana ká guru gobardhana dása.

Gobardhan Dás is the spiritual guide of all.

Used to denote the greatest person (the chief) in any business or profession. This is equivalent to "the paw of an elephant covering that of all other animals."

23. आपणा पैर जाणो पराया पैर औणो। Ápaṇá paira jáṇo paráyá paira auṇo.

One goes on his own feet, but he has to come back on another's feet.

I.e. If one goes to another of his own will for some object, it depends on the other to do the business sooner or later.

24. भूत पुजाइ। Bhúta pujái.

Material for ghost-worship.

A ghost is worshipped with half cooked *khicharhi* (made of two parts of rice and one part of *Dála* (pulse) and hastily. For the superstition is that while being thus worshipped the ghost might take possession of the soul of the worshipper, hence his worship is performed in a jungle, or in a place where four roads meet, and very hastily at night. Hence the proverb is applied to half-cooked food.

25. लुण्यू साग तेरि बोइ न निकयो आंख मैकु तकणि। Lun̠yú sága teri boi na nikayo án̠kha maiku takan̠i.

Your mother has not put salt in the vegetables, why do you stare at me with red eyes?

Spoken by the wife to her husband, who is blaming her on account of the food which has in fact been cooked by his mother.

Used in convincing one of his fault or in proving one's own innocence.

26. जोगि का चेला तुमड़ा का मेला। Jogi ká chelá tumarhá ká melá.

The disciples of a Jogi (ascetic) are as numerous as the seeds of a gourd i.e. too many to count.

Used to denote a Jogi's popularity.

27. कां राजा भोज कां गंगा तेलि। Kán̠ rájá Bhoja káṇ Gan̠gá teli.

What comparison is there between Rája Bhoja and Gan̠gá Teli.

E.g. Gan̠gá was a king whose dominion was seized by Rájá Bhoja, who in addition to this had his hands and feet cut off, and left him in the jungle. A *Teli* (oilman) who happened to see Gan̲gá in such a pitiable condition took compassion on him, and also thinking that he could be made use of in driving his bullock, carried him home, and got his wounds healed up by putting him under the treatment of a physician. When the *Teli* died his house was made over to Gan̲gá, hence he is called "Gan̲gá *Teli*". Thence forward Gan̲gá always ridiculed all the acts of Rájá Bhoja and, though himself now only an oilman, tried to oppose him as much as he could on account of the ill-treatment he received from him. Seeing this disposition in Gan̲gá (and finding him always against the Raja) people used to say among themselves Gan̲gá *Teli* cannot be compared with Rájá Bhoja.

Used whenever a small man attempts to measure himself with a greater.

28. नानि पूजा पांचै भांडा ठुलि पूजा पांचै भांडा। Náni pújá pán̲chai bhán̲ḍã ṭhuli pújá pan̲chai bhán̲ḍá.

Five vessels needed in small worship, and five vessels in great worship.

E.g. The same number of utensils are necessary to cook food for one person or many. All men whether great or small have the same necessities and the same fate.

29. लोटियो गोरू छ मणियां। Loṭiyo goru chha maṇiyáṇ.

A cow which has fallen down the hill (and been killed) is always said to have been a good cow, or to have given three seers of milk.

A thing not to be had any more is always praised.

30. कोढ़ि मरि सकनु न बाटो छोड़नु। Koḍhi mari sakanu na báṭo chhorhanu.

The leper can neither die nor get out of the way.

E.g. A leper lay down on a road in such a manner that he almost closed it, every one disliking to pass that way for fear of touching him.

Used of persons or things disliked.

31. गधा पचीसी। Gadhá pachísí.
The donkey age, up to twenty-five years.
Youths are awkward and silly until that age.

32. नौ भरीलि तबडुवली। Nau bharíli taba ḍubalí.
The boat will fill before it sinks.
A man will continue to prosper under iniquities for some time, i.e. his sins and injustice will accumulate before he is ruined by them.

33. पेड़ भ्रष्टा च पांगरौ नर भ्रष्टा तु डांगरौ। Perha bhrashṭá cha pa̲ngarau nara bhrashṭá tu dáṇgara.
A tree depraved becomes a chestnut tree (useless) and a man depraved becomes a Dáṉgara, i.e. one who professes to be inspired by a deity.
E.g. Some people feign to be inspired by gods, and while under their influence dance and predict things, though their prophecies generally turn out false.

34. बूड़ा मरनी भाग सरनी। Búḍhá maraní bhága saraní.
Old people die, but their sayings descend to the progeny.
That is, oral traditions are supposed to be based on facts.

35. ढुंगा में धरनो। Dhu̲ngá me dharano.
To place one on a stone (to ruin him or to deprive him of his wealth).
To eject a man from his house and reduce him to the greatest want.

36. खल साटी भोल ब्याउ। Khala sáṭi bhola byáu.
Paddy in the mortar and marriage tomorrow.
Applicable to any important business for which the people concerned are unprepared as yet.

37. कोई बोद क्या खाऊं कोई बोद के मा खाऊं। Koí boḍa kyá kháúṇ koí boda ke má kháúṇ.
One says "What shall I eat?", another says "What sauce shall I eat with my food?"
Used to compare poor people with those who have plenty.

38. काचो न पाको भसभसो। Kácho na páko bhasbhaso.
Neither raw nor well cooked, but half done.
Applied to a man who is neither one thing nor the other.

MISER

1. हींग कि डलि फुट नी बिन हींग को साग होनी। Hínga ki ḍali phuṭa ní bína híngo ko sága ho ní.
The ball of asafoetida (a spice) must not be broken, but the pottage must nevertheless be seasoned with it.
Applied to one who is a miser, but at the same time an epicure.

2. धेला को ल्यूं पुड़ा भरि खौं। Dhela ko lyúṇ purha bhárí khauṇ.
Would buy a dhela's worth, but would eat a plateful. (a dhela=1/2 of a pice).
Applied to one who is a miser, but at the same time an epicure.

3. लूण डलि फुटौ नै अलूणो साग होव नै। Lúṇa ḍali phuṭau nai alúṇo sága howa nai.
The lump of salt should not be used, but the food should not remain without salt.
Applied to one who is a miser, but at the same time an epicure.

4. खल खाणो कमल ओढ़नु रुपया के जोड़नु। Khala kháṇo kamala oḍhanu rupayá ke jorhanu.
What difficulty is there in earning money? One can earn it by eating chaff and covering himself with a blanket.
Getting rich by scraping and meanness.

MOCK MODESTY

1. नाचण निकसी घूंघट के। Náchaṉa nikasí ghúṇgaṭa ke.
If you have come out to dance why should you veil your face?
Applied to one who after having already undertaken a business abandons it for fear or shame or wishes to do it in private.

Women of good family wear veils, but if one of them comes forward to dance why should she in that case cover her face.

2. जोता खाया इज्जत बचि। Jota khàyá ijjata bachi.

I received a beating with a shoe, but saved my honor.

To be beaten with a shoe is considered very disgraceful. Persons are often purposely dishonoured in this way by their enemies, which is regarded as a public disgrace for them.

The proverb is used by one who is injured or insulted, but not in a public way, and so consoles himself.

MODESTY

1. शरम कि आंख जहाज है भारी। Sharama ki a̲nkha jahája hai bhárí.

An eye full of shame or modesty is heavier than a ship.

Fear of shame prevents many from doing work.

2. शरम की बोइ घड़ा पर मुह घाली रोई। Sharama kî boi gharhá para muha ghàli roî.

The mother of modesty hides her face in a jar when she weeps.

Used to denote that a modest person would rather weep in secret than expose the causes of his doing so.

Due reserve.

MONEY

1. जर में पर। Jara me̲n para.

Money has wings.

I.e. It can accomplish strange and seemingly impossible things.

It is also used to denote that money having wings does not stay, is soon dissipated, and so one ought to invest it in property or ornaments, and thus "cut its wings."

2. धन का अगाड़ि मक्कर नाच। Dhana ká agárhi makkara nácha.

Haughty and wealthy people will dance for the sake of wealth.

I.e. Everyone will condescend to do anything with a view to get wealth or money.

C.f. "It's money that makes the mare to go."

(Dancing in India is never indulged in by respectable people).

MOTIVES

1. चाट बड़ि कि चतुराइ बड़ि। Cháṭa barhi ki chaturái barhi.

Is cleverness greater, or necessity?

This means to say that necessity makes one do odd things in spite of the suggestions of his cunning or cleverness.

C.f. Necessity knows no laws.

A man's skill is not always a match for necessity.

2. पिना पाकदो रौ कवा ककड़ा दो रौ। Piná pákado rau kawá kakarhá do rau.

When the bruised oil seeds are heating in the sun, never mind the clamors of the crows (inviting other crows to eat it).

This is used to confirm another in his purpose against the criticisms of other people who have no concern in it.

3. पातल का चड़ा। Pátala ká charhá.

Chirping birds in the bushes.

I.e. Pay no heed to carping criticism.

MUNIFICENT MEN AND HEROES

1. शूरों का शिर नी दातों का घर नी। Shúroṇ ká shirani dátoṉ ká ghara ní.

Heroes have no heads, and munificent persons have no houses.

I.e. The former do not care for their own lives, and the latter for their own possessions, as in the story related below.:

Story : Shekha Nága is the name of one of the greatest snakes who bears on his head a most brilliant jewel called "Mani" and is so poisonous that any thing or animal that goes near him is burnt to ashes. He is said to be the monarch of all kinds of serpents who inhabit the world known as "*Pátala*" below this world. One day a munificent man of this world happened to go to Shekha Nága, before whom he stood for a minute uninjured, and paid him his obeisance. At this the Shekha Nága was greatly pleased with the man and gave him four rubies as a token of his favour. The quality of one of the rubies was to give its possessor as much grain as he wanted, and the second as much money, the third as large an army, and the fourth as much religious merit as he wished for at any time. As soon as the man with these four rubies came upon this earth he met with a very poor old man who made known his poverty to the munificent man, who at once offered to let him have his choice of one of the rubies, after describing the power and property of each. At this the poor beggar said he would take one after consulting his family, and so he went back to his house, and on consulting his family his wife insisted on having the one which gave the grain, saying that all the family was starving, his son longed for the one which gave the army, saying that by having the army he would bring empires under his subjection, and then would become an emperor; but his daughter-in-law asked for the one which gave money, saying that by having wealth they would live in splendour and comfort. In spite of all these demands the old man wanted virtue and piety. Thus they quarrelled for some time and each of the members insisted upon his own choice. After this the old man having become disgusted with his family went again to the munificent man and said that he would not take any one of the precious stones, but the liberal-minded man knowing the cause from his dejected countenance gave him all four rubies and went away. The poor man returned to his home in great delight, blessing the munificent man who had such little desire for such valuable things.

2. खड़ खाइक भड़ होंदान। Kharha kháika bharha hondána.
A hero is brave even though he has only grass to eat.
Bravery depends upon the disposition of the man, not upon the food he eats.

MUTABILITY OF WORLDLY WEALTH

1. जो देयो या खायो सो आपणो। Jo deyo yá kháyo so ápaṇo.

Only what one has given (in charity) or eaten is one's own.

C.f. "He that giveth to the poor lendeth to the Lord."

MUTUAL RESPECT

1. सास नि राख साड़ि बुवारि नि राख दाढ़ि। Sása ni rákha sárhi buwari ni rákha dáḍhi.

If a father-in-law does not hesitate to pull off the cloth of his daughter-in-law, why should the latter hesitate to pull out the beard of the former.

A father-in-law is a most venerable person to a daughter-in-law, who in turn is also an object of careful regard to him, and neither of them should touch each other.

Applied to mutual respect.

2. हम कसा जसा तुम। Hama kasá jasá tuma.

How am I? As you are to me.

Mutual treatment.

3. जो आपू कन नी चाव वीका बाप कणि नी चाणु जो आपु कन चाव वी का गुलाम कणि चाणु। Jo ápún kana ní cháwa wí ká bápa kaṉi ní cháṇu, jo ápuṉ kana cháwa wí ká guláma kaṇi cháṇu.

If a man dislikes me, I shall not like his father, but of one who likes me I will like even his slave.

C.f. "Love me, love my dog."

4. तू वेत भरि न्यूड़लै त मैं हाथ भरि न्यूड़लो। Tú beta bhari nyúrhalai ta maiṉ hátha bhari nyúrhulo.

If you bend (condescend) a span before me, I will bend (concede) a cubit before thee.

Used of mutual respect.

NATIONAL UNITY

1. जौं जौं राशी ग्यूं ग्यूं राशी। Jauṇ jauṇ ráhí gyúṇ gyúṇ ráshí.

Barley heaped on barley, wheat on wheat.

Applied to national unity or the unity of castes and races. *C.f.* "Birds of a feather flock together."

2. रुपया रुपया कमाव। Rupayá rupayá kamáwa.

Money earns money.

This is a common phrase shewing that money draws money and wisdom draws wisdom. *I.e.* Money goes to money.

NATURAL CAPACITY OR GENIUS

1. सूई को मुख ल्वार पल्यूंद कांडा को मुख को पल्यूंद। Súi ko mukha lwára palyúnda káṇḍá ko mukha ko palyúnda.

The point of a needle is sharpened by a blacksmith, but who sharpens the point of a thorn?

This is applied to a clever and able person who does not need to be tutored for any occasion. *C.f.* "Old foxes want no tutors."

2. खणुवा कुटलो। Khanuwá kuṭalo.

A digging hoe.

(A sharp and fault-finding person).

A nagging and inquisitive disposition.

NATURE OF WORLD AND HUMAN NATURE

1. आप डुबो तौ जग डुबो। Áp ḍubo tau jaga ḍubo.

The world is drowned to him who is drowned.

I.e. The affairs of the world are of no interest to him.

Story : Once a jackal was drowning in a lake, and kept crying "The world is drowning," "the world is drowning." On hearing such an extraordinary exclamation the by-standers (other jackals) wanted to know the meaning of this and asked their dying brother how the world was about to perish. To this the crafty jackal said that he could only tell them from the shore. This made the other jackals all the more inquisitive and impatient, and so by their united endeavours they got their brother ashore, and then asked him the same question again, to which he replied as in the proverb.

2. आप भलो तौ जग भलो। Ápa bhalo tau jaga bhalo.

A good man finds the world good.

C.f. "Good mind good find".

3. आपणा मन ले जाणनि परया मन कि बात। Ápaṇá mana le jánani paryá mana ki báta.

One's own feelings towards others suggest what others feel towards us.

3. वार कौणी पार कौणी पकोड़ी जोलि कखि नि पौणी। Wára kauṇí pára kauṇí pakorhí joli kakhi ni pauṇí.

Kauṇi (a coarse kind of millet grown in the hills) here, kauṇi there, but sweetmeats are no where to be had.

This is used to denote that there are many people in the world, but none who are willing to help one.

NEW COMPARED WITH OLD

1. नोला गोरू का नौ पुला घास। Naulá goru ká nau pulá ghása.

Nine bundles of grass for a new cow.

Great care taken of any thing newly obtained.

2. नयां नौ दाम पुराणा छ दाम। Nayán nau dáma puráṇá chha dáma.

New coins fetch nine-fold, and the old ones only six.

E.g. New things are more valued than old ones. Here *"dáma"* means value.

NOVELTY

1. नि पौणियां ले पायो आधि रात उठि बेर खायो। Ni pauṇiyán le páyo ádhi ráta uṭhi bera kháyo.

One gets up at night and eats what was not procurable in his own home.

Eagerness for a new thing.

2. पूंजि है ब्याज प्यारो पूत है नाति प्यारो। Púnji hai byája pyáro púta hai náti pyáro.

Interest is valued more than capital, and a grandson is dearer than a son.

I.e. Any small addition to one's possessions is valued more than things already in hand.

OBSTINATE AND STUBBORN PEOPLE

1. गाली ढाली मैं नी दींदो पर पूस की पोली ना खाये। Gáli ḍháli mai ni dindo para púsa ki poli ná kháye.

I am not abusing you, but may you not live to eat the treacle cakes made in January.

E.g. Obstinate men pride themselves on not withdrawing the language they have used.

Once an obstinate beggar addressed a great man, whose complexion was black and who was mounted on an elephant, thus: "O, Mr. Charcoal (referring to the black colour of his skin) give me something." The great man, being provoked by this address, told him to hold his tongue. On this the beggar rejoined "O Mr. Charcoal, do not crackle." This stubborness on the part of the beggar astonished the great man and made him reflect. He concluded that the best thing to do would be to rid himself of the nuisance of the beggar's insolence by giving him money, so threw him two rupees. The beggar, delighted with the gift, blessed him saying "Remain red for ever," (again representing him as a piece of live charcoal).

2. राज हट जोग हट तिरिया हट। Rája haṭa joga haṭa tiriyá haṭa.

The firmness of a king, an ascetic, and a woman are alike.

They will prevail in the end.

3. लाटा कि कड़ कड़। Láṭá ki karha karha.

The indifference (stubbornness) of a dumb man.

I.e. A dumb man or an idiot will, in spite of instructions to the contrary, continue to do a thing in his own clumsy way. Used of one who spoils his work by disregarding the advice of others who are his superiors in knowledge and experience.

OLD AGE

1. जैको बूढ़ो तैको कूड़ो । Jaiko búḍho tai ko kúrho.

So long as there is an old person in a family the reputation and prosperity of the house is sure.

Story : Once a man went to espouse a daughter of another who granted his request on the condition that the bridegroom should bring no old man with him along with the marriage procession, but bring hundred strong men who should fulfil or accomplish all the conditions he might require of them, on the marriage day. On the fulfilment of all the conditions he would give his daughter in marriage, and not otherwise. On hearing this, the would-be bridegroom came home and consulted all the old and wise people. All were of one opinion that it was necessary for at least one old man to be present to give advice in a case of emergency. So they managed to take an old man to the bride's house by having him concealed within a drum. (According to the custom the bridegroom accompanied by his kinsmen, and friends, with drums, trumpets etc goes to the bride's house in order to bring her to his home. This procession is called *"Baryát"* (party of the bridegroom). This party is well fed, and gratifed with pecuniary presents or rewards by the father or guardian of the bride). As soon as the marriage procession arrived at the bride's house, the bride's father supplied hundred goats, fifty seers of rice, and a hundred seers of *Ghi* to the hundred strong men who had gone there with the bridegroom, and said that if they would eat all the food he had given they would obtain his daughter for the intended bridegroom in marriage, and if not, they should return to their home without the bride. At this the party felt perplexed, but kept silent in order to secretly obtain counsel from the old man. The old man told them, Do not be afraid of this, say to the man 'yes we will do so'. Then kill one goat and divide the meat among the hundred men, and each of you must then eat a little, concealing some in the mouth to be afterwards spitted out. In this way you will be able to consume the hundred goats, fifty seers of rice, and hundred seers of *ghi*. They acted as advised, and thus consumed the whole quantity. After this, when the marriage had been performed, the bride's father found out the trick which had been effected through the ingenuity of the old man whom they had secretly taken with them. But he was helpless, for then the marriage could not be cancelled on any account. Hence the necessity of old people as advocated by the proverb. *C.f.* "Old men for counsel, young men for war."

2. जैको बूढ़ो बौली तैको कुड़ो बौली । Jai ko buḍho bauli taiko kúrho bauli.

When an elder of a household becomes mad all the members of the family are sure to become so.

Hence the necessity that the head of a family should lead an exemplary life, as all his dependents will be sure to imitate his conduct whether good or bad.

3. बरस भया असी अकल गई नसी । Barasa bhayá asî akala gaî nasî.

When a man reaches the age of eighty his intellect leaves him.

It is said that God at first appointed forty years as the limit of life for men, bullocks, dogs, cats, and owls. In conversation together, man expressed to the other creatures his dissatisfaction with the brief age allotted to him, saying that forty years was too short for an intellectual being who had such responsibilities to fulfil both to God and man. On the other hand, the bullock, dog, cat, and owl were discontented because their age was too long, seeing that their life was so full of toils and annoyances; therefore they desired to be limited to twenty years of existance. God granted their wishes, and reduced the age of the four beasts to twenty years each, adding the surplus to man's life, which thus was extended to hundred twenty years. So it comes to pass that during the first forty years of a man's life (his own age) he lives happily and fortunately. During the next twenty years (the bullock's period) he is full of anxiety and ambition, toiling like a bullock for worldly advantages. From sixty to eighty (the dog's period) he is without sense of honour or discrimination, caring only to suit his own convenience. From eighty to hundred his character becomes like that of a cat, timid, humble and pitiable, and from a hundred to a hundred and twenty he resembles an owl, being purblind and stupid.

4. दाना को बोल्यूं औंला को स्वाद। Dáná ko bolyún̲ aun̲lá ko swáda.

The advice of an old man is like the Aun̲lá fruit (the tree emlia myrobalan, phyllanthus emblica).

I.e. Though unpleasant to the taste, if eaten yields good results.

5. बुढ़ो कौ तरूण नि सौ बुढ़ाकी लाख रौ। Buḍho kau taruṇa ni sau buḍhá ki lákha rau.

Whatever an old man says is unbearable by a young man, but the saying of the former turns out to be true in a lac of instances.

Young people ought to mind what old people tell them.

6. दानो दुशमन भलो नादान दोस्त बुरो। Dáno dushmaṇa bhalo nádána dosta buro.

An enemy in an old person is better than a friend in a child.

It is better to have an old (or wise) man for an enemy than a young (or foolish) person for a friend.

ONE IN DISTRESS WISHES ANOTHER TO BE SO

(a) नगर कि रांडौ मैं जसि होव। Nagara ki ránḍau mai jasi howa.

Oh cursed women of the town, be like me.

(b) है जा पड़ोसी मै जसो। Haijá parhosî mai jaso.

Oh, neighbour be like me.

A bad character or deformed person wishes others to be like himself.

The story narrated below will illustrate the proverb:

Once a man who had his nose cut off for some offence happened to come in a city, where he was teased by being given the nickname "Nakaṭá" (noseless). For some time he patiently endured the disgrace but eventually invented a plan of revenging himself upon the residents of the town. So he sat down like a saint in a conspicuous place of the city, and acted as if he was absorbed in the contemplation of God. Now and then he used to address the gods thus. "O Vishnu, you are welcome. O Mahadeva, you are welcome, O Párbati, (wife of Mahádeva), O Brahmáni, (wife of Brahma), (in this way addressing many important deities). "You are welcome, come and sit down here" pointing out a particular place for each with his two hands as a form of respect, and thanking them for their trouble and condescension in manifesting themselves to him. He did this constantly every day. This conduct attracted the attention of the passers-by, and gradually the news spread throughout the city and the country. At first the people did not believe him, but seeing him so firm in his faith, piety, and adoration, at last some people began to pay some attention and feel eager about the matter, and so they enquired from the feigned saint into the cause, and said that they did not see the deities while he was addressing them as if present. To this he said that no one could see the gods with the bodily eye until he got heavenly eyes by having become a devotee. This naturally induced some to become devotees of God in order to have a constant vision of Him like the man, and so many of them besought him that he would have mercy on them also. The man said that they should become his disciples by learning the religious enchantments (fascination of deities) from him. On this many of them volunteered to be his converts, but the noseless man said to then, "O my dear brothers, it is very difficult for one to become a truly religous man amidst the luxuries and endearments of worldly things. No one can ever see the deities unless he divests himself of all worldly ambition and desire for the sake of his god. The chief source of pride of these worldly honors is the nose (the root of haughtiness and vanities) which ought to be got rid of first of all in order to render man an humble and worthy being in the sight of the deities. This is the first (most important) preliminary ordeal one has to go through in order to deserve and merit personal conversation with the deities. For as soon as one's nose is removed or cut off he becomes absolved of all sins and sinful sensations." One man at first fell a victim to this plot, (i.e. became a convert by having his nose cut), and to his utter grief found his hopes of seeing the deities to be utterly false. On enquiry from his *Guru* (spiritual guide) the new disciple was told by the man, "O my dear son, (disciple) do you not know that a leper wishes to have the whole world become like himself, and so a sinner? Since you have been unfortunately imposed upon, now you should also make the same profession, so that more men may become like ourselves, and that then no one will have to cast a slur on any one of us singly, for then there will be more men like ourselves in the world." After this both of the men (*Nakaṭas)* began to play the trick conjointly, and thus entrap a good many men in their clutches, until the news reached the King and his wise statesmen, who at once put a stop to this misbehaviour of the noseless sect by driving them out of their city and country.

2. बूढ़ो बैल न आप लाग न औरन कणि लागण दे। Búḍho baila na ápa lága na aurana kaṉi lágaṇa de.

An old bullock being unable himself to woo prevents others from doing so.

A dog in the manger.

3. न आप काट न काटी सौ। Na ápa káṭa na káṭi sau.

He neither cuts himself nor suffers others to cut.

Used of a presumptuous and envious man who will neither do a thing himself, nor allow it to do done by others.

C.f. "A dog in the manger."

4. गिरि पड़छ्यूं सज अैगेछ। Giri parhachhyún saja aigechha.

I fell down, but found the place I fell on comfortable.

Once a jackal while walking along the top of a mountain accidentally fell down a precipice and was caught in the wild creepers below. In the attempt to get up, he got more and more entangled in the plants. At last, being quite exhausted in his efforts to get out, he was obliged to remain there. Other jackals who came by, on seeing their brother thus seated below, called out to him to come up and join their company. To this call of theirs, he said that he would not find a more comfortable place in the world, and so he would not quit it. This statement of his tempted the other jackals to fall down the precipice and be thus entangled like their brother who was greatly pleased at the success of his trick.

Applies to one who himself being in trouble desires that others should share it with him, or tries to get others into the same plight.

C.f. The fable of the Tailless Fox.

5. आपण जयां की नी कका का रयां की छ। Ápaná jayán kí ní kaká ká rayán kí chha.

I do not complain of my own ruin, but why in the world has my uncle escaped?

The regret of one fallen into misfortune that others do not share it with him.

ONE'S OWN DEEDS ETC. NEVER BAD

1. अपणा दै कणि खटो क्वे नि बतूनु। Apaṇá dai kaṉi khaṭo kwe ni batúnu.

No one calls his own curds sour.

E.g. A merchant never says his commodities are bad. *i.e.* no one exposes his own faults and defects. *C.f.* "Every cook praises his own stow." "No fishwife calls out stinking fish."

ONE'S OWN FAULTS AND FAILINGS

1. आपणो सुनो खोटो परखनेर के दोष। Ápaṇo suno khoṭo parkhanera ke dosha.

It is no fault of the assayer when one's own gold is counterfeit.

This proverb is generally used of one who rightly loses his case, or gets punished for his real guilt by a court of justice.

OPPORTUNE ACTS

1. बाप को ब्या करियुं सुबेर को मुख धोयुं। Bápa ko byá karyun̲ subera ko mukha dhoyuṇ.

A marriage arranged by one's father, and ablutions performed in the morning.

No Hindu according to custom can eat anything until he has washed his mouth, hands, and feet, after having got up in the morning: but if he has performed these ablutions in the morning he can eat anything at any time during the day; and in the same way, if one is provided with a wife by his father, he can utilize her services at any time and is also saved the trouble of providing himself with one afterwards.

OPPORTUNITY

1. बूंद गे बिलायत सो। Bún̲da ge biláyata so.

The drop has gone to a foreign country.

This proverb arose from the story noted below:

Once some perfumers brought perfume for sale to a king, who bought some, but out of what he had purchased one drop fell on the ground, and the king at once tried to take it up with his own fingers from the floor. This act on the part of the king was considered very mean by his ministers and all others including the perfume-sellers. In order to remove the impression, the ministers afterwards purchased many thousand Rupees' worth of perfume from the same strangers, and got it sprinkled all over the royal stables in order to augment their master's fame for munificence and liberality. Nevertheless the news of the drop had already gone to foreign countries through those foreigners. Hence this proverb suggests a careful, reserved and wise dealing with a stranger, and shows that an opportunity once lost cannot be regained. *E.g.* Ill news travels fast.

2. अपणो हाथ जगन्नाथ। Apaṇo hátha jagannátha.

One's own hand is as that of Jagannath, (the Lord of the world).

The word Jagannath means God. When God is pleased with a man, He showers wealth and blessings on him; so when a man has permission to help himself he will do so to the utmost. A man will bestow on himself benefits when he has the opportunity, as bountifully as God does.

Self-help.

3. बार बरस दिल्ली में रयो भाड़ झौंको। Bára barasa dilli mel̲ rayo bhárha jhauṇko.

He lived in Delhi for twelve years, only to heat the oven of a grain parcher.

I.e. He accomplished nothing for himself. Delhi being the capital of the Moghal Kings, people thought that by going to Delhi they could make their fortunes. This is applied to one who has not availed himself of a very good opportunity of bettering his circumstances.

4. बखत चूको जुग को फेर। Bakhata chúko juga ko phera.

One who loses an opportunity may be delayed for ages.

5. जब छयो रैंठो तब तू नि आइ बैठो। Jaba chhayo raiṉṭho taba tú ni ái baiṭho.

When I had Raiṇṭhá (a kind of savoury dish) you did not come.

You did not come to me when I was in prosperity, and could benefit you.

6. आपणा पास आई गंगा में नै लीणु। Ápaṇá pása ái gaṇgá men̲ nai lín̲u.

One ought to bathe in the Ganges when it comes to him.

Seize every opportunity (of gaining merit etc.)

7. घड़ि बचि त घड़ो बचो। Ghari bachi ta gharho bacho.

If a small pot escapes the large jar may escape.

I.e. If the critical or dangerous moment is passed then there is no danger thereafter for years.

(A gharhi is equal to twenty-four minutes).

This is a play on the words gharái a small pot, and gharho aa jar, gharhi a small and light copper cup with a hole at its bottom which is placed in a tubful of water in order to measure time. It will fill with water in twenty-four minutes and then sink down.

PARAMOURS

1. स्येणी को जार जूता को गार। Syain̲í ko jára jútá ko gára.

One's wife's paramours and pebbles in the shoe (are very troublesome and embittering to the heart).

2. बदल्यां देव की घाम चड़ाक ढांटा मैंस की लाठी धड़ाक। Badalyán̲ dewa kí ghháma charháka dhán̲ṭá maisa kí láṭhí dharháka.

Sunstroke on a cloudy day is like the stroke given by a paramour.

A woman can willingly bear the ill treatment of her husband, on the consideration that she is married to him, but a stroke from her paramour, (or one with whom she lives without marriage bond) is unbearable, as sunstroke on a cloudy day causes more harm than on a bright day.

PATIENCE

1. भूखो बोद वली गदनी अघाणो बोद पली गदनी। Bhúkho boda wali gadaní agháṇo boda palí gadaní.

The hungry traveller wishes to eat his food at the first spring he meets, but the one who is not hungry wishes to eat at the next.

The needy man has no patience.

PATRONAGE

1. पहाड़ कि ओट सीक। Pahárha ki oṭa sīka.

A small stick hides a mountain from one's eye.

E.g. A small stick if placed close to one's eye will conceal a mountain from his sight.

Used as an appreciation of patronage, however small it may be, which works miracles and gives one encouragement and consolation.

C.f. "A drowning man will catch at a straw." "Little strokes fell great oaks."

Used also in the same sense as, "To make a mountain of a mole hill."

2. कुकुड़ा कि फाल सिना का झाल। Kukurhá ki phála siná ká jhála.

The flight of a cock is only into the next bush of Sina.

The cock when alarmed takes shelter in the next bush. *i.e.* a poor man or any person in distress seeks the help of his immediate patron, whosoever he may be.

3. काजि कि दौड़ मसजिद तक। ·Káji ki daurha masajida taka.

The flight of a Cadi is as far as the Mosque (no futher).

I.e. The Cadi's course ends at the Mosque.

That is, one in need or distress resorts only to his patron for help.

4. किला का जोर बाछि बुरक। Kilá ká jora báchhi buraka.

The calf jumps with all his might because he knows the peg to which he is tied will keep him from falling.

Applied to one's firmness or zeal in a certain business, which he shows on account of the patronage or help of another greater than himself.

PECULIARITIES OF LOW HILL-PEOPLE

1. जां खसियाले द पै कयो फिर एक घड़ि नि माननो। Jáṇ khasiyá le da pai kayo phira eks gharhi ni mánano.

When a Khasiya says "Da Pai" then nothing will stop his rage.

A *Khasiyá* is an illiterate hill villager who when ill-treated will forbear for a long time, but when he is unable to control his anger any longer he will say "Da Pai" ("very good, see now") and then nothing in the world will stop him from assaulting the offender.

Used as a caution against enraging him.

(For Khasiya, see Introduction).

2. खसिया की रीस भैंस कि तीस। Khasiyá ki rísa bhainsa ki tísa,

The anger of a Khasiyá (a rustic villager) is like the thirst of a buffalo.

A *khasiyá* when in rage will not spare any one, just as a buffalo drinks up all the water of a pool from which he drinks.

3. ओछी जात करौ उत्पात। Ochhí játa karau utpâta.

A mean man raises quarrels, (and a noble person does what is noble).

Low birth will show itself in vile deeds.

4. पहाड़ि कि नै सौ रुपया कि। Pahárhi ki nai sau rupayá ki.

A hill-man's "No" is worth a hundred rupees.

E.g. If a hill man once refuses to do a certain thing, he will not do it, even if one tries one's utmost to pursuade him to do it.

5. पहाड़ समान दाता नै बिना लठी दिनेर नै। Pahárha samána dátá nai biná laṭhí dinera nai.

No country so liberal as the hills (hill-men), but they will not give any thing without a stick.

This is used to describe the nature of the hill-people, who will give a thing when they are forced to give it, but not otherwise.

6. सुंगरा का पोथिला छारा कि बाण। Suṇgará ká pothilá chhárá ki báṇa.

Young pigs are accustomed to ashes.

Applied to people of low and mean families, by way of criticism of their bad conduct and evil habits. For the evil and filthy habits to which they have become accustomed for a long time become a second nature which they are quite unable to forsake afterwards.

7. भाट का बाड़्या भितनाइ लींड गाड़्या । Bháṭa ká bárhyá bhitanái ľiṇḍa gárhyá.

If a beggar's (or bard's) family increases they ease themselves inside their houses.

I.e. People from a mean family are accustomed to live mean lives. A *bháta* is a particular caste of *Khassia Brahmans* who beg from any and everyone, by singing their praises, and will even take money out of a dead man's hands, a practice abhorrent to other Brahmanas.

8. भुजेलो बाढ़त बाढ़ नितर खरस्याणा तभि होव । Bhujelo báḍhata báḍha nitara kharsyáṇá tabhi howa.

Let a pumpkin swell as much as it will, whether it be large or small it will shrivel up all the same.

The nature of a thing cannot be changed. The evil nature of a man will not change in spite of all appearances to the contrary.

9. डूम की डुम्याण बोक्या कि बोक्याण कखि नीं जांदी । Ḍúma ḱi ḍumyáṇa bokyá ki bokyáṉa kakhi ńi jáṉḍi.

The peculiar smell of a Dúm and a he-goat never dies out.

The evil propensities of people of low families.

10. डूम की तौली बोद कि बिठाणा कबारि जौं । Ḍúma ḱi tauľi boda ki biṭháṉá kabári jauṉ.

The Ḍúm's vessel says, "When shall I go to the dwellings of the Biṭhas?"

A Ḍúm is always anxious to mix with the Biṭhas (Patricians) in any way possible. Applied to low caste people who are anxious to be allied with the higher castes. Even an injury done by a *Biṭha* to a Ḍum is welcomed by him so long as it also disgraces the Biṭha caste.

11. मेरो नौ छ भदू मैं क्या बोदूं क्या कदूं। Mero náu chha Bhadú mai kyá bodún kyá kadúṇ.

My name is Bhadú, what I say or do no one knows.

Applied to people of low family who cannot be trusted. For they have no sense of shame in them.

12. येकै बांस का डाला सूपा एकै बांस कि टोपरि। Ekai báṇsa ká ḍálá súpá ekai bánsa ki ṭopari.

Big and small baskets, and fans, are made of the same bamboo.

Similarly of members of the same family. *C.f.* "A chip of the old block."

13. येकै थैलि का बट्टा। Ekai thaili ká baṭṭá.

Weights of the same bag.

Same meaning as above. *C.f.* "Tarred with the same brush."

14. बांस का खूंट बांस। Bánsa ká khunṭa báṇsa.

A bamboo grows out of the stump of a bamboo.

As father so is son.

15. जैको जसो तैको तसो। Jaiko jaso taiko taso.

Such as his (father).

Same meaning as above.

16. जां बम्मण तां लंघण जां रजपूत तां मजबूत। Jáṇ bammaṇa tán laṇghaṇa jáṇ rajpúta tán majabúta.

Starving where Brahmans (reside), everything to be had where Rajputs (reside).

E.g. Brahmanas are very lazy, and therefore live on begging (priesthood) whereas Rajputs are very industrious and have every necessary in their homes available at any time. If a traveller happens to be in a village settled by Brahman's alone he is sure to starve there, but if he settles in one of Rajputs (now also called Khassias, *i.e.* coolie race) he will get all kinds of food.

This is also used by Rajputs in regard to Brahmanas, inasmuch as the latter being engaged in their religious duties take their meal late, while the former who have nothing of the kind to do take their meal in good time.

17. खसिया भोला देलो टोपि मांगलो चोला। Khasiyá bholá delo ṭopi ma<u>n</u>galo cholá.

The Khasiyá (coolie or rustic) is so simple that he will demand a long coat in exchange for a cap.

An ironical expression meaning that rogues combine great cunning with apparent simplicity.

18. पहाड़ को राजा खाति माल को राजा हाथि। Pahárha ko Rájá kháti mála ko Rájá háthi.

A Kháti king in the hills, and a wild elephant in the Bhábara (plains commencing from the foot of the hills).

E.g. Before the amalgamation of the kingdom of Kumaun by Rájá Kalyan Chand of the Chand dynasty into one state, Khati, a race of Rájput origin held sway for a time in the hills, while the plains below the hill ranges were full of wild elephants, and so people dreaded to pass through them. Hence the Kháti tribes of the hills was appropriately compared to the wild elephant of the Bhábar.

19. खसिया मित्र नै गाण पवित्र नै। Khasiyá mitra nai gáṇa pawitra nai.

The Khasiyá will never prove to be a friend, nor a croton holy.

20. जातन में बड़िया सागन में जड़िया। Játana me Barhiyá ságana me jarhiyá.

Of all castes the barhiyá (gardener) (is the worst) and of all vegetables the jarhiyá (roxburgh).

The gardener or *Máli* caste is very selfish and unworthy of confidence, and so is the vegetable *Jarhiyá* which is bitterish in taste and unwholesome owing to its generating catarrh, colic, etc. when eaten.

21. खसिया मनायो ठंगा ठंगो। Khasiyá manáyo ṭha<u>n</u>ga ṭha<u>n</u>go.

A Khasiyá (villager) when entreated becomes ungracious.

I.e. Polite requests are lost on the villager who will only serve you after being threatened.

PERSEVERENCE AND DETERMINATION

1. साक रौ संतान जनरौ। Sáka rau saṇtána jana rau.
Let fame or reputation be established, though sons should perish.
Applied by one who is determined to fight out his case to the end even at the risk of losing his own sons or property, for he wishes his own name to live after him on account of the affair.

2. शिर जाव शिरड़ी नि जाव। Shira jáwa shirarhi ni jáwa.
Let one's head perish, but not his determination.
C.f. "Try, try, and try again."
Illustration: Once a bird known as *"Sitolá"* had seven young ones in a nest built in one of the branches of a tree. She brought seven grains of millet to feed them with. Six of the young ones ate each its share, but the seventh grain fell into a crack of the tree from which the bird could not extract it. She went to a blacksmith and requested him to cut the tree, but he refused to do so. Then she appealed to the king of the realm to fine the blacksmith for his non-compliance with her request. But the king refused to do so. Then she went to a mouse and requested him to gnaw the bed of the king. The mouse also refused to grant her request. Then she went to a cat and requested her to kill the mouse, she also declined to do so. After this she entreated a crow to take out the cat's eyes, but the crow also refused to comply with her request. Then she went and requested the fire to scorch the feathers of the crow; the fire also refused. On this she went to the waterspring entreating it to quench the fire, and on its refusal she requested a ram to destroy the spring, on the refusal of the ram she requested a leopard to kill the ram, the leopard, on this, said "Very good, shew me the ram, I will do so." Then she brought the leopard to the ram, who

being frightened at the presence of the leopard agreed to destroy the spring, which in its turn to save itself from being injured promised to quench the fire. Then the fire promised to scorch the feathers of the crow, the crow, to pull out the eyes of the cat, the cat to kill the mouse, the mouse to gnaw the bed of the king, and the king to punish the blacksmith, and the blacksmith to cut the tree and take out the grain of millet from its crevice. So the bird succeeded in her determination.

PETTY TRANSACTIONS

1. तीन तेपौणा पोणे चार। Tína tepauṇá pauṇe chára.

Three Tepauṇa if added to Rs. 3 amount to Rs. 3-12-0 (three Rupees and twelve annas) only.

E.g. A *Tepauṇa* is 1/3 of twelve annas (or 3/4 of a Rupee). Rupee 3 is a very small capital. If one Rupee brings four annas profit (the highest) the whole will not amount in any way to more than Rs. 3-12-0.

Applied to a small business in derision. *C.f.* "Six of the one and half a dozen of the other."

POLYGAMY

1. एक ब्या चक्र बरती दुइ ब्या कुकुर गती। Eka byá chakra baratí dui dyá kukuragatí.

He who has one wife is as an emperor, but he who has two wives is treated like a dog.

Once a thief entered the house of a man who had two wives. One occupied the lower story of the house and the other the upper one. When the husband after taking his evening meal began to ascend the steps to the upper story (intending to go to his other wife) the one who lived below began to drag him down. Seeing this, the other wife, who lived in the upper story, came and began to pull him upwards. Witnessing the amusing scene for some minutes the thief left the house, and proclamied the proverb to the people at large.

POOR PEOPLE

1. जोगि जोगि लड़ा पत्तर पत्तर फुटा। Jogi jogi larhá pattara pattara phúṭá.

When Jogis (ascetics) fight with each other their vessels in which they collect their alms) are broken and being of little value no great damage is done.

Applied to quarrels or law suits between poor persons.

2. पांड़ा का सिखाया वोबरा का सठ। Pánḍá ká sikháyá wobará ká saṭha.

Those of the upper story were taught, but those of the lower story became clever.

Sons of rich and well-to-do men notwithstanding the care and expense bestowed on their education do not profit by it, whereas the sons of poor men who listen attentively to the instruction of the former become learned.

3. पतलि छांछ पाणी नि स्वाव। Patali chhánchha páṇí ni swáwa.

Thin butter milk does not admit to more water being mixed with it.

A very poor man cannot afford to support anyone but himself.

4. लेष्टिया की चरबी घेरचा में। Lesṭiyá ki charbi gherchá men.

The fat of the Lesṭiyá (a very small bird) is in its Ghercha, i.e. a small sac in the intestines.

Poor people need to hide away very carefully the little money they may have.

5. मारो वेसणि जैको नि रोदारो। Máro wesaṇi jai ko ni rodáro.

Kill or beat one who has none to cry for him, i.e., who has no one to support or protect him.

This phrase is ironically used when a helpless poor person is injured.

6. मडुवा को भाव को पूछ। Maḍúwá ko bháwa ko púccha.

Who will enquire the rate of Maḍúvá (millet)?

This means, who cares for a poor person? Maḍúwá is a very cheap coarse grain eaten only by the poor.

C.f. Rattle his bones over the stones.

"He's only a pauper whom nobody owns."

7. आरसि मुख सब देखनी तवा मुख क्वे नि देखनु। Árasi mukha saba dekhaní tawá mukha kwe ni dekhanu.

No one need look into an iron oven (which is sooty), instead of a looking glass.

E.g. No one sides with or helps a poor and distressed person, but every one naturally wishes to please a party in position and power.

8. गरीब ले भिड़ा में चढ़नु भिड़ो उधरि गयो त पलि पलि बैठि जाणु। Gariba le bhirhá maṇ chaḍhnu bhirho udhari gaya ta pali pali baiṭhi jáṇu.

A poor man may mount on a wall; but if the wall becomes insecure he should put himself in a safe place.

A poor man should not fight for a thing of which he has been deprived by force though it was his by right.

9. गरीब का दश काल। Garíba ká dasha kalá.

A poor person has ten deaths or oppressors.

I.e. Every man oppresses poor people.

10. गरीब का ब्या मैं नौ खेचला। Garíba ká byá men̲ nau khechalá.

There are nine obstacles in the way of the marriage of a poor man.

In arranging for a marriage many persons or relatives are concerned and have to be consulted. A poor man, not having the means to please all, cannot expect them to be in his favour, and consequently many obstacles are thrown in his way.

11. घोड़ा कि लात घोड़ै सहारंछ। Ghorhá ki láta ghorhai saharan̲chha.

A horse's kick can be borne by a horse only.

A poor person cannot fight with a stronger one.

12. घड़ा मा ढूंगो त घड़ा की रांड ढूंगा मा घड़ो त घड़ा की रांड।
Ghará má ḍhúngo ta gharhá kí ránḍa ḍhúngá má gharho ta gharhá ki ránḍa.

If an earthen jar is struck by a stone it will break, and if the jar strikes the stone, it will suffer the same fate.

Poor people have no chance against the rich. *C.f.* "It is useless striking your head against a stone wall."

13. नंगा सितनी उज्याड़ में। Naṇgá sitaní ujyárha men.

Naked men sleep in the jungle.

E.g. They have no fear of being robbed of any thing. Applied to one who has nothing to lose.

C.f. "You cannot take the breeks off a highlander." (Scotch proverb.)

14. निमनसी को मदन सिंघ। Nimanasí ko madana siṇgha.

Madan Singha (is called for) when no other is to be had.

Madan Singh is an inferior man.

15. कुकुड़ा सों तकुवा को डाम। Kukurhá soṇ ṭakuwá ko ḍáma.

The prick of a thin hot iron bar is enough for a hen to bear.

A *Takúwá* is a thin iron bar which is attached to the hand of a spindle. "*Dáma*" is a slight burn with a hot iron as a remedy for pain in different parts of the body. If a hen is burned even with the thin iron of the spindle it is enough for her. The meaning is that even a little loss is enough for a poor man.

16. ये जंगल में मै न बाप अलख निरंजन आपी आप। Ye jaṇgala men mai na bápa alakha niraṇjana ápí ápa.

Orphaned in this jungle, unnoticed, alone, entirely by himself.

This is said by one who thinks himself helpless in this world, which he considers as a desert.

17. अंधा की ज्वे कि पति परमेश्वर का हाथ। Aṇdhá kí jwe ki pati parmeshwara ká hátha.

God alone is the protector of a blind man's wife.

Said of poor people when oppressed by the rich.

18. स्वर्ग को छुटो पताल को फुटो। Swarga ko chhuṭo patála ko phúṭo.

Let fall from the sky, and broken on the earth.

Used of one who is extremely poor and has no one to support or help him. One who does not even know his own parentage or is ashamed of it, and is also in very poor circumstances.

19. मेरो नौ छ पदि इचे कदुं अलखण भिंडे होंद बदीं। Mero nau chha padi iche kadun alakhaṇa bhiṇde hoṇda badi.

My name is only Padi, but for my slight fault I am greatly defamed.

Said by one bemoaning himself as a poor and humble man who is constantly blamed for slight faults, while great men do much worse things with impunity.

One law for the rich and another for the poor.

20. गरीब का चेला नींद को पोश। Garíba ká chelá ní̱nda ko posha.

For the children of the poor, sleep is the only nourishment.

Poor people should not disturb their peace of mind by undertaking such works as lead to quarrels and risks which they are unable to cope with.

21. छोरा को ज्यू तुमड़ि को घ्यू। Chhorá ko jiú tumrhi ko ghyú.

The pluck of an orphan is only equal to the ghi contained in a tumrhi, i.e. very little.

A *Tumrhi* is a very small vessel cut out of a long pumpkin. A poor man has very little courage to undertake any thing.

22. ढोल दमांउ मा कमच्यों को राग। Ḍhola damaú̱n má kamchyo̱n ko rága.

The soft song of the Kimcha (fiddlers and minstrels) amidst the beating of big drums.

In other words the voice of a *Tuti* (a small bird) in a house full of sounding drums.

Applied by one who thinks himself too poor to have his prayers and petitions heard by a great man or officer, who is inaccessible to him. Khimcha means the players of musical instruments who accompany singing and dancing girls.

23. दुबला कि ज्वे पंचु कि भाबि। Dubalá ki jwe paṇchuṉ ki bhábi.

The wife of a poor man is addressed by all as "Bhábi" or "Bahu" (i.e. elder brother's wife).

Every one looks on her with bad intentions, and amuses himself by chaffing her, which he would not dare to do in the case of a rich man's wife.

24. नंगो कूद उज्याड़ में। Naṉgo kúda ujyárha meṇ.

One naked does not hesitate to trespass.

E.g. One who is very poor and has neither property nor family will not hesitate to commit a wrongful act for he has nothing to lose.

25. के पिद्दि के पिद्दि को झोल। Ke piddi ke piddi ko jhola.

What is a piddi, and how much soup can be made from it?

Piddi is a very small bird.

Used as ridicule when comparing small things with greater.

26. किरमोला सों मूत कि रेवाड़। Kirmolá soṇ múta ki rewárha.

A stream of urine is an unfordable river to an ant.

Used by poor people to express their helplessness to do even a small thing.

27. नंगा नौ निचोड़ के। Naṉgá nau nichorha ke.

What cloth will a naked man wring dry if he bathes?

Applied to one who, having no property whatever, incurs debt. He will have nothing to pay back.

Illustration. Once a washerman in hope of finding employ and livelihood repaired to a certain colony inhabited by naked people, called "Digambars", have nothing else but the eight directions (east, west, north, south, northeast, south-east, northwest and southwest) for their clothes. The man finding the inhabitants in such a condition lost no time in quitting the place.

POVERTY

1. आप मियां मागनु फिर भैर खड़ो दरवेश। Ápa miyán̲ maganú phira bhaira kharho darwaisha.

A beggar is standing at the door of a man who himself lives by begging.

C.f. "Beggars cannot help beggars."
"Can the blind lead the blind?"

2. ढुंगा में धोयो पोका में उबायो। Ḍhúngá meṇ ḍhoyo poká men̲ ubáyo.

Washed on a stone and dried on his loins.

E.g. A man is so poor as to have only one *dhoti* (cloth to cover the loins) which he is obliged to wash when bathing, but having only one he has to put it on again as soon as washed, before it is dry.

Extreme indigence.

3. पेट हैगईं टोटा करम हैगईं खोटा। Peṭa haigain̲ ṭoṭá karama haigain̲ khoṭá.

A hole in the stomach (always hungry), deeds bad.

One in poverty always feels hungry, and is therefore apt to resort to illegal or dishonest means of livelihood which are sure and certain signs of his total ruin.

Used as a caution against falling into such errors as will lead to destruction.

POWER AND POSITION

1. गुणी पूजा दोखी सजा। Guṇi pújá dokhî sajá.

A worthy man is respected and an offender is punished.

Used to pursuade boys to become skilled and learned men.

2. कुत्ता क्या देखणो कुत्ता को मालिक देखणो। Kúṭṭá kyá dekhaṇo kúṭṭá ko málika dekhan̲o.

It is not the filthy dog we respect but the position of the person to whom it belongs.

Used of a great man's unworthy relations and servants who are dreaded only owing to their family connections, or to their position in a great man's house.

3. नूर सों आदेश। Núra son̲ ádesha.

Bending (making obeisance) before a light or splendour (great man).

I.e. Every one respects or tries to please a prosperous person.

4. मुलक मा गांव नी दफतर मा नाम नी। Mulaka má gáṇwas ní dafatara má námá ní.

I have no village in the country and my name is nowhere in the office.

E.g. Every one who possesses an entire village or a portion of one has name recorded in the public office. He who has no land has no name in the office.

Used by one who laments his humble position in the world.

5. जसै देवता उसै पुजारि। Jasai dewatá usai pujári.

As is the god, so is the worshipper.

I.e., As is the head, so are his attendents.

Used to denote a man's position as well as character (either good or bad) judged from his servants and comrades &c.

6. मुखड़ि देखिक टुकड़ि। Mukharḥi dekhika ṭukarhi.

To give one bread after seeing his face.

E.g. A man gets regard or disregard from other people according to his position. To the great we give much, to the poor little.

7. जसि रू तसा फरिस्ता। Jasi rú tasá pharistá.

As is the soul (of man) so will be the angel (of death).

E.g. It is said that when a man dies angels come to take his soul. If he is a sinner the angels of hell will come and take him to hell, and if he is a righteous man an angel from paradise will descend from heaven to take him there.

This is used by one bemoaning that he is visited by sicknesses one after the other, or by distresses (or of another in such a condition) in consequence of former bad deeds.

8. गुड़ दगड़ी माखा। Gurha dagarhî mákhá.

Flies will flock round treacle.

Applied to one who while in power is crowded by followers.

9. घाम की तरफ सब बेठनी। Gháma kî tarafa saba baiṭhaṉî.

All sit on the side where the sun shines.

This is to the same purport as the preceding one.

10. फेचुवा की खेब कूड़ा मा। Phechuwá kî kheba kúrhá má.

Phechuwá's flight is up to the roof.

E.g. A small bird called "*Phechuwa*" can fly only as high as the roof of a house, hence the point of the proverb. It is applied to a poor man whose powers of action are limited.

11. मुखड़ी देखिक टुकड़ि चेतना देखिक ब्योहार। Mukharhi dekhi ka ṭukarhi chetaná dekhi ka byohára,

Alms according to appearance, and business dealings according to intelligence.

E.g. One gives alms or gifts to another according to the position of the receiver, and deals with him according to his skill or wit.

12. जसै जागद्यो तसै भट कि पखोल। Jasai jágadyo tasai bhaṭa ki pakhola.

As is the deity Jágdyo, such is the food made of Bhaṭa (a kind of inferior pulse) offered to him.

A man is honored or dishonored according to his position or qualification. *C.f.* "As is the garden, such is the gardener."

13. जसी रांड तसै दिसाण। Jasi ráṉḍa tasai disáṇa.

As the woman (dancing girl) so her carpet.

As a man is in character, position &c, so will be his circumstances.

14. खालि खसिया बुढ़ि पातर। Khalí khasiyá buḍhi pátara.

A Khasiyá (a hill rustic or a man of coolie race without employ), and an old prostitute) do not meet with regard).

Used of those or who are out of power.

15. पुछड़ झड़ि गयो नौ चौरिया रैगयो। Puchharha jharhigayo nau chauríyá raigayo.

Though the ox has lost his coloured tail he is still called "Chauriyá".

This is applied to one who is nominally called after his former post or position, of which he has been deprived now.

PRECEPT AND PRACTISE

1. मासू खाइक मसखरा। Mású kháika masakhará.

One who eats animal food condemns it in others.

Instead of this having any effect on the minds of people they laugh at the man.

The eating of animal food is considered sinful.

2. औरन सो नशीहत आप फजीहत। Aurana so nashíhata ápa phajíhata.

One who is himself of a loose character gives instructions to others (to no purpose).

I.e. No one will attend to him, knowing his character.

"Practise what you preach."

3. औरन देढ हाको डाको आप रांडन हुड़किया राखो। Aurana deṇda háko dako ápa ra̱ṇḍa na hurhakiyá rákho.

A female who lectures others (on chastity) is herself in love with a drummer, (Hurhakiyá is a man of the lowest caste even among the Dumas).

PRIDE AND HAUGHTINESS

1. अति चतुर का नौ ठौर गू। Ati chatura ká nau ṭhaura gú.

He who thinks himself very clever, will find filth in nine places on his own person.

E.g. A clever and proud man has many great defects in him, of which he is not conscious.

2. बटक्यारा भूख मरन चेड़वाल्यो भेल लोटन। Baṭakyárá bhúkha marana cherhwályo bhela loṭana.

One who is very fastidious about his food will starve, and he who thinks too much of himself (always looks up at the sky) will fall down a precipice.

This proverb advises one to be content with what he gets, and not to boast of any thing that he has in this world. *C.f.* "Pride cometh before destruction, and a haughty spirit before a fall."

3. बिगच्यूं डूम खिरि मा लूण। Bigachyún ḍúma khiri má lúna.

A very proud Dúma (low caste) who goes beyond the limits of his caste puts salt in the rice-milk (instead of sugar).

I.e. One who is puffed up or proud, does a thing beyond his power or position. A man who places himself out of his natural and proper station in life, does odd things.

4. भीं में आंखा नहातन। Bhín men ánkhá nahátana.

One never looking towards the earth.

Applied to a very proud person.

5. बांस में चड़ियो। Bánsa men charhiyo.

One mounted on a bamboo.

Denoting a very haughty person.

6. चूतड़ छारा मा शेखी घोड़ा मा। Chútarha chhárámá shekhî ghorhámá.

Haunches in ashes, but pride as if on a horse.

Applied to one in poor circumstances who becomes very proud. One who sits in ashes (*i.e.* who is extremely poor) is as proud as a man who rides on a horse. A beggar on horseback.

7. धेला कि डुमणि टका को मिजाज। Dhelá ki ḍumani ṭaká ko mijája.

A Ḍumani (female Dom) worth a quarter of a pice has the pride of two pice.

E.g. A poor man leading a life beyond his position or circumstances.

8. उतरायां उंदो लमडन चड़वाल्या कपाल फोड़न। Utaráyán̲ uṇdo lamaḍana charhawályá kapála phorhana.

Persons going out of their proper limits shall fall, and persons proud and haughty will come to grief.

Applied to those who lead extravagant lives as well as to those who are haughty.

9. पैली मियां बावलो तै पर खाइ भांग। Paili̇ mayán̲ báwalo tai para khái bhán̲ga.

One who is already insane eats bhan̲ga (hemp) for intoxication.

This is used when one noted for pride becomes much haughtier on account of increase of fortune. To add crime to crime, to act in a very senseless manner.

10. पैली बुढ़िया गितांग छि अब नाति जै हैगोछ। Paili buḍhiyá gitán̲ga chhi aba náti jai háigochha.

The old woman who always sang for gladness of heart has her joys increased by the birth of a grandson.

I.e. Excessive pride at one's good furtune.

11. आपूं सड़ियो घोड़ा में चड़ियो। Ápúṇ sarhiyo ghorhá men̲ charhiyo.

Himself rotten (utterly destitute) but riding a horse.

This phrase is used of a poor person who is haughty, or assumes the airs of a rich man.

12. आपणा मन ले गुना बौराण। Ápaṇá mana le guná baurán̲a.

Guná thinks herself the beloved wife of her husband (who, however, does not like her).

Self-praise is no recommendation. This is used of one who thinks too much of himself. *C.f.* "It is not good to eat much honey: So far even to search their own glory is not glory." "Let another man praise thee, and not thine own mouth, a stranger, and not thine own lips."

13. रांसी नजर छ बीच गंगा देखदो नीछ। Ránsí nazara chha bícha gangá dekhado níchha.

His eye is turned upwards and he does not see the deep river that is below him.

This is applicable to one who does not see how he is being ruined. *C.f.* Let thine eyes look right on and let thine eyelids look straight before thee.

14. शिकल चुरेड़ कि मिजाज परि को। Shikala churerha ki mijája pari ko.

Face of a hag and the pride of a fairy.

Ironically used in regard to one who being destitute of any qualification or worth assumes an air of superiority and haughtiness.

15. 1. राजा के धनि मैं धनि। Rájá ke dhani mai dhani.

2. राजा मेरा धन को धनि। Rájá merá dhana ko dhani.

3. लेछियो त खायोकन। Lechhioyo ta kháyo kana.

1. What is the king's wealth compared to mine.

2. The king is wealthy by my wealth.

3. If he took my wealth why could he not enjoy it?

The above are the three notes supposed to be sung by a small active bird known as *"Pyurarhi"* which dances about singing on the branches and twigs of trees.

Once while catching insects and worms on the ground she found a very small copper coin which she took in her bill and danced about singing note 1. The story reached the king, who being angry on account of her pride had the coin snatched away from her. After this the bird began to sing the second note. On hearing this, the king for fear of disgrace thought it advisable to return her the said coin. As soon as she got her wealth back she began to sing the third song. Whereupon the good king came to the conclusion that it was no use fighting with such a small creature as she was. Hence the proverb, teaching that no one can stop the mouth of the world, and that it is beneath the dignity of a great man to quarrel with, or tease, or oppress, poor people, for they have no strength or courage to face him, but will open their mouth to defame or revile him. They are puffed up with the little they have, and so the proverb is also used of poor people who become haughty.

16. धन धन किड़ि तेरो भाग त्वीप लीदेछ भेली। Dhana dhana kirhi tero bhága twípa lídechha bhelí.

O Kirhi, you are the more fortunate of the two that your husband gave you alone a Bheli (treacle or gagry cake).

A man had two wives, one of whom was Kirhi. The man, who had gone to a foreign country, returned home with money and jewellery. He made over all the valuables to his younger wife, but in order to prevent Kirhi from quarrelling he gave her a cake of gagry (Bheli). She in consequence became puffed up and showed her pride to her kinsmen and neighbours, who knowing what had taken place in the household ironically uttered the phrase which afterwards became a proverb. Applied to those who become proud by having a little property.

17. भीं न भाना डूम का हाना। Bhín̲ na bháná ḍúma ká háná.

Neither on the ground, nor in a vessel, but in the head of a Ḍuma (a low caste man).

This is made use of to represent a very haughty person who has no more reason to be proud than a *Ḍuma* has. A haughty person is represented by a *Ḍuma*.

Story : Once a low-caste man was spoken to by a king. The man after having been thus honored came to his house, and contrary to his usual demeanor sat down silent. His wife, brother, and sons addressed him as usual, but he did not speak or reply to them. They then thought him to be possessed by a demon, and his wife eagerly entreated him to speak to her, and asked the reason of his having become angry with her. On this he beat her with a stick and said, "O, cursed woman you are a foolish one, how can I speak with you, a poor woman, with the mouth with which I have spoken with the King?" Hence it is said that pride does not find a place for itself anywhere except in the head of a low person.

18. मेरा घर है आग लीगे नाम बैश्वानर धरो। Merá ghara hai ága líge náma baishwánara dharo.

You took fire from my house and then named it "Baishwánara." (As it is called in Sanscrit).

Used of one who ungratefully shows arrogance to another on account of the very thing which he had received from him. For instance a student will act proudly towards his teacher on account of the learning which he received from him.

19. ऊपर जाली नीस पराली मुंह में बांधा धोता। ये हाल हमारो तो नंगों का क्या नहोता। Úpara jálí nísa parálí muṇha meṇ báṇdhá dhotá. Ye hála hamáre to nangon ká kya nahotá.

I have a net over me and straw under me, and my mouth is covered with a Dhoti (a loin cloth). These are my conditions, but how do the naked live?

The speaker is really naked, but he thinks much of himself, and others to be naked. Applies to those who are puffed up at a little property they have, looking down upon others as their inferiors; as elsewhere it is said that the man of low descent when made a king, the son of an illiterate man, who becomes a *Pandita* by learning, and a poor man who gets money, consider the world to be like a piece of grass (nothing).

20. ऊ घोड़ा चडंछ मैं पाखा चढ़ूं। Ú ghorhá chaḍhanchha mai pákhá chaḍhúṇ.

If he rides a horse I shall mount a roof.

Applied to pride and haughtiness.

PROSPERITY AND AFFLUENCE

1. आया सराध फूला कांसा बामण कूदा नौ नौ बांस। Áyá sarádha phúlá káṇsa bámaṉa kúdá nau nau báṇsá.

At the approach of kanyágata (fifteen days of the Shráddha fortnight which according to astrological calculations occurs in the months of September and October) when the káṇsa grass used in sacrifices and religiously (Pod. cynosuroides) begins to flower, the Brahmans leap with joy nine bamboos (a bamboo=ten cubits) high.

This is an ironical phrase applied to the Brahmans by other castes who have to feed them during this period.

Out of the four months of the rainy season called "*Chaumása*" sixteen days are set aside for the worship of one's deceased ancestors for three generations back: these are called "the sixteen Shrádhas", Shrádha means a religious ceremony performed in the name of one's forefathers, the principal part of which consists in feasting as many Brahmanas, kinsmen and relatives with dainties as possible, and giving as much alms as one's circumstances permit to the Brahmanas. This is performed annually on the anniversary of the date on which one's father or mother died. It has also to be performed on the corresponding dates of the Shrádha period. According to the doctrine of transmigration every one that dies is said to enter into another body, and anything given to God in his (deceased's) name is enjoyed by him, and so every one wishing bliss and prosperity to his forefathers feeds Brahmanas with expensive food and gives them as much alms as he can.

In proportion to the number of Brahmins fed and the value of the offerings made to them will be the satisfaction and welfare of the forefathers, who in return will bring blessings on their descendants.

The proverb is also sometimes used to describe a piece of good luck.

2. चलती को नाम गाड़ि। Chalatí ko náma gárhi.
As long as the vehicle moves it is called the "gárhi."
A man is considered wise and good as long as he is prosperous.

3. तातो पाणि सेलो चोपड़। Táto pá<u>n</u>i selo choparha.
Warm water and cool oil.
This is quoted in regard to one who is in very prosperous circumstances, as well-to-do persons can afford to have warm water to bathe in and oil to rub over their bodies. The oil is rubbed over the body before they bathe in warm water.

4. पूसु कोली पूस ते रांच कूच तखि ते। Púsú kolí púsa teṇ ráṇcha kúcha takhi teṇ.
The weaver "Púsú" gets employment with his weaving instruments up to the months of Púsa (January).
After this the work of weaving is stopped.
"Make hay while the sun shines."

5. सराध सूखा बामण भूखा। Sharádha súkhá, bámaṇa bhúkhá.
When Shrádhas are ended the Brahmans are hungry.
Vide above for a description of the religious ceremony called *"Sharádha"*.

6. दूध घुटण कु भात थुकण कु। Dúdha ghuṭa<u>n</u>a ku bháta thukaṇa ku.
To drink the milk and to spit out the rice.
Well-to-do persons generally mix rice and milk together for eating. But after they have eaten enough rice they drink the milk only.
Applied to one who has enough and to spare.

7. चलती का सब क्वे। Chalatí ká saba kwe.
All are akin to the prosperous man, i.e. everyone seeks his friendship.
Story : Ráma Chandra king of Ajyodhyá (now known as Faizabad) during twelve years' banishment once happened to visit the

hut of the saint known as "Agasti." The saint paid no attention to him and did not receive him with the respect due to a king. But when after having killed Ráwana he was on his way to his capital Ajyodhyá to ascend his father's throne, then the same saint Agasti, along with the other saints also, came to pay his respects to the king (Ráma Chandra). At this time Ráma Chandra asked Agasti what was the cause of his being so courteous at this time, since both of them knew each other from the beginning; to which the saint replied "O King, one's circumstances are worshipped or respected, but not his body."

8. सराध लागा बामण जागा सराध निमड़ा बामण चिमड़ा। Sarádha lágá bámaṉa jágá sarádha nimarhá bámaṇa chimarhá.

The Sarádha commenced, the Brahmans awoke, the Sarádhas ended, the Brahmans became lean.

I.e. The Brahmans who live on invitations to Sarádhas or religious feasts rejoice and grow fat, while the festivals last, but they starve when the religious ceremonies come to an end.

A satire on Brahmans, and also applied to one's prosperous and adverse days.

9. कपड़ा बड़ि बस्तु। Kaparhá barhi bastu.

Clothes are the chief thing (for respect).

Once a man of some note went to a certain town in his ordinary dress, but was not saluted nor shown any respect by any person he met with. After some days he visited the same town dressed in sumptuous clothes, when he was greeted and saluted by every person he met. In reply to every salutation the man instead of uttering "*Ráma Ráma*" (the name of God), "*Áshirbáda*" (blessing, "Live long" "Be happy" &c (forms of salutation) said as above, to show the people that no one regards man or God but everyone has an eye to the apparent signs of one's prosperity which command the respect of mankind without any regard to his internal defects and failings.

10. हरबखत कुकुर ध्यू नि खानो। Harabakhata kukura ghyú ni kháno.

Dogs do not eat ghi every day.

One must not look for continual prosperity without a single cloud.

11. बिदा द्यो का मांडा। Bidá dyo ká má<u>n</u>dá.

A shed for bright days.

Houses in which one can find shelter only during fine weather and not on a rainy day when they leak badly. Summer friends, who fail in time of trouble.

PROSTITUTES

1. पातर को यो काम खै पी सटकौ चातुर कौ यो काम पातर सो नि अटकौ। Pátara ko yo káma khai pí saṭakau chatúra kó yo káma pátara so ni aṭakau.

It is the harlot's business to entice and rob a man and then discard him; but the wise man will not be tempted by her seductions.

Applied to all who selfishly wish to profit themselves at the expense of others.

2. पातर को यार मरो कै गली को। Pátara ko yára maro kai galí ko.

Who knows in what street a friend of a prostitute died?

This is used to show that prostitutes have no real friends as they themselves are not such to others. As they have a great many customers, no one knows the whereabouts of the one who died. This is used by one who having a certain interest in a joint matter thinks himself too poor to do any thing in the matter.

3. रांडी घर मांडी पतिब्रता को कड़ाका। Rá<u>n</u>ḍí ghara máṇḍí patibratá ko karháká.

It is strange that a harlot has an abundance of everything, and a chaste woman starves.

This is used to console one on account of the transient nature of worldly pleasures, and to base hopes on good deeds, which secure everlasting bliss.

Story : Once a servant of Mahádeva (called "Nandi") was rubbing the body of the god with oil. On hearing a cannon-shot he enquired from the deity as to its cause. The latter said that Ráwana was born. While continuing to serve him the servant again heard another shot. On enquiry he was informed that Ráwana was made king of Lanká (Ceylon). This news grieved him and caused him to repent of his long service rendered to Mahádeva, being envious of Ráwana, who was anointed king of Lanká so soon after his birth. While the servant was thus brooding over and lamenting his luck, he heard a third shot. He again asked of the deity the cause of it, and Mahádeva replied that Ráwana was killed, and his death was being announced. This pacified the man and brought him to his senses. Then he began to appreciate the immortal life he had gained in the divine service, and to despise the transient nature of worldly glory.

4. जो खाणो बणकी दारी न सो खाव घर की बुवारी। Jo kháno banakí dárí na so kháwa ghara kí buwárí.

Whatever money is spent on a harlot ought to go to one's wife.

Used as a caution against vicious folly.

PRUDENCE AND PRECAUTION

1. जोगी हगणै बटि भाज। Jogí haganai baṭi bhája.

The ascetic runs away from the place where he has eased himself.

Applied to one who has no family or property to bind him to one place, and so cannot be entrusted with a loan or anything.

2. ओछा को धन चुकिला को गन। Ochhá ko dhana chukilá ko gana.

The wealth of a poor person and the eructation from acid food.
C.f. "Great cry and little wool."

3. भागनेर भूत कि लंगोटी लाभ। Bháganera bhúta ki langoṭi lábha.

Even the rag of a flying goblin is a gain.

I.e. The smallest thing received from a person who is leaving for good, may be regarded as a gain.

4. निमड़ियां है चिमड़ियो भलो। Nimarhiyá hai chimarhiyo bhalo.

(Any thing) even in a rotten and bad state is better than its non-existence.

C.f. "Something is better than nothing."

5. ले कै बार नालि ल्यौ कै छ नालि। Le kai bára náli lyau kai chha náli.

If one is asked to take (purchase) he demands at the rate of twelve náils (twenty-four seers of grain): if he is asked to sell he will do so at six nális for the Rupee.

6. साग खाणो ब्यूणी बेर गौं खाणे न्यूड़ी बेर। Sága kháṇo byúṇí bera gaiṇ khaṇo nyúrhí bera.

The crop of vegetables is to be gathered by thinning, and life in the village must be passed with meekness.

Counselling thrift and caution.

7. भली छिपि जांछ्य नकि फैलनि छ। Bhalí chhipị janchhya nakị phailaní chha.

The goodness is concealed and the wickedness spread abroad.

E.g. Anything good done to one is confined to him, but any wrong done to him he will spread by informing everybody.

Used to deter persons against doing an evil act.
"The evil that man do lives after them."
"The good is oft interred with their bones." (Shakspeare).

8. भैंस को मोल भैंस क़ा ढमाण। Bhaiṇsa ko mola bhainsa ká dhamána.

The large quantity of a buffalo's dung (used for manure) repays one for feeding it only.

A large business requires a large capital, or large profits are the results of large outlays, also used to describe an unprofitable business.

9. पैली आहार तब ब्योहार। Paili áhára taba byohára.

First food then work.

Used of one who delays taking his food in preference to other things at the fixed or usual time.

Don't attempt work on an empty stomach.

10. पंच परमेश्वर। Paṇcha Parmeshwara.

God in five persons.

I.e. God's will shown in the opinion of the majority.

It is said that once a king in ancient times tried to prove the truth of this maxim by bringing a jar of money, with its mouth closed and sealed up, before a number of people who were required to guess what it contained. All of them said that it contained a snake. On opening and emptying the jar a snake came out as predicted by the majority, to the utter astonishment of the King.

11. टुका में टौर। Ṭuká men ṭaura.

(A stick of sugarcane) sour at the end.

A sugarcane is sweeter towards its root, and insipid towards the end.

Used of one who after having done some work cheerfully and carefully spoils it eventually by bad or unwise conduct.

12. चेलो बचौ छटि तक। Chelo bachau chhaṭi taka.

A son should live up to his sixth day.

On the sixth day after the birth of a son a religious rite is performed at which there are great rejoicings and festivities. The father distributes alms, feasts his relations, and gives dancing parties &c. The proverb means that it is better that a man should have a short life and a merry one, rather than live out a long and miserable existence.

Used to encourage sons to be industrious and wise with a view to their becoming wealthy and renowned.

13. जो गरज सो बरस नै जो बरस सो गरज नै। Jo garaja so barasa nai jo barasa so garaja nai.

The cloud that thunders does not rain, and the one that rains does not thunder.

C.f. "The dogs that bark most bite least."

14. मुंड की मुंडाइ घट कि पिसाइ। Munḏa kí munḍái ghaṭa kí pisáí.

The shaving of one's head and the grinding of one's corn (must be paid for).

This is applied to denote expenses which are unavoidably necessary. A man who does not pay for his shaving will become a barber in the next birth.

15. दुइ खाणो बार बार रूइ खाणो एक बार। Dui kháno bára bára rui kháno eka bára.

One can milk a cow again and again, but can break down a bough (of fruit) only once..

For instance living on the interest of money and not spending the capital itself, or living on the produce of land and not selling the land itself, enjoying the fruit of a tree without destroying it. To milk a cow gently and carefully. To break down, to use roughly so as to destroy.

Used to pursuade one to be satisfied with a little help given to him, giving hopes that he will be helped again and again if the helper lives.

C.f. "How lives the wise? How doth he use
"The gifts and sweetness of the world?
"E'en as the bee that takes the dews
"Of nectar in the flow'ret furled,
"But mars nor hue nor scent nor worth-
"So dwells the wise upon the earth."

The undernoted story will further illustrate the proverb.

Once a prudent man went to a foreign town with a pice in his hand, where he remained for twelve years. He lived on his earnings all this time, but took diligent care of what he had in cash (i.e. one pice). The man could only earn his food, but not money for firewood, and so he bought one pice worth of firewood with the pice he had, but as soon as he had cooked his food he quenched the fire and preserved the charcoal which he sold to a goldsmith and got a pice again. In this way he continued for twelve years, at the end of which he returned home with his pice still in his possession.

16. मर्द कि मौत नामर्द का हाथ। Marda ki mauta námarda ká hátha.

A brave person is often killed by the hand of a coward.

E.g. Great persons or plans are often thrown by trifling causes.

C.f. "A small leak will sink a great ship."

"The best-laid plans o'mice and men

"Gang aft agley." (Burns).

17. सत को सवाइ असत को डेवढ़ो। Sata ko sawái asat ko dewaḍho.

Profit of four annas in the rupee invested in trade is fair, but eight annas unfair.

Used to inculcate that unfair profit will tend to one's ruin, but the fair one will make the trader prosperous and happy.

18. खाणो सराखत रौणो फराखत। Kháṇo sarákhata rauṉo pharákhata.

One ought to share his food with others, but remain aloof.

A man should secure a certain amount of privacy for his own affairs even in his own house.

19. दांतन का अगाड़ि जीभ सयांणि। Dáṇtana ká agárhi jîbha sayáṇi.

The tongue is cleverer than the teeth.

The tongue remains unhurt though close to the sharp teeth.

Advice to deal wisely with the dangerous people among whom one has to live.

20. नैका अगाड़ि रास्ता नै। Naiká agárhi rástá nai.

There is no other way in face of a refusal.

I.e. If you refuse my request there's an end on't.

21. स्याप कि बराबरी कितौलो कर ताणि ताणि मर। Syápa ki barábarî kitaulo kara táṇi táṇi mara.

The insect or reptile called "Kitaula" (a miniature of a snake) in its attempt to compete with a snake drags itself to death.

An unequal match.

Used as a caution against competing with a greater person.

22. रुपया कणि और अकल कणि भेट निहुनि। Rupayán kaṇi aura akala kaṇi bheṭa nihuni.

Wealth and wisdom never meet together.

E.g. A wealthy man has no wisdom and a wise man no wealth. A person while in the possession of wealth has no sense to take care of it, but it comes to him (in the way of repentance) when he has squandered his wealth. So he uses this proverb bemoaning his conduct.

23. आपण तीलन बट तेल निकलंछ। Ápaṇá tîlana baṭa tela nikalaṇchha.

One gets oil from his own Tîla (i.e. sesame).

One may derive any amount of profit from his own property or money.

24. दिन दूसरा को रात आपणी। Dina dusará ko ráta ápaṇi.

Day another's, but night one's own.

Leisure comes to all when the day's work is over.

25. अघाणो नि छोड़नो सामल धाम नि छोड़नो कमल। Agháṇo ni chhorhano sámala gháma ni chhorhano kamala.

When one's hunger is satisfied he should not leave his provisions behind, nor his blanket because the sun is shinning.

E.g. Food and clothes are two things always needed, especially on a journey, where the traveller has to bear them on his shoulders. So the proverb tells one not to neglect to take these with him. It also teaches one to provide himself with all the necessaries of life for his future comfort while in good circumstances.

Improvidence.

26. गास दीणो बास नि दीणो। Gása ďiṇo bása ni ďiṇo.

Feed the wayfarer but do not lodge him.

For a stranger will find out the faults and failings of the owner of the house.

27. सुणनि सबन कि करनि आपणि। Suṉani sabana ki karani ápaṇi.

One ought to hear everybody, but do what he wishes to.

28. बिना गुरु अंधेरी बाट। Biná guru aṉdherí báṭa.

The path is in the dark without a teacher or spiritual guide.

I.e. Every one is ignorant of the way he wishes to go, until he is instructed or enlightened in the matter.

29. तीरथ में जाणु झोंपड़ि नि बांधणि। Tiratha meṇ jáṉú jhoparhî ni báṉdhaṇi.

One ought to visit a shrine or sacred place, but not build a shed there to live or settle in.

A man's religious zeal should not interfere with his other duties. Besides he is likely to commit fresh sins, if he protracts his stay there. For it is said that sins committed elsewhere can be absolved in a sacred place, but those committed in a sacred place are never forgiven, nor can be atoned for by any meritorious act.

30. पाप और पंथ काटियो सुख। Pápa aura paṇtha káṭiyo sukha.

One gets peace of mind as soon as his sins are forgiven (absolved), and his pilgrimage finished.

In other words so long as one's sins are not absolved or the necessary journey to a certain place not performed, they prick his heart, and remind him of the disagreeable necessity he is under to expiate them.

31. गू खाइक काल नि कट दो। Gú kháika kála ni kaṭa do.

One cannot pass over famine (get over the time scarcity) by living on human dung.

I.e. One's poverty cannot be overcome by resorting to wicked and unlawful means, such as theft, falsehood &c.

32. अति भलौ नै। Ati bhalo nai.

Too much (of a thing) is not good.

Once should not go to extremes in any thing.

Sitá the wife of Ráma, owing to her remarkable beauty was carried off by Ráwana. Ráwana, king of Ceylon, boasting of his great power, was slain by Ráma. Bali, an ancient Indian king, was very liberal in his charities. On one occasion in his form of dwarf Brahman went to him (Bámana Avatára) he went to Bali and asked for so much land as could be covered by his three feet. On receiving the boon he expanded to such an enormous stature that he filled the three worlds with his two feet alone and there remained no space for his third foot, for which he had stipulated. Therefore Bali in this excess of liberality proposed that the third foot should be placed upon his own head. Thus he was thrust down into the lower regions.

33. आपुं चैनु गौं नै गौं चैनु देश नै देश चैनु परदश नै। Ápun̠ chainu gaun̠ nai gaun̠ chainu desha nai, desha chainu paradesha nai.

What a man needs for himself should not be given away or sold to his village, and what is needed for the village should not be allowed to go out therefrom, nor what is needed for one's own country to go to a foreign land.

(Else the man himself or his neighbours will eventually suffer want or inconvenience).

A caution against exhausting the resources on which the people depend.

34. सारो ढेबरो मुडो माडो पूछ कि दांव लराट कराट। Sáro ḍhebaro muḍo máḍo púchha ki dán̠wa laráṭa karáṭa.

The sheep kept silent while its body was sheared, but made a great outcry when they sheared the tail.

Applied to one who after having almost settled or completed an affair, quarrels about some small detail.

E.g. They agreed upon the price of the elephant, but quarrelled about the Mahat's spear.

25. जैगौं नि जाणो वी कि बाट के पुछणि। Jaigaun̲ ni jan̲o wí ki báṭa ke puchhan̲i.

Why should one enquire after the pathway to a village he does not wish to go to.

Unnecessary interference.

36. तालो द्युं न चोरि लगुं। Tálo dyúṇ na chori laguṇ.

Neither will I give you my key nor accuse yoụ of theft.

I'll manage my own affairs.

37. न जौं आली न खौं गाली। Na jaun̲ álí na khaun̲ gálí.

If I do not trespass upon the land (belonging to another) why should I be abused by him.

Caution against trespass.

38. बाछि बाग लिगयो तब हलो हालणो सीखो। Báchhi bága ligayo taba hulo hálaṇo síkho.

One learns to bolt his door after his calf has been taken away by the leopord.

Wise after the event. *C.f.* "A stumble may prevent a fall."

39. मरीक बच सो दानो खाइक बच सो बीज। Maríka bacha so dáno khaika bacha so bíja.

He who has escaped from a fatal sickness is an experienced man, and the grain left after eating is for seed.

40. नाइ थैं सलाह निकरि मुनलो भिजै बैठो। Nái thain̲ saláha nikari munalo bhijai baiṭho.

Lathering one's head (for being shaved) without consulting a barber.

E.g. Whenever one wishes to get his head shaved he engages the services of a barber for the purpose, but if he lathers his head without doing so he subjects himself to laughter and ridicule.

One ought to make every arrangement necessary for a work or business before he starts, otherwise he will not get his work accomplished.

41. जुआरी को धन दोषिला का नाना तिना। Juárî ko dhana dokhilá ká náná tiná.

Wealth in the hand of a gambler and children of ghost-affected (diseased) parents will not last long.

42. मेरो खोरो सारो कि पाखाण सारो। Mero khoro sáro ki pákháṇa sáro.

Is my head harder or the rock?

Applied to one who wishes to fight a stronger man, to dissuade him from doing so.

43. मरना है बिगचणा कि डर। Maraná hai bigachaṇá ki ḍara.

To be ruined is more to be dreaded than to die.

44. दूद को जलियो छांस फुकि बेर पे। Dúda ko jaliyo chháṇsa phuki bera pe.

One who happened to burn his lips by drinking hot milk does not drink even Chháṇsa (butter milk) without blowing on it to cool it.

Applied to one who, once cheated or betrayed by another, is suspicious of every one. A burnt child dreads the fire. *C.f.* "A scalded cat dreads cold water."

45. जैको बाप रिख ले खायो सो काला खुंडा सो डरौ। Jaiko bápa rikha le kháyo so kálá khuṉdá so ḍarau.

One whose father was killed by a bear is afraid even of the black trunk of a tree.

(A stumble makes one careful).

46. रोक कि फोक फोक कि छुट्टि। Roka ki phoka phoka kî chhuṭṭi.

Cash (scattered and turned) into goods (purchased with cash) and the articles, if lent on credit, disappear or are lost through insolvent borrowers.

Precaution against imprudent speculations and loans to persons who are cheats.

47. नाज कणि दांत छन। Nája kaṇi dáṇta chhana.

The grain has teeth.

I.e. If you eat too much of it, it will kill you (in the way of indigestion).

48. कभैं बैगण पथ कबैं अपथ। Kabhain̲ bain̲gaṇa patha kabhain apatha.

Egg-plants wholesome at one time and unwholesome at another.

This vegetable when eaten is said to be injurious, but if one at any time eats it without any such effect this cannot be said to be proof of its wholesomeness. For evil things ought always to be guarded against even if they do not hurt one on one occasion.

49. आप डुबन्ते बामना ले डूबा जजमान। Ápaduban̲te bámaná le ḍúbá jajamána.

In trying to save his priest, the man himself was drowned.

Caution against rashly undertaking to help those in difficulties.

50. आसमान सों थूको मुंह में आयो। Ásamána son̲ thúko muha men̲ áyo.

Spitting towards the sky the spittle falls back on one's own face.

"Curses come home to roost."

51. अणथ जाणो आंगो बांगो दूली जाणो सामो। Aṇatha ján̲o áṇgo bán̲go dúli jáṇo sámo.

One should enter one's hole straight, even though moving zigzag elsewhere, as a snake does.

This enjoins submission and reserve with the strong and great, and simplicity towards the members of one's own family. As a snake wriggling about when abroad yet enters its hole straight; so a man should practice wordly arts in dealing with the world or with superiors, but be simple and natural with his own people.

52. अकल मंद कि लौंडि बेवकूफ कि राणि। Akalaman̲da ki launḍi bewakúpha ki rán̲i.

To be the maid-servant of an intelligent man is better than to be the queen-consort of a foolish king.

53. अघिल को लाकड़ो बलियो पिछाड़ि औंछ। Aghila ko lákarho balíyo, pichhárhi auṇchha.

The fire which burns at one end of a piece of wood will gradually come to the other end.

What is beneficial or the reverse to one will in the end be found the same for all.

54. आग लागी झोंपड़ि जो निकलो सो लाभ। Ága lágî jhoparhi jo nikalau so lábha.

Any thing taken out of a burning house is a gain.

"Something is better than nothing."

55. गौं को बास कुल को नाश। Gauṉ ko básа kúla ko násha.

To live in the country is to ruin one's own descendants.

The children of one residing in a village are liable to contract the unpolished habits of their neighbours, and are debarred from the advantages of education which in India are found only in towns. Village life also renders young people awkward and clownish.

56. बरोबरिया को सोनो गाड़ नि बगौ। Barobariyá ko sono gárha ni bagau.

The gold of one of equal rank cannot be swept away even by a river (if thrown into it).

A person of equal position cannot be imposed upon, as he can claim redress in case he is put to any loss.

57. जो धन जानो देखो आधा दीयो बांट। Jo dhana jáno dekho áḍhá diyau báṇta.

Wealth which is about to be taken away, give away half of it.

I.e. If a case seems likely to be lost, spend liberally in order to better your chance of winning it. Also applied to those about to become bankrupt.

58. जो नेड़ो सो पेड़ो। Jo nerho so perho.

One who is near is dear.

The converse of "out of sight, out of mind."

59. जब तक बालक नि रूनो मैं दूध नि दीनी। Jaba taka bálaká ni rúno mai dúdha ni ďiní.

A mother does not give her child milk unless it cries.

C.f. "Nothing ask nothing have."

60. आपणो खाणु खाणो डूम थें छुवे मांगणो। Ápaṇo kháṇú kháṇo ḍúma the̱n chhuwe mangaṇo.

To eat one's own food, after it has been touched by a "ḍúm".

The food of a Hindu of any of the higher castes *(Bíṭhas)* if touched by a *Ḍúma* is considered defiled and only fit to be thrown away. Whenever there is any trouble or inconvenience in the management of one's own property through having entrusted it to another, this proverb is used.

61. मरनेर के निकरनु। Maranera ke ni karanu.

One about to be killed, what will he not do?

A desperate plight.

62. मीठा का जड़ा ख़ैणि खांद कड़ा का टुकुलु निछेड़दो। Míṭhá ká jarhá khaiṇi kháṇda karhá ká ṭukulu ni chherhado.

The roots of a sweet plant are dug out and eaten, but not even the leaves or shoots of a bitter one are touched.

This is applied to a man of good temper who is always being troubled and resorted to, whereas a person of cross temper is shunned.

Story : Once the sweetmeat being oppressed and troubled by every one in the world went to one of the gods and laid her complaint before him saying that every creature in the world attempted to eat her. The god after hearing the tale of her woes was thereby tempted to taste her himself in order to find out whether the universal liking for her was justifed. Whereupon she returned to the earth in utter despair to undergo her fate.

63. थोड़ी कमूणो आफुं सों भौत कमूणो औरन सों। Thorhí kamúṇo áphuṇ soṇ bhauta kamúṇo aurana son.

One who earns a little has enough for himself, but one who earns much benefits others (rather than himself).

64. बेटी का मागदारा बलदों का लेवाक। Beṭí ká mágadárá baladon̲ ká lewáka.

Those who come to espouse a daughter and those who come to buy bullocks are alike.

In Garhwál, where daughters are sold like farm stock, those who come to make a bargain for a wife are treated like bullock dealers *i.e.* with scant courtesy.

65. बेटी को बैद्वालो बुवारी को पठ्यादारो। Beṭí ko baidwálo buwarí ko paṭhyádáro.

One who is sent to bring one's daughter from her father-in-law's house, and one who is sent to take one's daughter-in-law to her father's house.

These two persons should be most honest and faithful.

66. बाग टाट भेल कांद को लांद। Bága ṭáṭa bhela kán̲da ko láṇda.

Who will embrace a tiger or prop up a falling hill with his shoulder?

Dangerous attempts.

67. बिराणु सोनु नाख डा। Biráṇú sonú nákha ḍá.

Another's gold causes pain in one's own nose.

Applies to one who borrows and wears another's noserings (women do this on many occasions, especially during festivities and fairs) and thus suffer pain from the unaccustomed ornament.

C.f. "Borrowed plumes".

68. बलद निल्योणु ढांगो आपत नि करनु कांगो। Balda nilyon̲ú ḍháṇgo ápata ni karanú kán̲go.

Lean bullocks should not be purchased, and men in poor circumstances should not be made into relatives by marriage.

69. छोटो छोटो ना देख चपगाइ सौरा। Chhoṭo chhoṭo ná dekha chapagái saurá.

Do not think of him as a harmless man, he is the son of a wild bull.

A dangerous fellow.

70. अन्त छ्यो मरम घौ। Aṇta chhyo marama ghau.

Excessive abuse, and a wound on a delicate part of the body.

The effects of these are lasting and injurious. One can never forgive or recover from the effects of such abuse.

C.f. "Sometimes words wound more than swords."

71. गाड़ मै तेरा नजीक नै औंलो त कसीकै बगाली। Gárha mai terá najīka nai auṇlo ta kasīkai bagálī.

O river, if I do not come near you, how can you wash me away?

Safety by avoiding evil habits or men.

72. दुइ नाव पर पैर धरो डूबि मरो। Dúi náwa para paira dharo ḍúbi maro.

He who puts one foot in one boat and the other in another will be drowned.

Falling between two stools. *C.f.* "No man can serve two masters".

73. देश देशों का आला भांति भांति बुलाला। Desha deshon̲ ká álá bhán̲ti bhán̲ti bulálá.

People who come from different countries will speak in different dialects.

Tot homines, tot sententiae.

74. नौ नकद भला तेर उधार बुरा। Nau nakada bhalá tera údhára búrá.

Nine (Rupees) in cash are better than thirteen promised.

C.f. "A bird in the hand is worth two in the bush."

75. नि करेव भेख नि खायेव देश। Ni karewa bhekha ni kháyewa desha.

One who does not adopt the disguise (i.e. customs and habits) of a foreign country, will not be able to live there.

C.f. "In Rome do as Rome does."

Story : Once a man went to see his friend who lived in a foreign town. Not knowing his house he promised a by-stander that he would make him *"Khúsh"* (give him an appropriate reward) if the man showed him his friend's house. The native of that country accordingly led him to the house he wanted to go to. On his arrival there the man gave the native Rs. 5/- (supposing that sum would satisfy him), and the native was not satisfied. Then he offered Rs. 10/-, but the man was not satisfied with that amount even, and began to quarrel, and insisted on his being made *"khúsha"* (Which also means "glad"). His friend at last came to know of the quarrel and came out, and after listening to what they both said he gave his friend the necessary advice as to how he was to act in the matter, and went away. After this the man concerned took a club in his hand and saying that he would show how Hanúmána (the celebrated monkey spoken of in the *Rámáyana*) destroyed Lanká (Ceylon) began to destroy every shed and house like a madman. This play of his made all the people standing by laugh heartily. Among them the man also laughed, and was told that since according to promise he had been made *"Khusha"* (glad) he had nothing more to expect as a reward; the man was convinced that he had had the promised reward and went away!

76. ज्यान छौ तौ जहान छौ। Jyána chhau tau jahána chhau.

The world is of use to one only so long as he is alive.

"Let us eat and drink, for tomorrow we die." Carpe diem.

77. नौ मण नंदू का खावन छांस मांगण नंदू का घर जावन। Nau maṇa naṉdú ká kháwana chháṉsa máṅgaṇa naṇdú ká ghara jáwana.

Nandu's family eats nine maunds a day, and yet people go to him to ask for butter milk.

No one should go to ask a thing from a man who cannot afford to give it.

78. गांव खोब रांड साग खोव मांड। Gáṉwa khowa ráṉḍa sága khowa máṉḍa.

A widow ruins a village and the máṇḍa (water in which rice has been cooked) spoils vegetable food.

On the one hand widows being disappointed of their position, envy others, and so become very cross and quarrelsome. On the other, unending quarrels and dissensions arise owing to their having contracted intimacy with some one in the village. Here the word "widow" also includes an unchaste woman.

79. गजि गवाइ बणिया सयाणो। Gaji gaṇwái baṇ̃iyá sayáṇo.

The baniyá became clever after having lost his cloth.

Wise after the event.

80. घ्यू खाणु शक्कर साथ दुनिया खाणि मक्कर का साथ। Ghyú kháṇú shakkara sátha dúniyá kháṇú kháṇi makkara ká sátha.

Ghi should be eaten with sugar, and the world subdued by pride.

As *Ghi* without sugar cannot be digested or relished, so the world cannot be imposed upon without some pretence or assumption of pride.

81. घासी घोड़ो काफल्या पैक। Ghási ghorho káphalyá paika.

A horse fed only on grass and a hero on vegetable food are strong and capable of doing great deeds.

Refers to the swiftness of wild horses which live only on grass and to the bravery of soldiers who generally come from families that live on coarse food and vegetables. Implies that the swiftness of a horse and the heroism of a man are natural gifts and have nothing to do with food.

82. गाड़ का मुख पगार रांड का मुख गार। Gárha ká mukha pagára ráṇḍa ká mukha gára.

Who would build a wall across the mouth of a stream, and who would abuse a widow to her face.

One who abuses a widow brings upon himself a shower of abuse. Used of impossible or foolish attempts,

83. गोरु दिणो खडंयात नौनि दिणि नज्यांत। Gorú diṇo khaḍyánta nauni diṇi najyántá.

Cows should be sold to those who have plenty of grass and grazing ground, and daughters given to those who have much grain, otherwise the cows will suffer and their daughters starve.

84. हाथ कि गंवाइ भीड़ा की सान। Hátha ki ganwái bhírhá ki sána.

Having lost what was in his hand he begins to try to seize a wall.

Applied to one who has given or lent a thing to another which he cannot be sure of getting back when needed. "Catching at the shadow and losing the substance."

85. जल में रौणो मगर दगड़ि बैर। Jala men rauṇo magara dagarhi baira.

To live in water and bear enmity with a crocodile (is not wise).

This is used to dissuade or discourage one from contending with his superiors.

86. झूटा ब्या सांचा न्या। Jhúṭá byá sánchá nyá.

Marriages will be effected by false representations but justice will be obtained by speaking the truth.

It is difficult to get a poor man married unless he is falsely represented to be of high caste and a man of property and wealth.

87. जो दियो या खायो सो आपणो। Jo diyo yá kháyo so ápano,

Only what one has given (in charity) or eaten is one's own.

88. जो कौ सो घ्यू सों जौ। Jo kau so ghyú soṇ jau.

Whoever will talk of Ghi will have to go to fetch it.

E.g. Whoever will inform any man of *Ghi* to be had at a certain place will be told to bring it.

This is used to caution one against giving information of any thing in which he is not concerned; if he does, he will have the burden of procuring it or of proving it.

89. बाग कि कड़ि में हाथ हालनो। Bága ki karhi men̲ hátha hálano.
To touch the person of a lion.
To enrage a great man in any way is dangerous.
"To tread on the lion's tail."

90. झिमोड़ा कि पूड़ में हाथ हालनु। Jhimorhá kí púrha men̲ hátha hálanu.
To thrust one's hand into a nest of hornets.
I.e. To stir up a number of wicked people against one.

91. गुरु करनु जाणि पाणि पीणो छाणि। Gúrú karanú já̲ni páni píṇo chhá̲ni.
Strain your drinking water and use judgment in selecting your Gurú (spiritual guide).
Act with deliberation.

92. फाटो स्यूणों रूठो मनूणों। Pháṭo syúṇo rúṭho manú̲no.
That which is torn or ripped must be mended, and the angry must be soothed.
Applied especially to daily life in the family.

93. पैर रड़ाव जीभ डंडाव। Paira rarháwa jíbha daṇḍáwa.
The foot causes one to slip and the tongue causes one to be punished.
"Whosoever keepeth his mouth and his tongue keepeth his soul from troubles."

94. शत्रु साखि ढुंगो अचैणो। Shatrú sákhi ḍhhú̲ngo achai̲no.
To choose an enemy as a witness and to take a stone for a chopping block.
A fatal mistake.

95. सुधरौ तौ नाइ को बिगड़ तौ जाट को। Sudharau tau nái ko bigarha tau jáṭa ko.
If the shaving is well done it is creditable to the barber, and

if any injury be caused it is to the head of the man who is shaved.

Applied to people who are careless in working for others.

96. सस्ती रो बार बार महंगि रो एक बार। Sastí ro bára bára mahagi ro eka bára.

One who purchases a cheap thing has to weep constantly, but one who pays a good price for a food article weeps but once.

97. एसि खीर मैं नि खै सकूं। Esi khíra mai ni khai sakúṇ.

I shall not be able to eat rice pudding of that kind.

"Not if I know it!" "Not for Joseph."

Story : Once a blind beggar was promised a feed of *khír* (a pudding of rice and milk). The blind man enquired what kind of food *"Khír"* was. He was told that it was white. As the blind man had no notion of color, he asked what was meant by white; For answer he was referred to the color of the heron which is pure white. The blind man then asked what a heron was like. On this some one made a figure of the bird by putting up his forearm representing the neck, and his hand with his fingers pointing downwards representing the head and the throat of the bird, which the blind man touched with his hand, and finding it of a crooked form said that "He could not eat *Khíra* like that," for it would stick in his throat. Hence the proverb; which is applied to one's refusing to undertake any business which he thinks will go against his own interests or involve him in difficulties.

98. रांड भांड अरना भैंसा बिगड़ गया तो करणा कैसा। Ráṇḍa bháṇḍa araná bhaiṇsá bigarha gayá to karaṇa kaisá.

If a widow, a buffoon, and a wild buffalo, become mad or angry, what is to be done?

There is no remedy.

Caution to deal carefully with violent people. (The widow in Hindu society, being neglected and despised and made to do the most menial duties, usually develops a shrewish temper.)

99. गवार को मन ठवार। Gawára ko mana ṭhawára.

You can only manage a villager by professing to agree with him.

100. ठोकर खैबेर अकल औंछ्य। Ṭhokara khaibera akala aunchhya.

A stumble causes one to be careful in future.

C.f. "A stumble may prevent a fall."

101. सब है भलि चुप। Saba hai bhali chupa.

Silence is best of all.

Illustrated in the following story.

Bírbal or Bírbar the most intelligent and wisest man of his time, was the beloved minister of Akbar the great. In consequence of favour with the Emperor he was hated by the other ministers of the same court. As they could not surpass him in intelligence, wit, and capacity, they were always intent on finding out his flaws and faults. Failing in this, and knowing that his father was a stupid and ignorant man, they found a way of revenging themselves upon the hated minister by bringing Bírbal's father before the king so that he might see his failings. Bírbal was not unaware of the plot, and he instructed his father to shew all proper marks of respect and homage to the king, but to keep silent. Soon after this the contemplated meeting took place, during which Bírbal's father, in spite of the many questions put to him, on topics of conversation raised by the Emperor, remained perfectly mute as previously advised, to the great astonishment of the latter; who, at last, asked Bírbal himself for an explanation of his father's conduct. Bírabala said, "My Lord, what should one do if he happened to be in the company of a fool?" To this the Monarch readily replied "I presume nothing but maintain silence." (By this reply the King indirectly acknowledged himself to be a fool).

C.f. "Speech is silver, silence is golden."

102. वोबरावालान कन लीगयो बाग पांडा वालान पड़ी जाग। Wobaráwálána kana lígayo bága páṇḍá wálána parhí jága.

The tiger carried off the people of the lower story and those of the upper story awake.

Take warning from the distress of others.

103. माल जानू माल जानु सबन ले कयो उकाला होलारा कैले नि देखा। Mála jánú mála jánú sabana le kayo úkálá holárá kaile ni dekhá.

Every one without due regard to the difficult ascents and descents of the hills wishes to go to the plains.

I.e. One ought not to undertake a work without first acquainting himself with the obstacles that he is likely to meet on the way. *C.f.* "Look before you leap." (See Introduction for description of this feature of the country).

104. मुष्ठि को धन दृष्टि को ज्वे। Múshṭi ko dhana drishti ki jwe.

Money in one's hand, and a wife within one's sight.

This means that money is one's own possession and a wife kept under surveillance are safe. This corresponds with the Sanscrit proverb. "The learning in books and the money in the hand of another person are of no use in time of need."

105. जाणु ढांगु औणो आंगु। Ján̲ú ḍhán̲gú aun̲o áṇgú.

One who goes to Dháṇgú (a steep and precipitous portion of Garhwal) must came back carefully and slowly.

A perilous task.

106. नंग चुनणि कुल्याड़ा काटणि। Nan̲ga chunaṇi kulyárhá káṭaṇi.

The thing which could be nipped in the bud with the nails, if suffered to remain must be cut with an axe.

C.f. "A small leak will sink a great ship." "A stitch in time saves nine."

107. वला ढुंगा कि फटक पला ढुंगा पुजिगे पै हट्ट हड़ि कौणो। Walá ḍhuṇgá ki phaṭaka palá ḍhuṇgá pújige pai hatta harhi kauṉo.

One should leap from one stone to the other before he boasts of the deed.

C.f. "Praise not the day, till night comes."

108. गया गया गयै गया। Gayá gayá gayai gayá.

One gone to Gayá has gone for ever.

In former times when there were no railways people repairing to Gayá (a famous place of pilgrimage) had to travel for months on foot, and so only about one fourth of the average number used to return home and the rest perished. Still used to dissuade from undertaking a perilous pilgrimage or long journey.

109. गम खाणु या कम खाणु। Gama kháṇú yá kama kháṇú.

One ought to forbear or eat little.

To forgive and to eat little food are advised as the safest course one ought to take in this world. The first puts a stop to quarrels and contentions; and the second protects a man from the evil consequences of an over-loaded stomach.

110. रख पत रखाव पत। Rakha pata rakháwa pata.

Be charitable (courteous) to others and you will be treated charitably (courteously).

One morning in the month of May, the Emperor Akbar the Great, his son, and Bírbar his Prime Minister, went out for a walk. They walked several miles. As soon as the sun had risen the monarch felt his cloak heavy and relieved himself of it by putting it on the shoulders of Bírbal. As soon as he had done this his son also followed his father's example. On this the Emperor looking at Bírbal said ironically that the load was heavy enough for one ass, to which Bírbar said. "No Sire, the load I am bearing is properly speaking the load of two asses."

111. पक्का पान खांसि न जुखाम। Pakká pána kháṇsi na jakháma.

Ripe betel causes no cough or catarrh.

Applied to dealings with, and the society of, old people. This proverb teaches that friendship and dealings with boys should be avoided. Indians eat the leaf of the betel when they have cough or cold.

112. गया बजाया अन्यारिया कणि औणो चितया। Gayá bajáyá anyáriyá kaṇi auṇo chitayá.

Sing and beat drums, but be warned of the approach of Anyáriyá.

Caution against the consequence of a dangerous and troublesome undertaking.

The proverb has its origin from the undermentioned tradition : Aneriyákot is a village on the banks of the river known as "Swáṉla." On the bank of the same river is a *Gháta* called Bishwa Nath about two miles east of Almora where all the dead bodies of the town of Almora are cremated. The road from Almora to Aneriyákota passes close to the *Ghát*. The Gháts where dead bodies are burnt are supposed to be haunted by ghosts or evil spirits. It is also supposed that these ghosts occasionally, and generally on the day Amábáshyá or the 30th of the lunar month (when the moon is invisible) rise up and beat their drums and dance after midnight. On one occasion a villager of Aneriyakot happened to go to his home from Almora late in the night and by mischance met with their procession and was greatly frightened at the horrible sight. For some of them were without heads, some without legs, some without arms, some with eyes jutting out and bleeding, some with eyes depressed looking like two holes, some with bleeding hair, some in huge shape with frightful faces and teeth, some walking on the ground and bearing their king (who was in a still more appalling form), others flying and dancing round him, but all in hideous and prodigious human form with their feet turned backward. In the desperation of his terror he rushed forward and seized the leader, and notwithstanding the threats of the ghosts kept hold of him, until at last the king of the demons was forced to submit and asked him what he wanted from him. The villager thereupon conceived the happy idea of demanding from the demon king the greatest favour that he could imagine, viz. that all manure heaps should be carried from the village of Khatyárhí near Almora to his own village, and that all the millet crops in his village should be weeded. The king of evil spirits agreed to do this and pledged his faith for it, whereupon he was released by the man. On the morning of the next day to his satisfaction he found his village full of heaps of manure, but to his utter grief saw all his millet crops uprooted (instead of being weeded, as promised by the king of the devils). He then started from his village and again laid wait for him, and overtaking him reproved him for the damage done to his crops, but the devils pleaded their innocence since they did not know how to weed. So the process was explained to them. They also gave their sacred vows to the villager that any person taken possession of by ghosts would be cured if he or any member of his village or their descendants should touch him, and that they would remain at their will and pleasure in future to do any service for them. So the man releasing the king of ghosts returned to his home and found his crops properly weeded. Since that time the residents of the village have become famous and successful mendicant exorcisers of evil spirits and are employed as such wherever their services are required. At the same time the ghosts have become so cautious of the residents of the village that they never appear in their sight and always warn each other with these words, which have become proverbial.

113. पैली आत्मा तब परमात्मा। Pailí átmá taba paramátamá.
First one's own soul, then God (are to be regarded).
That is one ought to take care of his own life before he under-

takes to please God. For only so long as he is alive he can remember God.

114. बड़ा मैस का निजाणो डीठ काना को बोज नि लगोणो पीठ। Barhá misa ká nijáṇo ḍīṭha káná ko boja ni lagoṉo pīṭha.

No one should go in the sight of a great man, or take a load of thorns on his back.

Great men have to be obeyed and heeded. If a poor man does not obey him he will be a marked man. In the same way load of thorns if taken on one's back causes inconvenience.

115. रिण मिलिजा तिण निमिल। Riṇa milijá tiṇa nimila.

One can get a debt, but not grass (in the cold season).

Used to warn people to provide grass for their cattle during the winter.

116. अन्न परमेश्वर। Anna Parmeshwara.

Grain too is a God.

Used to caution one against wasting grain, which supports life.

117. पाप प्रगट धर्म गुप्त। Pápa pargaṭa dharma gupta.

Sin comes out, but righteousness remains silent or hid.

That is, howsoever one may conceal his sins they will find him out eventually.

Also that one ought to expose his sins to evade future punishment, and to conceal his virtuous deeds; since it is supposed that a good deed if done in public is rewarded less than if done in private.

118. लौंडन दगड़ि खेलि धिंगड़ि आज नि बिगड़ि भोल बिगड़ि। Launḍana dagarhi kheli dhiṇgarhi ája ni bigarhi bhola bigarhi.

Dealings with boys will bring evil tomorrow, if not today.

Cautioṇ against dealing with boys.

119. दरबार परिवार तलवार। Darabára, pariwára, talawára.

A Court, a household, and a sword (are difficult to manage).

Used to denote that the management of each of these things requires a great amount of intelligence, care, and skill.

120. रिण गाढ़नु पूरा को दगड़ो करनु शूरा को। Rin̲a gárhanu púrá ko dagarho karanu shúra ki.

Borrow money from a really rich man and have a hero for a companion.

I.e. An ordinary money lender is troublesome, not so a hereditary rich man (banker). In the same way one is safe in the company of a hero or brave man.

121. खाइ जाणो केला को पात निखाइ जाणो कपालि हाथ। Khái jáṇo kelá ko páta ni khái jáṇo kapáli hátha.

If one knows how to eat his food on a plaintain leaf he can eat, but if he does not know it then he may put his hand to his forehead (a sign of disappointment).

E.g. One who is eating from a plaintain leaf must be very careful or the leaf will split and the food be spoiled.

The need of carefulness in everything.

122. कुकुर बोद कि हडि तें कौलो पाणितें सारो कुछ नीं। Kukura boda ki haḍi teṇ kauṇlo páṇi ten̲ sáro kuchha ní.

A dog finds nothing softer than a bone and nothing harder than water.

I.e. He loves bones and hates water.

Applied to people who go contrary to custom in everything.

123. खाणु घटकाइक मरनु भटकाइक। Kháṇu ghaṭakáika maranu bhaṭakáika.

To eat voraciously and die with difficulty.

Used to teach that one should do everything bravely. (A quiet death is considered a cowardly one, while it is thought a brave thing to die with difficulty).

124. खाणो नी फसाकू त रोणो दशा कू। Kháṇo ní phasákú ta roṇo dashá kú.

When I cannot get even plain tabacco to smoke why should I not lament?

Tobacco is prepared for smoking by mixing it with treacle. Hence to be unable to get even plain tobacco is a sign of extreme poverty.

125. कवा चलो हंस कि चाल आपणि लग भुलो। Kawá chalo haṇsa ki chála ápani laga bhulo.

The crow copied movements of the swan and forgot her own.

Applies to one who in imitating the actions of greater people neglects his own business and is thus ruined.

126. कुत्ता आयो भुकदो भुकदो बाग आयो लुकदो लुकदो। Kuttá áyo bhukado bhukado bága áyo lukado lukado.

The dog came barking, but the leopard came silently.

One who rebukes or reprimands does not wish to injure, but one who is intent to injure does so secretly.

127. कालो चोर अंधेरि रात। Kálo chora andheri ráta.

A thief in black and dark night.

E.g. A thing difficult to be found out or discovered.

QUARRELS AND DISCORD

1. एक हाथ ले तालि निबाजनि। Eka hátha le táli ni bájani.

Clapping cannot be done with one hand only.

"It takes two to make a quarrel".

2. ज्वे खसम एक छुयाल रांड छेक। Jwe khasama eka chhuyála ráṇḍa chheka.

The wife and husband are one, and let the scandal-monger be accursed.

Applied to dissuade people from raising quarrels among relatives.

3. ज्वे खसम की कल दूध भात की बेल। Jwe khasama ki kala dúdha bháta kî bela.

The quarrel between a husband and wife ends like a meal of rice and milk (i.e. quickly over, and will not last long).

E.g. As elsewhere said, the fighting of goats, the ceremony performed for one's forefathers by a saint or hermit, a cloudy morning, a quarrel between husband and wife, will not last long.

4. ठिनका पड़ाइ। Ṭhinaká parhái.

Striking a spark with flint and steel.

(Villagers still get their fire in this way).

Applied to quarrels which unexpectedly take place between parties without any evident or palpable cause. A sudden quarrel.

5. डूम दगड़ि गूगेलि। Ḍúma dagarhi gúgeli.

A quarrel with a low-caste man is like playing with human excreta.

I.e. Degrading to oneself.

6. तु दंडा मैं त्रिशूल नाचण बैठा तीनू कुल। Tú ḍaṇḍá mai trishúla náchaṇa baiṭhá tinú kula.

You are a club, I am a Trishula (trident) three generations began to dance.

Among illiterate folk, deities and ghosts are supposed to possess people and make them dance. During festivals the people of every village assemble at night near the village temple, and a great fire is lighted (called *Dhúni*) in the centre. One of the people gathered there, stands up and takes hold of the wooden club, while another takes the three-pointed iron bar which belong to the temple, to represent the deities. The drummers beat their drums; the two men begin a wild dance. This stimulates and excites all the other people to dance and make a great shouting and noise. Thus the combination of two big persons is able to excite the whole population of a neighbourhood. That is, two persons combined and united can play a far better part than a single person can. "Two heads are better than one." This is also interpreted to mean that when two persons begin to quarrel one thinks or says that he is in no way inferior to the other; if one claims to be the club the other says he is the *Trishúla* (trident) and so the quarrel or contention arises. Hence the proverb. *C.f.* "If you are Turk I am a Tartar."

7. सुचो न कपास कोलि दगड़ि करछा कर्छ । Sutro na kapása koli dagarhi karchhá karchha.

Neither thread nor cotton quarrel with the weaver.

Applied to one who quarrels with others for no cause.

8. तेरी मेरी कब बिगड़लि जब लेन देन होलो । Terí merí kaba bigarhali jaba lena dena holo.

When shall we quarrel with each other? When we begin to lend to and borrow from each other.

Another proverb says that three things destroy friendship:

1. To converse with a man's wife in his absence;
2. To lend to or borrow from him,
3. To debate with him.

9. तेरा पिसिया में मेरो मिसियो । Terá pisiyá meṉ mero misiyo.

Your grist and mine are ground together.

It is difficult to separate grist belonging to two or more parties without some disagreement. Hence the proverb refers to cause of quarrels.

Applicable to division of joint property or cited to warn one against running the risk of such liabilities or to advise him to abstain from such a bargain.

10. त्वे कु न मैं कु भुईचला रास । Twe ku na maiṉ ku bhuichalá rása.

Neither for thyself nor for myself, but for the earthquake.

This means that the thing which we are quarrelling about neither remained with you, nor with me, but was taken away by a third person while we were disputing.

The lawyer milks the cows whilst the disputants struggle for its possession.

11. झाड़ कुटि झगड़ो । Jhárha kuṭi jhagarho.

One raises a quarrel by beating grass.

Beating grass is nobody's business at all, or is a useless act, so if one beats it he does it to raise some contention without cause.

Applied to those who are fond of quarrels, and seek an occasion of offence, or to critics who are always ready to find fault.

12. तालि द्वि हाथन ले बाजंछि। Táli dwi háthana le bájanchhi.
Two hands are needed for clapping.
Applied to quarrels in which both parties are to blame.

13. कल्यारी कलकरी मरम आंखर नाबोली। Kalyári kalakarí marama áṇkhara ná bolí.
Quarrel, but do not say anything that may give mortal offence.
Quarrelling is allowable if it is not carried too far.

RASH AND FOOLISH ACTS

1. आ बैल मैं कणि मार मेरा गला में फंदा डाल। Á baila mai kani mára merá galá me phandá ḍála.
Come, bullock, beat me, and put the yoke on my neck.
I.e. A bullock is generally yoked and beaten.
If one unnecessarily and rashly undertakes the liabilities of the bullock (another person) he will be treated accordingly.

2. छंदा करछुला हाथ डडोणो। Chhandá karchhulá hátha ḍaḍono.
In spite of having a spoon (to stir up the food in the pot) he gets his hand burnt.
Applied to one who rashly endangers himself by attempting unnecessary work, or to one who instead of taking a safe path goes by one which is evidently perilous.

3. चतुर का चार जगा लाग। Chatura ká chára jagá lága.
A wise man feels four difficulties.
Before starting a thing a prudent man will reflect over its present and future consequences to himself and other people, whereas a fool will attempt a thing rashly and without any deliberation at all.

4. छन आंखान का भेल पड़नु। Chhana áṇkhána ká bhela parhanu.
Falls down a precipice in spite of having eyes.

Applied to one who does an evidently foolish thing rashly and without deliberation.

5. औ खुंड म्यरा मुंड। Au khuṇḍa myará muṇḍa.

O log, strike my head.

I.e. No one should endanger himself by meddling in another's affairs.

6. आला काचा खै नाख मुख अै। Álá káchá khai nákha mukha ai.

The food raw and half-cooked if eaten comes out through the nose and mouth.

E.g. As it is not digested it produces colic, causing vomiting and derangement of the stomach.

Used to warm people not to do anything without deliberation, for one who does a thing rashly eventually sufers in consequence of it. "Look before you leap". "Haste makes waste". "The more haste the less speed".

7. ताते खौं जलि मरूं। Tátai khau̲n jali maru̲n

One who eats hot food is sure to burn his mouth or lips.

Used of one who unwisely and reshly is determined to do a ruinous work without regard to its consequences.

Caution against doing a thing rashly or without prudence. *C.f.* "Hasty climbers have sudden falls."

8. खसम बोलिक डूम पर हाथ। Khasama bolika ḍúma para háthá.

A caste woman lays her hand upon a Duma (low caste man).

Applied to one who thoughtlessly does something wrong.

READINESS FOR CONTINGENCIES

1. श्याल की लड़ाइ शेर को ठान। Shyála kí larhái shera ko ṭhána.

One who goes to hunt a jackal must provide himself with weapons to fight with a tiger.

Be ready for all possible emergencies.

REGRET, REPINING OR DISSATISFACTION

1. सीली वोबरी झीली खाट। Síli wobarí jhíli kháṭa.

A damp cellar and loose bed.

Destitution, or untoward circumstances.

2. सांज का मरिया कु कबतें रोणो। Sánja ká mariyá ku kaba ten rono.

How long will kinsmen and relatives weep for one who dies in the evening.

E.g. When one dies his kinsmen immediately take him to the *ghata* for burning, and so long as the body is in the house they weep over him, and as one who dies in the evening cannot be removed until the next morning it has become a question "how long will his people mourn over him".

Applied by one, who is either disabled or made unfit for any business in his early life, or is in constant distress, for his own consolation.

3. काणो बिरालू मांड ले पत्यायो। Káno birálu máṇḍa le patyáyo.

A one-eyed cat is deceived by rice water (because it looks like milk).

Applied by one (bemoaning his ill luck) who is obliged to be satisfied with a little in place of much, or by one who has been misled by false hopes, or has been deceived through his simplicity.

4. लाग लागौ न धात पहुंचौ। Lága lágau na dháta pahuṇchau.

I have no mediator, and no one hears my cry.

Used by one who considers a certain thing totally out of his power.

5. पहाड़ निजनमौ चेलो देश निजनमौ बेलो। Pahárha nijanamau chelo desha nijanamau belo.

Let me not be a man in the hills, or a he-buffalo in the Plains.

Men in the hills have to carry heavy loads up the steep paths while those in the plains have not to do so. In the same way a he-buffalo in the hills has no work whatever to do, whereas in the plains he is always employed in heavy labour.

Used by a Pahárhí grumbling at his lot.

6. माछा को बोइ कु सदा शोग। Máchhá kí boi ku sadá shoga.

The fishes' mother is always in sorrow for her children. (for they are caught).

Applied to one who is incessantly in adverse circumstances.

7. चणा का पेड़ में गाड़ि अटकी। Chaṉá ká perha meṉ gárhi aṭakí.

A cart stopped by a stalk of gram.

E.g. Great affairs hindered by trifles.

8. छप्पन टका। Chhappana ṭaká.

Fifty-six ṭakas i.e. 112 pice the maximum amount of a gift.

In ancient times when money was scarce 112 pice was the greatest amount one could give another. This is still used by one who is not satisfied with what he has received, and says he expected at least 56 *Ṭakas*.

9. से रुणो तेरा बाबा का सांथ नहै गोछ हड़ी रुणो छ। Se ruṉo terá babá ká sáṉtha nahai gochha harhí ruṇo chha.

Sleep for me has gone with thy father, now I can only lie (like a log).

Spoken by a widow to her son who tells her to sleep.

This is made use of by one whose prosperity or happiness has left him, and who can do nothing but grieve and repine.

10. दुख सुख कै पैं नि कौणो सुखि साखि लाकड़ो है रूणो। Dukha sukha kai paiṉ ni kauṇo sukhi sákhi lákarho hai rúṇo.

Better to shrivel up like a log of wood than to tell one's distresses to another.

This is applied by one who bemoans his having no real friends and relatives, and so makes up his mind not to expose himself to others, who, having no interest in or sympathy with him, are likely to laugh at or take advantage of his weakness.

11. ज्वे जै हुनि त रोइ केछि। Jwe jai huni ta roi ke chhi.

If I had a wife, what should I cry for ?

A wife is a very useful article to the *Pahárhi,* as she does nearly all the work.

12. जेठा ज्यू कि खोरि फुटि टिका लेणि ठौर। Jeṭhá jyú ki khori phuṭi ṭiká laiṇi ṭhaura.

The husband's elder brother hurt the middle of his forehead (or defamed himself).

I.e. When any great man does anything bad it becomes widely known.

13. सिनालु का पिनालु पिनालु को भेल पापड़। Sinálu ká pinálú pinálú ko bhela páparha.

Sinálu (yam or big sweet potatoes) if neglected (not cultivated, allowed to grow wild) degenerate into Pinálus (small roots); and if Pinálus grow wild they become like grass and not fit for food.

Used by one bemoaning his degraded position due to his friends not taking proper care of him.

14. बड़ा बाप का चेला बड़ा पापले हुनि। Barahá bápa ká chelá barhá pápa le huni.

To be the son of a big (rich) man is the consequence of great sins committed in a previous state of existence.

E.g. The son of a rich and great man who is brought up in luxurious and lavish habits takes no trouble to learn any useful profession and consequently is not in such easy circumstances as his father. After his father's death when he is unable to go on as before he feels ashamed and regrets bitterly that he was born a rich man's son, seeing himself now reduced to poverty.

15. जेठा ज्यू फूं फां करि गया मेरि खोरि फोड़ि गया। Jeṭhá jyú phúṇ pháṇ kari gayá meri khori phorhi gayá.

My husband's elder brother in gratifying his own wish broke my head (I suffered much loss).

E.g. If the husband's elder brother going here and there on his own ends happens to touch the younger brother's wife (which is forbidden) then she says, you have hurt my reputation. Used by one who suffers in consequence of the doings of others.

16. मोर अपणा खुटा देखि क रोव। Mora apaṇá khúṭá dekhi ka rowa.

The peacock looking at his own feet wept.

The peacock was cheated out of his beautiful feet by a partridge, and in lieu of them he received the ugly ones of the partridge; he mourns over his deception, of which his feet remind him whenever he sees them. (The fact is: While dancing the peacock is pleased by looking over the other parts of his beautiful body, but tears flow from his eyes when he sees his feet).

Story : Once a peacock and a partridge proposed to have a dancing party in a forest; the condition entered into was that one should dance before the other by turns. The peacock was the first to please his comrade, the partridge, with his dancing, but when the partridge's turn came he refused to dance unless the former exchanged feet with him for the dance, to which the peacock agreed and gave away his feet to the partridge. The partridge after dancing a while flew away to the jungle with the borrowed feet and left his own with the peacock, leaving him to disappointment. Hence the proverb applied to one who regards his own foolishness in having lost something.

17. न होइ खील की कौणी न मंडल की भीख। Nahoi khîla kî kauṉî na maṇḍala kî bhîkha.

Neither did I get any kauṇí (a kind of millet) out of the jungle fields (newly cultivated in the jungle) nor have I been able to collect grain by begging from inhabited places (villages).

Used by one bemoaning that his labours and efforts to get a livelihood have been in vain.

18. घर में रइ न तीरथ गइ मुंड मुडै बेर फजीत भई। Ghara me rai na tíratha gai muṇḍa muṇḍaibera phajíta bhaí.

Neither remained at home nor went on a pilgrimage, but was disgraced by having her head shaved.

The heads of those who become ascetics are first of all shaved, and after that they are ordered to quit their homes and spend their time in visiting sacred places. If one does not do this after having his head shaved he is regarded as depraved, being neither an ascetic nor a family man.

19. हाथ न गात ढुंगा माथ। Hátha na gáta ḍhuṇgá máṭha.

Neither in his hand, nor on his body but spilt on a stone.

Applied to things lost and wasted without being in any way used or enjoyed.

"Spilt milk."

20. जैकि गाड़ि अटकि वी को नाम चुतिया। Jaiki gárhi aṭaki wí ko náma chutiyá.

The man whose cart sticks in a rut is called a stupid man.

Unfortunate men are generally considered fools.

21. जड़िया के खायो कड़िया खावो। Jarhiyá ke kháyo karhiyá kháyo.

Why did I eat jarhiyá (a vegetable, a kind of mustard)? it proved to be an unholy thing to me.

Applicable to one who repents for some acts of his which has resulted very differently from what he expected, to his trouble and harm.

22. जख सोनो छ तख नाख नी जख नाख छ तख सोनो नी। Jakha sono chha takha nákha ní jakha nákha chha takha sono ní.

Where there is gold there is no nose, and where there is a nose there is no gold (nose-ring) for it.

A rich man without a wife, or a man with a wife and family

but no wealth. So a rich man without children or without culture. Plenty with ill health &c.

23. थेचा कूटी ये अछाणामा। Ṭhechá kúṭi ye achháṉá ma.

This wooden block (on which all the chopping of firewood, meat etc, is done) gets all the beating and cutting.

The head of the family is made to bear all the expenses incurred by every member of his family.

Used by the head of a family who grudges the expenditure which his household is incurring. "The willing horse is always burdened."

24. खुदा बख्श का दिन भला मौला बख्श का दिन भला दिन बुरा मेरा जो तेरो घड़ौ को पाणि पियो। Khudá bakhsha ká dina bhalá Maulá bakhsha ká dina bhalá dina burá merá jo terá gharhau ko paṇi piyo.

The fate of thy sons Khudá Bakhsh and Maulá Baksh will be good, but mine is evil, because I have drunk water out of thy vessel.

E.g. The Hindus are prohibited from drinking water out of the vessel of a Mahomedan; if any one does so he is excommunicated. Once an astrologer travelling in the plains grew very thirsty. He happened to meet a woman, who enquired of him who he was. He said that he was an astrologer. On which she requested him to kindly predict the future of her sons, after consulting their horoscopes. To this the *Pandit* replied in the affirmative, and asked her for water (taking her to be a Hindu woman, as the Plains Hindu and Mahomedan women wear clothes of the same fashion). As soon as the Pandit had drunk the water given by her, she laid the horoscopes of her two sons before him, and he began to examine them. He found one was that of Khudá Bakhsh and the other of Maula Bakshsh. At this he was astounded (fixing his eyes on the said names) and did not know what to do. She, seeing the attitude of the *Pandit,* supposed that he was absorbed in contemplation of the horoscopes, and therefore addressed him thus: "Panditji! what is the future of Khudá Bakhsh and Maulá Bakhsh?" To this earnest enquiry of hers the Pandit replied thus: "The days of thy sons Kudá Bakhsh and Mulá Bakhsh are fortunate, but mine are the evil days, inasmuch as I have drunk water out of thy pot." Hence the proverb. Applied by one who regrets the evil consequences of his errors.

25. पूत कपूत पठायो चोरी झुसल्याणा आरू ल्यायो टोड़ी। Púta kapúta paṭháyo chorí jhusalyáṇá árú lyáyo ṭorhí.

A bad son sent to steal brought back only green apricots.

This is applied to one's own relations or kinsmen, who though they have had recourse to evil ways of getting money, are yet poor.

26. सूत कातिक कोली की भौदि पूत सैंतीक बुवारी की भौदी। Súta katika kolí kí bhandi púta saiṇtika buwárí kí bhaudí.

The thread spun is made over to a weaver, and the son nourished is made over to a daughter-in-law.

Natural regret of parents.

27. आज न पूती, काल न पूती, केसों फूली तौ न पूती। Ája na pútí, kála na pútí, kesoṇ phúlí tau na pútí.

Today childless, tomorrow without issue, and when turned grey still without issue.

This is applied to one who is never successful in any undertaking, or one who never grows wiser or learns from experience.

28. आज का पिनालु खाड़ै भोल का पिनालु खाड़ै। Ája ká pinálu khárhai, bhola ká pinálu khárhai.

The Pinálus (sweet yams) dug up today are buried, and those dug up tomorrow will also be buried.

This vegetable root is generally covered over with earth after being dug up, otherwise it dries up or rots. Infant children when they die are buried under ground. So this proverb is cited with regard to one whose all children have died in infancy. It is also applied to one who has failed in all his efforts to obtain some object.

29. अर्थ पायो न गोबिन्द गायो। Artha páyo no gobiṇda gáyo.

No wealth earned, nor yet a pious life led (the praises of Goviṇd not sung).

Regret for having lost both this and next world. For the theory is that one must either get his human birth blessed by the adoration of God with a view to the next existence, or by the accumulation of wealth for comfort and reputation during the present life.

30. बापू का घर निलाइ चोलि पयाल का भर नि खाई पोलि। Bápú ká ghara niláî choli payála ká bhara ni kháî poli.

No good clothes when in my father's house, and no sweet-meats when in my father-in-law's house.

"Poli" is a cake made of *gurha* (treacle) and is given to young girls in order to make them grow up quickly.

This proverb expresses regret at one's continued bad fortune.

31. बाप की कटारी नी मां की पिटारी नी। Bápa kí kaṭárí ní, má kí piṭárí ní.

I have received no kaṭári (a three-edged knife kept by Kshetrias or Rajputs), from my father, and no box (in which women keep cash and valuables) from my mother.

Used by one who complains of his poor unlucky circumstances, or by one who boasts of his own earnings.

32. दांतन है छुटि गयो त ओंठन ले नि पकड़ीनो। Dáṇtana hai chhuṭi gayo ta oṉṭhana le ni pakarhíno.

A thing that has slipped from one's teeth cannot be held by the lips.

Applied by one who bemoans that he has lost the favour of a greater man, which cannot be made up for by the favour of poorer people. This is also spoken of lost opportunities.

33. परलोक को चोर। Paraloka ko chora.

The thief of the former existence.

The theory is that one who does not get a thing in this life is supposed to have robbed another of it in his former life.

Used to express regret and grief of one who is destitute and in want.

34. ताता तवा को पाणि। Tátá tawá ko páṇi.

Water on a red-hot oven.

Used to represent one's insignificant income which is insufficient to meet his large expenses.

35. दै मैं को माखो। Dai mai ko mákho.

A fly in curd.

E.g. If one finds a fly in curd he immediately throws it away in disgust.

Used by one who is disliked, being a stranger and looked upon as an intruder.

36. कसा कसा कां गया मुसा का चेला दिवान भया। Kasá kasá káṇ gayá músá ká chelá diwána bhayá.

What has become of others that the sons of a mouse have become statesmen.

Used to express regret as to one of low family rising to an important post.

37. कनाली खै भूटी रड़गे टूटी। Kanálí khai bhúṭi rarhage ṭúṭi.

He longed for nettles and ate them, but afterwards his longing was changed to aversion.

One who follows after evil will suffer in the end. Also that all inordinate desire should be repressed.

38. खाणि पिणि गढ़ रैगे रौंत्यालो कुमूं। Kháni piṇi gaḍha raige rauṇtyálo kumún.

Food and drink is left in Garhwal, but beautiful scenery in Kumaun.

A Garhwali saying, Garhwalis in Kumaun cannot get as good food and water as when at home.

39. खाण कमूण कु बिडोली का डांग देखण दर्शन कु गोस्तु की बाड़े। Kháṇa kamúṇa ku Biḍolí ká ḍánga dekhaṇa darshana ku Gostu kí bárhe.

The story land of the village Biḍoli is cultivated profitably, but pleasant to be looked at is Gostu-ki-bárhe.

These two villages are in Garhwal. All is not gold that glitters.

40. खल का गुसाईं डडवार की स्याणे। Khala ká gusáî ḍaḍa-wára kí syáne.

One who was once the owner of threshing floors now longs for Ḍaḍwara (alms).

E.g. When the crops are threshed and winnowed the village blacksmith, the drummer who beats his drum before each house on festival days, the priest who performs the religious ceremonies, the tailor, the weaver, the oilman, the ploughman etc, and other poor men go and get some grain from the owner of the threshing-floor as a gift; this gift is called *"Ḍaḍwára"*. Hence the proverb which is applied to one who being once the master of wealth has now become a beggar.

41. खै आले बुआरि पी आले ससुर। Khai ále buári pí ále sasura.

What shall the daughter-in-law eat and the father-in-law drink?

An ironical phrase used when there is very little to eat, or expressing regret and surprise when the supply is very small.

42. काटियां माछा धार। Kaṭiyán máchhá dhárá.

Fish cut in pieces (for cooking) fled away to a ridge.

An impossible or astonishing thing.

43. काल मु बिनती करीत रोजाही लीग्यो। Kála mu binatí karíta rojáhi lígyo.

Death on being requested to spare one took away the best.

REJOICING AT OTHER'S CALAMITY

1. भलदा मरि गयो भली भै डुम कुड़ि आगो लागो भली भै। Bhaladá marigayo bhalí bhali bhai ḍuma kurhi ágo lágo bhali bhai.

That our elder brother the bear (a complimentry term, used now when the bear is dead) was killed, was a good thing; but that the house of the Ḍúma (a lower caste) was burned down was also a good thing.

This saying originated from the story of a bear who once entered the house of a *Ḍúma* after honey in a hive, and accidentally set fire to the house by stirring up the cinders. So, according to the higher castes, *(Biṭhas)* of Gangoli, "Two birds were killed by one stone."

2. बैरी को बाछरू पिजायो सुख। Bairí ko báchharú pijáyo sukha.

It is pleasant to see the milk of an enemy's cow drunk up by its calf.

Rejoicing at the injury done to one's enemy.

3. मूसा का जिया पर बिरालु का खेल। Músá ká jiyá para birálu ká khela.

The rat's painful death is the sport of the cat.

This proverb has the same meaning as Esops' fable of the boys and frogs. "What is fun to you is death to us."

RELATIONSHIP

1. अपणो पालो पोसो परायो खाड़ कोच्यो। Apaṇo pálo poso paráyo khárha kochyo.

One cherishes one's own, but beats to the ground another's.

I.e. No one is as careful of another's property as he is of his own.

2. आपणा गोरू दिया को पुण्य और पोश। Ápaṇá goru diyá ko punya aura posha.

He who feeds his own cow, obtains virtue and nourishment.

I.e. To feed the cow is an act of merit, and also repays one by supplying milk. Applies to maintaining one's own kinsmen and relatives.

3. आपणो आपणु बिराणु माचोद। Ápaṇo ápaṇú biráṉú máchoda.

One's own people are dear, a stranger is cursed in comparison.

4. आपणो मारिबेर पालो बिराणो पालिबेर मारौ। Ápaṇo máribera pálau biráṇo pálibera márau.

A man will continue to love his own even if beaten by him, but an outsider even if tenderly cared for, will beat (not love) the benefactor.

5. आपणो मारिक ऊंडो परायो मारिक फूंडो। Ápaṇo marika úṇḍo paráyo márika phúṉḍo.

One's own, even when beaten, will come closer, but a stranger, if beaten, will leave.

This teaches that we should chastise our own kinsmen for their good, but not beat strangers who are employed as servants &c.

6. आपणा बलद का पैना सींग। Ápaṇo balada ká painá sı̃ṇga.

The horns of one's own bullock are always considered very sharp by every one.

I.e. Every one thinks his own wit to be better than that of others. A man thinks that he possesses one full wit and that half a wit is spread over the rest of the world, since God has bestowed only one-and-a-half wits on the world.

7. आपणा को मुनकि टोलो भलो। Apaṉá ko múnaki ṭolo bhalo.

A tadpole caught by one's own child is considered a good fish.

I.e. Even a mite earned by the industry of their own children is considered great gain by the parents.

8. जो बाप ल्याव स्या बइ जो राजा कर स्या सइ। Jo bápa lyáwa syá bai jo rájá kara syá sai.

Any woman taken by one's father should be considered equal to a mother, and the decision arrived at by a king must be right.

Inevitable respect due to the deeds of father and officers owing to there being no remedy for such grievances. *C.f.* "What cannot be cured must be endured."

9. आपणि जांघ कन्याइ छारो इ छारो। Ápaṇi jáṇgha kanyái chháro i chháro.

One gets but ashes (scurf) by scratching his own thigh.

E.g. By scratching the thigh streaks like ashes become visible. This proverb is applied to one who exposes the fault of his own kinsmen or relations, to dissuade him from doing so. "Fouling one's own nest."

10. बौल्या गिजौणो पर पौणो नि गिजौणो। Baulyá gijauṇo para pauṇo ni gijauṇo.

A labourer may be treated well, but not a guest who is a poor relative, otherwise he will come again and again, and become dependent on one.

11. छोटि चेलि नांगि बडि चेलि लाज। Chhoṭi cheli náṇgi barhi cheli lája.

Seeing her younger sister naked the elder one feels ashamed.

Blood sympathies are absolute. Applied to induce one to help his relatives who are in distress.

C.f. "Blood is thicker than water."

12. लुवा को काल लुवा सोरा को काल सोरो। Lúwá ko kála lúwá sorá ko kála soro.

Iron cuts iron, and a kinsman injures his own kinsman.

Applied to one who is injured by his own caste fellows. The trees of the forest heard that an iron axe was coming to injure them, but the old trees on hearing this said there was no danger as he belonged to another caste. But when they heard that the iron was joined to a piece of wood they were filled with fear.

13. जाग जाग के दगड़ो निहुनु मेरो छे मेरो छै कै आपणु निहुनु। Jága jága kai dagarho nihunu mero chhai mero chhai kai ápaṇu nihunu.

No one can be sure of his company by requesting other travellers to wait for him, nor can any one be certain of a stranger becoming his friend, by assuring him that he is so.

No one in the world feels true sympathy for another except a real relation.

14. दैणो हाथ बायां धोव। Daiṇo hátha báyáṇ dhowa.

The right hand washes the left.

E.g. The good deeds of a man cover his faults and failings; or a man ought to help poorer kinsmen, who will do the same in their turn.

15. घर छेदू लंका बिनाश। Ghara chhedú Laṇká binásha.

Laṇka (Ceylon) was destroyed through the information given by a traitor (member of the household).

Ráwana was killed and Ceylon taken by Ráma through the secret information given by Rawan's own brother Bibhíkhana (*vide Ramayan*). Applied to a member of one's family who has become estranged and turned an enemy and is dreaded in consequence. Once worst enemies are those of his own household.

16. मामा शरीको पौणो नि पितर शरीको देवता नी। Mámá sharíko pauṇo ni pitara sharíko dewatá ní.

A man has no better guest than his own maternal uncle (i.e. mother's brother), and no better deities than his own father and mother.

Used to induce people to honour such relatives. *C.f.* Honour thy father and thy mother.

17. हाणि मारनु बेचि खाणु। Háṇí máranu bechi kháṇu.

I can beat him or sell him.

Applied to one's own brother or son etc, whom one can treat as one likes.

18. जो महादेव घर बसौ सो पारबती। Jo mahádeva ghara basau so párabatí.

Any woman living with Mahádeva may be treated as Párbatí (the renowned wife of the God Mahádeva).

Applied to an unmarried woman who lives with a relative or some great man as a concubine, in regard to her being treated exactly as if she were married to him.

19. जां अपणियांट तां खणियांट। Jáṇ apaṉyáṭa táṉ khaṇyáṭa.

Where there is kinship, there is enmity.

Men of the same caste will be more bitter against one another than those of different castes.

20. लाठि मारी शिर अलग नै हुनु। Láṭhi márí shira alaga nai huṉu.

No one can be beheaded by the stroke of a club.

This is used to show that it is useless to try and sow discord among the members of a family.

21. लाठि मारी बेर पाणि अलग नि हुनु। Láṭhi márí bera páṇí alaga ni hunu.

Water cannot be divided by the stroke of a stick.

Applied to brothers and kinsmen who though they may sometimes quarrel among themselves will eventually get reconciled, and it is of little use to try and separate them by showing dissensions among them.

22. सौ धोती एक गोती। Sau dhotí eka gotí.

One hundred Dhotis (Brahmins) and one Goti (blood relation). C.f. "Charity begins at home."

Applied to pursuade one to give to or help his own kinsmen by saying that helping one kinsmen is equal to helping a hundred Brahmins.

23. ये लटुला कु कखि जगा नि होइ मेरा नाख भीतर होइ। Ye laṭúlá ku kakhi jagá ni hoi merá nákha bhītara hoi.

This cluster of hairs, having no other place, found place within my nostril.

Used by one who laments on account of a useless and trouble some member of his family.

24. ये देवता को कोइ नै भयो मेरा आंग आयो। Ye dewatá ko koi nai bhayo merá áṇga áyo.

This deity has no one else, and so he has come upon me.

E.g. Deities and ghosts are supposed to enter into people and make them dance. Used by parents with respect to worthless children or relatives dependent upon them.

25. मिया ज्यु घैल होला त हलुवा खूंला। Miyá jyu ghaila holáta halúwá khúṇlá.

If my husband is hurt I shall eat Haluwá (a dish made of flour, Ghi, and treacle or sugar).

This is a saying regarding a woman whose husband was a great miser, and who used to keep all supplies under lock and key, contrary to the common custom which allows such articles of food to be in the custody of the wives. Once the miser fell down a precipice and was advised by his physicians to eat *Haluwá* which is believed to cure hurts by dispersing bad blood in the body. The miser being unable at the time to give out the necessary ingredients himself was obliged to send the key of the store room to his wife, who instead of taking a little of each ingredient took every thing in plenty and so got much *Haluwá* cooked not only for the sick man but for herself also. The miser as soon as he was up took away the key from his wife and kept it in his own possession which induced the wife to pray that some accident might be fall her husband so that she might have the chance of eating *Haluwá*. The proverb is applied to persons who wish injury to their own people or family, and ironically to the miser as well.

26. स्यै बटि अै राजा को दार बिनसर बटि अै राजा को दार। Syai baṭi ai rájá ko dára binasara baṭi ai rájá ko dára.

The timber that comes from Syai (a great fir forest) belongs to the king, and that which is brought from Binsar (another great fir forest) also belongs to the king.

Used to denote that any expense whatever incurred by any member of one's family at any time or place devolves on the head of the family.

Syahi and Binsar are the two great forests which supply wood for building at Almora.

27. कुकुर चेला बिरालु चेला मैं रांडि चेला। Kukura chelá birálu chelá mai ránḍi chelá.

The dogs have sons, the cats have sons, I, an accursed (unfortunate) woman, have also sons.

This is a reply by a woman, indignantly mourning over her sons who proved useless and troublesome to her, to a query by another woman who asked her whether she had sons.

E.g. In India the birth of sons is welcomed generally whereas those of daughters are regretted, for the former are valued and the latter depreciated for the reasons noted below.

The sons inherit their fathers' property and remain at home, while the daughters have to be given away in marriage to others with a dowry; but the sons who bring disgrace on their parents or family, squander property, and are either disobedient or troublesome to parents, are much bemoaned.

28. पूत कपूत गू को वलाणो। Púta kapúta gúko waláṇo.

A bad son brings blame for excreta (trifling mischief).

I.e. He eases himself in a forbidden place and thus his parents are chastised for the act by his neighbours.

29. सोरो निखाणदे या खोरो निखाणदे। Soro ni kháṇade yá khoro ni kháṇade.

Neither will one's kinsmen of the same caste suffer him to enjoy or continue in his prosperity, nor the skull (the suture of the skull denoting good or bad luck).

Used by one bemoaning losses due to either of the above sources. For kinsmen envy one another's prosperity through jealousy, and so take steps to ruin one another.

30. बिगलिया भाइ सोरा बराबर। Bigaliyá bhái sorá barábara.

Brothers, when they get separated from each other do not treat each other as brothers but as kinsmen.

Living apart from each other they become wrapped up in their own interests.

31. काटण्या ल्वे हग्यां सुख। Káṭaṇyá lwe hagyáṇ sukha.

One gets relief as soon as he has discharged the painful blood (referring to dysentery).

Used of worthless and troublesome members of one's family whose absence or loss is welcomed instead of being regretted.

32. पीना पाणि एक तेल उपड़ैल। Píná páṇi eka tela uprhaila.

The chaff (the matter out of which oil has been extracted) and water become one, but the oil is a stranger (a separate thing).

Used by one bemoaning his estrangement from a friend or relation owing to another introduced by him to his friend having supplanted him in his esteem. For at first the chaff was part of the seed and united completely with it and water was a foreign element, but in the oil press water and chaff have become one, and the oil is driven away as a stranger.

33. केड़ै कि तापणि देवर कि आपणि। Kerhai ki tápaṇi dewara ki ápaṇi.

The fire of dried-twigs is like the endearment of the Dewara (husband's younger brother).

A husband will love his wife with the same tender love all along or with a lasting love. A husband's younger brother, after the decease of his brother, shews great affection towards his sister-in-law for a while in order to impress her with his solicitude, but soon neglects her as the fire of thin twigs burns up for a time and dies out.

Used by women only. Small thin dry twigs are called *"Kerhás."*

34. मैं बाप को गोत पाणी को सोत। Mai bápa ko gota páṇí ko sota.

The descent of one's own parents and the source of water (are never to be depreciated).

This also denotes that by descent from his parents one has connection with people far and wide as a source of water has with other waters and oceans.

35. जैको सोरो छुटो वी को खोरो फुटो। Jaiko soro chhuṭo wí ko khoro phuṭo.

He who is deserted by his relations is an unfortunate one.

For he will be rendered an isolated and weak party in the world, as every one consults his relations in family alliances and other matters.

36. अपणा पूत रखंता पराण पूता भखंता। Ápaṇá púta rakhaṇtá paráyá púta bhakhaṇtá.

To protect one's own son and to devour another's.

Used to represent the custom and nature of relationship in this world.

37. पैली गै सुख तव गर्भ सुख। Paili gaî sukha taba garbha sukha.

First wish comfort to the cow and then to its embryo.

If the head of a family is happy all the members are so, and if he is in trouble all share with him. This teaches that every one should take proper care of and look after the comforts of the head of the family.

38. मामा फुफू का भाइ कका बड़ों का दाइ। Mámá phuphú ká bhái kaká barhoṇ ká dái.

Maternal uncles' sons and father's sisters' sons act like one's brothers, but cousins act like enemies.

E.g. Generally the former live in separate villages and are entitled to alms and help from their relations, and so they are friendly with him (the speaker), but the latter, who have to live in the same village where he does, and have collateral and joint interest with him in every thing they possess, are liable often to have quarrels with him.

39. खालो पेलो मेरो गुजा छौं ढोलना सों तुजा। Khálo pelo mero gujá chhauṇ ḍholaná soṇ tujá.

My Gujá (friend or relative) will have to eat and drink, but you shall throw away the filth or do my drudgery.

Near relations are valued and well-treated, distant ones are of no consequence.

40. नजीक को दुशमण टाड़ को दोस्त। Najika ko dushamaṇa ṭárha ko dosta.

The one near is an enemy, and the one who is at a distance is a friend.

Used of troublesome neighbours or members of the same household. This is further compared to a troublesome disease contracted in one's own body which certain herbs foreign to him cure him of.

41. आंसु आंखन बटि औनी घुनन बटि नि औना। Áṉsu áṇkhana baṭi auní ghunana baṭi ni auná.

Tears flow from eyes and not from knees.

A man's own relations will sympathize with him, but not a stranger.

Story : Once a tyrannical king, not satisfied with taxing his subjects while they were alive, laid a tax on every dead body taken for cremation to the river side. After some years the king felt the approach of death, and sending for his eldest son instructed him to reign in such a manner that the people should praise his (the father's) administration. After his father's death the new king, in order to make his subjects regret the decease of their former ruler, issued orders to the effect that, in addition to the death tax no body should be burnt at any *ghat* (burning place) until a "coffin officer" had driven into it a wooden peg as a sign of final sanction having been given for the cremation. This new law caused great consternation among the people, for it was equivalent to a public disgrace to the body of every dead person. The king's subjects, therefore, began to lament bitterly the new reign, and long for the old king, who, though oppressive enough had, yet never imposed such a shocking order on his people. Thus the son shewed his filial obedience and piety by making his father's death regretted and his administration praised, though at the expense of his own propularity. Such a duty would have been fulfilled by no one except the king's own son. Hence this story is often told as an illustration of the proverb quoted above.

42. आ लक्ष्मी मेरा घर आ मेरा पड़ोस में आ मेरा देश में आ। Á Lakshmí merá ghara á, merá parhosha me á merá desha me á.

O wealth, come to me (to enrich), or to my neighbour (to enrich him), or my country (to enrich it).

Used by good and patriotic people who rejoice at the good or welfare of their kinsmen, neighbours and country.

43. होइया को बाब नि होईयै कि मैं आस कि बैणि नि आस को दोस्त। Hoiyá ko bába, nihoiyai ki mai, ása ki baiṇi, ni ása ko dosta.

The father likes his son if the latter is in good circumstances, whereas the mother does so even if he is in adverse circumstances, the sister likes his brother, if she has some hope of advantage from him, but a friend will love him even if he has no hope of him.

REMEDY

1. बहम कि दवा नहाती। Bahama ki dawá naháti.

There is no remedy for a (groundless) suspicion or presumption.

No one can know what suspicion another has with regard to him in his mind.

2. बिष का मुख चीस। Bisha ká mukha chîsa.

The poision will not heal without a scorch.

The bite of venomous creature must be cauterized. Serious maladies require sharp remedies.

3. बिष की औषध बिष। Bikha kî aukhadha bikha.

The remedy of poison is poison.

Once during the intense cold in the month of January the Emperor Akbar the Great, while taking a walk round about his city, saw a tank of water, and enquired of his chief minister Birbal whether any man would be able to live a whole night in the cold water of the tank. A person who had overheard their conversation on the road came forward, and said that he would be the man to do it, if he were given a good reward. The Emperor said he would give him Rs. 10,000 if he should find him alive the next morning. The poor man accepted the stake. Accordingly he was put naked into the pool, the water of which came up to his neck, and a guard was placed there to watch him. The poor man thus spent the night, and was brought by the guard before the Emperor the next morning to receive the promised reward. The Emperor asked him how he spent the night in the water in such unbearable cold. The man replied, "My Lord. I saw a fire at a distance of four or five miles just in front of me;" depending on which (in hope that he would have such a fire to warm him next morning) he had felt no cold during the night. At this the Emperor refused to give him any thing at all, since he had had fire before him during the night. But Birbal did not think the Emperor freed from his promise. He interceded and pleaded for the poor man, but in vain. After a few days the Prime Minister was ordered to accompany the king on a certain day at a given time. The statesman in the meantime had a bamboo 5 yards long split up into three pieces and then made a *Chúlá* (hearth stove) on them, which stood 5 yards high. On the top of this hearth he put the vessel containing rice and water, and lighted a fire below it on the ground. On the fixed day and at the appointed time Birbal was sent for by the Emperor. He gave answer that as soon as he had had his food he would present himself before the Emperor, who on hearing this waited for him for some time. As Birbal did not come, the Emperor sent the messenger again to command him to make haste. Birbal sent him the same message again. After waiting for some time further, the Emperor became angry at the delay, and went to Birbal's house, whereupon Birbal prostrated himself at the feet of the Emperor and asked forgiveness for the unaviodable delay, and shewed him the pot of rice on the bamboo *chúlá*, On seeing this the Emperor expressed his astonishment and said "What a fool you are; how can the rice be cooked with the fire lighted at such a distance from it!" To this Birbal said "My Lord, the rice will be cooked in the same way by the heat of the fire as the poor man in the tank was warmed by the fire so many miles away from him." The Emperor became convinced of his mistake, and at once ordered Rs. 10,000 to be paid to the poor man.

4. राकस को भै भेकस। Rákasa ko bhai bhekasa.

The brother of a goblin is one who assumes his guise (to subdue him).

A goblin can only be subdued by some one assuming the same form. *I.e.* A wicked man can be brought to his proper bearings by wickedness only!

5. रिसाड़ की लेणी स्वैण रोसाड़ को खाणो बांटो। Risárha ki leṇí swaiṇa rosárha ko kháṇo báṇṭo.

The wife of one, who falsely charges her with unchastity, should be taken by others, and the share of one who gets angry at dinner time should be eaten by others.

Ironical censure of such conduct.

6. सामी अंगुलि घ्यू नि औंदो। Sámí aṇguli ghyú ni auṇdo.

A straight finger cannot bring out any ghi (clarified butter) out a narrow vessel.

Simplicity cannot thrive in this world; trickiness is needed.

7. बिन भेद किड़ा नि झड़ना। Bina bheda kirhá ni jharhaná.

Worms cannot be extracted without charming.

I.e. Wickedness should be matched by corresponding arts. Worms infest sores in animals and incantations are used to exterminate them. "Diamond cut diamond."

Story : Once the Emperor Akbar the great ordered his prime minister Birbal to convert him into a Hindu. Fearing to offend the monarch by saying anything against his wishes he gave his assent. Next day Birbal stationed a man by the side of the road daily frequented by the Emperor, and ordered him to take a donkey with him, and to clean it by rubbing and scrubbing the animal with a stone. This process was going on, and owing to the rough usage that he was getting the animal was braying loud, when the monarch accompanied by Birbal approached the scene. Akbar asked what all this meant, and why the ass was being handled so cruelly. Birbal replied that the man was trying to turn the ass into a cow. On this the Emperor expressed his surprise and said that the man was attempting an impossible thing. To which Birbal replied "Nay, Sire, it is as possible as to turn your majesty into a Hindu." The Emperor convinced to the force of Birbal's reasoning remained silent.

This story is also applied to the proverb, "The remedy of

poison is another poison used." (under the head of "Remedy").

REPUTATION

1. आबरौ। Ába rau.

One ought to preserve his lustre i.e. reputation.

One who has lost his reputation is disregarded, as pearls having vivid lustre sell dear, while the same, though bigger, but wanting in splendour, sell cheap.

2. कोरो भानो मोसो। Koro bháno moso.

A new (unused) vessel (soon) gets black.

A new vessel quickly shows the soot.

A small fault tarnishes a good reputation, but it would not be noticed did a scoundrel commit it.

REQUITALS AND RETRIBUTION

1. जो कर टुणो उई सो हो रुणो। Jo kara ṭuṇo ui so ho ruṉo.

He who performs enchantments on another will (have to grieve or) suffer in the end.

E.g. One who wishes to injure another will himself meet with the reward of his endeavours to ruin another. *C.f.* "The righteousness of the perfect shall direct his way : but the wicked shall fall by his own wickedness."

2. दिन खैण्या राति पड़्यो। Dina khaiṇyá ráti parhyo.

Dug a pit (for others) during the day time and fell into it himself in the night.

3. जो औरन सों खाड़ खण उइ सो कुवा तयार। Jo aurana soṇ kháḍa khaṇa ui so kuwá tayára.

Whosoever digs a pit for another will himself fall down a well.

I.e. He who wishes to harm another will thereby achieve his own ruin. A bad deed has an evil end.

Ps. vii. 15. "He made a pit and digged it and is fallen into the ditch which he made."

RESPONSIBILITY OR LIABILITY FOR ONE'S DEEDS

1. अपणि करनी पार उतरनी। Apaṇi karaní pára utaraní.
One's own deed will save a man.
I.e. One will get salvation by his own deeds alone. Any thing good or high to which a man aspires must be attained by himself.
"Work out your own salvation."

2. भलो कर भलो होलो सौदा कर नफा होलो। Bhalo kara bhalo holo saudá kara naphá holo.
Do good so that you may get good; and trade so that you may get profit.
This is spoken to one who is engaged in good works or trade by way of encouragement. *C.f.* "Industry is never unfruitful."

3. चोरी को माल चंडाल खौ पाप को माल प्राचित जौ। Chorí ko mála chaṇḍála kháu pápa ko mála práchita jau.
Stolen property is (eaten) enjoyed only by low caste people (i.e. by mean men) but property obtained by sin has to be spent in atoning for the crime.
No good man can rejoice in the fruits of his evil doings, but suffers sooner or later. *C.f.* "Evil got evil spent."

4. काम कि पछाड़ पछा औंछ्य। Káma ki pachhárha pachhá au̲nchhya.
The effects of an act are felt afterwards.
E.g. In performing a ceremony such as a marriage or tonsure every one wishes to make it as splendid as he can, but afterwards when he has to pay for every thing he feels it bitterly, and so one who is wise restricts expenditure as much as possible from the beginning by thinking of all items which are absolutely necessary and which he has to pay for. Used as a precaution against acting, or incurring liabilities, without due regard to their consequences.

5. ढुंगि ढुंगि में चड़ि चड़ि में पाप शिर में। Ḍhuṇgi ḍhuṇgi meṇ charhi charhi meṇ pápa shira meṇ.

The stone to stones, the birds to others birds, but the sin on his own head.

E.g. One threw a stone at a bird but missed his aim. The bird flew and joined other birds, the stone fell among the other stones, but the sin of wishing to kill the bird remained with him, for the Hindu Scriptures strongly condemn the taking of animal life.

6. द्यो देवता अपणा घरूं गया मेली लीपणी मैकु कै गया। Dyo dewatá apaṇá gharaúṇ gayá meĺi ĺipaṇí mai ku kai gayá.

The gods and spirits have gone away to their homes, but I have now to replaster (repair) the floor of my house.

E.g. People said to be possessed by deities and spirits, dance inside a house with such wild force that they break up the floor (which needs repairing) and so the mistress of the house complains of the trouble she has in consequence.

Applies to one's feasting the people and making them merry with eating and drinking but having to bear the expenses etc. consequent on it. *C.f.* "Dinner over, away go the guests."

"Having to pay the piper."

7. नाइ शिर में बाल कतुक छन हाजर औनी। Naí shira meṇ bála katuka chhana házara auní.

O, barber how many hairs have I in my head?

Answer. They will soon lie before you.

To be over-anxious about things which time alone can disclose. Also used of the consequences of one's dark deeds, which are certain to appear at some time.

8. नियत का सांथ बरकत। Niyata ká sáṇtha barakata.

A man is blessed in proportion as he uses his property well.

9. गंगा नाणि अपणा वास्ता गधेरो नाणो अपणा वास्ता। Gaṇgá náṇi apaṇá wástá gadhero náṇo apaṇá wástá.

One who bathes in the Ganges does it for his own benefit, and one who bathes in a rivulet (not in the Ganges) does it for his own purposes.

Applied to one's being answerable for his own deeds.

10. कलि युग नहाति कर युग छ एक हाथ ले दे दुसरा हाथले ले। Kali yuga naháti kara youga chha eka hátha le de dusará háthale le.

This is not the "Iron age" but "the age of the hand;" if you give with one hand you will receive with the other.

Used against the teaching of the Hindu scriptures which says that in this age one who does evil will prosper but those who do good will come to trouble in this existence, as illustrated by the story No. 1; but the proverb which says this is not the iron age is illustrated by the story No. 2 narrated below.

Story No. 1 : It was at the time when the third age, known as *Dwápara Juga,* had departed and the fourth age called *Kali Juga,* had stepped in, that a man brought up in the righteousness of the former time felt exhausted and fatigued on account of hunger and thirst while journeying to a certain place distant from his home. He still travelled on in hope to find some village where he might refresh himself. But he could not find one. At last he saw a garden at a distance, to which he plodded on. On reaching the place he found the garden full of various kinds of trees bearing flowers and fruit, but no man or water were to be seen there. The honest man called out loudly, but no one answered him. He then, being compelled by hunger, plucked one citron and tied a gold *mohar* to the stem from which the fruit was taken, with a piece of cloth, believing that the price of the fruit did not exceed the gold coin, and that on looking for the fruit the owner of the garden would find the price, and so he (the honest man) would be justified in taking the fruit in the absence of the owner. After doing this he resumed his way, having the fruit tied up in his handkerchief, in hope to find water where he could eat it after performing the necessary ablution. When he had gone a few furlongs from the garden he was called on to stop by a dark-coloured man behind him, who charged him with having cut off his son's head, and taken it away. The honest man thinking himself innocent stopped at his call. The black-faced man coming near him said again. "O, good man, why did you behead my son and take away his head?" To this accusation the honest man related what he had really done. On this the black man said that it was not the fruit, but his son's head. After this the former put the handkerchief with its contents before the latter. On opening it to the utter amazement of the former they both saw the head of a boy freshly cut off (it was bleeding) in the cloth, instead of the citron. At this wondrous sight the honest man became convinced, and with great sorrow admitted his guilt. Then the black man said. "O, my good man, I am Kaliyuga (Iron age). My reign has begun now. Why should I be pleased with one who does an honest act such, as was becoming to my predecessors. I can be pleased only with the man who does wrongful acts which add to the dignity of my reign. They alone are becoming during my sovereignty. I am glorified by such dark deeds. Righteous deeds cast a slur on my rule, therefore I afflict and render poor those who do such things during my reign. Had you destroyed many trees, eaten much fruit, stolen it without putting any price thereon, and then said that you did not do it, but some one else, I would have been pleased with your conduct. Beware now that you do not annoy me again by a repetition of such honest deeds in future. I forgive you this first time; go to your home, good bye; and communicate my instructions to all whom you see, so that by following them they may become prosperous, and escape the punishment inflicted by me on those who observe the righteous laws of my adversaries (predecessors) during my reign.

Story No. 2 : There was once, some hundreds of years ago, a king named Narhachiyá, who, besides having a kingdom over which he ruled, was possessed of fifty six crores of Rupees in his treasury. According to the ancestral custom in vogue he used to distribute three handfuls of parched grain to those only who had no food at all during the past three days. Even this was felt as a hardship by the king, who was a great miser, and so he stopped this, in consequence of which God was very angry with the king. One day while the king was away from his palace, God sent anther man exactly of the same form, countenance, and stature as Narhachiyá. This new man sat on the throne and commenced the work of the realm as usual. All the people of the empire recognized him as king Narhachiyá without the least suspicion of his being a man other than the real Narhachiyá. Soon after this the real king returned to his palace, but was refused admission and reviled by the new king and the people of the kingdom as an impostor. As no one in the palace or kingdom discerned him to be the real king, he was obliged to take refuge in the jungles in order to save his life. While living in the forest he used to lead a secluded life, sustaining himself on wild roots and leaves. At last he came to his senses and sincerely repented of his wrongful conduct, and prayed to God saying, "O Lord, if thou wilt give me even one twentieth part of the money I had in my treasury, I will devote it to the maintenance of poor people." God approved of this conduct and told him to go to his throne, and when he did so, he ws greeted and accepted as a king by all the people. No sooner did he ascend his throne than he distributed all his wealth to the poor of his empire. Immediately after this he made over the kingdom to his heir, and himself became an ascetic. He began to live naked with a fire before him on the bank of a river caring for no wordly things whatever. After this one day a messenger came to him from another king to whom his own sister was married, and who hitherto was not aware of his brother-in-law having become a *Jogi*. The messenger came to invite him to visit the other king whose daughter had to be married on a certain day. Narhachiyá had nothing to feed the messenger with, and so he (Narhachiyá) told him to take any thing he wanted out of his *Dhúṇi* (fire). The man accordingly thrust his hand into the ashes of the *Dhúṇi*, and drew out some sweetmeats, to the utter amazement of the messenger. The envoy stayed then for some days with Narhachiyá and got all the food he wished for out of the *Dhúṇi*. At last he took leave of Narhachiyá and rẹturned to his own king. At the time the messenger departed Narhachiyá (having nothing else) gave the messenger three handfuls of the ashes as a gift, and a stone to be given to his niece on the marriage day as prescribed by the established usage, saying that he would be there on the fixed day, and would then present the stone to the girl personally. The messenger while on his way to his master found the ashes (given by Narhachiyá as a gift) to be gold dust. After this Narhachiyá arrived at his brother-in-law's house on the day his daughter was to be married. He was extremely sorry to see Narhachiyá as a *Faquir* and regretted his having invited him, for he supposed it would be very disgraceful to him to acknowledge Narhachiyá as his relation in the presence of the other kings who were also invited for the occasion. And so he got Narhachiyá lodged at some distance from his palace in a garden. But on that day God sent his angel with a gold chariot full of precious stones, clothes etc to Narhachiyá so that he might present it as a dowry to the daughter of the king. On this all the kings and other people left the palace and went to where Narhachiyá was with the angel, to see the scene, and everybody paid his reverence and homage to Narhachiyá and angel. The stone formerly sent by Narhachiyá to be presented to the girl had become a *Mani* (a gem). So Narhachiyá at the marriage presented all the valuables to his neece. Hence the proverb that this is not the iron age, but the hand age &c.

12. हर कसो जसा सों तसो। Hara kaso jasá soṇ taso.

God is to each as that person is towards Him.

C.f. With the pure Thou wilt show thyself pure, and with the perverse Thou wilt show thyself forward. (II Sam. 22: 27).

13. जो कर सो भर। Jo kara so bhara.

One will enjoy the fruit of his deeds.

As man does, so he will have to endure.

14. जैको पाप तैको बाप। Jaiko pápa taiko pápa.

The crime is the father of the sinner.

I.e. Whoever has committed the sin, the sin is his father. This literally means to curse (the father of) the sinner, for it says his father is sin, and sin's father is also sin which will be punished sonner or later. This is applied to an unknown offender.

Or, a man's sin is his father. *I.e.* He can never get rid of it. *C.f.* "Be sure your sin will find you out."

15. अन्त भला को भलो। Aṇta bhalá ko bhalo.

A good man's end is good.

I.e. One who does good deeds will have a good end, as illustrated by the following story.

Story : Once a goldsmith, a barber, a lion, and a snake had fallen into a deep well in a dreary jungle, where a good man happened to pass. On perceiving him, each of them cried out for help, and each of them promised to help the traveller in time of need. So, first of all the good man took out of the well the lion, who presented him with a diamond ring, promised that he would come to his help whenever he should remember him, and told him not to take out the barber and the goldsmith, and then went away. After this the good man got the serpent up, who also having promised his help in time of need went away, giving his advice to the good man not to take out the goldsmith and the barber. The good man contrary to the admonitions of the lion and the snake helped the barber and the goldsmith out of the deep well, who also took their way after promising to reward the services of the good man. After some years when the barber had become a *Kotwál* of a certain city, and the goldsmith was also trading at the same place, the good man, on arriving there, went to see his friends the barber and the goldsmith, who, though they knew him well, feigned ignorance of him, and, seeing the diamond ring on his finger, went straight to report him to the king, who, in the meantime, not knowing that his daughter who had worn the diamond ring on her finger had been killed by the lion, had issued proclamations throughout his kingdom that any one finding any clue to her ornaments would be rewarded. The good man was consequently arrested and put in charge of the Police, when the barber (now Kotwál) unnecessarily troubled and tortured him. After that in spite of his pleading innocence by representing all facts of the case the king sentenced him to be beheaded, on the proof of the diamond ring having been found with him. At this moment the good man remembered his friend the snake, who, after biting the queen, came to the good man, and said that the queen would die unless she was treated by him. The queen was senseless in consequence of the snake-bite. All remedies and charms were administered in vain.

Every one supposed her last hour had come. The next day, when the good man was about to be executed, he offered his services to cure the queen, and accordingly he was sent for and told to treat her. No sooner had he used his charms than she became quite convalescent. But the king, notwithstanding this, said that he would not spare the life of the man. Then the good man adduced the lion as his witness, and as soon as he remembered the lion a great number of lions came to his help, so that the city became full of them. At this spectacle the king became convinced of the truth spoken by the good man, though the barber and the goldsmith denied the fact, and ordered them to be beheaded in his place.

16. जैको चून तैको पुण्य। Jaiko chún taiko puṇya.

The reward is his who gives the flour.

Used to encourage charity.

17. जो कंज्या खाव तैकी गली डाड। Jo kaṇjyá kháwa taikí galí ḍáḍa.

Whoever eats kanjyá (a wild but sweet vegetable which causes irritation in the throat) will have his throat inflamed.

This teaches that every one will have to taste the bitter fruit of his own evil deeds.

18. राम झरोखा बैठ कर सब का मुजरा लेत। जैसी जैकी चाकरी तैसा वाको देत। Ráma jharokhá baiṭha kara saba ká mujará leta. Jaisí jaikí chákari taisá wáko deta.

The God Rama sitting at window sees every one's work, and gives wages for the work done by each.

This is quoted in regard to Rama who rewarded or chastises people according to the nature of the work done by each.

C.f. "The eyes of the Lord are in every place beholding the evil and the good."

19. तू खिलवाड़ो नि खणदो त तेरा बापु रिख नि खांदो। Tú khilawárho ni khaṇado ta terá bápu rikha ní khaṇdo.

Had you not cultivated a field in the midst of the forest, your father would not have been killed by a bear.

Applies to one who suffers for his own unwise conduct.

20. नाचणि खेलणि मुह सामणि। Náchaṇi khelaṇi muha sámaṇi.

The dancers and players will come in front of each one.

I.e. The result of each one's conduct comes home to him, just as in a dance the performers come in front of each of the spectators.

21. कुइराल खाइक खंकरियाल कद। Kuirála kháika khaṇkaryála kada.

Whoever will eat kuirála (a kind of wild tree the flowers of which are eaten by poor people) will be liable to catarrh.

I.e. Every one is himself responsible for anything which he does without due regard to its consequence.

22. जसो बोलो तसो लवालो। Jaso bolo taso lawálo.

As much as one sows, so much will he reap.

Applied only to giving charities. In a future existence a man will be blessed in porportion to his gifts in this life.

Illustration : Once there was a poor, simple and virtuous beggar living with his wife in a town. He used to earn only three Chhatáks of flour a day, whether be begged at five houses or fifty, but never more. One day when they had cooked one and a half cakes with the three *Chhatáks* of flour, a saint arrived there who said that he was very hungry. They gave him the one and a half (three chhatáks) of readymade bread, which the saint ate and departed. The hermit then went to God, and interceded for the poor man, but God shewed him the account-book and said that since he had given only one and a half rupees in his former existence, he was not entitled to more than what he received, and if he got that one and a half rupees at one time, after that he would get nothing more. The kind-hearted saint then petitioned god to let him have the one and a half rupees at once, the God gave it to him. Then the saint came back to earth again and advised the poor man that the one and half a rupees should be spent on charity, and whatever he got thereafter should also be devoted to the help of the poor. The beggar did as he was told. The very next day, having spent one and half rupees on charity, he earned three rupees, and this sum also having been given to the poor, the next day he got six rupees. In this way as his income increased he increased his alms also, spending all he received on charity. After this the same saint went to Paradise again, and saw God in the form of an old man, sitting in a bending posture. On his enquiring the cause of this, God said that the man who had received one and a half rupees, some time ago, had become very charitable, and that whatever he got he gave it away to the poor and that his charity had thus put a heavy burden upon himself. After this the saint came to the man again and said that he was a very pious man, and gave him advice as to his saving something for times of need. The man being puffed up with pride began to withhold his hand from charity and the consequence was that he became poor again very soon.

C.f. "Much is expected when much is given." "As you sow, so you shall reap."

23. जतुक कम्मल भिज ततुक भारि। Jatuka kammala bhija tatuka bhári.

The wetter the blanket gets, the heavier it becomes.

Used in reference to liabilities and debts, for the sooner they are discharged and settled the better; putting them off only makes them more burdensome. (The ordinary dress of a hill man consists of a blanket). Also used to denote that one's responsibilities increase with the increase of his family.

24. सासु बुवारी उंजो पैंजो बाप बेटा लेखो जोखो। Sásu buwári uṇjo paiṇjo bápa beṭá lekho jokho.

Mother-in-law and daughter-in-law borrow and lend, and accounts are kept between father and son.

The necessity of keeping accounts even in dealings with near friends.

25. नाना खोरा नानि पीड़ ठुला खोरा ठुलि पीड़। Náná khorá náni pírha ṭhulá khorá ṭhuli pírha.

The small skull has little pain (cares and anxieties) the big skull has great pain.

The burdens and responsibilities of wealth and position.

26. स्वर्ग नरक यैं देखींछ। Swarga naraka yaiṇ dekhiṇchha.

One finds paradise and hell here (while alive in this world).

E.g. The doctrine of the Hindu scriptures is that a man gets human life as a reward of good deeds after undergoing transmigration through eighty-four lacs of animal lives, as consequences of wicked deeds committed by him during his former human existence. So human life is said to be a period of probation (out of the eternity the soul has to pass through) and the last improved state in which he can either obtain salvation through virtue, piety and contemplation of God, or earn other future lives, or hells which are forty-five in number according to the sins he commits in human life. The illiterate or common belief is that one in blissful circumstances is enjoying his paradise here, and one in distressed circumstances is said to be enduring his portion of hell here (in the present human life).

27. केकु पोण्याली होइ ति केकु द्वार ढकदि। Keku pauṇyalí hoi ti keku dwára ḍhakadi.

Why did you make alliance with me, and why do you now shut your doors against me?

E.g. As you have intermarried with me I must be treated as a relative. A thing agreed to should be maintained at any cost of trouble, risk or loss.

RIDICULE AND LAUGHTER

1. अधिकारि को फथकारि कूकर को चाकर। Adhikári ko fathakári kúkara ko chákara.

The officer's servant keeps a servant for his own dog.

The dog-keeper is a very menial servant, but gives commands as if he were an officer oppressing the people.

Applied contemptuously to one who takes on airs of command (a gentleman's gentleman).

2. रोग को मूल खांसी झगड़ा को मूल हांसी। Roga ko múla kháṇsí jhagarhá ko múla háṇsí.

Coughing a root of sickness, and ridicule a root of quarrels.

An axiom cautioning people against mockery.

RIVALS

1. आग और सौत थोड़ी लग बुरी। Ága aura sauta thorí laga buri.

No one should despise a spark of fire, or a small rival wife (i.e. a second wife).

Both these things are capable of causing much mischief if left unsuppressed.

2. दूइ तलवार एक म्यान में नी रइ सकनी। Dui talawára eka myána meṇ ní rai sakaní.

Two swords cannot be kept in one sheath.

Two rivals cannot live in the same place without quarrelling.

3. सौत चून कि लग बुरि। Sauta chúna ki laga buri.

The rival wife, even if made of maḍuwa flour (inferior) is a nuisance.

This proverb is used with keen appreciation by women who have rivals; and is also applied to competitors in any business.

The first or chief wife of a Hindu naturally resents with bitterness the idea of a rival in her husband's affections. In Bengal, according to a native writer, girls of tender age are taught to pray against such a calamity in the future and to pronounce curses on the possible future rival.

RUINOUS AND FRUITLESS EFFORTS

1. बिछीं को निजाणो मंच सर्प का दुला हाथ। Bicchî ko nijáṇo mantra sarpa ká dulá hátha.

To put one's hand into the hole of a snake when one does not know how to charm a scorpion.

I.e. To attempt work which is beyond one's power and dangerous. It is supposed that the effects of the poison of a snake or scorpion can be removed by incantations.

2. बोज छोटो जगात बड़ि। Boja chhotí jagáta barhi.

A small load but a heavy tax.

I.e. Much trouble attended with small gain. *E.g.* A small share in a village gives a great deal of trouble.

3. ब्योन स्यो लौड़ि कि खुटा तोड़ाइ। Byona syo laurhi ki khuṭá torhái.

The legs of the daughter were broken, (through fatigue in visiting all her friends and relations to say Good-Bye) and after all no marriage.

Applied to some bargain which after having caused much trouble, does not come to any thing.

4. भीम सों भारत स्वर्ग सों लात। Bhîma soṇ bhárata swarga soṇ láta.

To wage a war with Bhîma is like kicking the sky.

Bhîma is another name of Bhîma Sena one of the five Páṇḍavas, a great hero, spoken of in the Mahábhárata.

Applied to fruitless attempts.

5. एक टका का तें जोगि भयो नौ टका जोग्यूणा लागा। Eka ṭaká ká teṇ jogi bhayo nau ṭaká jogyúṇá lágá.

One became a jogi (ascetic) for the sake of two pice, but his being made a jogi cost him eighteen pice.

A bad investment.

6. मेहनत बर्बाद गुना लाजम। Mehanta barbáda gúná lájama.

Labour misspent proves a man guilty.

One who is not successful in this world is generally blamed. Compare the expressions "Poverty is a crime." "Success justifies anything."

7. गू खाण बाट। Gú kháṉa báṭa.

By eating excreta he gained nothing.

Applied to atrocious conduct by which no advantage is gained.

8. तिमिला का तिमिला खतैया नांगे का नांगा देखैया। Timilá ká timilá khataiyá náṇge ká náṇgá dekhaiyá.

All the figs collected fell down, and at the same time the body was exposed.

The hill women wear only a small sheet wrapped round their loins and passed over their head. One climbing up a tree to collect figs in her sheet, the sheet slips out of her hand and so she loses the figs, and at the same time the upper part of her person is exposed.

A double calamity, failure involving personal loss or disgrace.

9. ऊन कि खातिर ढेबरी लाया स्या दाम दाम कपास खाव। Úna ki khátara ḍhebari láyá syádáma dáma kapása kháwa.

A sheep was kept for the sake of her wool, but she ate up seers of cotton.

Dáma--Garhwal weight. An unprofitable speculation.

10. या बुवारि कुछ कुनि होइ पर छौं बरजण कु होइ। Yá buwári kuchha ku ni hoi para chhauṉ barajaṉa ku hoi.

This bride is of no other use except that I have to take care not to touch her.

Applied to a woman who instead of helping the family turns out useless and troublesome. The wife of a younger brother must on no account be even touched by the elder brother, nor may she touch him.

11. उड़ाया पोथलू घोल्यारा। Urháyá pothalú gholyárá.

Young birds that had flown away return to the nest.

Applied to grown up children who after they are married become dependent on their parents.

12. फरफतें मेरि कुंडली कथे। Pharphaten̤ merí kun̤dali kathen̤.

Where is my wooden bowl.

A *Dúm* (a low caste man) is in the habit of using this phrase all day and night, going in and out of his house asking "where is my wodden dish".

This proverb is applied to one who is moving here and there in vain in search of employment. The *Dúmas* are in the habit of eating a little food many times during the day, and as many times they need their respective dishes.

13. पैसा को कोदो टका पिसाइ। Paisá ko kodo t̤aká pisái.

One pice of millet (maduwá) but two pice for grinding.

C.f. "The game is not worth the candle."

14. पोयो पकायो सगलीणा घागरो डोयो बत्तीस हाथ। Poyo pakáyo sagalín̤á ghágaro d̤oyo battísa hátha.

The whole shirt after being sewn and washed measured only thirty two handbreadths.

This is used for any business which takes much trouble but affords little gain. *C.f.* "Great cry and little wool."

15. सुख की खातर बुवारी ल्यावा स्या रोज उठि मलार गावा। Sukha ki khátara buwári lyáwá syá roja ut̤hi malára gáwá.

A daughter-in-law was brought to increase our comfort but when she rises in the morning she does nothing but sing.

Applied to articles procured for the sake of comfort, but which prove to be sources of trouble and loss.

16. उधार निकालनु सों गया पैच याद करै आयो। Udhára nikála nu son̤ gayo paicha yáda karai áyo.

One went to borrow from a certain person, but only received a reminder to pay up a former debt.

C.f. "Going out for wool and coming back sheared."

17. गुड़ बेचि बेर गना नफा में चुसणा। Gurha bechi bera ganá naphá men̲ chúsan̤á.

One who barters his treacle for sugarcanes has the extra trouble of chewing them.

Unprofitable bargains.

18. खणिन पीणि घुना घुना ठिण। Kháṇina píni ghuná ghuná ṭhiṇi.

Feet benumbed to the knees but nothing to eat and drink

Great pains, small gains.

19. चौबेज्यू छबे हुणा सों गया आव दुबे ज्यू बैठो। Chaube jyú chhabe huṉá soṇ gayá áwa dube jyú baiṭhau.

A Chaube (once) went to another's house in the hope that he would be taken there for a Chhabe (would be more respected), but the man said to him "O dube, come and sit down."

A Chaube = one who has read four vedas.

A Chhabe = one who has read all the six vedas.

A Dube = one who has read two vedas.

Excessive ambition meeting with a fall.

20. बेला भरि नौणि नालि भरि कुकौणि। Belá bhari nauṇí náli bhari kukauṇi.

A cupful of butter and one Náli (2 seers) of dirt.

Used of work or business which is more troublesome than profitable. This is also used of a person in whom there is a little good and much evil.

21. अब कि जै खोलो कुंछ्यूं बबा कि जैगे। Aba ki jai khauṉlo kúṇchhyúṉ babá ki jaige.

I wished to earn for myself, but the undertaking deprived me even of what I inherited from my father.

Used of business which proves ruinous.

22. कान लगुंणा सों गयो नाख काठि लिगयो। Kána laguṇá soṇ gayo nákha kaṭi ligayo.

One set out in order to fix or replace his ear (which was cut off), but his attempt to do so deprived him of his nose.

Used of business which proves ruinous.

23. कम्मल को सातु। Kammala ko sátu.

The flour of parched grain kept in a blanket.

If the flour of parched grain is kept in a blanket, nearly all of it sticks to the blanket. Bad investments.

24. भारो छोटो जगात बड़ि। Bháro chhoṭo jagáta barhi.

A little load but heavy toll.

Used of work or business which is more troublesome than profitable.

SECRETS

1. एक कान दुइ कान तीन कान मैदान। Eka kána dui kána tína kána maidána.

One ear or two ears, but if three ears, then the open plain.

This is applied to secrets which should be confined at most to two persons. If it reaches a third ear it will become public.

2. सौज्यू कि फिलंग पाकि जाणिय। Sau jyú ki philaṉga páki jáṉiya.

The private disorder of a Baniyá is made known when it comes to a head.

A *Baniyá* is said to suppress the disease he is labouring under for fear of exposure, but when it comes to the worst stage he cannot hide it any longer.

Applied to secret dark deeds or evil designs which are known only when their result appears.

3. माछो पाणी कै बगत पीव। Máchho páṉí kai bagata píwa.

No one knows when the fish drinks water.

Used to enjoin proper secrecy.

4. दाइ मु पेट छिपोणु। Dái mu peṭa chhipoṇu.

To hide the person from a midwife.

Applied to those who keep any business in which they are concerned secret from their parents, or superiors.

5. दाड़िम खै दाड़िमै अै। Dárhima khai dárhimai ai.

One ate pomegranate and discharged the same entire, (i.e. could not digest its seeds).

Used of one who breaks secrecy and promise.

SELF-ESTEEM

1. सईसी इलम दरयाव छ। Saisí ilama daryáwa chha.

The work of a groom is like a deep stream.

Once a Syce was asked by a gentleman to bring another Syce for him: the Syce replied that the work of Syce is like an ocean; *i.e.* requires great talents, and therefore one could not be found, though clerks were plentiful everywhere. This is used ironically to ridicule the qualifications of one who himself boasts of them.

SELF-HELP AND EXERTION

1. बुटि का भरसा निरौणु हाथ पैर हिलोणा। Buṭi ká bharasá ni rauṇu hátha pair hiloṇá.

Do not trust altogether to charms, but use your hands and feet.

E.g. A certain saint gave a man a talismanic herb which would secure his prosperity. The man was delighted with the boon and asked leave to return home, whereupon the saint told him that he should not place his confidence alone on the herb, but also exert himself to attain his purpose.

C.f. "God helps them who help themselves."

Or, as Cromwell once said to his soldiers, "Trust in God, and keep your powder dry."

2. बापु ब्या कदौ सनेहू नि लांदो। Bápu byá kadau sanehú ni láṇdo.

The father can arrange for the marriage (of his son) but cannot create affection (in his son towards his wife).

A teacher can do his utmost in teaching, but cannot make his pupil clever. This is equivalent to. "One man can bring a horse to the water, but ten men cannot make him drink."

3. हिम्मत बंदा मदद खुदा। Himmata banḏá madada Ḳhudá.

God helps a brave man.

A man prospers through his own exertions and the help of God. *C.f.* "God helps them who help themselves."

4. जथगा हाइ को मनूणो ततगा गरज्योड़ी कन्यूणो। Jathagá háî ko manúṇo tatagá garjyorhî kanyúṇo.

Instead of exerting yourself to entreat another (to scratch you) use your efforts in scratching yourself.

This teaches that one should take the trouble himself of his own work instead of taking the trouble of inducing and entreating another to do the work for him.

5. पाणी कि धौ पन्यारा मु। Páṇi ki dhau panyárá mu.

One has to satiate his thirst by going to the spring itself.

This is used to encourage one to take the trouble of representing his own case personally, and not through others, to the highest officer, who is a fountain of justice. If you want a thing you must exert yourself to get it, and not expect it to come to you of itself.

6. माल कि लै कब कब खै। Mála ki lai kaba kaba khai.

How seldom do we eat the mustard produced in the Plains.

I.e. One ought not to depend on others for help, because it cannot always be depended upon, for one will give help only for once, as we can get the mustard of the plains only occasionally since it requires to be fetched from the plains.

7. घोघंत बिद्या खोंदत पाणी। Ghoghaṇta bidyá khodaṇta páṇi.

Learning to be had by repeating lessons, and the water by digging.

C.f. "No gains without pains." "There is no royal road to learning."

8. अकल ले परमेश्वर मिलंछ। Akala le parameshwara milanchha.

Genius and wisdom will even gain God.

Used as an encouragement to one to exert himself to find out the causes of things and to surmount difficulties instead of being daunted by them.

SELF-INTERESTEDNESS

1. बनजारा कन टांडै सुजंछ। Banajárá kana ṭáṇḍai sujaṇchha.

A Banjára looks always towards Ṭánḍá, (i.e. the place from which he set out).

Banjárás are Plains grain-dealers who take grain to sell in the hills. *E.g.* The Banjárás of Tándá village on the road to Moradabad are indefatigable grain dealers, but they love their home.

Every one looks forward to the accomplishment of his undertaking.

2. खाणो बाडि आपा चाड़ि। Kháṇo bárhi ápaṇá chárhi.

One eats bárhi (food made of millet flour) for his own purpose.

I.e. One takes trouble for his one sake. Bárhi is a very inferior kind of food which no one would eat who had not some special object in doing so.

3. परमेश्वर है मतलब बड़ो। Parmeshwara hai matalaba barho.

One's object or purpose is greater than God.

Every one cares more about his own desires than about God.

Illustration : Once the Prime Minister Birbal was deprived of the post by the Emperor Akbar in consequence of the back biting of his Mahomedan Ministers, who could not bear a Hindu being above them. Soon after this the Emperor asked the four Mahomedan Ministers who was the greatest man in the world. To this they replied the emperor was above all, then he put another question to them as to who was above him; they said "God". After this the Emperor asked them what was above God; they were unable to reply to this, but they said they would answer the question within one month, the king granted them the time. In the meantime they consulted many wise men about the matter, and fed many *Faquirs* in order to take their opinion about the question, but all in vain. On the last day of the month they left their home at night under the guise of *jogis* and went to the jungles. But Birbal being aware of this movement went ahead disguised as a *jogi* and stopped on the side of the road they had to come by, seating himself on a *Chárpái* (bed-stead). The Ministers while going along that way saw the *Faquir* (Birbal) and taking him for a real *faquir* told him of the difficulty they were labouring under. The *Faquir* consoled them and told them that if they would take him to the king he would give him the proper answer to his question. The ministers were only too happy to do this, and after stopping there for the remainder of the night they lifted up the *Chárpái* and conveyed him to the Emperor the next morning while he was sitting in his Court. Birbal while thus being conveyed to the *Darbár* upon the *Chárpái* put on his own clothes before he reached the *Darbár*. Then he saluted the king and told him that man's object or purpose was greater than God, for had the ministers not had an object they would have not borne him on their heads to the Court. With this the Emperor was fully satisfied and reinstated Birbal and the other ministers in their respective posts.

4. पातल का चड़ा। Pátala ká charhá.

Chirping of birds in the bushes.

Applied to the criticisms of various people to which one should pay no more heed than to the different notes of the various birds in the bushes, but go on with one's work. *C.f.* "Many men many words."

5. तेली तेल की नौना बालों खलाकी। Telí tela kí nauná bálon̠ khalákí.

The man who is grinding oil seeds is thinking of his oil, but the children are anxious for the chaff or husks.

When oil is ground the children eat the husks.

Used to show that every one is interested in his own affairs. *C.f.* "Every one for himself and God for all."

6. ज्यान छ त जहान छ। Jyána chha ta jahána chha.

The world is in existence or of use to a man so long as he is alive.

Used to induce one to take proper care of himself and enjoy life.

7. आपणि चाड़ि गधा जवारणि। Ápaṇi chárhi gadhá jawaraṇi.

One salutes an ass for a purpose of his own.

E.g. Hindus do not touch donkeys, and consider them to be impure.

Used to teach one to condescend to do everything possible in order to attain his object. As elsewhere said that one truly intent on a purpose ought to get it by placing disrespect and contempt in front of him and respect and courtesy behind him.

SELFISHNESS

1. जो मै कन देव सो मेरो ठाकुर जो मै कन निदेव सो मेरो कुत्ता। Jo mai kana dewa so mero ṭhákura jo mai kana ni dewa so mero kuttá.

The man who gives me anything is my master, but he who does not give me anything is as a dog to me, (for which I care nothing).

2. बदरीनाथ अपणा घर मै कन क्या देलो मेरा घर क्या ल्यालो। Badari nátha apaṇa ghara mai kana kyá delo merá ghara kyá lyálo.

What will Badarinatha give me if I go to his house, and what will he bring me if he comes to my house?

The shrine of Badari Natha is considered by the Garhwalis as their own peculiar shrine, and they do not have to present any offerings to it like other pilgrims, but instead ask something from it.

Addressed by poor persons to the rich and great.

Applied as a slur to one who is very selfish.

[See Introduction].

3. बाखरा को पूछ बाखरा का गिचा। Bákhará ko púchha bákhará já gichá.

The goat gets its own tail.

Each limb of a he-goat, which is sacrificed, is offered to different deities. The tail is assigned to Vishnu, who alone has power to give salvation. Its tail is therefore cut off and put into its mouth so that the goat may get salvation as a compensation for having been killed.

Applied to selfish people or when a thing taken from one is given back to him as a *present*.

4. गंगा गयो गंगा दास जमुना गयो जमुना दास। Gaṇgá gayo Gaṇga dása Jamuná gayo Jamuná dása.

When he goes to the Ganges he becomes Gangá dás (i.e. the slave of the Ganges), and when to the Jamuna he becomes Jamuná dás.

Applied either to a fickle-minded person, or to one who is selfish or time-server.

5. हुक्का का सांथ नातो चिलम का सांथ बैर। Hukká ká sánṭha náto chilama ká sáṉtha baira.

Friendship with the Hukká, but enmity with the Chilam.

The *Hukká* and the *Chilama* are two parts which together form the pipe for smoking used by natives of India.

Applies to one who bears enmity to a father, but befriends his son in order to gain some selfish ends.

6. हाथ कि तेरि तवा कि मेरि। Hátha ki teri tawá ki meri.

The loaf which is being kneaded is yours, that in the oven is mine.

E.g. The cake on the cooking-pan is sure to be ready sooner than the one which is being made ready: used when one is intent on having his own object attended to first; putting off the interests of other people to a future time.

7. हसण की दारी देण कु चूमड़। Hasaṇa kí dárí deṇa ku chúmarha.

A fairy to laugh, but a miser in giving.

Applied to people whose manners are very pleasant, but who are selfish and good for ṇothing.

8. फते नगारची। Phate nagárchí.

The drummer of one who is victorious.

Time-servers.

9. सारा सारा म्यारा मुख में पौला पौला माधरचोद का। Sárá sárá myará mukha meṇ paulá paulá mádharachoda ká.

Put the best into my mouth, and give the refuse to others.

10. सबै जोगी मरन मेरो हि पत्तर भरन। Sabai jogí marana mero hi pattara bharana.

A Faquir wishes that all other Faquirs should die so that his own dish may be filled.

Applied to one who wishes to be profited by the ruin of others. Faquirs always inherit the possessions of their desceased relations. *E.g.* Every Hindu puts a little food into the dish of a Faquir. If all other Faquirs were to disappear from the world by dying, householders would give the surviving one plenty (a dishful or plateful).

11. तू मेरो यबारी चूस मैं औंदा भादो चूसलो। Tú mero yabári chúsa mai auṇdá bhádo chúsalo.

If you work for me now I will work for you in the month of Bhado (August) next, i.e., a long time hence.

Illustration : A man once cried out in the Bazar, will any rascal lend me a *lákh* of rupees, I will pay him in the next world? Some one replied yes, why not, you can have it, for your words are so nice, the amount you ask for is so small, and the time of repayment is so near.

12. लाला ज्यु गिरला ढब संग। Lálá jiu giralá ḍhaba sanga.

A baniyá is willing to fall if he can profit by it.

E.g. Whatever a *Baniyá* may do or whatever course he may take it will not be without a motive.

Story : There was once a *Pandit* who for some months had been reading and expounding religious books in a temple. One day when a *Baniyá* went to pay his homage to the deities therein one of the idols said to the other "whenever the *Pandit* finishes his book he must get one thousand rupees." After hearing this the *Baniyá* enquired from the Pandit when he would finish the book. The Pandit informed him. Then the *Baniyá* said that he would give the *Pandit* one hundred rupees in lieu of all the offerings that he might get on that day. The *Pandit* who did not expect even a few rupees, and who was not aware of the promise of one thousand rupees made by the deity, gladly accepted the offer and received one hundred rupees from the *Baniyá* in advance. The latter stayed there until the former finished his book. But to the great disappointment of the *Baniyá* the Pandit did not get a single rupee on the appointed day. On this the *Baniyá* being exasperated slapped the idol with his hand, and said "the god is false." But his hand stuck to the face of the idol, and he could not take it away. After this, one of the gods asked this god whether the *Pandit* had received his one thousand rupees. He replied that the *Pandit* had already received one hundred rupees, and for the remaining nine hundred rupees the *Baniyá* had been arrested. On this the *Baniyá* was obliged to effect his release by paying nine hundred rupees.

13. मतलब की दुनियां। Matalaba kî duniyáṇ.

A selfish world.

14. खाणा सों पूत लड़ाना सों भतीजो। Kháṇá soṇ púta larha ná soṇ bhatîjo.

One feeds his sons but employs his nephews for fighting.

15. तेरो घट पिसी या नि पिसी ल्या मेरि भाग। Tero ghaṭa pisî ya ni pisî lyá meri bhága.

Whether your watermill may or may not grind your grain give me my right or wages.

Used of over-selfishness.

16. राणी मु नि दीनी छांस कुमहारीं मु दही। Ráṇí mu ni ďiní chhaṇsa kumahárí mu dahí.

The queen is refused butter-milk, but the potter's wife gets curds.

Selfishness conciliates those who are wicked and given to slander.

17. पिणा बखत का बाछा चढ़नि बखत का बहड़। Piṇá bakhata ká báchhá chaḍhani bakhata ká baharha.

Like a calf to suck the milk but like a bull to mount.

Applied to selfish people who are meek and humble in adversity or when asking favours, but violent and offensive when solicited for favours in return, or when they get other people into their power.

18. पै हालो मेरा मलुआ निपै भेल हलुआ। Pai hálo mero maluá ni pai bhela haluá.

If I get something from him he is my sweetest friend, if not, he should be thrown down a precipice.

A selfish disposition.

19. बानर कि गाल भरीणि गात कि कुशल। Bánara ki gála bharíṇi gáta ki kushala.

The monkey's filling his cheeks (mouth with food) is only for himself.

E.g. The monkey cares only for his own carcass and not even for his own young ones. No sooner does he find food than he will fill his mouth with it without regard to his young ones though present there.

Used of selfish persons.

20. लौ लेट खल उचेड़। Lau leṭa khala ucherha.

Grasping or sticking to one closely and then taking off his skin.

Used of one who is shamelessly selfish, and who would not leave another without extorting his object from him even to his ruin or detriment.

SHAMELESSNESS

1. अणन्यूतो भाट नौटी का सार। Aṇanyúto bháṭa nauṭi ká sára.

A bard or Brahman uninvited is like the land of the village of Nauti (in Garhwal).

I.e. An uninvited Brahman receives no attention from the people of the feast just as the land in the village of Nauti is always uncared for and uncultivated (on account of its being too high to produce any thing).

2. बेत भरि नाख काटो हाथ भरि बढ़ो। Beta bhari nákha káṭo hátha bhari baḍho.

The nose though cut down to a span, grew to one cubit length.

I.e. When one after being reprimanded or punished for a crime instead of repenting commits others much worse. This proverb describes a shameless man, the nose being regarded as a seat of honour or sense of shame.

3. बेसरम का नाख में रूख जामो कौण बैठो कि शेल बैठुंलो। Besarama ká nákha meṇ rúkha jámo kauṇa baiṭho ki shela baiṭhuṇlo.

A shameless person says he will sit under the shade of the tree which has grown on his nose.

This is exactly to the same purpose as the preceding one. A tree growing on one's nose is figuratively used of one who has been disgraced by committing a sinful act, and regardless of the warnings or punishment given for it, gives himself up to an evil life.

E.g. A man once conviced of theft determines to live in future by stealing.

4. नाख कटै नाम शोभा राम। Nákha kaṭai náma shobhá ráma.

After having his nose cut off calls himself Shobhá Ráma (i.e. full of grandeur and honour).

Ironically applied to one who, after having his character tarnished, puts on the airs of a gentleman. The nose is considered to be the sole glory of the human face, and a sense of honour, (as represented by the nose) is the chief ornament of a man's character.

5. नकटि बेटि उजला नाम। Nakaṭi beṭi ujalá náma.

A nose-less daughter called by a good name.

The explanation given above holds good here also.

6. नकटो नाख चंदन को टीका। Nakaṭo nákha chaṇdana ko ṭíká.

One having no nose adorns his forehead with a Tika of sandal.

Used to denote that people destitute of the sense of honour do many odd or pompous things to hide their defects. *Tika* here means a small dot of paint on one's forehead as an adornment.

7. शरमदार कन शरम बेशरम कन दुबलाई। Sharamadára kana sharama besharama kana dubaláí.

A good man is ashamed of wrong, but a shameless person minds it not.

Caution against dealing with one who is reckess and has no sense of shame.

8. सबन सों सकी बेशरम सों नि सकी। Saba̲na soṇ sakí besharama soṇ ni sakí.

One can conquer everyone by proper reasons except a shameless person.

For no arguments whatever will previl upon one who is devoid of common sense. Being deprived of the sense of honour or dishonour, nothing in the world can stop him from doing anything.

Used of shameless persons.

9. खंकल का काखा मोलका। Khankala ká kákhá molaká.

A shameless man's coat is very loose in the arms.

E.g. When one's coat is very tight his movements are restricted by it. A careless shameless man who is afraid of nothing is not restrained from doing whatever he wishes.

SIMPLETONS

1. गोबर गणेश। Gobara Gaṇesha.

An idol of Ganesha, made of cowdung.

Applied to a very simple man who can be moulded into any form i.e. made to do anything one wishes.

SLANDERERS AND WHISPERERS

1. बाप बेटा एकै छुयालों न खै मैके। Bápa beṭá ekai chhuyáloṇ na khai maike.

Father and son being one, the man who tries to create discord between them is cursed (deserves to have his mother abused).

2. फांकण बैठ्या माई को जार बांटण बैठ्या चूलि को छार। Pháṇkaṇa baiṭhyá maî ko jára báṇṭaṇa baiṭhyá chúli ko chhára.

One accustomed to slander will abuse his own mother by naming her paramours, and one accustomed to give will not spare even the ashes of his kitchen.

3. सासु बुवारि एक छुयाल रांड छेक। Sásu buwári eka chhuyála ráṇḍa chheka.

Mother-in-law or daughter-in-law are one, the woman who caused them to quarrel is cursed.

C.f. "Whisperers separate chief friends."

4. मारनेर को हाथ पकड़नु बोलानेर को के पकड़नु। Máranera ko hátha pakarhanu bolánera ko ke pakarhanu.

You can catch the hand of one who is about to strike you, but who can seize the tongue of the slanderer?

5. मरिया स्याप का आंखा खचोरना। Mariyá syápa ká áṇkhá khachoraná.

To prick the eyes of a dead snake.

Applied to one who slanders or insults an enemy who is dead or is in distress or poverty.

C.f. "To kick a man when he is down."

SOCIAL HABITS AND CUSTOMS

1. आव बैठो पीव पाणी तीनू बस्तु मोल नि आणी। Áwa baiṭhau píwa páṇí tinú bastu mola ni áṇí.

"Come, sit down, and drink water." This invitation costs nothing.

Nothing is lost by a kind word.

2. ब्याह बैर और प्रीत समान सों करनु। Byáha baira aura príta samána soṇ karanu.

Marriage, hostility and friendship ought to be between equals.

The infringement of this maxim entails penalty, and so it becomes the subject of a proverb. Natives generally attend to equality in caste and not in social status, hence the hindrance to civilization.

3. जां सो देश तां तसो भेश। Jáṇ jaso desha táṇ taso bhesha.

One ought to adopt the guise of the country in which he lives.

C.f. "One in Rome must do what Rome does."

Story : A man once arrived in a foreign country to visit a friend. He enquired for the road leading to his friend's house from a boy standing by, telling him that on arrival at his host's house he would give him plenty of sweetmeats. The boy led him there. The man before entering his friend's house gave him one rupee to buy sweetmeat. The boy did not accept it, saying that it was not enough. The man, for fear of disgrace, offered him five rupees but still the boy refused, and becoming very obstinate, began to quarrel with him. He was at a loss what to do. At last the noise of the quarrel reached his friend, who came out and enquired into the whole matter, and then told him the proverb and gave him advice adapted to the occasion. The man according to his friend's advice bought some sweet-meats for one pice, and then divided it into two portions i.e. one greater and the other smaller, putting a portion in each hand he told the boy to take whichever he pleased, the boy took the greater portion with satisfaction, and then went away.

4. ज्यूंदा जोगी चाबा चाब मूआ जोगी दाबा दाब। Jyúṇdá jogî chábá chába múá jogî dábá dába.

A jogî while alive is constantly munching, but when he is dead he is buried again and again.

This is applicable only to a *jogi's* fire; for while alive he is in the habit of eating as many times as he gets alms, and when dead he is buried by those of his disciples or relations who are present; but whenever an absent disciple or near relation arives at his tomb he also according to the custom adds earth to it or enlarges the tomb.

5. उत्तर को तालो पछम को नालो। Uttara ko tálo pachhama ko nálo.

A thin hot iron bar with which infants are scorched on their stomachs is called "Tálá" and a thin stream of water poured on the head of infants is called "Nálá".

This maxim advises application of the "Tálá" (in the north=cold) and that of the Nálá (in the west=heat) as established remedies for infant children against the attacks of diseases.

Note : On the occasion of the Bikh Sankránt (festival held at the time when the sun passes from one constellation into another) an iron rod is heated and applied to the navels of children in order to drive out the poison (bikh) caused by windy colic.

Vide Gazeteer of N.W.P. Vol. XI. p. 698.

6. रण मुख क्ष्यत्री तीरथ मुख ब्राह्मण। Raṇa mukha chhyatrí tíratha mukha bráhmáṇa.

A Kshatri in a conflict or a Brahman before a shrine should never turn his face.

This is a maxim for persuading Brahmins to visit shrines and perform religious acts and to stimulate Rajputs to go to battle. It is said that if a Brahmin refuses to visit a shrine or a Rajput refuses to go to war their faces should not be looked upon by others.

7. रांति चलणो भांति बोलाणो। Ráṇti chalaṇo bháṇti boláṇo.

Follow established customs and speak in a pleasant manner and to the purpose.

8. देश काणो एक आंख ले चाणु। Desha káṇo eka áṇkhá le cháṇu.

One ought to look at the country of one-eyed men with only one eye.

C.f. "In Rome do as Rome does."

Once a man happened to arrive in a village which was peopled only with noseless men (who had their noses cut off for some crimes). No sooner had he arrived than he was ironically addressed by the nickname *"Nacku"* or the man having a nose. As the stranger was obliged to stay there for his livelihood he was contemptuously treated and tormented by the villagers until he also had his nose cut off.

9. पौणा की खातर मागणा है पैली। Pauṇá ki khátara mágaṇá hai pailí.

Courtesy to a guest before he asks for it.

10. जोगि और स्याप एक ठौर नि रूना। Jogi aura syápa eka ṭhaura ni rúná.

A Fakir (an ascetic) and a snake do not stay at one place constantly.

This being contrary to their natural habits.

11. मलो भिड़ो उधरि तला भिड़ा में औंदो। Malo bhirho udhari talá bhirhá meṇ auṇdo.

The wall of an upper field comes down into the lower one.

Used only as a lame excuse by certain sects of inferior Rájpúts in Garhwal who keep the wives of their deceased elder brothers as their own without bringing any disgrace on their families. The practice would be considered as an incest by people of other castes, and would degrade the culprits.

12. मा मुचि मौनि फागुण मुचि गै। चैत मुचि बनरा फल टिपि खै। Má muchi mauni phaguṇa muchi gai. Chaita muchi banará phala ṭipi khai.

Bees after Má (January) cows after Phaguna (February) and monkeys after Chaita (March) enjoy fruits well.

Strictly speaking this is a hill song but used as a proverb as well in consoling and encouraging one is distress, indicating that one has to suffer only for a brief period, which is sure to be followed by plenty and pleasure. Bees are hard-up for food for want of flowers in January, cows in February for want of grass, and monkeys in March for want of fruits. After this period of scarcity each has plenty of good cheer and is happy and content.

13. शोर कि नालि कत्यूर को माणो ज्वे जै ठूलि खसम जै नानो। Shora ki náli katyúra ko máṇo jwe jai ṭhúli khasama jai náno.

The standard Náli of Shora and the standard Máná of Katyúra are here compared to a wife and a husband when the former is older than the latter.

E.g. According to the measure of capacity obtaining here :

4 maṇas make	1 nali.
16 nalis make	1 pirhai or duna.
20 nalis make	1 bista.
20 bistas make	1 khára or khári.
20 kháris make	1 biswá.

The standard *náli* in use in Parganá Shora (Kamaun district) consists of eight handfuls of any grain, whereas the standard *máná* used in Patti (circle) Katyúrá (Parganá Dánapúra

Zillah Kumaun) contains twelve handfuls. Thus the *máná* of Katyúrá is larger than the *náli* of Shora. Hence the people commenting on the extraordinary usage compare it to an ill-matched pair, a grown up wife having a minor as a husband. So a *náli* ought to be greater than a *máná* the latter being only one fourth of a *náḷi*. This proverb is therefore used to denote things not fairly matched. *Máná* is also known by the names of *Baikara Belá* or *Chhapiya*.

15. खत्याड़ि को साग गंगोलि को बाग। Khatyárhi ko sága Gaṇgoli ko bága.

Khatyárhi for vegetables and Gangoli for tigers.

The tigers in Gangoli are as common as vegetables in the village of Khatyárhi (almost the whole town of Almora is supplied with vegetables by this village). Conseqently the people of that part of the district hardly dread the animal. Once hearing screams and yells the neighbours went to see what was the matter, but finding that a tiger was the only cause of all the uproar they regretted coming there, and said that they thought that a court peon (messenger) had arrived, which prompted them to go to their help, and that, if they had known that it was only a tiger that was the cause of alarm they would not have come. At the beginning of the British rule in this province people used to dread a court peon far more than a tiger.

16. खसिया नै जाड़ो बामण खै जाड़ौ। Khasiyá nai járho Bámaṇa khai járho.

A Khasiyá feels cold after bathing, and a Brahman after dinner.

E.g. A Khasiyá usually does not bathe at all, but when he does so on some festival or religious day he feels very cold, being uninured to the practice, while a Brahman accustomed to bathing does not find it troublesome, but he takes his meals after putting off his clothes and so when done eating he feels cold, while a Khasiya (coolie caste) who eats his food with his clothes on, does not feel cold.

17. शोर हराम खोर बाप भडुवा बेटी मैतोर। Shora haráma khora bápa bharhuwá beṭí maitora.

Shor's livelihood is an evil one, fathers give their daughters to shame.

The people of Shora, a parganá of Kamaun, are said to prostitute their own daughters, who therefore remain in the parental home (a great disgrace in India).

18. कै रांड दिवरा भौज नि सुवाव। Kai ráṇḍa diwará bhauja ni suwáwa.

Is she not a cursed woman who does not like her brother-in-law, and vice versa.

Among lower classes of Hindus these persons are allowed much freedom of intercourse, and hence such conduct approved.

SOCIETY

1. असल बटि खता नि कमसल बटि वफा नि। Asala baṭí khatá ni kamasala baṭi waphá ni.

A noble man will not play false (betray) but a mean man will not prove true.

A warning against friendship with the latter.

2. एक माछो ताल खराब कर। Eka máchho tála kharába kara.

A single fish infects the whole tank.

C.f. One sickly sheep infects the flock.

3. दूध भात छोड़नो संग नि छोड़नो। Dúdha bháta chhorhano saṇga ni chhorhano.

One may give up rice milk, but never a companion on the road.

A companion on a journey is considered to be a great support.

4. नकटि देवि को पदु पुज्यारि। Nakaṭi devi ko padu pujyári.

Padu is the worshipper of a Goddess who has no nose.

The name "Padu" signifies a mean or inferior person who is therefore fit to worship a goddess who has no nose (sense of shame). Worthy men have worthy companions and servants, and unworthy men have unworthy companions.

SOLITARY MAN

1. बचलो त नाटो कति खालो आटो मरलो त नाटो किरिया न काटो।
Bachalo ta naṭo kati khálo áṭo maralo ta náṭo kiriyá na káṭo.

One without a family may live to eat as much food (flour) as he can, but when he dies no one will perform his funeral ceremony.

Used in ridicule of one who is unmarried and has no children to urge him to marry.

2. आपी नेक आपी पैक। Ápí naika ápí paika.

Himself a master as well as a hero (servant).

E.g. A king has an army to fight with, and as the head of a family has many members of his family to execute his orders. But the proverb is applied to a solitary man who has neither family nor servants to help him in any business.

STOLEN PROPERTY

1. चोरी को गुड़ मिठो। Chori ko gurha mitho.

Gurha (treacle) obtained by theft is sweeter.

C.f. "Stolen waters are sweet."

SUSPICION

1. दाल में कालो। Dála meṇ kálo.

Something black in the Dál.

(*Dál* is a pulse cooked in turmeric etc and eaten with rice), when cooked it becomes yellow, so the smallest speck of black in it is easily seen. Hence it means a cause of suspicion.

Story : A Brahman being conscious of the intrigues and stratagems of the other sex repaired to a dense forest and began to live there quite concealed from everybody. The man used to bring in *khicharhi* (raw rice and *dala* mixed together) by begging, and his wife used to cook it for herself and her husband. In this manner they lived for some years there. One day his wife instead of the *khicharhi* he had brought, and against his wish, put the *dala* and rice, cooked separately, before her husband as a dinner. This made him suspicious, and so he said. "There is something black (suspicion) in the *dala*." He left the food and went away. Subsequently by patient enquiries from the shepherd-boys, who used to graze their herds there, he found out that his wife was in love with a hermit (*jogi*) living in the same jungle, whom she used to feed with part of the *khicharhi* she used to cook for herself and her husband. And the hermit being tired of the *khicharhi* requested the woman one day to get him rice and dál separately. She did not hesitate to undertake the trouble of separating the rice from the *dál*, and cooking them thus in order to satisfy her paramour.

Used to express suspicions rising from odd circumstances occurring in the usual course of events.

2. सौगंध खैबेर कस्तूरि बेचणि। Saugandha khaibera kastúri bechaṇi.
One who sells musk with an oath as to its genuineness.
I.e. One who recommends himself or his wares with suspicious eagerness. The scent of the musk should be sufficient recommendation.

SYMPATHY

1. दि धित्यूणो या बोली पत्यूणु। Dí dhityúṇo yá bolí patyúṇu.
Either satisfy a man by giving him something, or let him be assured (of future help) by kind speeches.

2. दुसरा को दुख को जाण। Dusará ko dukha ko jáṇa.
Who knows the pain of another?
C.f. "None can feel the weight of another's burden." "The heart

knoweth its own bitterness and no man intermeddleth with its joy."

3. जो मर सो तर। Jo mara so tara.

A dead man has passed over pains.

Used to console the relatives of the one who is dead.

4. एक घर का नौ मता कुशल कां बटि होलि। Eka ghara ká nau matá kushala káṇ baṭi holi.

A household which is governed by nine (different) opinions will not thrive.

Used by members of a family when one of them dissents from another in regard to domestic affairs, in order to bring them to understand that disagreement among themselves is a sure sign of their impending ruin.

C.f. "A house divided against itself cannot stand."

5. गाव एगला बिगला रीत भांत एकै। Gáṇwa egalá bigalá ríta bháṇta ekai.

Villages are scattered here and there, but the customs and manners of all are the same (i.e. they are in similar circumstances).

Used to induce people to help and sympathize with others in matters that affect the general welfare.

6. बाला कि नि मरौ मैं बूढ़ा कि नि मरौ ज्वे। Bálá ki ni marau mai buḍhá ki ni marau jwe.

May the mother of an infant child, and the wife of an old man not die (otherwise no one will take care of them).

These events render them helpless.

7. छोटो बढ़ौ न बड़ौ घटौ नै। Chhoṭo baḍhau nai barho ghaṭau nai.

May a mean man not be a power (for he will do mean things), and a great man not come to poverty (otherwise he will suffer bitterly).

TEMPTATION

1. हांडी को मुख खुलो छ पर बिल्ली को शरम चाहेंद। Háṇḍi ko mukha khulo chha para billi ko sharama chaheṇda.

The mouth of the pot is open, but the cat ought to have some sense of shame.

The good man will often be tempted, but he should obey his conscience and resist evil. *C.f.* "An open door will tempt a saint."

2. जुठो खाणो मिठा का लोभ। Juṭho kháṇo miṭhá ká lobha.

One eats the leavings of another person in the hope of finding something sweet therein.

Men will condescend to do mean things for the sake of gain.

THIEVES, PICKPOCKETS AND BAD CHARACTERS

1. चोर को साखि गठकटो। Chora ko sákhi gaṭhakaṭo.

A thief calls a pickpocket as his witness.

Applied to the combination of wicked persons.

2. चोर कि नजर बोगचा में। Chroa ki nazara bogachá meṇ.

A thief's eye is on the baggage.

I.e. Waiting for an opportunity to take it away.

Applied to a wicked man who waits for an opportunity to put his evil plans into execution.

3. चोर चर चरो जार जर जरो। Chora chara charo jára jara jaro.

A thief loses his temper, and a paramour becomes indignant.

I.e. Both try to hide their crimes under a mask of apparent innocence.

4. हाथ में चोरि सरिन सचो। Hátha meṇ chori sarina sacho.

The stolen property in his hand, but the thief says he is an honest man.

Applies to persons who try to hide their sins and crimes.

5. चोर चोर सांक जार जार सांक। Chora chora saṇka jára jára sáṇka.

All thieves are real brothers, and so are all paramours.

This is applied to all bad characters as being unworthy of any trust. *C.f.* "Birds of a feather flock together."

6. वार खंडवार पार खंडवार तेरि मेरि एक अन्वार। Wára khan̠ḍwára pára khan̠ḍwára teri meri eka anwára.

Ruin here, ruin there, you and I have similar faces.

I.e. You are ruined and I am ruined (our character is stained) and so we are in the same box. Union of bad characters.

7. खै हालो बागले लाल खाब नि खै बागले लालै खाब। Khai hálo bágale lála khába ni khai bágale lálai khába.

The tiger's mouth is red whether he eats animal food or not.

Used to denote those who have tarnished their character, for they are always taken for criminals, without any regard to facts.

THINGS IN WHICH ONE HAS NO CONCERN

1. तुलि मु न कैण मु। Tuli mu na kaiṇa mu.

Neither scales nor weights.

An unfit or insignificant person, or one who has no concern with the matter in hand.

2. कैको ब्याउ कैका आंखों डाउ। Kaiko byáu kaiká áṇkhoṇ ḍáu.

Whose marriage and who got pain in his eyes.

Who share the marriage fest and who get pain in the eyes. People who are simply spectators of a marriage get nothing but aching eyes.

Used when one gets trouble from an affair in which he was not concerned.

TRUST IN PROVIDENCE

1. परमेश्वर की लंबी बांह। Parameshwar ki lambi báṇha.

God's arm is long (either to punish or to help).

I.e. He is mighty to accomplish anything that seems impossible to a man. One already ruined or in distress draws hope from this phrase, which is also used in encouraging or consoling one in poor circumstances, so that he may have patience in distress and trust in the mercy of God for better days.

2. खवया बेटा कणि देवया राम। Khawayá beṭá kaṇi dewayá ráma.

A voracious eater is fed by God.

This means that God supplies the wants of every creature in the world.

TRUST AND SINCERITY

1. यार न सो चोरी पीरन सो दगाबाजी। Yárana so chorí pírana so dagâbají.

Cencealing things from friends, and acting deceitfully with one's elders.

2. जै मुं नी सत ऊई को नौपत। Jai muṇ ní sata úi ko ní pata.

The man is whom there is no truth cannot be trusted. Honest and truthful persons are trusted by every one.

3. सांच में क्या आंच। Sáṉcha meṇ kyá áṇcha.

There is no danger in the truth.

This is used in encouraging one to speak the truth and act truthfully for his own safety. *C.f.* "The wicked fleeth when no man pursueth, but the righteous are as bold as a lion." "Tell the truth and shame the devil."

Illustration : During the reign of native princes various crimes against the person were tried by means of *"Dipa"* a red hot iron ball. If any body was accused of such a crime his innocency had to be tried by his taking the red hot iron ball in his hand with seven green leaves of the *pipala* (ficus religiosa), the holy fig tree, beneath it, and then going round the parties and people where they had stopped. If this ordeal did not scorch the palm of the accused he would be acquitted of the charge, and considered innocent. In case the ball scorched his hand the accused had to be punished for the crime, and was made to pay compensation to the aggrieved party. Hence the proverb says that truth does not harm.

4. सांची बोलणु सुखि रौणो। Sáṇchi bolaṇu sukhi rauṇo.

One who speaks truth remains in peace.

C.f. "Lying lips are abomination to the Lord; but they that deal truly are his delight."

5. पौ रति बाउन तोला। Pau rati báuna tolá.

One fourth of a Rati is equal to fifty-two Tolas.

E.g. There are thirteen *máshás* in a *Tolá*, and eight *Ratis* in a *Máshá*. (Two grains make a *Rati*).

A hyperbolical expression denoting that a genuine unadulterated article, though small, is worth more than a spurious one valued at fifty-two *Tolas,* or that the smallest thing if it is genuine is equal to fifty-two tolas, *i.e.* has its own excellence or worth.

6. एक बाचा द्वि बाचा त्रि बाचा बचन टले नरक पड़े। Eka báchá dwi báchá tri báchá bachana ṭale naraka parhe.

I give my word once, twice, and the third time. If I break it I incur the punishment of hell.

Used as an oath to assure another that he will be faithful to his word.

7. इमान जुबान। Imána jubána.

Honesty and one's word (ought to be kept true).

Used to induce one to act up to his words.

8. खस खाणो भस बुलाणो। Khasa kháṇo bhasa buláṇo.

Eat what you get and speak what you think.

Do not be fastidious, and speak the truth.

UNANIMITY

1. सात पांच कि लकड़ी एक जणि को बोझ। Sáta páṇcha ki lakaṛí eka jaṇi ko bojha.

When five or six persons gather each one stick it makes a load for one man. ("every little helps").

C.f. "Union is strength."

2. द्वी राजी त के कर काजि। Dui ráji ta ke kara káji.

If two are agreed they have no fear of the cadi (magistrate).

"Union is strength."

3. कांधे पर धनुष हाथ में बाणा कहां से आये दिल्ली सुलताना।
बन के राव बिकट के राणा आंखर बड़े को बड़ेने पहच्याणा।
Kaṇdhe para dhanusha hátha me báṇá kaháṇ se áye Dilli sulatáná. Baṇa ke Ráwa bikaṭa ke Ráṇá áṇkhara baṛhe ko baṛhe ne pahachyáṇá.

Having a bow (plough) on your shoulder and an arrow (a stick to drive bullocks with) in your hand, where do you come from O, Emperor of Delhi? O, Lord of jungles and master of opportunity you are a great personage. Take me also for a great one.

Used of wicked and mean unions.

Once in a narrow ravine a fox unexpectedly met a ploughman. Having no opportunity to run away, and fearing that he would be beaten or killed by the ploughman, the fox began to flatter him, as in the first half of the proverb, but the ploughman at the same time was also frightened at the sight of the fox, taking him for a tiger, and flattered him as in the third verse of the same. Thus each of them passed on their way unhurt. But at this moment another man who had observed the scene ironically uttered the fourth verse, *i.e.* A great man discerns a great man.

4. सोना में सुहागो। Soná meṇ suhága.

Borax in the gold.

Borax unites well with gold.

Used to describe unions when both parties have good qualities.

5. काला कालों की एक जात। Kálá kálon̤ kí eka játa.

All blacks are of one caste.

Applicable to the union of wicked persons.

C.f. "Birds of a feather flock together."

6. कूटी जुगत जाड़ी पूत जुगत बुवारी। Kúṭi jugata járhí púta jugata buwári.

A hoe suited to its handle, and a son fit for the daughter-in-law.

A good match,

UNAVOIDABLE EXPENSES AND THINGS

1. मुंड कि मुंडाइ घट कि पिसाइ। Muṇḍa ki muṇḍái ghaṭa ki pisáí.

The shaving of one's head and the grinding of one's corn (must be paid for).

This is applied to denote expenses which are unavoidably necessary. A man who does not pay for his shaving will become a barber in the next birth.

2. मरी के लै सास नी। Marí kelai sása ní.

Why did you die? Because I had no breath.

Applied to one's being unable to do a thing.

UNCERTAINTY OF LIFE AND WORLDLY THINGS

1. आकाश का फल। Ákásha ká phala.

The fruits of heaven (may or may not come down).

Used to denote uncertainty of success in a case which is in the hands of another person, in whom one has no confidence.

2. नौ क्वांरिन को ब्या। Nau kwánrina ko byá.

The marriage of nine virgins.

E.g. The marriage of a single girl takes a considerable time in selecting bridegroom for her, and then arranging for the marriage, notwithstanding objections brought forward by relatives of both parties who wish to cancel the arrangement made. Thus of course the marriage of nine maidens must take a considerably long time. Used to denote delay and uncertainty.

3. आव को नाव चोर को साहु। Áwa ko náwa chora ko sáhu.

The (serviceable) boat is called Náwa, and the thief gets the title of sahu (good man).

Náwa means a boat, but is in form the negative of *Áwa* which means honour and blessing; so that a boat which is really a useful thing is by its name said to be the opposite of a good thing. *Sáhu* means a rich and honest man, but is a title given to *Baniyás* who are notorious for their false dealings.

Good things are called bad, and bad things good by the world.

4. स्वीण कि सम्पत्ति। Swíṇa ki sampatti.

Wealth of a dream.

Applied to one's life and possession, and other short-lived things.

5. तितिरा का मुख की लक्ष्मी। Titirá ká mukha kí lakshmí.

Wealth is the mouth of a partridge (very difficult to get).

E.g. Titirá is a very shy kind of partridge which flies away on the least alarm, and one cannot expect it to chirp its notes just when we wish it.

Used by one who is very uncertain of success which depends on the judgment or discretion of another (a judge etc) who is not to be cajoled or influenced by any means.

6. छिन घड़ि में कैको पहरो। Chhina gharhi me kaiko paharo.

After this moment whose turn comes next?

Utter uncertainty as to what will happen in the immediate future.

C.f. "After that—the Deluge."

7. नौकरी की जड़ ढुंगा में। Naukarí kí jarha ḍhungá me.

The root of service is on a stone.

I.e. It may wither at any time.

Applied to its instability, uncertainty of duration.

8. अैल को मैस पाछिय को राकस। Aila ko maisa páchhiya ko rákasa.

A man now, but a ghost this evening.

Applies to the uncertainty of life. A man now living may be found dead in evening. *C.f.* "Death keeps no calendar." "Here today and gone tomorrow."

9. पौ तालि मौत। Pau tali mauta.

Death lurks under one's foot.

Uncertainty of life.

10. रौकि जगा ढाण ढाण कि जगा रौ। Rau ki jagá ḍháṇa ḍháṇa ki jagá rau.

Sand in place of pools, and pools in place of sand.

The transient nature of worldly goods.

C.f. "Boast not thyself of tomorrow; for thou knowest not what a day may bring forth."

11. धारमा को दिन गलमा को गास। Dhárамá ko dina gala má ko gása.

The sun on the ridge of a hill and a morsel in the throat will both soon disappear.

Applied to short-lived things, or to those who have but short time to continue.

12. पुरुष की माया वृक्ष की छाया। Purusha kí máyá briksha kí chháyá.

Wealth lasts as long as a fortunate man lives, like the shadow of a tree disappears with its removal.

The transient nature of a man's wealth or prosperity which disappears with his life. Anything amassed by him for the use of his posterity is squandered by his sons.

13. जां तक निभि तां तक। Jáṇ taka nibhi táṇ taka.

A man should go on as long as he can.

I.e. Every one ought to take advangate of his opportunities, and retain his advantages as long as he can in view of the uncertainty of worldly things.

A story is related in connection with this saying.

Once a rich Hindu, wishing to gain merit and salvation, employed a number of Brahmans to repeat *"Mantras"* or invocations of the divine name from the *Shastras*. Having secured the services of several Brahmanas, he seated them in a row before himself to begin their *"Japa"* or invocations, which are repeated thousands of times in a low voice. Among the Brahmanas was an illiterate poor Brahman who was anxious to secure the fee, but had no knowledge of the Vedic scriptures. However, having already engaged himself for the sacred service and seated in the row with others concerned, he at first felt himself at a loss how to behave in this difficult position, but having no alternative (as he was too prudent to confess that he did not know the Sanscrit verse which was being repeated) he at last began to encourage himself by muttering the above proverb in a low tone (for during all this time he was in constant fear and trembling lest his ignorance should be found out, with the risk of his being expelled from the company). Meanwhile his client and others thought that he was performing the work assigned to him. Afterwards he acknowledged the ruse to a friend, who informed the rich man. The latter, instead of being angry, declared that the saying was a very good one, and applicable to every condition of life.

UNGRATEFULNESS

1. मेरी मथुलि मैकु नख चौल। Meri nathuli mai ku nakha chaula.

My own nose-ring sneers at me.

This is applied by a mother to her own daughter when she becomes proud and turns up her nose at her after having been married into a rich family; or to a woman to whom the nose-ring has been lent, and who is vain of herself although wearing a borrowed nose-ring. Also to a student who disdains his teacher.

2. आज को दिनेर जी रयै बेलिया को दिनेर मर जायै। Ája ko dinera jī rayai beliyá ko dinera marajáyai.

Let the man who gives me to-day live long, but let the one who gave me yesterday die.

Ingratitude.

3. शिकार का बखत कुतिया कन हगण लागी। Shikára ká bakhata kutiyá kana hagaṇa lágī.

The bitch in the chase wants to ease herself.

Used of one who has been fed and maintained for years, but when his services are needed makes some excuse.

4. तेल मा डुबाव पर रूखो ही रूखो। Tela má ḍubáwa para rúkho hī rúkho.

After being bathed in oil he is still found stiff.

A most ungrateful person.

5. लूण खाइक लूण हरामी। Lúṇa kháika lúṇa harámi.

One who eats another's salt to ruin him.

Once a man while reposing on his bed at night asked his servant to go and see whether it was raining. The servant instead of obeying the order said that it was (without going out of the door) for he had just seen that the claws of a cat were wet. The master remarked his conduct and remained silent on that occasion. On another occasion the same servant was told to put out the lamp, on which he said to his master, "Sir, it is needless to do so, you should close your eyes and sleep." Though this exasperated the master he nevertheless kept silent. After this one night the master encamped in a field, below which there was a deep precipice. The master after taking his evening meal went to bed, and told the servant to shampoo his legs. (As customary among the well-to do men in camp). The servant at first sat by the feet of the gentleman to do the work, but after having placed his master's luggage near his feet quietly withdrew from the place, and seated himself at a distance. The man repeatedly called on his servant to rub his feet, but the servant did not reply to his calls. He then thought that the servant was asleep near his feet; mistaking the packet for the servant and remembering his former ill-conduct and words intending to kick the servant he gave a kick to the packet and threw it down the precipice. After this the servant quietly deserted his master, leaving him alone without any property.

6. सूम कणि एक नाम दिनेर कणि भौत नाम। Súma kaṇi eka náma dinera kaṇi bhauta náma.

The miser is only blamed once (for being a miser) but a munificent person many times.

The recipients of a generous man's bounty are often dissatisfied in various ways.

Used by one who is troubled by beggars for more alms.

7. जै पातलि में खाणो वी में छीन करनु। Jai pátali me kháṇo wî me chhîna karanu.

He destroys the leaf from which he eats.

Poor people in villages generally take their food on leaves sewn together, instead of on dishes, if one pierces or tears the leaves, the food (especially fluid food) is lost.

Applied to an ungrateful person.

8. खैपी बेर ये रांडि को खटो दै। Khai pí bera ye ráṇḍi ko khaṭo dai.

After eating and drinking my curds you say they were sour.

Used by a woman who, after having rendered long and good services, is at last rejected on the ground of some pretended fault.

UNREQUITED AFFECTION

1. मैं झुरूं यार सों यार झुर आपणा घरबार सों। Mai jhuruṇ yára soṇ yára jhura ápaṇá gharabára soṇ.

I long for my lover, who longs for his own family.

Said to one who loves those who do not care for him.

2. मा रोव धीकु धी रोव जार कु जार रोव घरबार को। Má rowa dhí ku dhí rowa jára ku jára rowa gharbára ku.

The mother cries for her daughter, the daugher for her paramour, and the paramour for his own family.

Unrequited affection.

USEFULNESS

1. घर में घोड़ो मट्टि में मोल। Ghara men̲ ghorho maṭṭi men̲ mola.

A pony in the stable, and manure in one's field.

Will both be of much use. Always serviceable.

2. सग्बाड़ा को साग अगेला कि आग। Sagwárhá ko sága agelá ki ága.

The vegetable of fields close to one's house, and the fire in the flint and steel (are always at hand).

Applied to their usefulness.

3. वड़ियाल है पडियाल भलो। Waḍyála hai paḍyála bhalo.

The stranger, who is of use to me, is better than the person with whom I have collateral interests or whose boundaries affect my lands.

E.g. One is liable to have friction with the latter, while he is safe in dealing with the former.

4. घ्यु गिरो खिचड़ि में। Ghyu giro khicharhi men̲.

The Ghi has fallen into the Khicharhi.

E.g. Khicharhi consists of two parts of rice and one part of *dála* (pulse) cooked together. It is delicious when eaten with *Ghi* mixed with it. If *Ghi* by chance falls into the food it makes it better. Hence the point of proverb.

Applies to a loss which results is some good thing.

C.f. "All the fat's in the frying-pan now."

5. नि मैस है कुमैस को आसरो। Ni maisa hai kumaisa ko ásaro.
In a place where there is no one, even the presence of a bad man (not fit for one's society) is a support in a journey through a desert.
C.f. Something is better than nothing.

6. काली कंबल कुचल जोई जां बिछाई उत्तम होई। Káĺi kan̲bala kuchal joí jáṇ bichhái uttama hoí.
Black blanket and dirty wife are the best for use every where.
Applies to usefulness of things without any regard to their beauty.

7. खेती हालि द्यो घर हालि बौ। Kheti háli dyo ghara háli bau.
It rains after the tillage is spoiled (for want of rain) and the bride after splitting the house (becomes useful).
I.e. As soon as a man is married he is separated, as a married man, from his parents (household). The rain is wished for, but comes at the wrong time or inconveniently, yet afterwards will be useful; so in the house a young wife causes sorrow at first (to her husband) but afterwards joy.

8. खाणी को पथर जाती को मनखी। Kháṇí ko paṭhara játí ko manakhí.
Stone from a quarry and a man from a good family.
Showing the advantage of good descent.

USELESSNESS

1. अन्यारा पट को भौं मटका। Anyárá paṭa ká bhaun̲ maṭaká.
Making signs with one's eye-brows in the dark.
This is quoted of one who is doing any thing uselessly. "A wink is as good as a nod to a blind horse."

2. अरण्य रोदन। Aran̲ya rodana.
Crying in the jungle is not heard.
Saying or doing what will have no affect.

3. बांस डूबन पोरियुं को हिसाब। Bánsa ḍúbana poryun ko hisába.

If the whole bamboo goes down, what is the use of counting the knots?

Bamboos are used in measuring the depth of water, etc.

E.g. If a man is losing the whole of his property what is the use of troubling about small parts of it?

4. धौड़ी का उपर मूंज को बखिया। Dhaurhî ká upara munja ko bakhiyá.

Dhaurhi (inferior and cheap kind of leather) sewn neatly and carefully with Múnja (in the way in which good leather ought to be sewn).

E.g. Much labour spent on a worthless object. A poor man sumptuously dressed in a manner unsuited to his circumstances.

"No man putteth a piece of new cloth on an old garment."

5. देखणी दरसनी दाबा सी छड़ करना कमूण सों आटा की सी लड़। Dekhaṇî darsanî dábá sî chharha karaná kamúṇa soṇ áṭá kî sî larha.

To look at a very beautiful woman, like a reed of dábá, (a kind of long grass that flowers in September), but for usefulness or worth like a string of paste.

Applied to a lazy woman, more ornamental than useful.

6. नाज कु नाज डूमण मोटी। Nája ku nája ḍúmaṇa moṭî.

The grain is bad, and the woman is a fat and strong Ḍumani (a low caste woman).

These are of no use. Applied to a useless person.

7. जैकि राणि तैकि राणि खंकल रयो आंखा ताणी। Jaiki ráṇi taîki ráṇi khaṇkala rayo áṇkhljá táṇî.

She is the queen of somebody or other, but a wicked man fixed his eyes on her.

Caution against looking at another's wife.

8. टटुवा खाय बटुवा फिर टटुवा को टटुवा। Taṭuwá kháya baṭuwá phira ṭaṭuwá ko tatuwá.

A pon after eating up a purse of money is still only a pony.

Caution against spending money uselessly and to no purpose.

9. पकायूं अन्न मरियूं मनखि। Pakáyúṇ anna mariyúṉ manakhi.

Cooked food and a dead man (should be disposed off quickly or else they will rot).

10. सिमल को हड़ो सूखो न सड़ो। Simala ko harho súkho na sarho.

The trunk of the Simal tree, silk cotton tree (Bombax heptaphyllum) neither dry nor rotten.

This is applied to one disliked for his being lazy and useless. The useless man neither does his work nor dies.

11. लंका को सुनो। Laṇká ko suno.

Gold at Lanká (Ceylon).

It is supposed that the earth of Ceylon is all gold dust which to one who is not there is useless, for it is out of his reach. Hence the point of the proverb applied to a thing which, though it is his own, is out of reach at the time he needs it. *C.f.* "Like the Dutchman's anchor."

12. मरिया चेला का बर्स गणना। Mariyá chelá ká barṣa gaṇaná.

To count the age of a son who is dead.

Used when one occupies himself with things that have passed beyond control or are out of his reach.

C.f. "It is no use crying over spilt milk."

13. खालि खसिया बुढ़ि पातर। Kháli khassiyá budhi pátara.

A Khassiyá without employ, and an old harlot, are useless.

Spoken to a useless person with a view to goad him to industry.

14. हाथ कंकण सों आरसि के। Hátha kaṉkaṇa soṇ árasi ke.

No looking glass is needed for putting on bangles.

No further proof is necessary.

"Clear as a pikestaff." "Plain as the nose on one's face."

15. कालो लड़ीक खोटो पैसा। Kálo larhîka khoṭo paisá.
A dumb and deaf son and a counterfeit pice.
Both are useless.

16. खाड़ दियो बखला लूण। Khárhú diyo wokhalá lúṇa.
One gave a ram salt in the wokhala (mortar).
E.g. The horns of the ram made it impossible for him to reach the salt with his mouth.
Applied to useless benefactions.

17. कोढ़ि मर न बाटो छोड़। Koḍhi mara na báṭo chhorha.
The leper neither dies nor gets out of the way.
An expression of displeasure applied to one who is both troublesome and useless.

18. कै बिरसा को तातो पाणि। Kai birasá ko táto páṇi.
For what consideration or inheritance should I give you warm water?
(A rich man gets warm water for bathing. Here it is a symbol of comfort.
Applied to one who is of no use to any one, and so why should people render him service or help?

19. द्वि भाइ रामा का कौड़ि न काम का। Dwi bhái Rámá ká kaurhi na káma ká.
Both brothers of Ráma have neither money nor industry.
Used when all the sons of any one are idle and worthless.

20. काटिया आंगुला में मुति नि दिनो। Káṭiyá á̱ngulá me̱n muti ni dino.
He won't even make water on one's finger that is cut or hurt.
E.g. It is believed that when the finger gets cut it is quickly healed if immediately washed with fresh urine, which costs nothing (a common practice). So if one refuses to render this small service in time of need he is considered a worthless being.
Used of one who is totally useless.

21. पिष्ट पेषण। Pishṭa peshaṇa.

To grind flour, i.e. to repeat a request already rejected, or to say something over and over again.

22. कै कै कन्या राशि। Kai kai kanyá ráshi.

Told and told again but proved to be a virgin.

Used of one who is instructed to no purpose.

Told something over and over again, but either not attending to it or not understanding. "A virgin" here means a minor, a useless bit of a lass, unable to understand anything or do any work.

23. भौण न भास जिया को उपास। Bhauṇa na bhás jiyá ko upása.

Neither good words nor tact, but grieving (fasting) of the soul.

Used of one disliked both for his bad temper and incompetency by another interested in him by relationship, and who laments that he is good for nothing.

VACILLATION

1. दुबिधा में दुवै गया माया मिली न राम। Dubidhá meṇ duwai gayá máyá mil̆i na ráma.

Vacillation loses both wealth and salvation (lit. Rám).

The hesitating and undecided man can neither be successful in worldly affairs nor can he devote himself thoroughly to the concerns of eternity.

C.f. "Unstable as water, he shall not excel."

2. दुवै दीन है गयो पांडे हलुवा रयो न मांडे। Duwai d̆ina hai gayo páṇḍe haluwá rayo na máṇḍe.

The Páṇḍe has lost both worlds (objects), neither is he Haluwá (a valuable sweet) nor mande (the water in which the rice was cooked, or in other words "too fluid a Haluwá").

Applies to one who spent money on works, or laid it out in, speculations, which have failed. The business did not yield any profit as anticipated, and he lost both capital and interest.

3. धोबि को कुत्ता घर को न घाट को। Dhobi ko kuttá ghara ko na gháṭa ko.

The washerman's dog is neither at the Ghát (river-bank or landing-place where he washes clothes) nor at home.

I.e. A vagrant, belonging to nobody. On seeing a bundle on the shoulder of a washerman a dog followed him from a town to the *ghát* in the hope of getting something to eat when the parcel, which, the dog supposed, contained food, was opened. When the dog arrived at the *ghát,* to his utter disappointment he saw nothing but clothes. The dog then returned to the town, but before his return the people had done taking their meals, which threw him into a state of despair. As an act of charity, when Hindus finish their meals they bring a handful of the remaining food to be thrown out to the dogs and crows, etc. The vagrant dogs live on these morsels.

Hence the proverb, the meaning of which is that by vacillation one loses everything.

VANITY, ASSUMPTION AND PRETENSION

1. आंखन को अंधे नाम नैनसुख। Áṉkhana ko aṇdho náma nainasukha.

A man devoid of sight is named "Nainasukha."

This phrase is made use of in two ways.

First, that a blind man cannot get into troubles due to the "lust of the eyes," so he is called Nainasukha, which means "fortunate as to his eyes." Secondly, to express the inconsistencies of life, e.g. when a rogue is called good etc.

2. बाप नि मारो गीदड़ बेटा भयो तिरंदाज। Bápa ni máro gídarha beṭá bhayo tiraṉdaja.

The father has never killed even a jackal, but the son calls himself an archer.

The son of a poor man who puts on airs and behaves haughtily.

3. भला भला मुख चानी कातरि कि लाज। Bhalá bhalá mukha cháñí kátari ki lája.

When big people look at me I feel ashamed of my rags.

The desire of having things better than they are when visited by superiors, or by one whose favour we wish to gain.

4. दुख न सुख बुखडो सी मुख । Dukha na sukha bukharho sî mukha.
Without (cause for) either pain or pleasure yet with a face like a devil's.
One who always looks angry without cause.

5. पोथि न पातड़ो नरैण पंडित । Pothi na pátarho naraiṇa paṇḍita.
He has neither book nor almanack, but is called Narain Pandit.
An illiterate pretender, a quack.

6. तलब न तनखा भज राम हौलदार । Talaba na tanakhá Bhaja Ráma Hauladára.
Neither pay nor wages, yet is called Bhaja Rama Havildar.
This is said by a man when he is made to work without pay for another on account of friendship or relationship: or when one make pretensions which are beyond one's deserts.

7. मेरा बाबु ले घ्यू खायो मेरो जोर देखौ । Merá bábu le ghyú kháyo mero jora dekhau.
My father ate ghi, now see how strong I am!
Applied to one who boasts of past prosperity or strength.

8. भेकाना लग जुखाम लागो । Bhekáná laga jukháma lágo.
A frog even caught cold.
Applied to one who makes undue pretensions, or assumes the airs of a great man.
A common saying throughout India.

9. मेरा बापु ले घ्यू खायो मेरा हाथ सूंगौ । Merá bápu le ghyú kháyo merá hátha sungau.
My father ate Ghi and now there is the smell of Ghi in my hand.
This is applicable either to one who demands respect on account of his ancestry, or is suspected for the faults of others.

10. छोटो मुख बड़ि बात। Chhoṭo mukha barhi báta.

Small mouth, but big words.

An insignificant fellow who talks of great folks and censures them, or comments on their actions.

11. पौ भरि चून तेबारि में डेरो। Pau bhari chúna tebárî me ḍero.

Only four chhaṭákas of flour (the smallest quantity necessary for one person) but cooked in the Tebári. The Tebári is that portion of a house which is visible to all who pass by.

This is used of one who being very poor has haughty airs and makes vain shows.

12. ऊंचि दुकान फीका पकवान। Úṇchi dukána phîká pakawána.

A lofty shop but tasteless sweets.

This is applicable to a man of note whose dealings are not good, or to one who is great in name only but has no wealth or property to maintain it.

13. मा भटियारिणि पूत फतेहखां। Má bhaṭiyáriṇi púta Fateh Kháṇ.

His mother is but a Bhatiyarini, but the son calls himself Fateh Kháṇ.

Applied to one who comes of a poor family, but shows great pride, and bullies his neighbours. A Bhaṭiyáriṇi is a poor woman who waits on travellers at an inn. Fateh Khan is a boastful title.

14. भीख का टुकुड़ा बजार में डकार। Bhîkha ká tukurhá bájára men̲ dekára.

The man who lives on scraps obtained by begging belches in the bazar, (showing that he has had enough).

Making a great show of a very little.

Note : Belching after eating is a sign of satisfaction in India, and after dining at a friend's house it is considered polite to show that one has had a good meal in this way.

15. दारु न गोली खिमा तोपजी। Dáru na goli khimá topajī.

Having no powder or bullets Khima calls himslef "Topaji" (a crack shot).

People who are of no use but pretend to be, or wish to be considered expert.

16. डेढ़ टट्टु बाग में डेरो। Derha ṭaṭu bága meṇ ḍero.

A pony and a half encamped in a garden (or large camping ground).

Applies to one who makes a great show of a very little property.

17. दिन में गुड़िया गुड़ नि खाव रात गुलमिणा चाट। Dina men̲ gurhiyá gurha ni kháwa ráta gulamin̲á cháṭa.

One who does not eat treacle in the day time licks the refuse of treacle at night.

Used of one who assumes a haughty or fastidious air in the presence of people, but his circumstances are totally incapable of maintaining his pride or his pretended position.

18. काल को जोगि आज को सिद्ध। Kála ko jogi ája ko siddha.

The ascetic of yesterday has become a saint today.

An ascetic becomes a saint after a long preparatory course during which he has to lead a pure and pious life, undergo penances, practising abstinence from worldly things, and subjecting or controlling his senses for the sake of meditation and devotion.

Used of one who assumes an air of pride or is puffed up by the little he possesses.

19. मूसा का हाथ हलदा कि गांठ लागि पसारि बणि बैठो। Músá ká hátha haladá ká gánṭha lági pasári baṇi baiṭho.

A mouse that happened to find a root of tumeric became a grocer.

Conceit of small people.

20. ढकीण न बिछोण मरोड़ बड़ि। Ḍhakiṇa na bichhoṇa marorha barhi.

Nothing under nor over him, yet very proud.

C.f. "Pride and poverty."

21. बाग मारि बगंबर में बैठो। Bága mári baganbara men baitho.

One kills a leopard and then sits on its skin.

Used of one who after some achievement grows proud and consequential, and does not remember his former position.

Also applied to cheats and selfish persons who after obtaining their ends become stiff and unyielding.

22. घर न बार मुहल्लादार। Ghara na bára muhalládára.

A man having no house and family is called "Mohalládár".

Applied to so called great persons, who have no property.

23. गुड़ खाणो गुलगुलन को परहेज। Gurha kháṇo gulagulana ko paraheja.

One eats gurha (treacle) but abstains from sweet loaves (made with gurha).

C.f. "Strain at a gnat and swallow a camel."

Applied to showy and fastidious people.

24. हाथि निंगलनु मच्छर गला लागणो। Háthī níṇgalanu machhara galá láganọ.

To choke over a fly and swallow an elephant.

E.g. To make much ado about the performance of unimportant duties, but to make no difficulties about neglecting much more important things.

Applied to fastidious, haughty people.

25. काल को जोगि कब कि जटा। Kála ko jogi kaba ki jaṭá.

An ascetic of yesterday but with very long hair.

Applied to one who makes great pretensions with small foundation.

26. कांडा को घागरो। Káṇḍá ko ghágaro.

A skirt for Káṇḍá.

Káṇḍá is a village in Garhwal near Srinagara where the annual fair is held on the last festival day of *Diwáli* (October). Women always wear their gayest clothes at this fair, and often wear borrowed clothes.

Applied to one who makes a great show of himself though he may be destitute of the necessaries of life.

VIRTUE OF NECESSITY

1. चिफलि पड़ो त हर गंगा। Chifali parho ta Hara gaṇgá.

One slipped into water and called out "Hara Gaṇgá."

People say "Hara Gaṇgá" when they bathe. This man had no mind to bathe but accidently fell into the water. He at once took the opportunity of performing a religious act. In the same way when one loses anything he says that he has offered it to God. For they say that anything burnt, drowned in water, taken by thieves or kings, the owner will get back in the next existence, together with everything lost, except in gambling.

It is used now a sarcasm on greedy people. One who makes a virtue of necessity.

2. उड़ती चून पितरन का नाम। Urhatí chúna pitarana ká náma.

The wind takes away the ancestor's share of the flour.

Small balls (*pinda*) are offered to the manes of ancestors by the nearest surviving relatives. When a portion of flour has been blown away by the wind, the owner hastens to say that that portion was intended for making *pinda*, and thus secures himself from any loss, the ancestors being the only sufferers. Applied as above.

VISITING FOREIGN COUNTRY

1. नजीक को जोगी टाड़ को सिद्ध। Najíka ko jogí ṭárha ko siddha.

An ascetic in his own village will be considered a saint in another village.

"A prophet is not without honour but in his own country." "Familiarity breeds contempt."

2. देश भिक्ष्या परदेश चोरी। Ḍesh bhikshyá paradesha chorí.

To beg in one's own country and steal in a foreign country.

A man should not beg in his own country, where he would be disgraced by doing so, and so one who steals should not steal in a strange land where he will have no one to defend him or his cause.

3. जो जाव कलकत्ता गू खाव अलपत्ता। Jo jáwa Kalkattá gú kháwa alapattá.

One who goes to Calcutta will have to eat human dung.

Used to dissuade orthodox Hindus from going to Calcutta.

4. राज रजणु अपणा देश भीख मांगणि परदेश। Rája rajaṇu apaṇá desha bhíkha maṉgáṇi paradesha.

To reign in one's own country and to beg alms in a foreign country.

I.e. Seek fame and good repute in your own country: it does not matter what you do in a foreign land, where nobody knows you.

WANT OF APPRECIATION

1. अंधा का हाथ आरसी। Aṇdhá ká hátha árasí.

A looking glass in the hand of blind man.

Want of appreciation. Giving a thing to one who does not know its value.

2. बानर के जाण आदा को सवाद। Bánara ke jáṇa ádá ko sawáda.

A monkey is no judge of the taste of ginger.

C.f. "Throwing pearls before swine."

3. भैंस का अघाड़ि मृदंग। Bhaisa ká aghárhi mirdaṇga.

Drumming (playing music) to a buffalo.

C.f. "Throwing pearls before swine."

4. निमखणा भैंस कि भैसैनि खीर। Nimakhaṇá Bhaiṉsa ki bhaisainí khíra.

Rice pudding prepared with the milk of a buffalo which one dislikes smells of the buffalo.

Applies to the work and good services of one who is disliked being unacceptable. *E.g.* If a *Zemindar* (agriculturist) who keeps three or four wives to work for him in the fields dislikes one of them, he will never be pleased with her work, and she will quote this proverb.

5. गना डूमको गाइयो नि गाइयो। Ganá ḍúma ko kaiyo ni gáiyo.

The singing of a Ḍúma (low caste) having a goitre in his throat is no singing at all.

Used by one who being disliked by his superior finds that the work done by him is not appreciated.

WANT OF SYMPATHY

1. अंधा का अगाड़ि रोया आंख अपणा खोया। Aṇdhá ká agárhi royá áṇkha apaṇá khoyá.

To cry before a blind man is but to pain one's own eyes.

I.e. Nothing should be asked of a man who has no sympathy in the matter. Generally used when a reasonable request is rejected without consideration.

2. अपणा काला रोवावन बिराणा काला हसावन। Apaṇá kálá rowáwana biráṇá kálá hasáwana.

One's own dumb children cause us to weep, but those of others make us laugh.

Applied to one who gloats over the distress of another.

3. बालक नि देख आपणो घर पौणो नि देख परायो घर। Bálaka ni dekha ápaṇo ghara pauṇo ni dekha paráyo ghara.

A child does not know what there is in his own house, nor a poor relative who comes as a guest what there is in the house of his host.

E.g. A child asks for things which the father cannot afford to give. So a poor relative often makes preposterous demands.

4. देखंछु कि पिहल पट खांछु कि अलूण पट। Dekhaṇchhu ki pihala paṭa kháṇchhu ki alúṇa paṭa.

Quite yellow to look at, but to the taste without any salt.

Applied to one who is very polite and gentlemanly but good for nothing, i.e. has no sympathy or consideration for others. Nearly every kind of vegetable food has turmeric put into it which gives it a yellow colour.

5. गांठ में नै लूण कि डलि लड़का मागंछ घ्यु खिचड़ि। Gaṉṭha meṉ nai lúṇa ki ḍali larhaká mágaṇchha ghyu khicharhi.

He has not even a bit of salt (tied up in a corner of his sheet) but his son asks for Ghi khicharhi (an expensive article of food).

6. जैको जाव तैको जाव धोबी का बाप को क्या जाव। Jaiko jáwa taiko jáwa dhobī ká bápa ko kyá jáwa.

A dhobi washes clothes by beating them on a stone with such force that they are torn, since they do not belong to him, but to other people.

Applied to one who injures the property of other people which has been consigned to him.

7. लूट का धान फुफु का सराध। Lúṭa ká dhána phuphu ká sarádha.

One offers "sarádha" to his "phuphu" (father's sister) out of the rice he obtained by plunder or for nothing.

E.g. The religous rites performed for one's forefathers, during which balls of rice are consecrated to them, and Brahmins and relatives are fed with rice &c. are called *Sarádh*. No one ever performs this ceremony for his father's sister. But when he gets rice for nothing he remembers even his fathers's sister; which he would not do if he had furnished the rice at his own expense. Such wealth inclines a man towards extravagance. This is an equivalent of the Persian proverb which says that one's heart becomes cruelly liberal with the money or property of another which has cost him nothing.

What is called "cheap kindness".

8. लै पिछो जानरो। Lai pichho jánaro.

Take the mill stone on your back.

E.g. One who was carrying a load on his head was told by another to take his mill stone on his back also.

A good-natured man is imposed on.

C.f. "Riding a willing horse to death."

9. मेरि घाण अैजाव बाड़े का बलद बाग लीजाव। Meri gháṇa aijáwa bárhe ká balada bága lījáwa.

If my fields are ploughed I do not care if the Dum's bullocks be killed by a leopard.

This is applicable to one who after borrowing and using another's property, takes no care of it.

10. मा मौस्याण बाप कठ बाप। Má mausyáṇa bápa kaṭha bápa.

(I am in sad plight) my mother is a step mother and I am but the bastard of my father.

This is used whom one represents his helpless condition, having no one to sympathize with him.

11. निमखणो घट बूस का वेरा। Nimakhaṇo ghaṭa búsa ká werá.

The water mill which has no master (or no one to look after it) is made use of by putting into it handfuls of chaff (for grinding, instead of grain).

Used to denote the treatment an orphan or poor person generally gets in the world.

12. बानर कि सुख पुछै। Bánara ki sukha puchhai.

Enquiring after one's health like a monkey.

E.g. A pet monkey taken into one's arms at first bites and scratches. So the proverb refers to a friend who either makes but one visit or commences his visit by quarrelling. Want of sympathy.

WICKEDNESS

1. आपणो नाख काटि बिराणो असकुनु। Ápaṇo nákha káṭi biráṇo asakunu.

To cut one's own nose in order to act as a bad omen for other people.

I.e. To injure oneself in order to bring trouble on others.

2. बुरा देखि करतार डर। Burá dekhi kartára ḍara.

Even the creator fears a wicked man.

I.e. Every one is afraid of a tricky person.

3. लंका में जो सबन है छोटो सो बाउन गज लंबो। Laṇká men̲ jo sabana hai chhoṭo so báuna gaja lambo.

The shortest monster man found in Lanka (Ceylon) measured fifty-two yards.

This is used to signify a very atrocious iniquity perpetrated by the smallest person of his class or caste.

4. राम मिलाइ जोड़ी एक अंधा एक कोढ़ी। Ráma milái jorhî eka aṇdhá eka korhi.

A God-made pair, one blind and the other leper.

By chance a blind man and a leper met and struck up friendship. This is applied to bad and mean people when they are in concert with each other for evil designs. Spoken ironically of two persons when one is as bad as the other. *C.f.* "Birds of a feather flock together."

5. सोना कि छुपाई पेट नि मार कोई। Soná ki chhupâî peṭa ni mára koî.

A knife will cut even when made of gold.

A man who is dangerous and untrustworthy must be avoided though he be of noble descent.

6. कालि भली न सेत द्वियै मारौ एकै खेत। Káli bhali na seta dwiyai marau ekai kheta.

Neither the black nor the white are good, both should be killed (at once) at the same place.

Applied to two persons who are alike in wickedness. (The black and white refer to two insects that destroy crops).

7. माइ अपणि भिक्ष्या नि दे आपणा कुत्ता कणि थाम। Mái apaṇi bhikshyá ni de ápaṇá kuttá kaṇi tháma.

O, mother never mind giving me anything, but do not let your dog bite me.

A beggar once went to the house of a woman to ask the usual alms, who instead of giving him anything set dog upon him to drive him away. He entreated her to keep her dog back, and he would not ask for alms. Hence the proverb is applied to one who instead of complying with the request of another tries to do him an injury.

8. काला कालों कि एक जात। Kálá kāloṇ ki eka játa.

All black people belong to one caste.

I.e. All who have evil designs in concert with each other remain in unity among themselves.

C.f. "Birds of a feather flock together."

"Honour among thieves."

9. स्याप का पैर स्याप पहचाणौ। Syápa ká paira syápa pahacháṇau.

A snake discerns the way of (another) snake.

C.f. "Set a thief to catch a thief."

10. पत्थर है ईंट नरम। Pathara hai ĩṇṭa narama.

A brick is softer than a stone.

Used in comparing two wicked persons or actions, which though both bad, differ in the nature or degree of atrocity, for instance a theft is less atrocious than a murder, a slanderer than a thief.

11. जो अपणा को खाव सो औरन क्या राख। Jo apaṇá ko kháwa so aurana kyá rákha.

One who devours his own people will hardly spare others.

Applied to an extravagant and wicked person.

WILFULNESS

1. मन को सौदा। Máṇa ko saudá.

One's own choice, or such is my wish.

Used when anyone acts in an unusual or irrational manner asserting his own independence.

WITNESS

1. चूलो बोद कि मैन बार पकवान करेन औंदो बोद मैं दगड़ी छौं।
Chúlo boda ki maina bára pakawána karena auṇdo boda maiṇ dagarhī chhauṇ.

"Chúlá" (the oven) said that it had cooked 12 kinds of sweetments. "The Aundo" (which is adjoining) said "I was near at hand".

Anything done in the presence of two or more persons cannot be concealed. Don't boast unless there have been no witnesses. *Aundo* is a small compartment adjoining to and behind a *Chúlá* enclosed with the *Chúlá* wall or stone.

The custom of making a *Chula* or open oven upon the ground *having an empty space behind* is peculiar to Gaṛhwal. The reasons of this arrangement are (1) to provide a receptacle for cooked food, and (2) to avoid the "evil eye". Cooked food thus "overlooked" is supposed to be injurious.

WOMEN

1. तिरिया चरित्र जाने न को खसम मारि सत्ती हो। Tiriyá charitra jáne na ko khasama mári sattī ho.

Kills her husband and then becomes a satti: who knows the ways of women?

A certain woman being in love with another man killed her husband at night at the instigation of her paramour, giving out that thieves had done it. But in the morning she went as a *Satti* with the body of her husband.

2. स्यैणि लीबेर घर। Syaini lībera ghara

One's household depends on a woman.

If a woman is not dexterous in the management of the household affairs, or being clever, does not give her attention to it the house will not thrive or prosper. The story noted below will illustrate the proverb.

Once a king with his queen consort was taking a drive along a public road. Seeing a man in rags with a load of firewood on his head, he remarked to the queen that this was evidently an improvident man, but the queen instead of maintaining the king's opinion about the man said that he was not to be blamed for his poverty, but it must be due to his wife, who must either be a foolish woman or indifferent to her duty. The noble pair began to dispute about the matter. At length the king in anger directed his queen to go and manage the man's affairs for a certain time. The queen was very glad to obey this command of her husband. Accordingly she went to the house of the poor man and found his wife a lazy woman, and ascertained that the poor man used to earn only two pice a day by the sale of fuel, with which he used to buy flour whereon the man and his wife could barely subsist. The first thing the queen did was to direct the man to sell two loads of wood in a day instead of one as he used to do, and to get two pice worth of wheat instead of flour, and his wife was made to grind the wheat. This arrangement secured them enough food, and saved two pice a day. After a time the saving amounted to five rupees, with which the queen bought him an ass for conveyance of firewood. By this arrangement the poor man was enabled to sell sixteen loads of wood instead of two. Thus after some time she effected a further saving, with which she purchased many oxen and asses to convey the fuel to the capital town for for sale. She also employed many men to cut and prepare firewood in the jungle. In this way the poor man monopolized the whole trade of firewood in the town. Soon afterwards the jungle caught fire. On hearing of it the queen ordered that all the charcoal made by the fire should be brought to the poor man's house. All this charcoal, on being carried to his house, became gold (i.e. sold at a high rate). In this way the poor man became very rich. One day by the advice of the queen the man invited the king to a feast at his own house, when, seeing the immense wealth of which the man had become possessed, the king admitted the truth of what the queen had said. The king then took away his queen to his own palace.

3. भै रांड नारि गे लाज सारि। Bhái ráṇḍa nári ge lája sári.
No sooner does a woman become a widow then she loses all shame.
I.e. Having no one to control her she does what she pleases.

4. रांड न को पांजो गौं पड़ो बांजो। Ráṇḍa na ko páṇjo gauṇ parho báṇjo.
If women manage a village it will become a desert.
This corresponds with what is elsewhere said, that one who acts on the advice or direction of woman, boy, or enemy is sure to meet with ruin eventually.

WORK AND WAGES

1. उन्ने गांगुली की छाकुली उन्ने टुकन्या को हल। Unne gáṇguli̇ ki̇ chhákuli̇ unne Ṭukanyá ko hala.
The ploughing of Ṭukanyá is as the food given him by Gáṇguli.
As the wages so will be the work (the man hired for ploughing is fed by those who hire him).

WORLD

1. ततः किं या फिर के। Tatah kiṇ yá phira ke.
What is to be done then? or what to do in the end thereof?
E.g. This means that if one succeeds in his enterprise what will he do thereafter since all wordly things are of transient nature and will vanish some time.
Consolation used at a time of loss.

2. जे संसार ते मनसार। Je saṇsára te manasára.
What there is in my mind is also in that of the world (what I wish is also wished by the world).
Used to indicate that one can judge the state of the world by the suggestions of his own mind.

3. दुनियां साझि। Duniyáṇ sájhi.
The world is the joint property of all human beings.
E.g. An act either good or bad, done by one individual affects others in this world. *C.f.* "As the world leads we follow."

Used to induce people to be careful of what they do, and also to do what the world does. *C.f.* "We are members one of another."

4. चार दिन कि चांदनी फिर अंधेरि रात। Chárá dina ki cháṇḍani phira aṇdheri ráta.

Moonlight for a few days and then the dark fortnight.

This is used to impress on one's heart that prosperity and adversity will not last, but are of transient nature. *C.f.* "Make hay while the sun shines." "Work while it is called today, for the night cometh when no man can work."

5. बिराणो मन परदेश। Biráṇo mana paradesha.

The mind of another is as a foreign land.

I. e. We do not know what is in the mind of others.

6. सपक स्वाद झलक संसार। Sapaka swáda jhalaka saṇsára.

Taste in a morsel, and the world in a glance.

The saying of an ascetic, who declares that just as a man can tell from the first taste of a dish what all the rest will be like, so from a very brief or slight experience of the world he can find out its nature, the vanity of its pleasures etc.

7. संसार सिसण को पात। Saṇsára sisaṇa ko páta.

The world is (like) a leaf of nettle (pricking on both sides).

No one can escape criticism, however he may act.

8. कांको ईंट कांको रोड़ो भानमती ले कुटम जोड़ो। Káṇko ỉṭa káṇko rorha bhánamátỉ le kuṭuma jorho.

The bricks of one place and stones of another formed the conjurer's family.

I.e. The conjurer makes up his show from bricks and stones. This proverb declares that all human relationships and friendship are merely imaginary conditions, like the toys with which the conjurer constructs his plays. All is a dream.

APPENDIX

1. बिनाश काले बिपरीत बुद्धि। Binásha kále biparíta buddhih.

He who is about to perish becomes demented.

Illustration : Rám Chandra when in exile in the jungle of the Deccan was allured by a deer of golden hue, which was really a demon or phantasm. In pursuing this, Rám wandered far from his home, and Ráwan took this opportunity to carry off Ráma's wife, Sitá. Had not Rám lost his senses and gone after this imaginary and impossible animal he would not have lost his wife or rather had that loss not been fated, he would not have been so senseless.

2. चुगलि लागिजा बिनती निलाग। Chugali lágijá biṇati ni lága.

Backbiting leaves an impression in the mind (of the hearer) but entreaty (makes no impression).

We remember a fault when it is told us regarding some one, but we soon forget a request made for or recommendation of that person.

3. पहरो करनु भलो कि खोज करनु भलो। Paharo karanu bhalo ki khoja karanu bhalo.

Is it better to watch one's possessions, or to search for them when lost?

Prevention is better than cure.

4. भैर गौं को भसाड़ जेठ न असाड़। Bhaira gaun̲ ko bhasárha jeṭha na asárha.

A villager and clown who does not know Jeṭha (the month of May) from Asárha (June).

A stupid fellow, unable to discriminate.

5. ज्वे का दैजा ले बाबु का धन ले को खांछ। Jwe ká daijá le bábu ká dhana le ko kháṇchha.

Who will live on his wife's dowry, or on his father's wealth?

Every man must earn his own living, and not depend on such sources of income.

6. जाणि मार बणियां पछाणि मार चोर। Jáṇi mára baṇiyáṇ pachháṇi mára chora.

A banya will cheat only those will whom he is well acquainted, and a thief will rob only those whom he knows (cannot bring him to justice or overpower him).

7. घटि गया त फकीर बढ़ि गया त अमीर मरि गया त पीर। Ghaṭi gayáta phakíra baḍhi gayáta amíra mari gayáta píra.

Mussalmans, when they have no property, call themselves faqirs; if they are rich, they call themselves Amir (nobleman); and when they die, they are called Pir (saints).

A satire on Mohammedans.

8. छाला घाम हालनि। Chhálá ghárna hálani.

To expose a man's hide to the sun.

To reveal a man's faults and secret crimes.

9. तराजु का पलड़ा। Taráju ká palarhá.

The scales of the balance.

The alternation of prosperity and misfortune in people's lives. "The turning of the tables."

10. पल में पुणि। Pala me puṇi.

A small wisp out of the bundle (of cotton, in spinning).

I.e. A very small part of the work done.

11. आंखा बुजणा। Áṇkhá bujaṇá.

To close (lit. quench) the eyes.

Not to listen to or grant a request.

12. काल का दिन पूरा करना। Kála ká dina purá karaná.

Completing the days of Fate (or Death).

Said by an unhappy man, waiting for deliverance from this life.

13. टेकण सों जांठि नै खोलण सों गांठि नै। Tekaṇa so̱n jáṇṭhi nai kholaṇa soṇ gaṇṭhi nai.

No stick for support, no knot to unloose (i.e. no money, which is usually tied up in the cotton garment).

Weak and patronless.

14. गांठा गणना। Gáṇṭhá gaṇaná.

To count knots.

Build castles in the air.

15. जो कुत्ता पाल सो कुत्ता जो कुत्ता मार सो कुत्ता बैंणि घर मैं कुत्ता ससुर घर जवैं कुत्ता। Jo kuṭṭá pála so kuttá jo kuttá mára so kuttá baiṇi ghara bhai kuttá sasura ghara jawaiṇ kuttá.

He that cherishes dogs is a dog; he that beats dogs is a dog; he that lives in his sister's house (spunges on his sister) is a dog; and he that lives in his father-in-law's house (too long) is a dog.

A satire on spunges of this kind, who are considered disgraceful.

16. जो पंत कौ सबन ले करनु जो पंते कर कैले नि करनु। Jo pan̲ta kau sabana le karanu jo paṇta kara kaile ni karnu.

Whatever the Pant says, do it; but do not do what he does.

The Pants are powerful caste of Brahmins, and so can do much as they please.

17. छ्यूं करनि। Chhyúṇ karani.

To sneeze.

Sneezing is regarded as a bad omen, on setting out on a journey or commencing a business, if anyone sneezes, the project must be laid aside for a while. A man beginning a march and stopped in this manner will return for a few paces and then go on.

The proverb means 'to dissuade' one from his purpose.

18. गया जाया म्यरा बबा को पिंड बाटि आया। Gayá jáyá myará babá ko piṇḍa báti áyá.

Go to Gaya and offer Pind to my father.

The ceremony of shraddh can only be performed by the son,

grandson, nephew or other near relations of the deceased. Hence to request a stranger to perform the ceremony is absurd.

Means "Look after your own affairs." If you want anything done, do it yourself.

19. घोड़ा जुजीणा दूब को नाश। Ghorá jujĩṇá dúba ko nása.

When two horses fight, the dub grass is destroyed.

That is, when great powers come into collision, common folk suffer.

A caution to poor people against interfering in the quarrels of their betters.

20. खसिया मनै ठंग ठंगो। Khasiyá manai ṭhaṉga ṭhaṉgo.

The Khasiya (rustic hill-man) the more he is besought the surlier he becomes.

I.e. The only way to manage him is by threats and compulsion.

21. नकटो नाख परमेश्वर देखलो। Nakaṭo nákha Parameshwara dekhalo.

A nose cut off (secret sin) is known to God.

Cutting off the nose is a common figure of speech meaning to lose one's character, become disgraced, as in former days the punishment for shameful actions and heinous crimes took this form. Here the meaning is that though a man may conceal his evil deeds from his fellow-men, God sees his wickedness, he` is disgraced in the sight of God.

Ironically used in speaking of a person's secret or supposed sins.

22. ज्यूनु जिया को मेलो। Jyúnu jiyá ko melo.

Life is a fair.

I.e. As long as men are alive they meet. Spoken when acquaintances come across each other.

23. पोत पुरि करनि। Pota puri karani.

To fill up one's basket.

To do well by oneself, to look after number one.

24. तीनतेर। Tinatera.

All at sixes and sevens (lit. three thirteen).

Utterly ruined and done for.

25. छक्का पंजा। Chhakká panjá.

Pitch and toss (gambling with shells).

Means playing tricks, practising by dishonest methods.

26. भैंस को सींग भैंस कणि भारि नि लागनु। Bhaiṇsa ko síṇa bhaiṇsa kaṇi bhári ni láganu.

The horns of a buffalo are not heavy to him.

One is not unwilling to incur cost or trouble for his own people.

27. पुवा पाकणा। Puwá pákaná.

Cooking sweetmeats.

Spoken of one raised to sudden prosperity. Having a "good time."

28. छल झाड़नु। Chhala jhárhanu.

Exorcising demons (or "devil-driving").

A class of mendicant doctors profess to exorcise evil spirits by using force. *E.g.* burning, beating, shouting loudly in the ear of the possessed person etc. When one is threatened and bawled at by another the bystanders facetiously use this proverb.

29. पुजनै पुजनै आज काम लागो। Pujanai pujanai ája káma lágo.

After I have worshipped you so long you are of use to me only today.

The Bairagis or Vaishnavs (devotees of Vishnu who worship the god in the form of a black stone called Sáligrám, found at Damudhar Kund on the banks of the river Sáligrámá in Nepal), are exceedingly strict in their religious duties, and will not eat or do any work until they have offered the food to the Sáligrám stone or worshipped it. Once a Bairagi who had worshipped such a stone for many years was cooking his cakes in the Plains. After cooking he placed all the cakes in front of the stone by way of offering, when a dog coming along suddenly snatched one of the cakes and made off. As there were no stones near, the man could not resist the temptation to fling his Sáligrám at the dog, who dropped the cake and fled. The Bairagi then made use of the above words.

30. हाड़ गाड़ माटो गांठो। Hárha gárha máṭo gánṭho.

Bones go into the river, but earth remains in one's knot.

I.e. Cattle will die and their bones will be swept away into a river, but land property or money invested in land is an enduring possession.

The knot is equivalent to "the pocket", and hence often means "money". The poorer class of Hindus carry their money tied up in a knot of their sheet.

Used to encourage people to buy land and not to invest their money in cattle.

31. आपुं मरि बेर लग बैरि मारनु। Ápuṇ mari bera laga bairi máranu.

One should kill himself in order to bring death on his enemy.

It is a popular belief that if a man is unable to revenge himself on the enemy in this life he will be able to do so in the next life, if he has a strong desire to that effect on his death-bed. It is also believed that a man can torment his enemy after death by taking possession of him or bewitching him.

Once there were two sworn enemies living in the same village. One of them went to the temple of a goddess to pray for blessings, and the other, hearing of this, also went to the same shrine, and besought the goddess to give him the same boon which his enemy had asked. The goddess, knowing his thoughts, told him he would have whatever he desired, but that the first petitioner would get double of the same; whereupon the cunning fellow, after a moment's thought, prayed the goddess to deprive him of one of his eyes, so that his enemy might thus *lose both his eyes*.

32. फुटो ढोल। Phuṭo ḍhola.

A broken Drum.

I.e. A broken drum when played makes all kinds of unexpected noises. Applied to a talkative person who is always saying "awkward things," without due reserve.

33. गरीब ले बेचि आपणि ज्वे सौकार उधार मांग। Garibale bechi ápaṇi jwe saukára udhára máṇga.

The poor fellow was so hard up that he was obliged to sell his wife, but the rich man to whom he was going to sell her wanted her on credit.

Used when a man wants his money badly, but is put off to a future date.

34. कौड़ि को पूत। Kaurhi ko púta .

The son of a shell (cowrie).

A miser; one who will do anything for money; or who will not spend a fraction.

35. थूक का थेकला। Thuka ká thekalá.

Patching with spittle.

Torn cloth if mended by sticking bits of material upon it with saliva used as paste will soon be as bad as ever. This is used of baseless statements or groundless pleas.

36. लाटा ले लगड़ देखो बगड़ बगड़ै दौड़ो। Láṭá le lagarha dekho bagarha bagarhai daurho.

A dumb idiot found a cake on a river bank, and ran along hoping to find more.

One who pursues a foolish or useless course because he has been benefitted once by it.

37. बैरि मरि बेर लग दुख दिछ। Bairi mari bera laga dukhu dichha.

An enemy, even when dead, will give trouble.

A noted bad character once lived in a village, and was a great pest to all his neighbours, lodging false information against them at the police-office etc, and being in every way a public nuisance. When on his death-bed he sent for all his neighbours and implored them to have mercy on him and save him from penalties in the future existence on account of his many crimes. He besought them for this object to drag his corpse round to every house in the village before cremating it. Being touched by this his last request they all vowed to do so, and accordingly when the breath was out of the sly rogue, they began hauling him along the street. Here they were met by some police and "chaukidars", who, supposing that they had beaten and killed the man, arrested them all and took them off to a magistrate. They were all sentenced to a long term of imprisonment. Thus their enemy had his revenge on them even after he was dead.

38. सै को सोरो लाख को मित्र। Sai ko soro lâkha ko mitra.

A relation of the same caste (with whom one has collateral interests) is worth a hundred rupees, but a relation by alliance, or a friend, (who is a stranger) is worth a lac of rupees.

Used to appreciate the genuine usefulness of an allied relation or friend.

39. मैं चाकलो बाजार सांगुड़ि। Mai chákalo bázára sáṇgurhi.

He is too big for the bazaar and the bazaar is too narrow for him.

A conceited person, puffed up with pride.

40. वोड़ कोढ़। Worha koḍha.

A mason or the leprosy (both very difficult to get rid of).

The masons of this country are often very cunning, delaying the completion of their work from day to day, so that they may get the extra pay. Until their work is completed their employer cannot well dismiss them, and so is at their mercy, even though they add only a single stone to the wall in a day's work. In the same way leprosy, an incurable disease, is a simile for anything that cannot be got rid of.

41. अकल ले परमेश्वर मिलंछ। Akala le Parameshwara milaṇchha.
God is found out by wisdom.
By close application of the mind a man can rise even to the knowledge of the divine things. An exhortation of wisdom or mental activity, which gains all things.

42. ये बस्ति का लोग बड़ा बेकूफ छन कभैं ये तरफ कभैं वी तरफ बसनि। Ye basti ká loga barhá bekúpha chhana kabhaiṇ ye tarapha kabbaiṇ wí tarapha basani.
The people of this place are great fools, sometimes they live on one side of the street, sometimes on the other.
A blind man led by another went begging. He found it troublesome to pass from one side of the road to the other, and thus apostrophized the people of the village, instead of acknowledging his own defect.
The unreasonable criticism of ignorant and conceited people.

43. माल है जगात बांकि। Mála hai jagáta báṇki.
The commodity not worth the tax or duty upon it.
"Not worth the candle."

44. द्वी पर द्वी। Dwí para dwí.
Two for two.
When an inferior puts himself on an equality with his superior or withstands him. Insubordination.
"Jack's as good as his master."

45. संसार को मुख क्वेनि थामि सकनो। Sansára ko mukha kwe ni thámi sakano.
No one can stop the mouth of the world, (or men's criticism).
A man should not heed people's remarks, but go his own way.
An illustration is given as follows: according to the story of the Ramayan the god Ráma took back his wife Sita after she had been carried off by Ráwan. Once a *dhobi* (washerman) was seen beating his wife, telling her that he was not like Ráma who took back his wife under such disgraceful circumstances, he could not behave in such a way etc. Thus

even the gods are not exempt from criticism. In consequence of this unfavourable popular opinion Ráma was compelled to put his wife away.

46. तीतिरो । Titiro.

A titira (lit. a partridge).

A knowing person, wide-awake; cunning.

47. भेकुला कि जांठि । Bhekulá ki jánṭhi.

A stick of bhekulá (a kind of tree, the fibres of which are very slippery) when used as a staff it slips from the hand of the holder.

An untrustworthy man, who cannot be depended on for support, a broken need.

48. गुसैं कि देलि बढ़ौ मेरो गास बढ़ौ । Gusaiṇ ki deli badhau mero gása baḍhau.

गुसैं का आंखा फुटि जाना त मैं चोरि करन्यु । Gusaiṇ ka áṇkhá phuṭi jáná ta mai chori karanyu.

The dog wishes the increase of the family (so that his food or leavings may thereby increase, but the cat wishes that all the members of the family should become blind (so that she may steal with impunity).

The dog is considered a grateful animal and auspicious, while the cat is regarded as ungrateful and unlucky. The cat is supposed to be the maternal aunt of the leopard, whom she has taught all the evil he knows, except the trick of climbing a tree, according to the saying that "one thing should be reserved from a pupil." The leopard formerly used to feed on *dead* cattle, but the cat instructed him to kill *live* cattle, so that she also might have a share; since that time the leopard has preyed on live animals. This is quoted as a reproach to the cat.

The dog is supposed to have remarkable powers of hearing, and the cat of sight. Once a king set a dog and a cat to watch his horse. At night the dog began to bark, hearing some sound. The cat reproved him for making such a noise, saying that she had seen (in the dark) only a hair falling from the horse.

Evil spirits are supposed to appear often in the form of a cat, but never of a dog.

49. सौ की साट आधा की नाट दश द्यूंलो दश देउलो दश को केलीणो के दीणो। Sau kí sáṭa ádhá kí náṭa dasha dyúṇlo dasha deuṇlo dasha ko kelíṇo ke díṇo.

Out of a hundred, sixty: out of that sixty, half lost; I will give you ten rupees and have ten given to you by some other person; then the remaining ten is not worth talking about.

A man sent one hundred rupees by the hand of one of his countrymen to his family in another country. The bearer of the money on arriving said he had only set out with sixty rupees, and half of that had been lost on the way. He very generously promised to give ten of the remaining thirty at some future time, and said he would cause some other men to pay them another ten. As for the remaining ten, he said it was not proper that they should take such a paltry sum, nor for him to give it, so he ended by giving them nothing at all.

Ironically applied to dishonesty, and "cooked" accounts etc.

50. मुडियो जोगि पिसी औषध। Muḍiyo jogi pisí aukhadha.

A shaven jogi and powdered medicine (are not distinguishable).

No one can tell whether the jogi was a Brahman or Dom or to what caste he belonged, as all jogis are alike; and so powdered medicine is difficult to analyse.

Used of these two things.

51. आदमि कि कसौटि मतलब। Ádami ki kasauṭi matalaba.

Motive is the test of a man.

We can only know whether a man is good or bad by knowing his real motives.

52. अकाल धणियां द्वी कपाड़ि सुकाल धणियां द्वियै कपाड़ि। Akála dhaṇiyáṉ dwí kapárhi sukála dhaṇiyáṉ dwiyai kápárhi.

In time of famine dhanyá (coriander seed) has two capsules, and in time of plenty two also.

Coriander seed when pressed or pounded separates into two parts.

Used to express dissatisfaction with a small fixed income.

53. दिन नि रूना बात रै जांछि । Dina ni runá báta rai ján̲chhi.

The time (of need) passes away, but the fact remains (for ever).

When some one has asked another for help and been refused, he tells him my time of need will soon be over, but your refusal will always be rememebred.

Used to induce another to give his help.

54. रावण रो आपुं सुणि हनुमान रो आपुं सुणि । Ráwaṇa ro ápuṇ suṇi Hanumána ro ápuṇ suṇi.

Rawan cries for himself, and Hanumán cries for himself.

Hanumán was the hero-monkey in the Rámáyan, sent by Ráma to look for his wife Sita, who was in the power of Ráwan, King of Ceylon. Ráwan tried to slay him with his wonderful sword with which it is said he could cleave mountains and even earth into two parts. With this sword he struck Hanumán, who turned his back, so the stroke fell on his tail, and cut only one and a half hairs from it. Ráwan was grieved at the failure of his sword, and Hanumán at the injury done to his tail.

Used when both parties in a business are dissatisfied or unfortunate.

55. पर घर को भानो । Para ghara ko bháno.

Vessels of another's house.

Daughters are thus spoken of a depreciatory sense, inasmuch as they do not stay in their father's house, but go to another family on their marriage.

56. बांस बालड़ो । Bán̲sa bálarho.

The ear of a bamboo.

When a bamboo grows ears, it is regarded as an omen portending that it will soon be destroyed or uprooted.

Used on seeing evil deeds and habits springing up in a family, regarded as signs of approaching ruin.

57. थूक का आंसु। Thúka ká áṇsu.

Tears of spittle.

Unnecessary grief, or sorrow at the good fortune of others.

58. निमुवा पिछाड़ि को बनौलो। Nimuwá pichhárhi ko banolo.

The dwarfed after-growth of the lemon crop.

Lemon trees sometimes produce a second growth of fruit, but this is always of a very stunted and poor description. The simile is used to represent the last child of a married pair, or the last yield of anything.

59. दोफर तक माला दोफर माथ चाला। Dophara taka málá dophará mátha chálá.

Málá, friend in the morning, enemy in the afternoon.

Málá is a village in Patti Boráki Rau, parganáh Báramaṇdal, Kumaun, the people of which have the reputation of being very untrustworthy and cunning.

60. अैगयो मेरो मलुवा नि अै भेल हलुवा। Aigayo mero maluwá ni ai bhela haluwá.

If it comes back, it is my Maluwá; if not, let it fall down a precipice.

A certain man had an old and useless ox named maluwá (sweet one). One day the poor animal did not return home from grazing. Instead of going to seek it, the owner expressed himself as in the proverb.

Used of a person or thing little cared for.

61. वला कि टोपि पला का खोरा पला कि टोपि वला का खोरा। Walá ki ṭopi palá ká khorá palá ki ṭopi walá ká khorá.

Putting the cap of one man on another's head, and vice versa.

Double-dealing.

62. ये मुरदा का पिहला पैर तुलै शिर पिटनै आ। Ye muradá ká pihalá paira tu lai shira piṭanai á.

This dead body has yellow feet, come along, beating your head.

Expresses suspicion.

The following story is told relative to the cunning and dishonesty of goldsmiths. Once a king required a number of ornaments made. In order to secure himself against dishonesty on the part of the goldsmiths employed, he had them fastened up in a room, and stripped and searched when they went home at night. One day, however, they represented that one of their number had died, and asked permission to carry out his corpse. In the meantime they had made a figure of solid gold, fetched from the treasury of the king, and dressed up this figure of gold in a winding sheet and carried it forth. As they were leaving the palace, a man caught sight of the golden feet of the figure, and cried out. "This dead body has yellow feet." On hearing this from him the goldsmiths said, "Come along, and join the procession crying for the dead, you also will get a share."

63. अमृत लपेटियो विष विष लपेटियो अमृत । Amrita lapeṭiyo bikha bikha lapeṭiyo amrita.

Outside, nectar; inside, poison. Inside, nectar; outside, poison.

The first is applied to gram, the husk or skin of which is considered good and digestive, while the inner part of gram causes dyspepsia.

The second clause is used of uṛd dál, the inner part of which is considered very nutritive while black covering or shell is regarded as poisonous.

Simple villagers relate the following about the respective merits of dál, wheat and rice. Once these three cereals had a dispute as to their relative superiority, and it was at last agreed to refer the matter to a king. The king at first put them off by saying that he would require twelve years to consider the case. At the end of the twelve years the three grains again went to the king and begged him to give his decision. This time the king said that they must go to a sick man, and ask his opinion, and on that opinion the case must be decided. They accordingly repaired to the house of a sick man, and laid the matter before him. He replied that he could not give the palm to uṛd dál because it disordered his stomach whenever he ate of it, nor to wheat, because he found it very difficult to digest. The only grain which he could eat with safety and comfort was rice, and therefore he considered rice to be the best. On this wheat was so enraged that he tore open his own body, and hence the form of the wheat grain with its split body; and uṛd dál banged his head so severely against the ground that he broke his pate, and ever since has had the mark of the wound (a white speck) on his head.

64. के मैं गोठ ब्यानेर छूं। Ke mai goṭha byánera chhúṇ.

Am I one who has to lie-in the lower story?

A protest against ill-treatment.

In ancient times men of wealth used to purchase girls and boys as slaves. The females were not permitted to give birth to a child in the upper story of the house, this being reserved for the lawful wife, and they were otherwise ill-treated.

65. मुख राखि न्यो हाथ राखि घौ (बिगड़ौ)। Mukha rákhi nyo hátha rákhi ghau (bigarhau).

He who speaks awry will not win his case or get justice, and he who strikes unskilfully will miss his aim.

(Literally will make a bad wound in the material in which he is working).

66. सुन हो राजा भील जसा कू तसा मील। नौ मण लुवा घुनतो खौ लड़का लीगयो चील। Suna ho rájá Bhîla jasá kú tasá mîla. Nau maṇa luwá ghuṇato khau larhaká lîgayo chîla.

Hear, O king Bhil, as a man is so he gets. Nine maunds of iron were eaten up by worms, and the eagle in like manner has carried off the child.

A certain man deposited nine maunds of iron with a friend for safekeeping. On asking for his iron some months afterwards he was told that it had been devoured by insects. As he had no means of proving the deposit, he contrived a plan for forcing the dishonest friend to give up the property. He one day saw his friend's infant playing outside in the sunshine, so darted upon him and carried him off. The father of the child appealed to the king, and the other man on being brought before the court declared that just as his iron had been eaten by insects, so the child had been carried off by an eagle. The king, seeing how matters stood, ordered the man to give up the child, and the dishonest friend in turn to give up the iron.

67. नर कौनि दिन गया दिन कौनी नर गया। Nara kauni dina gayá dina kaunî nara gayá.

Men say that time passes. Time says that men pass away.

A warning that death comes to all. Each day brings a man nearer to his end.

68. चेलो बढ़ौ आपणा घर पैसा बढ़ौ बिराणा घर। Chelo baḍhau ápaṇá ghara paisá baḍhau biráṇá ghara.

A son will flourish in his own (father's) house, but not in a stranger's, but money will increase in another's house.

Referring to putting money out at interest.

69. आपणि आपणि सब गानी। Ápaṇi ápan̲ saba gánî.

Every one sings his own song.

Illiterate but shrewd men in the country, seeing the strange variety of opinions among learned men and professors of different religions, are often quite sceptical, and they assert that the doctrines of punishment for sin in the future world etc. are all inventions for the purpose of frightening people into good conduct. But they have never known any one return from the next world, and so they disbelieve in a future life. There are many of these *nâstiks* or *atheistic* philosophers, who attribute everything to chance, in Kumaun and Gaṛhwal. They observe no sacred days, and are frankly Epicurean. They say a tree has many leaves, which all fall in autumn, but the same leaves will not grow next spring. So men are like leaves, which flourish and decay, and the memory of them is lost.

They quote in derision the story of the sweeper's religion, as follows:

The sweepers are considered lowest of all in the social scale : even the doms will not eat with them. Their spiritual guide is called Lal guru or the Red Teacher, who presides over the sweepers of a large district. When he visits a station all the sweepers gather around him with presents of sweet-meats etc; and treat him with great reverence. He preaches to them on an appointed day, and also acts as a judge or umpire in cases of misconduct among the sweepers. He fines the culprit a certain sum which is spent in feasting all the sweepers, and then the offender is readmitted into their communion. In addressing them he tells them they are the best people in the world, and God honours them above all nations, and they alone with go to Heaven. Their souls will have to pass three terrible rivers in going to Heaven, one consisting of cow's blood, the second of pig's blood, and the third of filth. The Hindus will be unable to pass the first, the Mohammedans the second, and the Christians will stop at the third, but the sweepers will go boldly on and attain felicity. (This is a keen sarcasm, no doubt, on the cow worship of the Hindus, the Mohammedan dread of the pig, and the Christians' zeal for sanitation, to which they themselves owe their living).

70. बाप मरत मर कैंजा सत्ति जालि मेरि मै रोटा पकूण हुणि रै जालि।
Bápa marata mara kaiṇjá satti jáli meri mai roṭa pakúṇ huṇi raijáli.

If my father dies let him die. Then my stepmother may perform satti for him, but my mother will be left to cook my food.

A man had two wives, one of whom he liked, but neglected the other. The latter wife had a son, whom he also disliked. The son when his father was in distress and about to die, thus speaks. By Hindu custom both wives are obliged to perform satti, that is, to be burnt with their husband's body, but in this case, the youth considers that the wife who was beloved should accompany her husband, while the ill treated and neglected wife (his mother) should be allowed to live.

Illustrates the truth that selfish conduct produces like selfishness in others also.

71. गोरू मर त मर बाछो मर त मर सेर भर दूद दिजीकर। Goru mara ta mara báchho mara ta mara sera bhara dúda diji kara.

Let the cow die and the calf too, but we must have a seer of milk every day.

In India, when a cow has a female calf, two teats of the udder are left for it to suck, when the calf is male, only one is left. As a rule the hill cows do not give more than one seer a day. If the calf should die through want of nourishment the cow will refuse to give milk. Thus the foolish man in the proverb demands an impossibility. Since no milk will be left for the calf, which will certainly die, and so the supply of milk will be lost altogether. (The man is supposed to be addressing his wife).

Demanding an impossibility.

72. नौमि का बामण घुणतिया का कवा। Naumi ká bámaṇa ghugatiyá ká kawá.

On the 9th of Asoj (dark fortnight) Brahmans (are to be got with difficulty) and on the Makar Sankránti (12th Jan) crows are scarce.

On the former date the shraddh or memorial rites for mothers is observed, when in almost every family the presence of Brahmans is required and so their services are greatly in request. On the latter date it is the religious custom to feed the crows. If the crows come to take one's offerng it is considered auspicious, if not, it is ominous of evil. So on that day the crows finding abundance of food everywhere, are not so eager to come round the houses and pick up the food.

Used ironically when the abundant and common article is suddenly found wanting.

73. हाथ को मैल। Hátha ko maila.

The sweat, dirt of one's hands.

Used to describe money—filthy lucre—when a man has lost a sum and pooh-poohs the loss as trifling.

74. नि पौणिया ले पै नाख मुख अै। Ni pauṇiyá le pai nákha mukha ai.

He got what was beyond his reach, and it came out at his mouth and nose (he could not manage or digest it).

When a man exceeds the allowable limit on getting opportunities which were formerly beyond him. Want of self-control under new circumstances.

75. कांकड़ बासि गोछ। Káṇkaraha bási gochha.

The Kákar (wild sheep) bleats.

Applied in an abusive way to denote a man's inaptitude or failure. "The thing has turned out to be a jungle in which the voice of the Kákar only is heard." (A Gaṛhwál proverb).

76. कपूवा बासि गोछ। Kapuwá bási gochha.

Same meaning. "The cuckoo utters his voice."

In the Bhábar the people work diligently until about April: when they hear the cuckoo's voice they give up work, regarding it as a sign of the approach of the hot season, when they must retire from their field etc. (A Bhábar proverb).

Used also to denote hopelessness or inability.

77. दातुलो आपणा तर्फ काटंछ। Dátulo ápaṇá tarphá ká ṭaṇchha.

The sickle cuts (grass) to its own side (inwards).

Applied to clannishness.

78. खलुवा कुभागी। Khaluwá kubhági,

Khaluwá is a wretched bungler in speech.

E.g. A man seeing a new house in process of erection by his neighbour finds fault with the arrangement of the doors, and makes the ill-omened remark, "when one of the members of your family die, how will you carry the body out of those doors"? Such an unfortunate speech would be considered as most ill-omened and in the worst taste, and the proverb above-quoted would be used.

79. ले घोड़ो खवे घोड़ो। Le ghorho khwe ghoro.

Take my horse and spoil it.

A thing which no sensible person would do, as a horse is a valuable piece of property in the hills. Applied by a person who is asked to do hastily something damaging to himself.

80. बीठ को निछनु डूम को मरनु के निजाणनु। Bíṭha ko nichhanu ḍúma ko maranu kwe nijáṇanu.

No one believes the poverty of a Bith (patrician) or the dying (from starvation) of a Dom.

Bíthas are always supposed to be wealthy, and Doms are a low and disregarded class, whose death is a matter of no concern.

Used by these two classes of each other.

81. गाहक को मन काल को मन के ठीक छ। Gáhaka ko mana kála ko mana ke ṭhíka chha.

No one knows the mind of a customer or the will of Death.

Both choose in an indiscriminate and uncertain way, and just as every article of goods in a shop will be sold some time or other, so every man will be taken by death some day.

82. मेरो छै मेरो छै कै आपणो निहुनु जाग जाग कै दगड़ो निहुनु।
Mero chhai mero chhai kai ápaṇo nihunu jága jága kai dagarho nihunu.

No one becomes our (relation) by our telling him "You are mine, you are mine," and we cannot make friends (on a journey) with others by saying "Wait for me, wait for me," (for each man is bent on his own purpose).

83. सौ सयाणा एक मतो। Sau sayáṇá eka mato.

Wise men (though there be a hundred of them) are of one opinion.

Good sense always finds out the right course.

A story is sometimes told in connection with this proverb as follows. A king once had a small tank made, and having collected ninety-nine of his wisest subjects and one foolish man ordered them all to pour in a certain quantity of pure milk at night time. The simple man did so, but each of the others thinking that a single seer of water would not be observed in so much milk, poured in water, so that in the morning there were ninety-nine seers of water and only one of milk. Thus the truth of the proverb was established.

84. गरज बौली। Garaja baulí.

A man in need is a man insane.

He will go any length to obtain what he wants, without regard to right and wrong.

85. जूवा जबान। Júwá jabána.

Gambling and making a promise (are equal).

That is, when a man loses in gambling he must certainly pay, so a man who has made a promise must keep it. Used to urge another to keep to his engagement.

86. हाथ सूखो जोगी भूखो। Hátha súkho jogí bhúkho.

As soon as the jogi's hand is dry, he becomes hungry again.

That is, an soon as he has eaten the portion given him by some benevolent person, he goes to another and begs, without telling him that he has already been fed.

Applied to greedy and ungrateful people.

87. सिसणो को पात। Sisaṇo ko páta.

A leaf of nettle (stinging on both sides).

Applied to a tricky, untrustworthy person, who will injure both parties.

The fact noted here is that the nettle leaf stings on whichever ṣide it is touched. So people say, "The world is like a nettle leaf." *I.e.* Whatever one does, people censure and criticize.

88. कोटिश्च कीटायते। Koṭishcha kíṭáyate.

There are millions of insects of the same kind.

A phrase used to one who is boasting about something, to take down his pride; or spoken by one who complimented.

89. गू निखौं गू निखौं गू निखौं त कैखों। Gú nikhauṇ gú nikhauṇ gú nikhauṇ ta ke khauṇ.

The sitola chirps, I won't eat dirt, I won't eat dirt. (Then he says). "If I don't eat dirt what shall I eat"?

Used of force, coercion; *E.g.* When a man has lost his caste, and at first refuses to eat the food and follow the customs of his new associates, but is at last compelled to do so, nolens volens.

90. बूस बैठि गेछ। Búsa baiṭhigechha.

The chaff has got into the mill.

The ordinary water-mill will grind grain, but if chaff creeps into the aperture the mill will be stopped.

Applied to inability or obstruction.

91. कवा कि ब्याण। Kawá ki byáṇa.

Giving birth to a crow.

The crow is supposed to have offspring only once in its lifetime.

Applied to a woman who bears only one child.

92. धुंवां देखणो। Dhuṇwáṇ dekhaṇo.

Watching the smoke.

Seeing others in trouble or labouring hard, and not helping them.

Derived from the analogy of a house on fire, which it is the duty of persons concerned to help to put out.

93. बिरालु को घा। Birálu ko ghá.

A cat's eating grass.

Cats are sometimes observed eating a particular kind of grass, which is regarded as unnatural. Used of a man's beginning to contract bad habits.

94. छैं चितोणो। Chhaîṇ chitoṇo.

Smelling one's object.

Eager for a thing, like a cat scenting a mouse etc.

95. कान आंगुलि। Kána áṇguli.

Putting a finger in one's ear.

At ease after an object is attained.

96. रस में कस। Rasa me kasa.

Adulteration of a pure or genuine thing.

This is considered a sin, *E.g.* putting water in milk &c.

97. नचनची। Nachanachî.

The habit of dancing.

Applied to established bad habits, which a man will practise even if he gains no profit thereby.

Once a king was much pleased with the performance of a dancing girl, but contrary to custom he did not give her a present, but told her, "If ever you feel inclined to dance again, you may come here," implying that a bad habit is practised for its own sake.

98. कौ लाटा काथा माथा सुण काला तू। अनालाले घर मुसो दौड़ डूंडा तू। Kau láṭá káthá máthá suṇa kálá tú. Análá le ghara muso daurha ḍúṇḍá tú.

O dumb man, tell stories. O deaf man, listen to them; O blind man go a thieving, and lame man, run away with the spoil.

Bad choice of agents, or faulty management.

99. रूप रीश नै कर्म बांटो नै। Rúpa ŕisha nai karma báṇṭo nai.

No one should envy another's fair countenance, and no one can share another's fate.

100. हलि हाल जू माल हलोन पर्सा का सेत हलिया बमोरखेत बलद गोरु का पेट। Hali hála jú mála halona parsá ka setá haliyá bamorakheta balada goru ká peṭa.

The plough share is being hardened in the fire, the yoke is in the Bhábar, the handles are being matured in the dung hill, the ploughman is in Bamorkhet (in the plains) and the bullocks are yet unborn.

A man wants his field ploughed at once, although none of the requisites are at hand.

The plough is made of three different kinds of wood. The share has to be hardened in fire, the yoke is made of shisham or sál wood, brought from the Bhabar, and the other parts are made of another wood, which is fitted for use by being buried in a dunghill for several months.

Foolish and improvident haste.

101. बहडसु धारियो को बलद लोड़ा नालि को के। Baharha sudháriyo ko balada lorhá náli ko ke.

The Dom employed to castrate a steer demands a castrated steer as wages, and wants something to pay for his tools as well. That is, he wants wages exceeding the value of the property to be dealt with.

Expresses astonishment at the exorbitant rate of interest or wages demanded by one who has a monopoly of his particular business.

102. जब मांगो तब भोल। Jaba máṇgau taba bhola.

Whenever he is asked, he says he will pay tomorrow.

Breach of contract.

103. लेखो पल पल को लिजी जालो। Lekho pala pala ko lijî jálo.
Every moment will have to be accounted for.
Divine judgment on all actions, moral responsibility; used as a religious admonition.

104. इशक मुशक खांसी खुर्रा नी छिपना। Ishaka mushaka kháṇsî khurrá nî chhipaná.
Love, musk, and a cough cannot be suppressed or concealed.

105. ऊं कि टूं नि जाणनु। Úṇ ki ṭúṇ ni já_nanu.
He doesn't know úṇ from tuṇ i.e. the similar signs or letters ऊं and टूं.
That is, cannot tell a bee from a bull's foot; a simpleton, ignoramus.

106. काठ को उल्लू। Káṭha ko ullú.
A wooden owl.
A perfect body.

107. पुरा पड़ि गेछ। Purá parhi gechha.
You've finished it.
You have been and gone and done it, made a fine mess of it. Used ironically.

108. कभैं गाड़ि में नौ कभैं नौं मे गाड़ि। Kabhaiṇ gárhi me nau kabhaiṇ nau me gárhi.
Sometimes a boat is carried on a cart, and sometimes the cart is carried on a boat.
Mutual help or usefulness.

109. आसमान पाताल। Ásamána pátála.
(Makes) Heaven of Hell.
Makes black white, a liar.

110. राजा का मारिया कि हिला में लोटिया की लाज नै। Rájá ká mariyá ki hilá me loṭiyá kî lája nai.
There is no shame is being punished by a king, nor in falling on a slippery place.

111. करो छीयो करि निजाणि। Karo chhíyo kari nijáṇi.

He did it, but bungled in the attempt (lit. did not know how to do it).

112. जोड़ि जोड़ि महरूड़ि। Jorhi járhi maharúrhi.

Maharurhi (was made) by gathering from here and there.

Maharúrhi is the name of a small parganah of the Kumaun district.

Formerly it did not exist, but when the Gurkha Government was obliged to assign villages, for the feeding of pilgrims to Badrinath and Kedarnath, this new parganah was formed by cutting off portions from the neighbouring ones.

Used by one who tries to raise money from all quarters (by begging etc) for some purpose.

113. नौ दिन चले ढाई कोश। Nau dina chale ḍhaî kosha.

Nine days for going two and a half kosh (five miles).

There are temples at the sacred places Kedarnath and Badrináth which formerly were connected by a road only five miles long. These temples were at that time served by the same *pujári* (priest), but he grew weary of having to perform service at both places on the same day. So the gods Kedarnáth and Badrínáth caused a huge landslip which made the road impassable, and the two temples are now separated by a nine-days' journey.

Used by a traveller who misses his way.

114. खेल खेलारि को घोड़ो सवार को। Khaiḷa khilári ko ghorho sawára ko.

Plays are for players, and horses are for riders.

Things are only of value to those only who know their use and are able to handle them.